Artisanal and Small-Scale Mining Formalization in Ghana

African Worlds: New Interdisciplinary Perspectives

Series Editor:
John Stanfield II, Director of African Studies at ASARPI: Advanced Study of African Renaissance Policies Ideas Ltd // ASARPIversity, Mauritius and South Africa

The African Worlds: New Interdisciplinary Perspectives privileges the Indigenous and otherwise community-grounded voices of African and global African Diasporas peoples through utilizing new and critical epistemologies, theories, methods, and policy evaluation strategies drawn from the social sciences and humanities.

Volume 2
Artisanal and Small-Scale Mining Formalization in Ghana
A Decolonial and Legal Pluralist Analysis
Linda Mensah

Volume 1
Colonial Intervention and Destabilization of African Identities
Contours of Trusteeship and Organized Infantilism in Sub-Saharan Africa
Obed Mfum-Mensah

Artisanal and Small-Scale Mining Formalization in Ghana

A Decolonial and Legal Pluralist Analysis

LINDA MENSAH

berghahn
NEW YORK • OXFORD
www.berghahnbooks.com

First published in 2026 by
Berghahn Books
www.berghahnbooks.com

Library of Congress Cataloging-in-Publication Data
Names: Mensah, Linda author
Title: Artisanal and small-scale mining formalization in Ghana : a decolonial and legal pluralist analysis / Linda Mensah.
Other titles: African worlds v. 2.
Description: New York : Berghahn Books, 2026. | Series: African worlds: new interdisciplinary perspectives ; v. 2 | Includes bibliographical references and index.
Identifiers: LCCN 2026000644 (print) | LCCN 2026000645 (ebook) | ISBN 9781836955122 hardback | ISBN 9781836955139 epub | ISBN 9781836955146 adobe pdf
Subjects: LCSH: Mining law--Ghana--History | Small-scale mining--Ghana | Customary law--Ghana | Ghana--Colonial influence
Classification: LCC KRX1006 .M46 2026 (print) | LCC KRX1006 (ebook) | DDC 343.667077--dc23/eng/20260121
LC record available at https://lccn.loc.gov/2026000644
LC ebook record available at https://lccn.loc.gov/2026000645

British Library Cataloguing in Publication Data
A catalogue record for this book is available from the British Library

EU GPSR Authorized Representative
LOGOS EUROPE, 9 rue Nicolas Poussin, 17000,
LA ROCHELLE, France
Email: Contact@logoseurope.eu

ISBN 978-1-83695-512-2 hardback
ISBN 978-1-83695-513-9 epub
ISBN 978-1-83695-514-6 web pdf

https://doi.org/10.3167/9781836955122

To my children, Joy and Kwasi, what a journey this has been for us! Thank you for making it all worthwhile.

When they ask what you saw today, Akyaamah of Obuase
With your eyes drenched in tears and the summery dews of Kew
Your heavy heart longing for silence from the blasts of the Adanse hills
Searching for stories you never knew

Tell them you saw your ancestor today
Hair gathered in locked glory
Guiding you to the lost treasures of the Prah
Mourning the waters our gods can no longer drink

So wake up child of the Tuesday Sun
And gather the children raised on the stories of the mines
Before you pour a drink to the gods today
Remember to tend to the lands of your ancestors and the waters that cleanse your pain.

—Linda Mensah, 2021

Contents

Figures

Acknowledgements

To Dr Saskia Vermeylen and Dr David Wilson, for always championing my research with immense kindness, guidance and patience.

I am thankful to the Socio-Legal Studies Association (SLSA) for their grant, which enabled me to complete the archival research for this project. The process of researching, data gathering and completing this work was hampered by many challenges, including the COVID-19 pandemic. I do not take for granted the patience and support of the SLSA and all others who held space for me during those difficult times as I navigated parenting in addition to my research work.

To my dear family, most especially my brother, Ebenezer Ankapong, and to my friends, Azeb Walday, Dr Vera Hayibor and Edna Okine, thank you for remaining steadfast in your support.

To the chiefs and people of Adanse, Amansie and Obuasi who co-produced this knowledge with me, I am grateful for your time, reflections and critique, without which this book would not have been possible. *Aseda!*

Legislations and Cases

Legislations

Constitution

Constitution of the Republic of Ghana, 1969
Constitution of the Republic of Ghana, 1992, arts 1(2), 11(2), 11(2)(3), 20(1)(a), 20(2), 36(8), 257(6), 242(d), 267, 267(1), 270, chap 20

Acts of Parliament

Administration of Lands Act, 1962 (Act 123)
Akim Abuakwa (Stool Revenue) Act, 1958 (Act 8)
Ashanti Stool Act, 1958 (Act 28)
Chieftaincy Act, 1961 (Act 81)
Chieftaincy Act, 2008 (Act 759)
Chieftaincy (Amendment) Law, 1985 (PNDCL 107)
Chiefs (Recognition) Act, 1959 (Act 11)
Concessions Act, 1962 (Act 124)
Ghana Geological Survey Act, 2016 (Act 928)
Land Act, 2020 (Act 1036)
Local Governance Act, 2016 (Act 936)
Minerals Act, 1962 (Act 126)
Mercury Law, 1989 (PNDCL 217)
Minerals and Mining Act, 2006 (Act 703) ss 1, 38, 81–94, 111
Minerals and Mining Law, 1986 (PNDCL 153)
Minerals Commission Act, 1993 (Act 450)
Precious Minerals Marketing Corporation Law, 1989 (PNDCL 219)
Small-Scale Gold Mining Law, 1989 (PNDCL 218) s 21
Stool Lands Control Act, 1960 (Act 79)

Colonial Legislation

Ashanti Concessions Ordinance, 1903, s 55
Concessions (Amendment) Ordinance, 1901 s 25(1)(a)(b)
Concessions Ordinance, 1900 ss 31(1), 33(1), 34, 41(1), 50
Concessions Ordinance, 1939 ss 11(3), 36(1)(a)(b), 36(2)
Criminal Procedure Ordinance, 1876
Crown Lands Bill, 1894
Foreign Jurisdiction Act, 1843
Forest Bill, 1910
Lands Bill, 1897
Mercury Ordinance, 1932
Minerals Duty Ordinance, 1952
Native Authority (Colony) Ordinance, 1944 ss 2(1)(a), 30, 31
Native Jurisdiction Ordinance, 1878 ss 5, 6, 9 and 10
Public Lands Ordinance, 1876 s 7(6)
Superior Court of Judicature Act, 1874
Supreme Court Ordinance, 1876

Secondary Legislation

Adansi West District Assembly Executive Instrument, 2003 (EI 15)
Obuasi Municipal Assembly Legislative Instrument, 2004 (LI 1795)
Minerals and Mining (Health, Safety and Technical) Regulations, 2012 (LI 2182)

Minerals and Mining (Licensing) Regulation, 2012 (LI 2176)

Obuasi East Municipal Assembly Legislative Instrument, 2018 (LI 2332)

Minerals and Mining (Mineral Operations-Tracking of Earth Moving and Mining Equipment) Regulations, 2020 (LI 2404)
Water Use Regulations, 2001 (LI 1692)

Other Jurisdictions

Cameroonian Mining Code, 2001 art 2
Ecuadorian Mining Law, 2009
International Treaties
Minamata Convention, 2013 Art 7(3) Annex C

Cases

Sustaining the Wild Coast NPC & 6 others v Minister of Mineral Resources and Energy & 4 others, High Court, Eastern Cape Division, Grahamstown Case No. 3491/2021.

Shilubana and others v Nwamitwa, Constitutional Court of South Africa, Case CCT 03/07 [2008] ZACC9.

Nana Gyamena Kwabena Oyiakwan II, Chief of Kwapia and Nana Anokye Ababio, Krontihene of Kwapia v Lan Haisong, Li Dehao, Huang Shen Gjun, Wen Shli, Obuasi Municipal Assembly, Asamoah Gate, Simon Kwadwo Antwi, Minerals Commission, Leap Palm Oil Company, Justice Ofori Ampofo and Environmental Protection Agency (EPA Obuasi), High Court Obuasi 2021.

Abbreviations

AGA	AngloGold Ashanti
AGC	Ashanti Goldfields Corporation
ARPS	Aborigines' Rights Protection Society
ASM	Artisanal and Small-Scale Mining
CeSIS	Centre for Social Impact Studies
CHPS	Community-Based Health Planning and Services
CLS	Customary Land Secretariat
CMS	Community Mining Scheme
COCOBOD	Ghana Cocoa Board
CPP	Convention People's Party
EPA	Environmental Protection Authority
EU	European Union
GEF	Global Environment Facility
GDP	Gross Domestic Product
GNASSM	Ghana National Association of Small-Scale Miners
IIED	International Institute for Environment and Development
ILO	International Labour Organisation
KVIP	Kumasi Ventilated-Improved Pit
LAP	Land Administration Project

NDC	National Democratic Congress
NREG	Natural Resource and Environmental Governance
NPP	New Patriotic Party
NYEP	National Youth Employment Programme
OASL	Office of the Administrator of Stool Lands
PIS	Participation Information Sheet
PMMC	Precious Minerals Marketing Corporation
PNDC	Provisional National Defence Council
PNDCL	Provisional National Defence Council Law
PTP	Pompora Treatment Plant
SLSA	Socio-Legal Studies Association
SOAS	School of Oriental and African Studies
SODEMI	Société pour le Development Minier en Côte D'Ivoire
SSMP	Small-Scale Mining Project
TWAIL	Third World Approaches to International Law
UN	United Nations
UNDP	United Nations Development Programme
UNEP	United Nations Environment Programme
UNITAR	United Nations Institute for Training and Research
WACA	West African Court of Appeal
WBCSD	World Business Council for Sustainable Development
WLSA	Women and Law in Southern Africa

Introduction

Towards a Decolonial Examination of ASM Formalization in Ghana

This book concerns informalized and criminalized small-scale miners in Ghana, and it begins with the story of a child raised on the stories of the gold mines of Obuasi.[1] Mine was a childhood filled with the voices of playful children, the delightful sounds of Ghanaian highlife music and the excitable chatter at the Obuasi Central Market where I helped my paternal aunt ply her tomato trade on Saturdays. Atop the hills surrounding the Anyinam township where I lived with my aunt stood the imposing mine shaft towers of the Ashanti Goldfields Corporation (AGC). Here, it was not uncommon for us to be awakened by the deafening blasts of the mine rocks vibrating through our roofs. There were also other frighteningly unforgettable sounds that interrupted my peaceful memories of this gold-mining community, such as the occasional pandemonium from small-scale miners, locally known as the *galamsey,* fleeing from AGC's concessions, and the sounds of despair amongst neighbours wondering who had been shot, killed or injured in the chase.

These firsthand glimpses of the world of friends, family and neighbours, who, as *galamsey*, had to live daily on the edge of state criminality and corporatist brutality, stood in sharp contrast with the disembodied mainstream narratives about local small-scale mining. To many on the outside of this world, the *galamsey* were nothing more than the scourge of the earth, a band of irresponsible individuals polluting the environment, or a marauding gang of criminals trespassing and bothering the operations of respectable mining corporations. A walk into the archives to reconcile the disconnect between my embodied experience of the *galamsey* and the dominant narratives left me with an unbearable heaviness regarding the massive scale of the destructiveness of resource extractivism in historic mining communities like Obuasi. I was met with many lost and forgotten stories shoved under volumes of state legislations and re-emergent concepts like formalization. These stories matter and, as I will argue in this book, need to be retold through the lens of the local miners and their communities as counterhegemonic to the prevailing narratives on (il)legitimacy in the artisanal and small-scale mining (ASM) discourse.

Researching ASM in the Golden City

Before I delve into the specificities of my theoretical and empirical analysis on the legal framework of ASM formalization, I first present an introduction to the historic gold-mining town, Obuasi, as the case study area for this work. About 64 km south of the Asante capital of Kumasi, one is met with a makeshift police barrier bearing the inscription, 'Welcome to the Golden City'. When I was growing up, this barrier's arch was known to be of paling wood, and the dusty, pothole-ridden road upon which it was installed became the memento of the sad irony of this mineral-rich community and the deprivation that had become symptomatic of many other gold-mining towns in the country. Obuasi, also known locally as *Sikakrom* ('the Golden City'), is located in the Ashanti Region of Ghana. The name, spelt '*Obuase*' in Asante Twi, literally means *Ɔbɔɔ* ('rock') *ase* ('under'), an indication of its derivation from the expansive quartz mountains and gold-mining activities in the town. Writing about his first trip to Kumasi in 1839, Wesleyan missionary Reverend Thomas Birch Freeman recorded his observations about the quartz mountains of Adanse, noting how the rocks in the province were 'granite with croppings of ironstone and small erratic blocks of feltapar [*sic*] prevailing in some parts which are considered by the natives to indicate the presence of gold'.[2] Geologically, Obuasi falls within the Birimian system, which is known to contain erratically distributed, high-value gold ore in dense quartz and sulphide reefs with significant occurrences of arsenopyrites, carbonates, silver and copper-bearing sulphides (Taylor 2006).

The indigenes of Obuasi are primarily Adanse people, a subset of the larger Asante nation. Obuasi is therefore an Akan community and forms part of the largest ethnic group, which makes up nearly 47.5% of Ghana's population of thirty-three million (Davies and Maier 2024; Ghana Statistical Service 2024). I highlight this to clarify the disparate geographical, ethnic, cultural and socioeconomic realities prevalent in Ghana and to emphasize this book's focus on the Akan – and more specifically the Adanse – society of Obuasi. A noteworthy caveat here is that while this book's decolonial approach to ASM formalization may offer relevant insights for mining communities in formerly colonized societies, its attention to the geographical and cultural setting of Obuasi emphasizes a focused interest in ASM within chieftaincy contexts. As I will show in the following chapters, this rejoinder is crucial, having regard to this book's departure from the imperialist preference for cultural monoliths and, within Ghana, the 'Akanization' of customary laws in erasing the distinct customs of minority ethnic groups (Mensah-Bonsu 1993–1995; Kludze 1988; Nii-Aponsah 1978).

Gold has always been an important feature of the political, religious, social, economic and cultural lives of Adanse people, forming part of vital rituals and ceremonies from birth to death. As the southernmost border community of the Asante Kingdom, the Adanse people's control over goldfields and trade routes to the coast played a significant part in the Battle of Feyiase around 1700, in which the Asantes were eventually freed from the throes of their Denkyira overlords, galvanizing the establishment of Asante as an empire (Ofosu-Mensah 2010). The famous Golden Stool of the Asante Kingdom, the unifying symbol of the soul of the nation, which was obtained after Asante established control over Adanse from Denkyira, serves as a further example of the relevance of gold to the Asante society (Kyeremanten 1969).

According to Boahen (1975: 4), gold was exploited long before the arrival of Europeans, and it formed one of the principal trade items between the areas of the Niger Bend, Mali, Songhai and Hausaland on the one hand, and the forest areas of Ghana on the other hand. Boahen's work confirmed thirteenth- and fourteenth-century Arabic accounts of gold being exported in large quantities across the Sahara to the Barbary states and Europe, a significant volume of which proceeded from modern Ghana. This aligns with oral-historical accounts of gold mining in Obuasi, where Indigenous practices of mineral extraction and processing were long established before the arrival of AGC in 1897. Tradition has it that the Akan states of Bono-Manso and Adanse were the first to emerge during the first half of the fifteenth century, with Adanse deriving its greatest wealth from the north–south trade in gold (Boahen 1975: 10–11). In describing Obuasi in the 1890s, a newly arrived AGC manager detailed the workings of Indigenous miners who had sunk shafts along the outcrops of the gold reefs in the community. According to *The Gold Coast Aborigines* (7 January 1899: 4), this European mine manager observed how the Indigenous miners harvested stones that were then carried down to a neighbouring pool by women, to be ground on granite slabs.

Obuasi is essentially what one will call a 'mine-town' since the socioeconomic lifeblood of the community revolves around the main gold-mining operations in the community (Ofosu-Mensah 2011). In addition to mining, the people of Obuasi are also involved in both subsistence and cash-crop farming,[3] petty trading and artisanry such as masonry, carpentry and mechanics. Obuasi acts as the administrative capital of the Obuasi Municipal Assembly, which was carved out of the erstwhile Adansi West District Assembly under Executive Instrument (EI 15) of 2003 and Legislative Instrument (LI 1795) of 2004. In 2018, Obuasi East Municipal Assembly was also carved out of the Obuasi Municipal Assembly by Legislative Instrument (LI 2332). The Obuasi Municipal and Obuasi East Municipal Assemblies have grown to become major cosmopolitan communities with populations totalling 110,263 and 97,686 respectively (Ghana Statistical Service 2024).

Despite the rise in Christianity and Islam, traditional belief systems – such as veneration for *Onyankopɔn* (the Supreme God), *Asaase Yaa* (Mother Earth), who nourishes the earth with mineral wealth, *nsamanfoɔ* (the ancestors), *abosom* (the lesser deities) and *mmoatia* (dwarves and forest deities) – are still deeply rooted in the community. Abraham (1962: 46) has explained that Akans do not have an attitude of externality to the world because to them, the world is metaphysical: what exists is, in the first place, spirit. For instance, the Akan state was considered as sacred and conceived as falling inside a world inhabited by human beings, spirits and gods who owed specific duties to one another through the performance of appropriate rituals and constant communion. According to Boahen (1975: 6), accounts of oral tradition indicate that the cradle of the Akan people is located at the confluence of the rivers Pra and Offin, to the north of the Twisa hills – namely, the area of modern Adanse and Amansie. It is believed that the different waves of Akan migrations began from these regions, demonstrating how pivotal Adanse is to the ultimate formation of the Asante nation and its cosmology.

In Asante cosmology, the entities in the universe – men, women, spirits, skies, waterbodies, animals, plants, mineral resources – each possess their own identity; these identities are differentiated but relationally non-oppositional, serving to mutually define and unite one another. Every child is born into a totemic identity given by the clan, through which he holds association with the community, the earth and the ancestors (Adom et al. 2018). This, as Jamaican scholar Sylvia Wynter (2003: 257) observes, differs from the Western construction of man as solely a political and economic subject of the nation-state. This is further underscored by the ancestral veneration and the belief that the spirits of the ancestors are always around and within call, ready to be summoned at will through ritual invocations (Wiredu 1998: 17). The *akomfoɔ* (priests and priestesses) serve in this metaphysical world as special connections to the minor deities and hence directly to God. They are consulted as unfailing oracles, a hand-dip into the omniscience of the Supreme God (Abraham 1962: 57).

In respect of gold mining, this Indigenous spirituality anchors both the earthly and the transcendental, nourished by rituals and sacrifices overseen by the *akomfoɔ*, the chiefs and the elders (Rosen 2020: 49). Among the Adanse people, the territorial deity, Bona, is highly revered and believed to grant his blessing to all activities on Adanse lands including fishing, farming and mining. The Bona shrine and those of the other deities in the community remain regular spots for many small-scale miners who visit to offer sacrifices in anticipation of the blessings of the gods and the ancestors. Productivity at the mine sites is said to be dependent on the propitiation of the gods, without which it is believed the gold veins will not manifest (Sarpong 2017).

Ritual ceremonies in Asante are not mere abstract performances but essential enactments of the past instantiated by the particularities of present events. Furthermore, the writing system of the Akans expresses their philosophies through the timeless elemental powers of art, sayings, songs, poems, riddles and craft (Abraham 1962: 16). Across Africa, colonization tried to erase these Indigenous knowledges through legislative prohibitions, use of state force and fetishization (Dube 1999: 213). For instance, in addition to policing their Indigenous lands under the aegis of protecting the propertied concessions of European mining corporations, the colonial government was described in *The Gold Coast Leader* (14 January 1922: 4) as further authorizing its police force to enter the streets and homes of the local people – whips in hand – to control the singing of sacred songs and the performance of rituals, dances and ancestral invocations.

The story of Obuasi has for long been told through the lens of the mining corporation and the state, even where the narrative is supposedly about ASM in the community. It is almost always about violence, 'clashes', military presence and the constant vilification of the *galamsey*. In this book, I draw on decolonial theories to bring a critical focus to these narratives and the laws that engender them. Black feminist scholar bell hooks teaches us that marginality is not simply a site of deprivation but also a site of radical possibility, a space of resistance and a central location for the production of counterhegemonic discourse (hooks 1989: 15). Thus, in approaching the narrative of ASM formalization in Ghana through a decolonial lens, I bring in the particular stories of a historic gold-mining town still grappling with ongoing colonialities, as well as the resilience of a community that is incredibly endowed with a plethora of situated Indigenous knowledges and is capable of addressing its challenges. Ultimately, I chose to honour this land of my birth by deploying its Indigenous spiritualities, philosophies and epistemologies in my examination of ASM law and formalization.

Figure 0.1. A map of Ghana showing Obuasi. © Linda Mensah.

Formalization and the Question of ASM Informality

As Hilson (2020) examined in one of his recent analyses on the subject, formalization has, over the past three decades, and under the direction of the World Bank, European Union and other donor agencies, been generally presented as a panacea for addressing the host of social and environmental challenges associated with ASM. Formalization briefly entails the integration of small-scale miners into the formal legal system as a pathway for monitoring and ensuring compliance with environmental and tax obligations, as well as securing access to tenure security, legitimacy and government support (Siegel and Veiga 2009). This, according to Hilson (2013: 51), is a result of the representation of informal small-scale miners as a 'developmental problem' that the formal state needs to governmentalize. Although Lahiri-Dutt (2014: 6) explained informality as a defining condition that intersects with, but is not the same as, illegality, Hilson and Maconachie (2017: 443) observed that to key actors in ASM governance such as donors and governments, legalization and the acquisition of permits were pivotal to formalization. In this focus on legalization, any operation outside of the prescribed state law on formalization is simply a legal violation that ultimately renders informality an illegality. Within this bifurcated hierarchy, unlicensed small-scale miners are deemed as illegals and are met with repressive policies such as state criminalization and militarized evictions.

This fixation on state centralism in ASM formalization, however, fails to recognize the rather crucial history of the state and its legal apparatus in the ASM regime. More importantly, it overlooks the fact that informal small-scale miners may be robustly complying with established customary laws and practices. Postcolonial analysis of informality has sought to disrupt the formal/informal binary and its dualistic reproductions on the basis that informality is neither the preserve of the poor nor the absence of law (Varley 2013: 4). The prevalence of law and legitimacy within the informal ASM space, therefore, represents one of the core issues I address in this book as I examine the tensioned intersection between state-centric formalization and the reality of a plurally determined living customary law on the ground. This opens up the overarching inquiry of this book and its contribution to broadening knowledge on the much-needed legal reforms for the ASM sector.

The core objective of this book is to problematize ASM formalization and its underlying state-centric legal frameworks. This exercise is achieved through the novel use of decolonial legal pluralism as a discursive and analytical tool to interrogate the systemic conflation of (il)legality with (in)formality within the Ghanaian ASM landscape. One of this book's distinctive contributions to ASM scholarship lies in this decolonial approach to unsettling the colonial entanglements of formalization. In doing so, this book situates the failures of ASM formalization within a wider sociopolitical context spanning colonially inherited, state-centric notions of legality that are incompatible with the actual lived realities of local small-scale miners.

This decolonial lens sheds light on two things: the state absorption of governance in Indigenous mining; and the longstanding history of colonial interferences in customary land tenures, and traditional mineral resource governance. Here, I seek to demonstrate that in Ghana's mining regulatory infrastructure, the problematic narratives which underpin the criminalization of ASM informality are rooted in a failure to critically historicize concepts of (il)legality within the operationalization of formalization. This also shows that notwithstanding decades of political independence, Ghana's dual-mining economy remains underpinned by ongoing colonialities and a colonial legal pluralism that continues to legitimize the marginalization of local small-scale miners, their criminalization and their deprivation from state support and access to geologically productive lands. Ultimately, the purpose of this book is to highlight and dismantle these colonial legacies within the ASM regulatory framework and to propose more locally determined, communally focused, non-extractive and environmentally responsible approaches to addressing the challenges associated with ASM in Ghana.

To achieve this, I invite a pause and reflection on the following important questions:

1. What is formalization and why ASM formalization?
2. What does formalization's legal framework entail? What are its origins and methods of constructing, interpreting and applying law?
3. In what ways do these laws impact small-scale miners' operations and access to lands?
4. What other alternative legal frameworks are there and how do we conceptualize, gather and deploy these legal possibilities for the benefit of miners and their local communities?

Through a decolonial approach to intersectionality, this book unpacks the colonial, racialized and classed matrices of domination that intersect within contemporary ASM spaces. By tracing the linkages between colonization, the emergence of ASM informality and the discernible patterns of subjugating poor and vulnerable small-scale miners, this book will scrutinize how the state got to centre itself in ASM regulation to the exclusion of other culturally situated forms of governance, and how the state's conceptualization of legitimacy perpetuates heightened classed and racialized inequalities within the sector, ultimately reinforcing, rather than addressing, the negative environmental and social impacts associated with the sector.

This further presents an opportunity to introduce the living customary law into the ASM discourse as a timely intervention through which the lived realities of small-scale miners can mediate the contested gap between formalization and the so-called persistent ASM informality. To generate these local knowledges, this book makes a further contribution by critiquing extractivist and Eurocentric approaches to knowledge production in ASM, and by advancing Indigenous knowledges such as the Akan philosophy of *Sankɔfa,* which serves as the overarching methodological framework to this book. This pioneering methodological approach offers a thoughtful reflection on epistemic violence, issues of positionality and reflexivity and the ethics of researching ASM in formerly colonized societies of the Global South. It further advances an excavation of Indigenous knowledge systems in reimagining the living customary law and traditional institutions like chieftaincy as alternative legal possibilities for ASM reform in Ghana.

Scope and Overview of Chapters

Chapter 1 engages with the key themes and debates on ASM formalization in the mainstream literature. I explain the concept of formalization in greater detail, highlighting its unilinear approach towards state-centric legalization of informal ASM. I make the connection between this dominant approach to law and the challenges faced by informal small-scale miners, particularly their land struggles and state criminalization. This chapter further highlights the intersectional complexities within ASM by illustrating how local elites and their foreign collaborators have positioned themselves within ASM informality enabling them to benefit from and circumvent statutory rules through their financial and social capital. I emphasize this to show the limitations and inequities of state absorption of ASM governance, drawing from Banks et al.'s argument (2020: 223) that so-called 'illegals' within the informality discourse are often those on the wrong side of the formal rules who lack the power to negotiate around them, and are thus rendered most vulnerable to stringent state enforcements and crackdowns. This sets the stage for a reflection on the origins of

ASM state laws, namely, who makes them, what informs their designation as 'formal' or 'official' law and whom they serve. Through this approach, I am able to dive into my decolonizing probe of the history of ASM law, thereby generating empirically valid and theoretically sound insights towards reforming the ASM legal framework.

In Chapter 2, I examine the decolonial methodologies and epistemologies of my ASM research, which is guided by the Akan philosophy of *Sankɔfa*. *Sankɔfa* ontologically explores a reflection on the present, a retreat into the past and a reclaiming of Indigenous knowledges relevant for reimagining liberatory futures. Through this approach, I retreat into the past using a combination of archival and qualitative materials to uncover silenced historical narratives and overlooked knowledge systems within the dominant epistemological framings of ASM law. This further enables me to reflect on the present and to show how colonially constrained knowledge production is within the ASM scholarship, thereby positioning my argument for a rethinking of methodology as an urgent, ethical, epistemic, ontological and political characteristic for reimagining liberatory futures for small-scale miners and local mining communities. The methodological enquiries in this book are further grounded in reflexivity and the enunciation of my positionality as a Ghanaian with family roots in the mining community. Here, I prop up my embodied experience of the *galamsey* as an entry point, using my birthplace and one of Ghana's oldest gold-mining communities, Obuasi, as a case study, to emphasize the relevance of situated knowledges in the construction of law. As Liboiron (2021) has rightly asserted, introducing yourself in your research is part of ethics and an obligation through which readers are made explicitly clear about where one is speaking from, what grounds one stands on, to whom one views their obligations, what structures and privileges one's current positionality affords and how these relate to the arguments being made.

In Chapter 3, I introduce legal pluralism as the conceptual framework for the arguments made in this book. I set out the dominant legal positivist notions of law, including the official customary law in ASM as a construct of the colonial state and its monist-pluralism. In doing so, I highlight the imperative need to reconstruct ASM law beyond state centralism, thereby advancing a decolonial legal pluralism as a more appropriate framework for navigating the enduring legacy of legal pluralism in formerly colonized societies like Ghana. I present Ehrlich's concept of the living law (1936), through which I conceptualize ASM law as situated within the social formations and associations of local small-scale miners, coexisting mutually and independently of the state. This emphasis on small-scale miners as a legitimate source of law fosters this book's critique of the formalist evocations of law underpinning ASM formalization. It further enhances my advancement of the living customary law as the more suitable alternative legal framework for ASM governance. This chapter also addresses concerns about legal pluralism and knowledge uncertainties (Delmas-Marty 2009) which, as I explain in Mensah (2021), I have encountered from reviewers in my critical reflections and use of legal pluralism in the ASM discourse.

Chapters 4 and 5 engage in the empirical analysis of data from the archives, oral histories and interviews. In Chapter 4, I focus on the colonial antecedents of contemporary ASM state law by tracing its historical emergence. In drawing out the history, this chapter presents a challenge to the axiomatic claim of state exclusivism to law by re-embedding local perspectives and resistances in the historiography of mining laws in Ghana. This chapter continues my critique of the rigid dichotomy between formality and informality by showing its history as integral to the colonial project of state suppression and criminalization of Indigenous gold mining. In Chapter 5, I demonstrate the enduring legacy of these colonial legal frameworks by highlighting their remnants in contemporary ASM governance. This chapter also emphasizes the resilience of the living customary law of local small-scale miners, showing how it has survived empire and the postcolonial state, thus articulating a critique of criminalization as a rational project.

In Chapter 6, I explore chieftaincy as a crucial traditional institution to the development of a decolonized ASM legal regime. In keeping with the *Sankɔfa* philosophy, I reflect on the contemporary position of chiefs in the modern nation-state and the scholarly criticisms of chiefly involvement in customary land administration and ASM. Through this, I present a decolonial perspective to the colonial and postcolonial state's manipulation of chieftaincy that has fostered the current weaknesses in accountability within the institution. I rely on *Sankɔfa* to offer a reconstruction of an egalitarian, communal and democratic chieftaincy system underpinned by the living customary law as relevant for reforming ASM.

This book concludes by reiterating how Western assumptions about law and governance permeate the ASM formalization discourse. It argues that formalization has failed to take root in formerly colonized mineral-producing countries like Ghana because its legal premises are predominantly Eurocentric and culturally incompatible with the conceptions of mineral rights, tenure security and access to lands in these societies. Moving forward, the conclusion offers some reflections on reconceptualizing formalization within legally plural contexts, and the ways in which we theorise and gather knowledges on ASM in formerly colonized societies. This chapter further provides an initial commentary on decolonizing legal education in Ghana, as a crucial pathway to teaching, researching and devising reforms capable of addressing the ongoing colonialities and shortcomings of the prevailing formalist approaches to law in ASM.

Notes on Terminology

In view of my decolonizing approach, I present at this point an overview of some key terminology and an explanation for my decision to use or not use certain terms in this book. I begin this exercise with the concepts of decolonization, decoloniality and their juxtaposition with postcolonialism. The difference between postcolonialism and decolonial studies is said to be mostly a difference in geographical origin and remit, that is, the geographical locations from where the scholars within the particular fields hail and the geographical focus of their studies (Bhambra 2014: 115). Bhambra (2014) traced postcolonialism as an intellectual movement that developed from diasporic scholars from the Middle East and South Asia, whereas the emergence of decoloniality is traced from the work of diasporic scholars from South America.

In terms of timeline, postcolonialism generally refers to the nineteenth and twentieth centuries, whereas decolonial thinking addresses a much longer time frame spanning from the very inception of modern forms of colonization in the late fifteenth and early sixteenth centuries (Nelson Maldonado-Torres 2011). While many contemporary decolonial thinkers are postcolonial people and most postcolonial scholars share a decolonial agenda, there are still spaces and conceptual tools within each of these discourses that, according to Tlostanova (2020: 165), remain opaque to the other. While decolonial scholars like Walter Mignolo (2011a: 55) view the postcolonial and decolonial as complementary trajectories with similar goals of social transformation, which walk in the same direction but follow different paths, the decolonial option is often positioned as a critique of, and an alternative to, postcolonial theory. This notwithstanding, postcolonial and decolonial arguments have been most successful in challenging the troubling notions of 'modernity' and Western universalism by demonstrating how the idea of the 'universal' was based on an analytic bifurcation that removed the colonized 'other' from the production of an effective history of modernity (Bhambra 2014: 116). This is particularly pertinent to the African context, where the darker side of Western modernity in the form of mercantilism, slave trade, colonialism, missionary work, imperialism, apartheid and neocolonialism led to, and continues to perpetuate, underdevelopment on the continent (Ndlovu-Gatsheni 2013).

Another noteworthy point here is the difference in the decolonization movements of the second half of the twentieth century and contemporary decolonial thoughts. For Indigenous Peoples in Africa, Asia and South America, the objective of the earlier decolonization projects was ending colonialism and taking back control of the state. This, according to African feminist scholar Patricia McFadden (2007: 36), was partly a failure because it resulted in a neocolonialist era where the local elites who replaced colonial administrators captured the state and perpetuated the exact same structures of privilege, institutionalized exploitation, classed accumulation and domination through the enactment of legal and policy frameworks within relevant sectors such as mining. The participation of independent African states in the political and economic structures established and maintained by the colonial machinery, without changing the fundamentally unequal relationships of power between the state and the poor and vulnerable, continues to create new terrains of foreign interests and classed struggles.

The concept of coloniality (Maldonado-Torres 2007; Quijano 2000; Mignolo 2011b) was introduced to highlight the continuity of established patterns of power between colonizer and the colonized, and how that power shapes the understanding of culture, labour, intersubjectivity and knowledge production. It underscores the argument that political independence is not enough and that there needs to be a more active, transformative and interventional process in identifying and addressing current colonial tendencies, including those perpetuated and facilitated by local elites. Here, decoloniality intervenes as an epistemological project to understand and 'delink' from the colonial condition. By using Audre Lorde's (1984) famous statement that 'the master's tools cannot dismantle the master's house', Tlostanova (2020: 167) presented a critique of the ultimate failure of postcolonialism, which she described as its attempt to use the methodological tools of the master to dismantle his house. According to Tlostanova, this is impossible, and decolonial theories intervene by performing a different epistemic operation that does not start with Western theoretical frameworks or modifying them to fit the analysis of post- and neocolonial reality. Rather, decolonial theory focuses on the genealogy of decolonial thinkers and their epistemic tools from the start, hence transcending Western convention and epistemology. This analogy of dismantling the master's house and undoing the persistent Eurocentric epistemological scaffolding underpinning African institutions is invoked in Wakunuma et al.'s (2025) differentiation between decolonization and decoloniality. Here, the authors characterize decolonization as the process of ensuring that the stranger in our house leaves, while decoloniality involves 'cleaning the house in the aftermath of the stranger leaving, including repairing damages, renovating the house to our specific needs, context and taste, and ensuring that whenever the stranger returns it will only be for a visit and no similar damages will occur again'.

I am also guided by my decolonizing approach to avoid common terminology such as 'sub-Saharan Africa' in this book. Adebisi (2016) has argued that 'sub-Saharan Africa' is neither an accurate geographical term nor a reliable scientific unit, but a classification that accords with Hegelian ideas about Africa and the colonial library. As historian Howard French (2021) posits, the use of the term is problematic and roughly coterminous with the notion that this part of the continent is composed of senselessly warring tribes who are without literacy or history. 'Sub-Saharan Africa' strongly overstates the racial distinctions between societies located on either side of the Sahara Desert and overlooks their heterogeneity. These imperialist ideas are views that I vehemently confront in this book, hence my avoidance of the term. Additionally, while the archives and historical literature are replete with the term 'native' in reference to the colonized African, I avoid it; this is in following with Mamdani's (2012) well-detailed analysis where he drew on Maine's description of the native as a creation of the colonial state, pinned down, localized, thrown out of civilization as an outcast, confined to an ossified custom and then defined as a product. In doing so, Mamdani addressed the term as a designated condition that is neither original nor authentic. Accordingly, my reference to the term will only be in respect of its use in the archives and nothing more.

Finally, within the array of controversies surrounding the difference between ASM and *galamsey*, where the latter term is used exclusively to refer to the predominantly informal and illegal form of ASM, I will be using both terms interchangeably in this book. As I explain in the next chapter, this serves as a way of reclaiming the local term *galamsey* from its criminalized positioning within mainstream narratives on ASM formalization.

Notes

1. This work will feature the typical local spellings of names such as Obuase, Kumase, Adanse and Asante. Where relevant, their modern or historical representations in the archives (Obuasi, Obuassi, Kumasi, Coomassie, Adansi and Ashanti) will be used.
2. MMS/Special Series/Biographical/West Africa/597B; Extract of typescript manuscript of the journals of Reverend Freeman's visits to the Kingdoms of Asante and Dahomey, and to Abeokuta, Lagos and Bagadry between 1840 and 1843, p. 84. Wesleyan Missionary Archives, SOAS, London. The final work was published in London as Thomas Birch Freeman (1844), *Journals of Various Visits to the Kingdoms of Ashanti, Aku, and Dahomi in Western Africa*.
3. Songs by Ghanaian highlife musicians, such as Tommy Wiredu's '*Fa ɔdɔ bɔ dɔm*' and Nana Romeo's '*Obuasi ankaa*', refer to Obuasi *ankaa woɔ* ('the honeyed oranges of Obuasi') as a metaphor for the sweetness of romantic love. This is also indicative of the popularity of orange farming mainly by the surrounding villages in the Obuasi area.

CHAPTER 1

Against 'Paper' Formalization in Ghana

Critical Reflections on ASM Informality and Alternative Legal Possibilities

Introduction

Over the past decades, artisanal and small-scale mining (ASM) has grown exponentially, emerging from the shadows of invisibility to policymakers and subsidiarity to highly incentivized large-scale mining corporations. International donor agencies, research organizations, local and national policymakers are now paying closer attention to the sector as a significant livelihood venture with viable developmental potential for both domestic and global economic growth. This widespread attention has also exposed ASM to intense scrutiny for its negative social and environmental externalities, prompting diverse interests in the development of an effective regulatory framework that will ensure better sustainability for ASM. Consequently, formalization was presented as an axiomatic pathway for remedying the social and environmental challenges of the sector, as well as promoting tenure security and a rewarding asset capitalization for local small-scale miners. Investment was poured into licensing and registration schemes that were rolled out in response to formalizing the ASM sector, many of which, as Verbrugge (2015: 1023) categorically put it, have failed tremendously to achieve their set objectives.

A recent reflection by Hilson et al. on ASM formalization in Ghana (2022) revealed similar systematic failures, beginning with the short-lived Small-Scale Mining Project (SSMP) that was established in the early 1990s as the blueprint for facilitating the legalization of ASM and administering assistance to small-scale miners. An overwhelming number of ASM operations continue to take place outside of state purview, and the state's deployment of increased criminalization, militarized evictions and other carceral responses have achieved little in deterring ASM informality or addressing the challenges of the sector. This tensioned intersection between ASM formalization and what is deemed the persistent informality of the sector brings into focus the dire need for a critical rethinking of formalization as an intervention and its underlying legal framework.

Rather than rehashing the extensively researched factors relating to its limited success, I will examine in this chapter the causal link between formalization's state-centric legal framework and its stringent conflation of ASM informality with illegality. I then draw a connection between this informality–illegality narrative and the land struggles facing small-scale miners. In doing so, I interrupt the insistence in the prevailing scholarship on state-centric formalization, particularly amidst the evidence of alternative legal frameworks that can effectively be harnessed for ASM reform. The deliberations I present in this chapter are aimed at setting the scene for the decolonial, legally pluralist analysis I proffer in advancing the living customary law as an alternative legal framework for ASM governance in the subsequent chapters.

In the first section following this introduction, I provide an overview of ASM, including a quick survey of the debates surrounding its definition and characterization. I also discuss the cultural and socioeconomic relevance of ASM, as well as the environmental challenges that render it a crucial subject of study under the theory of informality. In the next section, I introduce the concept of formalization, its different conceptualizations and its relation to ASM. I proceed to provide an overview of ASM formalization in Ghana, with specific emphasis on the construction of illegality as an expression of informality. I address the core issue of access to land for ASM operations and the delegitimization of small-scale miners' resort to customary land tenures as a further expression of state hegemony over mineral-rights governance. In the third section, I provide a summary of the key recommendations for legal and policy reform in the literature, drawing upon these to present my arguments about alternative legal possibilities to the prevailing state-centric ASM formalization.

Artisanal and Small-Scale Mining Defined

Drechsler (2001), Hentschel et al. (2003) and Zvarivadza and Nhleko (2018) have respectively established that there is not a single, universal definition of ASM. Rather, it is mostly context-specific and generally left to national legislations that utilize the level of sophistication, size of the mine, workforce, level of production and even incidence of formal regulation to define or, in some cases, differentiate between 'artisanal' and 'small-scale' mining. In Cameroon, for instance, article 2 of the 2001 Mining Code defined artisanal mining as including all mineral extractions involving manual methods and procedures with the use of little or no mechanization (Funoh 2014). The 2009 Ecuadorian Mining Law characterized artisanal mining as a subsistence-based manual activity, while small-scale mining, on the other hand, was defined as mineral extraction up to 300 tonnes per day and involving the payment of a 5% tax. Everything above this capacity was considered large-scale and subjected to higher taxes (Marshall and Veiga 2017). In countries like India and Zimbabwe, small-scale mining is associated with mining organized and undertaken under statutory control with permits, while artisanal mining is usually uncontrolled and unauthorized (Zvarivadza and Nhleko 2018: 78). 'Artisanal mining' thus generally refers to the more rudimentary form of mining, which connotes labour-intensiveness and low capital and investment, while 'small-scale mining' references the more mechanized and semi-industrial form of mining (Ferring, Hausermann and Effah 2016).

Seccatore et al. (2014) have challenged the characterization of ASM based on the level of sophistication as simplistic, maintaining that small-scale mining can refer only to the size of the mine, which can be operated using either conventional or rudimentary mining methods. For Marshall and Veiga (2017: 302), such miner definitions in legislations were inutile, as the authors believed that the production level was much more important. Such debates about the definition and characterization of ASM were particularly predominant in the 1970s, before giving way to more focused attention on the socioeconomic and environmental impacts of ASM in the 1980s (Hentschel et al. 2003: 13; Hilson and McQuilken 2014: 104). By the early 1990s, the conversation had shifted towards legalization of ASM as the first of many steps towards ASM formalization (Buxton 2013).

In Ghana, the term 'artisanal mining' does not feature in state mining legislations; the more popularly used terminology is 'small-scale mining'. Small-scale gold mining was first defined under section 21 of the Small-Scale Gold Mining Law 1989 (PNDCL 218) as 'the means of mining gold by a method not involving substantial expenditure by an individual or group of persons not exceeding nine in number or by a cooperative society made up of ten or more persons'. What constituted 'substantial expenditure' was not clarified under the law. Under section 111 of the current Minerals and Mining Act, 2006 (Act 703), small-scale mining operation is defined as 'mining operation over an area of land in accordance with the number of blocks prescribed'. The Ghanaian legislative definition therefore characterizes small-scale mining based mainly on the size of the land, the number of people involved and the level of expenditure. Small-scale mining in Ghana is locally known as *galamsey,* an adulteration of the English phrase 'gather and sell', in reference to the gathering and panning methods originally used in the mining process (Aubynn et al. 2010).[1] This term has become coterminous with the unlicensed and illegal forms of small-scale mining operations in the country.

The search for more sustainable measures to address the environmental challenges presented by the sector has reignited debates on ASM definitions in the Ghanaian ASM discourse in recent times, with the argument being that a definitive, legislative reclassification of ASM is a necessary condition for ensuring environmental sustainability and accountability in the sector. The differing characterizations notwithstanding, there is the defining commonality of ASM as a predominantly manually intensive, low-tech, low-capital form of mineral extraction and processing (Banchirigah and Hilson 2010). I use the terms 'ASM', 'small-scale mining' and '*galamsey*' interchangeably, with clarifications where necessary to highlight the ever-evolving complexities brought about by the increasing sophistication and mechanization of the sector. The use of '*galamsey*' in particular is aimed at reclaiming the terminology from its negative connotations of illegality.

ASM Challenges as an Expression of Informality

Two dominant narratives that have characterized debates in the ASM literature revolve around the sector's economic relevance on the one hand, and its widely publicized negative environmental impacts on the other hand. While the global burgeoning of ASM has brought the sector's economic contributions and vast developmental potential into prominence, this broad socioeconomic significance, according to Hirons (2020), is often pitted against the environmentally damaging practices associated with the sector. The environmental harm and social ills of ASM, characterized as 'expressions of informality', continue to form the predominant focus of the mainstream literature (Hilson and McQuilken 2014: 105). These negative portrayals of ASM are not only fuelled by a superficial understanding of the dynamics and nuances of the sector, but also compounded by what Hilson and Gatsinzi (2014) described as the shortsightedness of the policy creation of informality. Ultimately, this deliberate focus on the harmful expressions of ASM is deployed in criminalizing and undermining efforts towards understanding how small-scale miners adapt and innovate within their informal settings.

Globally, ASM involves a wide range of low-value minerals such as salt, limestone, marble, sand and clay, as well as high-value minerals such as diamonds, gold, bauxite, gemstones, aluminium and manganese. The majority of ASM operations are of the high-value minerals that also form the predominant focus of the literature, with the exception of an emerging scholarship that addresses the relevance of low-value development minerals (Afeku and Debrah 2020; Torvikey, Gyapong and Adomaa 2024). ASM is a significant contributor to the global mineral output, accounting for 30% of gold, 20% of diamond and 80% of sapphire production globally (World Bank 2013; Lahiri-Dutt 2018). In 2018, ASM accounted for 43% of Ghana's total gold production (Adu-Baffour, Daum and Birner 2021). Within that same year, Ghana overtook South Africa as Africa's top gold-producing country, demonstrating ASM's contribution to the total national gold output (Whitehouse 2019). The evidence further suggests that ASM contributes to rural economies through financing the building of schools, clinics, housing and local infrastructure, invigorating farming, associated service industries and local markets (McQuilken and Hilson 2016: 5). Unlike large-scale mining, where a huge proportion of revenue generated is repatriated to foreign shareholders, foreign-based suppliers, bankers and expatriate workers, income from ASM is generally retained and spread within the local communities, thus supplying sustenance to local vendors, manufacturers and other service providers (O'Faircheallaigh and Corbett 2016: 961).

Across 110 countries, ASM provides direct employment to an estimated forty-five million people, with additional indirect livelihood support to over 150 million people (ASM Inventory 2018). In Africa, there are close to twenty million people involved directly in ASM, with over 100 million others indirectly dependent on ASM for their livelihood (Clifford 2022). In Ghana, the ASM sector covers gold, diamond, bauxite, manganese and other low-value minerals, where an estimated one million people – accounting for 60% of the country's mining workforce – are directly employed. The majority of ASM's job creation reportedly occurs in its downstream employment, with approximately 4.5 million people working as cooks, food vendors, drivers, clothing merchants, machine operators, repairers, bookkeepers, accountants and other technicians (Centre for Development Studies 2004; Boafo, Paalo and Dotsey 2019). With increasing global mineral prices, combined with transnational capital flows, migratory low-cost workforces, poverty, youth unemployment and the low barriers to entry, this high turnover of ASM workers is expected to expand in unprecedented numbers in the coming years (Fold, Jønsson and Yankson 2014; O'Faircheallaigh and Corbett 2016).

These economic contributions are overshadowed by reports of ASM's environmental damages, such as land degradation, water pollution and other socioeconomic issues (Hilson and Gatsinzi 2014; Bansah et al. 2018; Zolnikov 2020). For instance, there remains an unceasing buzz about the increased mechanization and intensified production from the introduction of dredging machines by Chinese and local ASM firms, which have generated an alarming rate of pollution in waterbodies, causing high levels of turbidity and loss of aquatic life (Crawford and Botchwey 2017). The severity of the water pollution from ASM activities is said to have led to increased costs of chemical treatment needed to render such waters potable for the local communities. There are even concerns that Ghana may have to import drinking water from neighbouring countries if the situation is left unmitigated (Eduful et al. 2020). Regarding deforestation and land degradation resulting from ASM, a study conducted by Mantey et al. (2016) estimated that it would take a total of $198 million to remedy the ASM-affected lands in the Western Region of Ghana alone. Furthermore, the irreversible transformation of large tracts of arable farmlands used for cocoa and food-crop production into ASM sites has not only had an adverse effect on food security and the country's foreign-currency earnings, but it has also brought with it intense land-use conflicts between ASM and agriculture (Baddianaah, Baatuuwie and Adongo 2022).

Prominent among concerns about ASM's environmental impacts have been its mercury use and the attendant health consequences. Telmer and Veiga (2008) described the mercury amalgamation technique of separating gold from the ore as widely used by small-scale miners because it is 'cheap, simple, fast, independent and reliable'. This inexpensive and easily accessible mineral-processing mechanism has, however, been found to present dire outcomes to direct users and nearby communities. Mercury never disappears from the environment once emitted, and the discharge of large amounts poses a serious threat to land and waterbodies, rendering them unfit for food-crop production and aquatic life (Clifford 2017; Esdaile and Chalker 2018). As a neurotoxin, mercury causes deformities in foetuses and pregnant mothers, as well as neurological damage to people exposed to it in high doses, including fish-eating populations and the small-scale miners who use mercury on a daily basis. With ASM's mercury use alone accounting for two-thirds of anthropogenic global mercury pollution, the sector was singled out in the multilateral environmental response to tackling the mercury crisis during negotiations for the 2013 Minamata Convention on Mercury. Article 7(3) and Annex C of the Minamata Convention endorse formalization as a relevant national action plan towards reduction of mercury use in ASM (Spiegel et al. 2014; Veiga, Angeloci-Santos and Meech 2014).

As a signatory to the Minamata Convention since 2014, Ghana has adopted several strategies for achieving controlled mercury use in ASM, including statutory control of the purchase and quantity of mercury use under section 99 of the Minerals and Mining Act, as well as technical education and promotion of cleaner technologies (Basu, Renne and Long 2015; Rajaee et al. 2015). However, Hilson et al. (2018) noted that these measures have not been entirely successful due in part to the state's limited capacity, lack of political will, the technicalities of alternative technologies and the general scepticism of local artisanal miners. As I will explain later in this chapter and in subsequent analysis in this book, the national mercury action plans (as with all environmental protection measures relating to ASM) largely ignore the vital historical aspect of state law and its criminalization of environmental pollution attributed to local small-scale miners.

This attention to ASM's negative impact is also seen in the sector's association with child labour, substance abuse, prostitution and a high incidence of HIV/AIDS. These are said to arise from the increased population growth accompanying new gold finds (Hentschel, Hruschka and Priester 2002), or what Savornin, Niang and Diouf (2007) referred to as an illustration of the 'tragedy of the commons'.[2] Further to this, ASM is known for exploitative labour practices and occupational risks associated with precarious working conditions, and poor health and safety standards that often result in high levels of diseases and deaths from collapsing pits. Relatedly, the absence of post-mining reclamation means that many abandoned ASM pits are left uncovered, leading to health hazards such as the spread of malaria, and posing a danger to local residents, some of whom have lost their lives from falling into these pits (Bansah, Yalley and Dumakor-Dupey 2016). As governments seek to boost revenue from mineral exploitation, there has been increased attention on informal gold trading in ASM, which is conducted through middlemen. This is noted as not only being exploitative to the local miners, but also causing huge revenue loss to the state, since these minerals are smuggled through a network of unregulated channels and high-powered black-market operatives (O'Faircheallaigh and Corbett 2016: 962). There are even fears of armed groups using ASM to launder money and other criminal organizations using these untraceable mineral transactions to fund terrorism and civil unrest across the world (Maconachie and Hilson 2011a; Echavarria 2014: 23).

While these environmental and social impacts of ASM are a key concern, fixation on them by the government, researchers and policymakers has suppressed other equally crucial discussions, such as local miners' participation in ASM law-making and the construction of a more culturally situated, context-specific, long-term solution to the challenges of the sector. ASM's informality is cited as the root cause of the sector's social and environmental ills, poverty and land struggles, as well as of the government's inability to address the many challenges associated with the sector. For instance, in their analysis of the state's complicity in the influx of Chinese miners into the Ghanaian ASM scene and its attendant social and environmental repercussions, Crawford and Botchwey (2017: 459) posited that the corrupt and rent-seeking practices of power holders was reinforced by the informality of the sector as well as the generalized informal functioning of the state. According to the authors, ASM's informality served as fertile ground for bribery and corruption, more so than in the formalized large-scale mining sector, thus enabling illicit and unlawful activities to occur with relative impunity in ASM.

Furthermore, the prevalence of exploitative labour practices within ASM is highlighted as a symptom of an informal system where perpetrators ride on the casualization of work, the desperation of poor workers and the absence of recourse to statutory labour protection mechanisms (Arthur-Holmes and Abrefa Busia 2022a; Lahiri-Dutt 2008). This conceptualization of informality and its associated notoriety in ASM accounts for the literature's fixation on formalization, which, as I will show in the next section, is touted as the surest approach to addressing the host of environmental, social and health and safety issues associated with ASM.

Formalization Explained

Martha Chen's overview of the different theoretical approaches to the informal sector (2012) identified four dominant schools of thought, namely the dualists, structuralists, voluntarists and legalists. First, the dualist school viewed the informal sector as distinct from the formal economy with norms that are incompatible with the dictates of the modern capitalist economy (Hart 1973; Sethuraman 1976; Tokman 1978). According to Benton (1994), the concept of the informal sector, as it emerged in the 1970s in the analyses of urban economies in the developing world, dwelt on a dualist positioning of the informal sector as being opposed to the formal sector. Integral to this dualism was the notion that the informal sector was distinctively based on transactions and contractual labour relations that were not regulated by the state. This, as Benton (1994: 227) explained, could mean that workers did not make or receive social security and other tax contributions; it could also mean that work conditions did not fall within state purview not just for tax purposes but also for compliance with health regulations, union contracts, minimum-wage requirements and other restrictions on employment practices. Dualists viewed informality as characteristic of poverty-driven economic activities that operated largely as safety nets crucial for the survival of the poor in developing countries, rather than as a platform for wealth creation (Chen 2005).

Next is the structuralist school, which saw informality as being characterized by subordinated economic units (microenterprises) that served to reduce input and labour costs, thereby increasing the competitiveness of large capitalist firms. Closely associated with the works of Alejandro Portes, the structuralist approach drew attention to informalization as a long-term systemic process embedded within the material structures of global capitalism (Portes, Castells and Benton 1989; Portes and Schauffler 1993). Informal sector expansion was seen neither as a distinct set of economic activities nor a bottom-up reaction to economic crisis or overregulation, but as a capitalist response to a crisis of accumulation in the formal economy (Meagher 1995; Tabak and Crichlow 2000). From Meagher's analysis (1995), structuralist approaches focused on three main distinct features of the informal sector: the heterogeneous and segmented character, the intricate connection between the formal and informal economy, and the enabling role of institutions and social networks in the process of informalization (Biles 2009).

On their part, the voluntarist school of thought held the position of informality as a rational economic choice made by actors after calculating the costs and benefits of informality against formality. Their consideration of the fiscal and regulatory barriers in the formal economy was circumscribed by the understanding that informal entrepreneurs deliberately avoided regulation and taxation, and did not blame their choice on the cumbersome registration procedures, as long as they perceived the cost of formalization to outweigh its benefits (Maloney 2004).

Finally, the legalist school of thought, which is widely associated with the works of Peruvian economist Hernando de Soto (2000), viewed the informal sector as comprised of 'plucky' microentrepreneurs who lacked formal property rights because of various fiscal and regulatory barriers that prevented their entry into a formal sector dominated by mercantilist elites who deliberately excluded them. Informality, from the legalist point of view, is largely a product of hostile legal regimes. According to de Soto, the poor in developing countries control vast amounts of assets, all of which are tied up in 'dead capital' because of a lack of formal representation accorded by deeds, titles and statutes of incorporation. This discrepancy, he argued, limits the poor from capitalizing their assets to access credit, insurance and profitable contracts in the modern economy. His solution, couched in the concept of formalization, was to integrate the rights associated with these assets into the formal property system. The crux of de Soto's thoughts was that the formal legal economy was more orderly and coherent as opposed to what he viewed as the anarchic state of informality, which he referred to in terms of extra-legality. Accordingly, extensive registration and titling were viewed as the default pathway to ensure tenure security, to legitimize and protect the property of the informal economy and ultimately to alleviate their poverty (de Soto 2000: 6).

According to Benton (1994), it is politically naïve to characterize informality as a transitory phenomenon that would substantially change if provided with initiatives like legalization. She critiqued how the dualist conceptualization underpinning structural notions of informality categorized behaviours as either legal or illegal by definition, with little room for nuanced analysis of how people perceived what they were doing in relation to the law, or of how their 'illegalities' may have been shaped by efforts of compliance that were nevertheless left incomplete. This is upheld by a structural notion of legal pluralism, where the economic and legal levels are closely tied together, with state law hovering above a regulatory sphere defined by the absence of state authority, and the relationship between the two sectors structurally defined as one of dominance and subordinance. By representing rulemaking in the informal sector as a negation of, or response to, the absence of state regulation, attention was shifted away from both the influence of state law and the ability of other cultural practices to generate frameworks for ordering economic activity. In addition to shoring up the scaffolding of a system of class power, this image of stacked levels of law fit poorly with the perceived dynamics of the various ways of viewing and using law (Benton 1994).

In turn, Verbrugge (2015) criticized the homogenizing tendency of the leading approaches to informality, stating that their simplistic assumptions only provided a partial causal explanation for the rather heterogeneous and segmented character of the informal sector. In his view, these approaches shared a legalistic focus on entry barriers and political impediments that prevented or discouraged the formalization of poverty-driven operators, but failed to fully explain cases where ASM was characterized by differentiation between a poverty-driven workforce and a dominant stratum of ASM entrepreneurs. This point is echoed by Hilson, Goumandakoye and Diallo (2019: 259), who cautioned that the four dominant schools of thought on informality evolved without taking stock of the dynamics of an economic activity as complex, unique and diverse as ASM, and hence should be contextualized and not relied upon as wholesale explanation for the sector's informality. Verbrugge's proposal for a more integrative approach (2015) notwithstanding, the legalist framework continues to be the dominant approach adopted in the mainstream analysis of informality in ASM. This legalist approach also forms the basis of my decolonial examination of ASM formalization in which, through theories of intersectionality, I will address Verbrugge's concerns about simplistic dualisms, homogenization, differentiation and classed exploitation in ASM.[3]

With informality being invoked as the underlying factor to the social and environmental improprieties of ASM, researchers, policymakers, states and foreign donor agencies have become resolutely fixated on formalization, through which it is believed the sector can be effectively monitored and supported upon incorporation into the formal legal domain (Hilson et al. 2017; Maconachie and Hilson 2011b; Kumah 2022). Formalization is sold as a mutually beneficial policy framework through which small-scale miners can obtain licences and permits to operate legally on secured mineralized lands that can be further capitalized to access formal credit and state support (Hilson and Vieira 2007). Based on the reciprocal assumptions of formalization, it is also believed that the registration and licensing would render miners easily traceable and place the government in a better position to monitor and regulate their operations for environmental and tax compliance (Hinton 2005; Salo et al. 2016; Bansah 2019; Kinyondo and Huggins 2020).

Since the 1980s, formalization as a policy formulation has received wide support from international agencies like the World Bank, which has been particularly invested in legal reforms as well as technical and logistical support towards ASM formalization across the Global South (Bromley 2008: 20). A study by Hilson, Bartels and Hu (2022: 209) showed the US$16.88 million contributed by the World Bank in support of enhanced governance in sustainable ASM as part of the Ghana Landscape Restoration and Small-Scale Mining Project (GLRSSMP), which was launched in February 2022. The United Nations Development Programme (UNDP) has also spent US$6.35 million on a five-year project in Ghana aimed at optimizing ASM formalization, supporting operators financially, enhancing uptake of mercury-free technologies, fostering knowledge-sharing and building local capacity. These figures highlight claims about the emergence of ASM as merely indicative of the more recent attention from international agencies who have since recognized the sector's viability and potential for global economic development (Labonne 2014:121). ASM has been a longstanding part of the histories of many local mining communities where it is embedded in the cultural heritage, traditional legal systems, spiritualities and socioeconomic survival of the people, even when it was not fully recognized by foreign donor agencies and treated with pedestrian policies by national governments (Zvarivadza and Nhleko 2018: 78; Hilson and McQuilken 2014: 109; Hein and Funyufunyu 2014: 260). The incursion of resource extractivism and its attendant legal mechanisms have greatly altered the legal landscape and Indigenous governance systems of mining in these communities, with implications for contemporary ASM operations. This is particularly true for Ghana where, as I will explain in the next section, formalization continues to be the dominant government policy despite a longstanding history of its failures and restrictions on Indigenous mining.

Four Decades On: Formalization and the ASM Sector in Ghana

Siegel and Veiga (2009), Zvarivadza (2018) and Hilson and Maconachie (2020a) have respectively explained the global consensus on formalization as the first step towards transforming ASM and addressing the social and environmental issues associated with it. These hopeful iterations notwithstanding, there remains an equally general sentiment that ASM formalization across the Global South has been woefully unsuccessful (Marshall and Veiga 2017: 302; Kumah 2022: 2). Nearly four decades after its first rollout, and despite years of massive investment in its diverse legal, technical, financial and institutional components, ASM formalization remains an outlier for many small-scale miners as the majority of them continue to operate outside of state oversight and support. The factors accounting for this limited success have been extensively expounded by Spiegel (2015), Hilson (2016), Afriyie, Ganle and Adomako (2016) and Hilson et al. (2021a), among many others. These factors include the current legislation, overwhelming bureaucratic processes, prohibitively expensive registration fees, lengthy delays in the application process, acute shortage of mineralized lands and disjointed coordination amongst the different government agencies that oversee ASM policy implementation.

Pivotal to the concerns about formalization's failures, as raised by Van Bockstael (2014), has been the disjuncture between state formalization efforts and the actual realities on the ground. As already established, a fundamental aspect of de Soto's conceptualization of formalization was its emphasis on situated knowledges and the customary practices of the informal sector (de Soto 2000: 40). In that regard, formalization does not merely become a process of imposing state notions of law and formal property-rights systems but is an avenue to understand the underlying practices within the informal economy. This, according to Salo et al. (2016: 1060), however, has been rendered an uncertain political endeavour for governments and their key stakeholders. This is largely because formalization is often pursued as a control-oriented, information-intensive, top-down endeavour that ignores the preformalization order of affairs and local realities (Putzel et al. 2015). In other words, despite the emphasis on formalization as a concept that aims to understand, map and integrate the informal, customary practices of small-scale miners into the formal legal economy, the prevailing policy implementation has largely been the imposition of state-centric formalisms to the exclusion of existing structures, Indigenous knowledges and the practices and perspectives of key stakeholders like small-scale miners (Verbrugge and Besmanos 2016).

This miscoordination does not only show an insensitivity to local realities, but ultimately leads to a huge waste of resources in the production of regulatory frameworks that are remotely implementable and hardly a priority for local miners (Adu-Baffour, Daum and Birner

2021; Crawford and Botchwey 2017: 448). For instance, institutional and policy frameworks usually ignore the actual site-specific heterogeneities of ASM, its temporalities and transient nature as well as the motivations of small-scale miners. Instead, governments pursue ASM formalization based on wrongful assumptions about the sector, thereby failing to achieve any meaningful reform with the miners (O'Faircheallaigh and Corbett 2016). Elsewhere, Hilson and McQuilken (2014) observed that the dominant idea of artisanal miners as entrepreneurs, rather than individuals seeking to sustain their livelihoods and escape poverty, led to the formulation of policy measures such as the provision of assaying services to local miners. This move later proved inappropriate since the mining activities of the targeted group were mostly of the 'dig and wash' type and had no need for such sophisticated techniques. Furthermore, national strategies directed at the implementation of the Minamata Convention achieved little success because they failed to take into consideration the cyclic poverty of small-scale miners who often had no access to cheaper, user-friendly, low-tech processing alternatives to mercury (Hilson et al. 2018; Labonne 2014: 123). Accordingly, supporting technological projects under ASM formalization placed little emphasis on studying local cultures and using existing Indigenous knowledges to inform the design of assistance programmes for small-scale miners (Hilson and McQuilken 2014: 113).

This gap between ASM formalization and local realities is further felt within the underlying legal framework, where there is said to be a fixation on legalization, to the exclusion of other long-term measures necessary for institutionalizing reform in the sector, a phenomenon that has come to be known as 'paper formalization' (Kinyondo and Huggins 2020: 6; Martinez, Smith and Malone 2023). Hilson and McQuilken (2014: 111) noted that in their bid to formalize the industry, many African countries hastily enacted legislations with rigid licensing systems that had very little consideration for the people being targeted. Mutemeri et al. (2016) attributed this lack of consideration for local miners' realities to the pursuit of ASM formalization as an attempt to force small-scale miners to follow scaled-down versions of legislations designed for conventional, large-scale mines. This phenomenon was highlighted by the International Labour Organization (ILO 1999) decades ago, where they attributed the failure of many ASM projects to the treatment of ASM as a subset of large-scale mining. These sweeping regulatory procedures, according to Hilson and Maconachie (2020b), were galvanized to qualify for structural adjustment lending and failed to recognize that its conditions were largely constraining ASM operators from formalizing their activities. By revisiting de Soto's legalist school on informality, the authors concluded that the continued implementation of such restrictive and burdensome licensing schemes was not only inexplicable but a further indication that ASM informality was a deliberate creation of the state through stifling regulatory compliance measures.

A similar situation exists in Ghana, where the first point of reference for ASM formalization in contemporary literature begins with the passage of the Small-Scale Gold Mining Law, 1989 (PNDCL 218). This era coincided with the enactment of the Mercury Law, 1989 (PNDCL 217) and the Precious Minerals Marketing Corporation Law, 1989 (PNDCL 219), all of which formed part of the government's externally funded SSMP to formalize the ASM sector. The SSMP, according to Hilson, Bartels and Hu (2022: 208), was comprised of the Minerals Commission, the Precious Minerals Marketing Corporation (PMMC), the Mines Department and the Geological Survey Department. The Geological Survey Department now operates as the Ghana Geological Survey Authority, established under the Ghana Geological Survey Act, 2016 (Act 928). Nearly four decades after these legislative and institutional measures, and notwithstanding a reputation as one of Africa's mature mining regimes, more than 85% of ASM operations in Ghana continue to take place informally (Nwokolo 2019).

A review of PNDCL 218 expanded ASM formalization beyond gold mining to include the regulation of all other small-scale mining operations. It further embedded ASM into the broader mining regime under a singular legislative framework – the Minerals and Mining Act, 2006 (Act 703). This new legislation, like the erstwhile Small-Scale Gold Mining Law, explicitly set out the parameters of what constituted a formalized ASM operation and established a clear distinction between licensed and unlicensed ASM. Sections 81 to 94 of the Minerals and Mining Act provide that only duly registered and licensed individuals or groups of Ghanaians aged eighteen and above can lawfully undertake ASM in the country. In operationalizing ASM formalization in Ghana, these state laws institutionalized a rigid binary that conflated formality with legality and informality with illegality. Furthermore, they upheld the notion of the eminent domain where the state maintained control over the grant of mineral rights, permits, licensing, the facilitation of compensatory payments to landowners and the enforcement of environmental standards, through the concerted oversight of state institutions such as the Minerals Commission, the Ghana Geological Survey Authority, the Environmental Protection Authority (EPA), the Forestry Commission, the Lands Commission and the Water Resources Commission, among others (Mensah et al. 2015: 81).

On paper, ASM formalization appears to be a simple process. The licensing procedure, as set out under the Minerals and Mining Act and the Minerals Commission guidelines, begins with prospective miners submitting applications with the prescribed documentation (such as a site plan of the intended mining site) at a district office of the Minerals Commission within the jurisdiction of the proposed mining operation. The Minerals Commission was established under the Minerals Commission Act, 1993 (Act 450), to regulate and manage the utilization of Ghana's mineral resources. Currently, there are thirteen of such district offices set up in designated mining communities, with eighteen other satellite offices across the country (Hilson, Bartels and Hu 2022: 215). These district offices are a remnant of the erstwhile SSMP and were created to serve as decentralized centres for the Accra-based Minerals Commission headquarters.

The application form and accompanying documents are forwarded from the district offices to the head office of the Minerals Commission, where the Minerals Titles Department conducts an initial review, generally to ensure that the area of interest is georeferenced and earmarked for ASM, cross-referenced against existing mineral rights and confirmed for no conflicts of interest. Following this review, the Minerals Commission issues notices through the municipal and district assemblies and in public locations in the host mining community for twenty-one days. In the absence of any objection to the notice, a recommendation is made, and the sector minister approves the prospecting minerals right. Subject to approval by the sector minister, a final mining operating permit is issued to the applicant by the Inspectorate Division of the Minerals Commission. These licences are granted for assigned concessions not exceeding 25 acres (Minerals Commission of Ghana 2021).

Owing to the increased attention on ASM's negative environmental impacts, applicants for small-scale mining licences have, since 2001, been required to obtain an Environmental Permit to Undertake Small/Medium-Scale Mining to be issued by the EPA. Prospective small-scale miners are required to apply following receipt of their small-scale mining licence. The mainstream media campaign on the damaging effects of ASM on waterbodies also led to a growing pressure to revive the provisions of the Water Use Regulations, 2001 (LI 1692), which, although technically applicable to ASM, were rarely enforced. These regulatory requirements were enhanced under the Minerals and Mining (Licensing) Regulation, 2012 (L1 2176), and

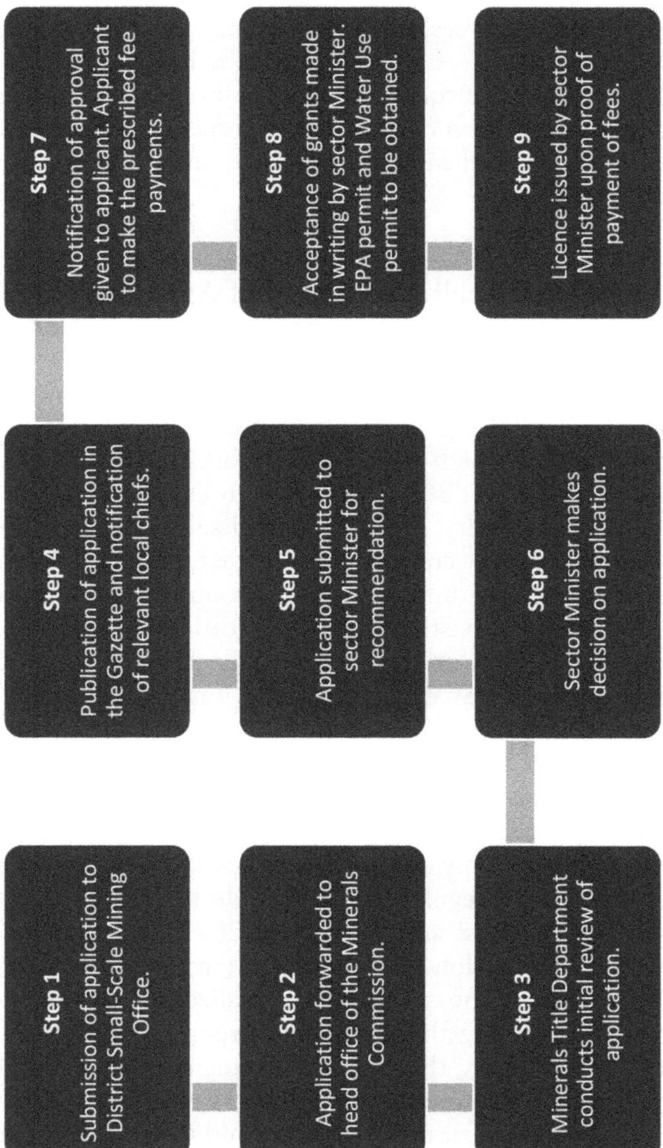

Figure 1.1. A chart of the ASM formalization procedure in Ghana. © Linda Mensah.

have meant an additional Water Use Permit for ASM activities from the Water Resources Commission (Hilson, Bartels and Hu 2022: 209).

In practice, however, the outlined formalization process remains much more tedious, rendering it impractical and alienating for a significant number of small-scale miners (O'Faircheallaigh and Corbett 2016: 962). In the next section, I highlight the linkages between this failed policy and the construction of ASM informality as an illegality, through the criminalization of ASM's environmental pollution, which further reinforces the exclusion of Indigenous knowledges, customary practices and realities.

'Fixing' ASM Informality: Creation of ASM Illegality and the Criminalization of Environmental Pollution

ASM formalization does not only aim to usher in new working rules but is also connected with pre-existing identities and memories in the mining communities, which it inevitably works to disrupt (Salman, Carrillo and Soruco 2015: 360). According to Damonte (2016: 956), the procedural complexity of ASM formalization ignores the important situational aspect and informal characteristics of the mining practices it addresses, leading to ambiguous outcomes of top-down measures that disturb existing customary orders. Ultimately, such superimposed ASM regulations do not only impede the intended formalization process, but end up making unregistered small-scale miners 'illegal' (Hilson and McQuilken 2014: 111). In this regard, formalization represents an example of a mainstream framework that is portrayed as a means to reform an economic activity and empower its marginalized actors, but which ends up as a policy failure and an institutional misfit that only controls, punishes and sentences many to illegality in the face of regulations impossible to comply with (Salo et al. 2016; Huggins, Buss and Rutherford 2017). Salo et al. (2016: 1065) note that the tension at the intersection of this legal impasse does not only prevent the success of formalization on the ground, but reinforces a stalemate that leaves little room for the creation of alternatives. Consequently, the strategy to integrate the informal, customary practices of ASM into the formal legal economy remains stuck with no clear theoretical direction (Hilson and Okoh 2013: 138). As Marshall and Veiga (2017: 301) put it, there appears to be no sound alternatives despite the overwhelming criticism of ASM formalization.

This deadlock is traceable to the dominant conflation of ASM informality with illegality. Informality is generally framed as a chronic, developmental problem to be fixed (Chen 2007), and in the ASM context, informality is viewed as the epitome of all that is wrong with the extractive industry. This notion is used to sanction the exclusion and criminalization of local informal miners. As Salo et al. (2016: 1061) explained, governments' response to the growing negative impacts of ASM has been the adoption of a dual strategy of promoting formalization and implementing interdiction. The former features a technical, bureaucratic process, and the latter offers increased criminalization, policing and militarized evictions. In Ghana, interdiction measures manifest in the combative language used in framing the government's responses to ASM, which are seen as a 'war', a 'battle' and a 'fight' against *galamsey* (Hilson 2017; Ullo 2022). Bockstael (2019) has described this as governments' appropriation of the environmentalist vocabulary of anti-mining activists for exclusive use against ASM. In the literature, media and policy documents, it is not uncommon to find references to ASM as a 'wicked problem' (Bansah, Acquah and Assan 2022); a 'menace', 'headache' and 'threat' (Tschakert 2009); 'a cancer that literally eats the land and the rivers' (Kaufmann and Côte 2021); an 'unruly and messy sector' (Labonne 2014); a 'thorn in the flesh' (Zvarivadza and Nhleko 2018); and an 'environmental menace and criminal activity' (Sojková 2022) perpetuated by individuals who have no respect for law or regard for the dangers they pose to the environment.

This perception of ASM's informality as a harbinger of illegality extends to the customary laws, Indigenous knowledges and practices adopted by local miners in their operations. From this perspective, the design, implementation, monitoring and enforcement of ASM governance is exclusively (or largely) placed in the hands of state institutions where punitive interventions – such as the enactment of more stringent legislation, imposition of bans, forfeiture and burning of ASM equipment, and militarized evictions – are sanctioned as imperative for flushing out informal ASM and its harmful environmental footprints (Hilson and Yakovleva 2007; Okoh and Hilson 2011; Asamoah and Osei-Kojo 2016). This posturing underplays the many challenges that are left in the wake of state-centric formalization as a remediation policy.

Studies respectively conducted by Owusu, Bansah and Mensah (2019), Eduful et al. (2020), Bansah, Acquah and Assan (2022) and Hilson and Maconachie (2020c) provide recent overviews of such crackdowns in the legal and policy direction of Ghana's efforts to formalize ASM. They outline how public outcry against the catastrophic spate of water and land pollution from ASM activities precipitated into a nationwide #StopGalamseyNow campaign spearheaded by the Accra-based media firm Citi FM and the Ghana Media Coalition Against Galamsey in 2017 (Adogla-Bessa 2017). These anti-ASM protests successfully galvanized widespread support from a section of Ghanaian society – including politicians, civil society organizations, pro-environmentalist groups, media, faith-based organizations and think tanks – who mounted pressure on the government to address the environmental devastations of ASM (Armah-Attoh 2017). This campaign eventually prompted the government to impose a ban on all ASM operations; it also served as a precursor to subsequent military sweeps such as 'Operation Vanguard' in 2017 and 'Operation Halt' in 2021. These militarized operations formed a continuity of state-sanctioned evictions, such as the erstwhile 'Stop Illegal Mining' campaign, 'Operation Flush Out' and similar military endeavours launched between 2006 and 2013. For Operation Vanguard alone, about four hundred military personnel were deployed across various mining communities in what the government described as sanitizing the local communities against the ASM menace responsible for environmental degradations (Hilson 2017).

In addition to this, specialized 'Galamsey Courts' were established across the country and tasked with the specific mandate of trying mining-related offences, particularly the operation of informal ASM (Shaban 2017). In response to arguments that there was little incentive for ASM formalization as the risk of it being sanctioned was minimal, a 2019 amendment to the Minerals and Mining Act was passed, which increased the penalties for informal ASM to a minimum of fifteen years' imprisonment and/or a prescribed fine. A study conducted by Bansah, Acquah and Assan (2022) highlighted the more recently enacted Minerals and Mining (Mineral Operations-Tracking of Earth Moving and Mining Equipment) Regulations, 2020 (LI 2404), which prescribed the confiscation of *galamsey* equipment by the state. Many excavators seized under this regulation were subsequently burnt and destroyed, a situation described by the authors as an unreasonably showy destruction of equipment that could otherwise have been used for other economically beneficial purposes in the local communities.[4]

Among other things, the failure of these highhanded measures to deter informal small-scale miners is a testament to the inefficiencies, corruption, classed disparities, exclusions and marginalization within the state's formalization and compliance mechanisms. The legal recognition granted under formalization, coupled with the increasing capitalization, professionalization and mechanization in ASM, has led to a growing classed, gendered and racialized differentiation within the sector. As Fisher (2007) addressed in her empirical analysis of formalization in Tanzania, formalization efforts designed along the capitalist, entrepreneurial model often enact arrangements that are generally exploitative, discriminatory and exclusionary of the low-classed workers within the system. For instance, within the state criminalization of ASM informality, Eduful et al. (2020: 9) observed a 'catch and release' pattern where evictions, arrests and prosecutions were primarily targeted at the low-paid small-scale miners who did not have any political connections or the financial capacity to bribe their way out. Allegations of involvement by high-level government officials and local chiefs, as well as evidence of extortions by the military personnel, have marred the integrity of the entire criminalization and eviction process. This has further plunged the endeavour into a cacophony of blame games between sector ministers, local chiefs, police, politicians, local government officials and government agencies over who is most responsible for enabling ASM informality and its associated environmental consequences in the mining communities. Accordingly, ASM has become a site of intense political contestation, with local miners fighting for access to lands and opportunities to operate, and political elites exploiting the subject for votes depending on their stance to ban or improve access for operations (Ofori, Mdee and Van Alstine 2021).

Notably, many ASM operations take place in some of the most minerally endowed yet materially deprived communities, where local populations and migrant workers engage in ASM for various reasons (Arthur-Holmes and Abrefa Busia 2022b). Hilson and Maconachie (2020b) conceptualized the motivations underpinning peoples' movement into ASM as, to one extreme, poverty-driven groups or individuals whose primary motivation is to alleviate personal hardships, and at the other extreme, those seeking to 'get rich quick' or aspiring businesspersons whose reasons are purely profit-driven. The authors further identified a third category of hybrid entrepreneurs who viewed ASM as a long-term platform for wealth creation notwithstanding the hazards and lack of protection they faced within the informal sector. Despite claiming to have initially moved into ASM because of poverty, these hybrid entrepreneurs have accepted their fate as small-scale miners because they consider ASM to present the best income-earning option available.

For a long time, ASM was largely viewed as a poverty-driven venture undertaken as an economic necessity by families and individuals seeking to eke out a living, students raising funds to further their education and farmers supplementing their incomes (Bush 2009; Andrews 2015). While these poverty-driven actors remain the majority within the sector, ASM sites continue to evolve as an eclectic mix of individuals with classed and racialized heterogeneities (Hilson and Maconachie 2020b). While ASM was once regarded as the preserve of low-skilled rural workers with no or low levels of formal education (Twerefou et al. 2015; Mabe, Owusu-Sekyere and Adeosun 2021), it has now been noted to attract a wide range of formally educated individuals and other well-connected, rent-seeking and opportunistic entrepreneurs whose financial and social capital enable them to embed themselves within its complex sociopolitical and bureaucratic landscape (Hilson and Maconachie 2020b).

For instance, a study conducted by Hilson and Potter (2005) on the effects of the World Bank's Structural Adjustment Programmes on employment in Ghana found a declining standard of living that had driven many school graduates, former professionals, semiskilled labourers and retrenched large-scale mine workers to the rural areas for ASM. This classed livelihood diversification into ASM is further evident in a recent study by Arthur-Holmes et al. (2022), which revealed a significant exodus of undergraduate- and postgraduate-degree holders into ASM for reasons such as escaping the high rate of graduate unemployment and endemic poverty in their local communities. A racialized dimension to these classed complexities was identified by Hilson, Hilson and Adu-Darko (2014), and in subsequent studies by researchers such as Crawford and Botchwey (2017), Crawford, Agyeyomah and Mba (2017), Hausermann, Adomako and Robles (2020) and Antwi-Boateng and Abunga-Akudugu (2020), who found mass Chinese migration into Ghanaian ASM facilitated by local political and traditional elites despite the legislative reservation of ASM for Ghanaians. As McQuilken and Hilson (2016) observed, these classed and racialized incursions do not necessarily negate the centrality of poverty as a driving factor for a significant number of the workers involved in ASM. However, it has serious implications for law-making in ASM, opening up questions such as what constitutes law, who makes these laws, whose operations are deemed legitimate, who is protected and who is punished in the state's pursuance of ASM formalization.

As I will highlight later in this book, state law has historically been an instrument of the dispossession, victimization and marginalization of the poor, the colonized and other vulnerable groups. In recent times, a noticeable trend in ASM criminalization in Ghana shows the tendency for state law enforcement to target the minimally paid workers at the bottom of the ASM production chain, whose arrests are paraded in the front pages of mainstream media publications as evidence of the efficacy of state criminalization efforts. Meanwhile, the local elites and financiers and their foreign compradors largely remain unaccounted for (Tetteh 2021). ASM criminalization therefore entrenches the classed disparities and poverty gap in the sector, contrary to the government's own rhetoric of poverty reduction (Tschakert and Singha 2007). This was emphasized by Geenen (2012) in her examination of the detrimental outcomes of ASM bans in the Democratic Republic of Congo, which she described as not only a radical example of top-down formalization policy but also an illustration of a bureaucratic and technical measure that compounds but does not address the problems associated with ASM.

In Ghana, studies conducted by Zolnikov (2020) and Osei et al. (2021) have shown the untold financial hardships unleashed in the rural areas in the aftermath of ASM bans. Ofosu et al. (2024) recently conceptualized this mining ban and its consequent livelihood implications as a 'ban on mining as a ban on dining'. Pijpers (2014: 32) described ASM as an 'economy of dreams' for many miners – dreams of raising enough money for a better life, schooling, providing for family, building a house and even relocating overseas. These dreams are shattered following ASM bans, leaving many miners to navigate financial hardships by resorting to petty crimes or engaging in less lucrative yet more dangerous and physically demanding jobs to survive. This, as Tuokuu et al. (2020) noted, represents a situation where the law (in this context the state law apparatus) becomes a tool to criminalize the poor for being poor and unable to conform to the stringent demands of state-centric formalization. Furthermore, it amalgamates ASM as a site where only a certain segment of well-educated or well-connected individuals with sufficient social and financial capital are able to navigate the high threshold of state legislative prescriptions (Salo et al. 2016; Huggins, Buss and Rutherford 2017). Again, by targeting only licensed ASM operators in their multimillion-dollar assistance schemes amidst the procedurally bureaucratic and expensive registration fees, governments and their donor agencies are said to have rendered the benefits of formalization as theoretically possible for only a small fraction of people involved in ASM (Hilson and McQuilken 2014: 113; Salo et al. 2016: 1061; Hilson 2020: 1624).

Moreover, the deployment of military forces against informal ASM operators as an environmental protection mechanism has been critiqued by Hilson and Maconachie (2020c), who have described the entire militarized conservatism as a façade through which the state used environmental protection as a pretext for indulging in rent-seeking and securing the propertied interests of large-scale mining companies for revenue generation (see further discussions in Aryee, Ntibery and Atorkui 2013; Yankson and Gough 2019). Later on, I will unveil the historical continuity of the colonial use of mercury control and other environmental protection laws to ban, restrict, dispossess and marginalize Indigenous miners, while simultaneously creating a conducive environment for large-scale mining operations free from competition and interference from ASM. This is fundamental to the continued land struggles facing small-scale miners in the local communities. Besides, the linkages between legalization as a core tenet of ASM formalization and better management of natural resources, land tenure security and environmental sustainability remain unclear. Marshall and Veiga (2017: 301) were emphatic that the process of formalization currently being practised in many developing countries does not result in a reduction of bad polluting practices or better benefits for the small-scale miners or even the governments that implement these policies. Accordingly, the use of legal titles or 'paper formalization' has been unable to create the necessary conditions for accountability within ASM, contrary to the proponents of formalization and its legalist school of thought (Banchirigah 2008).

As a solution, Geenen (2012), Siwale and Siwale (2017) and Martinez, Smith and Malone (2023) have respectively emphasized the need for governments to focus on strong post-formalization mechanisms such as capacity-building, credit opportunities, land demarcations and the organization of small-scale miners into cooperatives or associations. Sadly, in Ghana such policy implementation measures largely overestimate the state's institutional capacity, as seen in the rise and fall of the SSMP (Hilson, Bartels and Hu 2022). As Verbrugge, Cuvelier and Van Bockstael (2015) have observed, the capacity of state regulatory machinery in many mineral-producing countries of the Global South stretches very thin and is unable to effectively administer its respective mandates, particularly in remote rural mining communities. In addition to issues of corruption, the main institutions with direct supervisory responsibilities over ASM are usually ill-equipped and lack clearly defined, cross-sectoral linkages with the other institutions needed to ensure the effective regulation and supervision of the sector (Akabzaa and Darimani 2001). For instance, the Ghana Geological Survey Authority, which was tasked with prospecting and demarcating suitable areas for ASM operations, has been gravely constrained by internal institutional deficiencies (Hilson, Goumandakoye and Diallo 2019). Furthermore, the PMMC's monopoly in the ASM purchasing system was hit by structural deficits and inadequate allocation of funds, which led to the agency reducing its offering prices and eventually driving local miners to alternative private buyers (Fold, Jønsson and Yankson 2014).

Moreover, the dominant notion of informality as the underlying factor to ASM's negative environmental impacts has been debunked by studies that point to alarming environmental improprieties committed by duly licensed, formalized ASM operators, without much intervention from the mandated state agencies (Weng 2015; Osei, Arku and Luginaah 2022). This reflects the varying spectrum of formality and the different layers of informality that permeate even the formal sector. Furthermore, it effectively defeats the problematization of ASM informality as a nonstatutory regulatory issue and the attempts to 'fix' informality through criminalization. Overall, eclipsing ASM's record economic contribution and its sociocultural significance by accentuating its environmental devastations through stringent state legislations, criminalization and evictions has proven counterproductive, short-lived and unsustainable (Crawford and Botchwey 2017). Criminalization begets the exclusion of local small-scale miners as key stakeholders in the ASM reform process, which goes against the grain of key research recommendations for a regulatory framework that is inclusive of the voices and realities of miners (Osei-Kojo and Andrews 2016). According to Kinyondo and Huggins (2020: 758), formalizing ASM, rather than criminalizing it, is now generally accepted as a global best practice by major organizations such as the African Union and the World Bank. Decriminalizing ASM informality will require a critical rethinking of the entire legal framework underpinning ASM formalization and the adoption of a more culturally situated system.

ASM Formalization and the Land Question

At its core, the ASM formalization discourse revolves around land, mainly the acquisition of tenure security on geologically productive lands. I have already established that formalization efforts are typically based on the assumption that ASM on secured property rights will empower the recipients of these rights with the opportunity to capitalize their possessions to access formal credit and generate revenue. This, according to Bromley (2008: 22), flows from a flawed inductive logic; vast empirical research has been unable to establish any robust and reliable connection between secured tenure and improved productivity. Bromley argues that the highly touted political legitimacy of formalization misses a central point, namely, that borrowers must have secured income streams before it will be possible to leverage credit out of a banking system. This is pertinent to the ASM context, where the promises of tenure security remain unfulfilled even for formalized ASM operators, mostly because banks and governments are generally unwilling to provide financial credit and support to artisanal and small-scale miners (Hilson 2011; Martinez, Smith and Malone 2023). After all, the title to a claim and some buckets and shovels, as Siegel and Veiga (2009) found, was hardly enough collateral to guarantee a loan. This situation is evidently more difficult for unlicensed miners, who have to resort to informal credit from gold buyers and other informal investors to finance their operations (Fold, Jønsson and Yankson 2014). As further observed by Amanor (2009b) in a study on the formalization of customary lands and tenure security in Ghana, the assumed relationship between registration, tenure security and capitalization was not supported by the evidence on the ground. Elsewhere, Amanor (2008) had argued that registration merely emphasized the favoured status of commercial interest groups who were more likely to register land and to protect the interests they often gained through expropriation from the less fortunate.

The universalist adoption of formalization has created unprecedented opportunities for states to consolidate their hegemony over mineral-bearing lands. These are usually backed by statutory laws rooted in colonially inherited legal conceptions of mining and property rights (McQuilken and Hilson 2016). By vesting all mineral rights in themselves, states assert sole regulatory oversight over access to, control and use of mining titles under a formalized, unitary property rights regime. Davidson (1993) had earlier addressed the need for governments to move beyond the establishment of legislative frameworks towards providing specially demarcated areas amenable to small-scale development, including preliminary evaluation of their technical and economic viability at different levels of operation. This advice was not fully heeded, and notwithstanding their control over mineralized lands, states are still unable to implement adequate spatial planning to address the land struggles of small-scale miners and avert other land-use conflicts.

In Ghana, the initiative to pursue an ASM formalization informed by geological knowledge began as far back as 1985, when delegates at the Joint Secretaries' Conference drew attention to the idea of blocking out gold deposits in which large-scale mining companies had not demonstrated any interest. In May 2009, the Minerals Commission produced a list of Designated Areas for Small Scale Gold & Diamond Mining in Ghana, which then stood at forty-six designated areas (now exceeding 144), to augment this policy intervention. This stemmed from complaints about ASM land allocations being unaccompanied by geological mapping and mineral inventory. Consequently, local miners were often left with lands that had marginal productivity and commercial viability (Hilson, Bartels and Hu 2022). More detailed policy frameworks evolved under the 2014 Minerals and Mining Policy, which outlined the government's commitment to undertake geological investigation and demarcation of areas suitable for ASM. This policy initiative was further elaborated under the Artisanal & Small-Scale Mining Framework developed by the Minerals Commission in 2015.

These attempts to address the land struggles of ASM through exclusive demarcations have proven not entirely successful, partly due to stiff competition from large-scale corporations and the government's hesitance to fully committing to land access for small-scale miners. The Natural Resource and Environmental Governance (NREG), which set out to implement the identification of mineralized lands capable of sustaining formalized ASM, saw the prospecting of only a few of the designated areas. Indeed, at the end of the third NREG project in 2012, only seven designated areas covering 349 km^2 had been prospected, and as of January 2014, no mining activity had commenced at any of these sites despite the huge investments by the World Bank. This can be contrasted with the eagerness with which the government allocates substantial concessions to large-scale mining corporations. Hilson, Bartels and Hu (2022) placed the current record of total land area held by large-scale mining ventures under different reconnaissance, prospecting and mining leases at 68,325.78 km^2 constituting approximately 30% of the country's total land area of 238,538 km^2. This underscores the longstanding land struggle of small-scale miners in what Hilson (2019) referred to as 'large-scale mining bias', where rent-seeking governments prioritize the attraction of large-scale mining corporations through the grant of sizeable fiscal and regulatory concessions.

One direct consequence of this large-scale mining bias has been the subjugation of ASM to an informal existence where much-needed policy measures such as access to land are relegated to the bottom tier of the country's mining initiatives (Hilson and Hilson 2017). Characterizing it as a 'legislative afterthought', Maconachie and Hilson (2011a) argued that legalization has done little to augment access to land for small-scale miners, since ASM legalization occurred three years after mining sector reforms had already yielded substantial mining concessions to large-scale mining companies. These asymmetric concessionary grants were the bedrock of the World Bank's Structural Adjustment Programmes, which promoted mining through large-scale corporations and associated elites. Fisher (2007) explained that in many cases, this prioritization enabled corporatist land grabs, where multinational mining companies were able to draw on the power of the state to acquire licences for lands over which so-called informal claims were already being held by local small-scale miners. Studies conducted by researchers using Landsat imagery and GIS technology revealed significant overlaps between ASM sites and large-scale mining concessions, with more than half of the studied ASM operations occurring within concessions granted to large-scale mines (Patel et al. 2016; Mitchell 2016). These spatial overlaps were observed to arise from expropriations and rezoning of ASM sites to large-scale mining corporations, or encroachment by small-scale miners.

While mining legislations introduced with the purpose of revolutionizing the mining sector largely targeted the improvement of conditions for attracting large-scale mining corporations, legislations and policies aimed at ASM were mostly punitive, prescribing more carceral responses than supportive measures. This deprioritization of ASM is unfortunate considering its socioeconomic relevance. For instance, an estimated 16,000 workers employed by large-scale mining corporations in Ghana (and the 66,000 supported indirectly) pales in comparison to the numbers employed by ASM. The latter includes the significant number of retrenched large-scale miners who found refuge in ASM, particularly during the era of the Structural Adjustment Programmes (Banchirigah 2006). The relationship between ASM and large-scale mining corporations is, as a result, characterized by intense land contestations that have rendered many mining communities a hotspot of violent clashes, military interventions and, in some cases, deaths (Akabzaa 2009; Ellimah 2017). Okoh's study of the Obuasi mining community (2014) – also the case study area for this book – shows such tensions to be even more pertinent in communities with a longstanding history of mining and substantially proven mineral deposits, where land conflicts between small-scale miners and mining corporations oscillate between latency and periodic outbursts of violent confrontation.

Following its failure to address land contestations in the mining sector, the state elected to have the matter addressed through negotiations between large-scale mining corporations and small-scale miners at the local level. As Hilson, Sauerwein and Owen (2020) observed, efforts to defuse the tensioned land conflicts have generally involved arrangements where large-scale mining corporations permit small-scale miners to operate on portions of their concessions. Examples of such working partnerships include the agreement between Ghana Consolidated Diamonds Limited and local miners, where the latter were allowed to work on the company's Akwatia diamond mine (Yelpaala and Ali 2005); Gold Fields Limited's agreement to allow nearly 740 small-scale miners to work on its Damang site (Aubynn 2009); and the allocation of approximately 5% of Bogoso Gold Limited's concession to small-scale miners (Hilson 2002a).

Hilson, Sauerwein and Owen (2020) have critiqued these land arrangements as shortsighted and farfetched cohabitations that are unsustainable as a development strategy. They argue that large-scale mining corporations are hardly ever altruistic, and that such arrangements never fully relinquish the apportioned concessions to the small-scale miners. The authors presented evidence of the temporality of such land arrangements, where mining corporations were quick to grant parts of their less productive concessions to small-scale miners, especially during periods of fluctuating gold prices, but were equally quick to evict these miners as soon as gold prices began to rise, or when the concessions proved to be much more geologically profitable to the local miners than earlier anticipated. Occasionally, new managements were also not keen on continuing with these negotiated arrangements (Hilson, Sauerwein and Owen 2020).

Amidst such tensioned complexities in obtaining lands for operations, small-scale miners are left to compete amongst themselves in a 'survival of the fittest' type of contestation for the limited available productive lands (Zvarivadza and Nhleko 2018). Without access to lands and supporting geological data, the ability of local miners to operate with the legitimacy prescribed under state law is effectively constrained (Siwale and Siwale 2017). As already established, prospective ASM operators receive little to no assistance from the state in their initial search for lands, as the formalization process only kicks in after the examination of already negotiated and acquired site plans of the intended mining area. Prospective small-scale miners are left to navigate what Hilson, Bartels and Hu (2022) described as a puzzling and ill-advised cross-ministerial licensing system where they face unprecedented bureaucracies and a host of fees for multiple permits. Local miners bear the entire cost of searching and negotiating for lands from customary landowners, engaging the Land Valuation Division in the event of conflicts over payment of compensations, engaging geological surveyors, registering their operations as legal entities with the Registrar-General's Department and payment for the publication of notices on their intended operations (Kumah 2022: 5).

It is therefore not surprising that ASM operators choose to bypass these processes and negotiate directly for lands with customary landowners, chiefs and other authorities who act as twilight institutions for small-scale miners without the added hassle of statutorily required, bureaucratic licensing procedures (Lund 2006; Fisher 2008). However, state-centric ASM formalization, as it stands, delegitimizes any such resort to customary land tenures that are not sanctioned by the state. This, according to Bromley (2008: 22), stems from a lingering uneasiness amongst Western-oriented development experts that Africa will never develop as long as it hangs on to its 'quaint' tenure regimes, where 'quaint' refers to the customary, communal land tenure systems. Bromley (2008: 26) cautioned against the push for formalization as a form of cultural imperialism, especially within contexts where customary tenure systems provide sufficient security to facilitate the level of transactions required.

The ASM land issue has also highlighted the rapid expansion of the sector into new frontiers that were traditionally dominated by agricultural activities (Ofosu et al. 2020). The interface between ASM and agriculture is a widely researched subject, which underscores the tensions, conflicts and complementarities between the two sectors. The evidence points to the seasonality of operations, where 'mining farmers' supplement their farm incomes with ASM during the dry season, and 'farming miners' undertake farming activities in the rainy seasons (Maconachie and Binns 2007; Bryceson and Jønsson 2010; Hilson and Garforth 2013; Mkodzongi and Spiegel 2019). However, the increasing competition over land has altered the synergies and created new forms of resource-use conflicts between these two relevant rural drivers of development. As a result of the sporadic proliferation of ASM in rural farming communities, for instance, concerns about deagrarianization – the reorientation of livelihoods away from the agrarian sector – have brought into focus the rapid loss of arable lands to ASM (Bryceson 1996). A study conducted by Schueler, Kuemmerle and Shröder (2011) using maps derived from satellite data revealed a 45% loss of farmlands to concession areas and 58% deforestation from surface mining in the Wassa West district, one of the most prominent ASM districts in the southern parts of Ghana. A similar study by Boateng, Codjoe and Ofori (2014) revealed that around 50 hectares of cocoa farmlands in the Atiwa district of Ghana had been lost to ASM.

In response to the huge and often irreversible transformation of cocoa farms into ASM sites, the Ghana Cocoa Board (also known as COCOBOD), the state agency responsible for regulating the production, processing, marketing and purchasing prices of cocoa and other cash crops, suggested the introduction of legislative and other policy interventions to prohibit cocoa farmers from granting their lands to informal ASM operators. This came against concerns that Ghana's cocoa might be banned from the European Union (EU) market owing to contamination with mercury from ASM. COCOBOD believed that local cocoa farmers were being forced to give away their farms due to low exposure and coercion from local chiefs (Lartey 2022). In doing so, COCOBOD dismissed the low cocoa prices and 'agricultural poverty' that, according to Hilson and Garforth (2013), epitomized the inability of subsistence farming to sustain the livelihoods of rural families, which leads farmers to branch into ASM or transact their lands for more lucrative returns from ASM operators. What this entanglement between ASM and agricultural land use reveals is that solutions are far more complex than formalization and should be integrated with other rural poverty alleviation measures and global processes on equitable and fair pricing for cocoa.

In all the suggestions for addressing the land question in ASM, a strikingly missing point is the fact that land in mineral-producing countries like Ghana is fundamentally shaped by a plural legal system where rights derive from both customary land tenure and statutory laws, with overlapping interests that intersect at various points in space and time. This should be of primary interest to ASM research, especially with the focus of emerging scholarship on the complex interplay of state and non-state legal frameworks in ASM governance (Nyame and Blocher 2010; Verbrugge, Cuvelier and Van Bockstael 2015; Persaud et al. 2017; de Haan and Geenen 2016; De Jong and Sauerwein 2021; Mensah 2021). In Chapter 4, I will examine a number of these studies and their ethnographic findings from Ghana, the Philippines, Liberia, Congo, Senegal and Côte d'Ivoire among others, with the aim of provoking a rethinking of how we approach the land issue in ASM. In doing so, I also aim to present key insights into ASM at the tensioned intersection of state and customary laws and to address the sector's heavy reliance on customary land tenures not as an 'informal illegality' but as a site of radical resistance, survival and expression of Indigenous knowledges, practices and customs that can be harnessed for ASM reform.

Artisanal miners are heterogeneous, just as their claims to mineralized lands are constrained by multiple, often competing claims and power relations. I argue that it is the disregard for this reality of legally plural, multiple, overlapping claims that forms the fundamental stumbling block to ASM in Ghana being more sustainable and transformative. In the next section, through a review of some of the pertinent scholarly recommendations for ASM legal reform, I provide a precursor to the possibility of an alternative system to state-centric formalization.

Another 'Law' Is Possible: Situated Knowledges and Deconstructing Legality in ASM Formalization

In this chapter, I have established how the crux of ASM's environmental problems and other related challenges are primarily attributed to its informality as well as the weak and stifling regulatory framework that hinders the enforcement of state mining regulations. Consequently, demands for regulatory reform have revolved around the need for stronger and more comprehensive legislation. This discourse has presented many suggestions, one of which is the re-emergence of proposals for multitier reclassification of ASM in the mining codes. Echavarria's (2014: 37) study of ASM in Colombia, for instance, registered that the absence of differentiation in the Mining Code for the diverse scales of artisanal, small and medium mining operations did not only leave local miners at a disadvantage when requesting mining concessions, but also negatively affected law and policy regulation of the sector. The demand for definition of the various forms of artisanal and small-scale mining in Ghana was one of the foremost suggestions during the #StopGalamseyNow campaign (Kpienbaareh et al. 2021). Pushing this further, Kumah (2022: 8) described the current legislative framework as homogeneous in the sense that it does not differentiate between the rudimentary and more mechanized methods of ASM operations in the country. This, he argued, was a regulatory gap inextricably linked to the high level of informality and illegality in Ghana's ASM sector.

For Hilson and McQuilken (2014: 106), the ASM definition debates that defined the 1970s discourse on the sector were 'fruitless' and 'mundane'. According to the authors, the preoccupation with compartmentalizing and defining 'artisanal mining' and 'small-scale mining' posed a major disservice to the sector, distancing it further from the global development agenda. From their studies in Sierra Leone and Liberia, Hilson and Maconachie (2020b) argued that legislative recategorization of ASM according to levels of production and mechanization was not a particularly effective formalization strategy. The authors identified that the separate licensing schemes rather stifled innovation across the sector and cemented the division between, on the one hand, subsistence ASM groups, and on the other, those who deployed advanced operations. In their rebuttal to Hilson and Maconachie (2020b), Arthur-Holmes and Ofosu (2024) contended that rather than inhibiting innovation in the sector, different categories of mining licences will enhance the dynamism of ASM operators and pave the way for innovation and the use of heavy machinery where necessary to increase ore production. In making the case for differentiation in the issuance of ASM licences, Arthur-Holmes and Ofosu (2024) argued that 'one size fits all' mining licences hindered the designing of context-specific land reclamation approaches, the development of appropriate environmental regulations and mine waste management practices, as well as the provision of logistics, training, and technical assistance to address the divergent environmental impacts from ASM.

This insistence on the compartmentalization of ASM and its licensing system is grounded in the argument that subjecting alluvial gold mining (which utilizes simple tools such as pots, pans, pickaxes and shovels) to the same licensing and legislative requirements as the more mechanized mining (undertaken with high levels of capital investment and sophisticated earth-moving machinery like excavators, drillers and trommels) is unreasonable due to their different levels of environmental impact (Ferring, Hausermann and Effah 2016; Kumah 2022; Arthur-Holmes and Ofosu 2024). Foreign (mostly Chinese) involvement in Ghanaian ASM has introduced increased mechanization and intensified production, which Crawford and Botchwey (2017: 454) believe have irreversibly changed the rudimentary nature of ASM such that the sector can no longer be described as artisanal. There are even concerns that these advanced technologies in ASM are displacing low-skilled workers in the sector (Damonte et al. 2013). To that end, differentiated legislative definitions based on the physical characteristics and level of sophistication are advanced as imperative for environmental compliance and accountability. These reignited debates on ASM definitions form part of the wider discourse on context-sensitive formalization measures towards strengthening the sector (Jønsson and Fold 2011).

On another front, Hilson, Bartels and Hu (2022) were emphatic that the impact of all these formalization measures will be negligible in the absence of decentralization. Proponents of decentralization argue that with the apparent failure of centralized resource management in delivering sustainable and equitable outcomes, a redistribution of decision-making authority, particularly in licensing, is more suited to an empowering, responsive, transparent and efficient natural resource management (Hirons 2014; Eduful et al. 2020). The current formalization system in Ghana is known to be heavily centralized despite the presence of District Small-Scale Mining Offices across the country (Osei-Kojo and Andrews 2016). This is unlike the situation in countries like Kenya where, as Huggins, Buss and Rutherford (2017) observed, county governments are authorized to issue licences.

The problem with decentralization of ASM administration, as Hirons (2014) found from his study in Ghana, was that such attempts were mostly inadequate and further exacerbated the complex nature of local resource politics surrounding ASM.

A recent attempt at decentralizing ASM governance in Ghana appeared in the Community Mining Scheme (CMS), which, among other things, aimed to create a more transparent and predictable framework for acquiring concessions, and to facilitate a more environmentally responsible ASM (Yeboah 2021). The government defined a community mining area as land that has been designated by the responsible minister in accordance with section 89 of the Minerals and Mining Act, or the portion of a concession of a large-scale mining lease that has been permitted for the purpose of the tributer system.[5] The maximum area to be granted under CMS is 25.2 acres, in accordance with Regulation 204 of the Minerals and Mining (Licensing) Regulations, 2012 (LI 2176).[6] In other words, this could be an area within a prospecting licence held by a large-scale mining company that has been relinquished or surrendered in accordance with section 38 of the Minerals and Mining Act and specifically requested and designated for small-scale mining (Hilson, Bartels and Hu 2022).[7] Small-scale miners interested in operating under the CMS are required to organize under a body corporate, cooperatives/partnerships or sole proprietorships and demonstrate the capacity to invest a minimum of GHS 100,000 (£538.86). Prospective miners are also required to register under the scheme and sign on to the Code of Practice developed by the Minerals Commission.[8] This Code of Practice was developed in accordance with Regulations 475 and 515 of the Minerals and Mining (Health, Safety and Technical) Regulations, 2012 (LI 2182), and governs every aspect of the mining operations, including the maintenance of buffer zones from waterbodies, measures to avoid the discharge of toxic chemicals during mining and processing, post-mining land reclamation, blasting, crushing, chemical processing, fire prevention, first aid and other health, safety and environmental rules (Minerals Commission of Ghana 2021).

Under this scheme, key roles in the formalization process are given to district assemblies, which form the centrepiece of Ghana's decentralization, but have been limited to onboarding and communicating ASM applications. As a start, interested miners are expected to share their proposals with their district assemblies. The district assemblies then make the applications to the Minerals Commission for licences on behalf of the small-scale miners in their constituencies and for ringfencing mineralized lands for ASM. The involvement of district assemblies is envisaged to alleviate the expenses involved in ASM formalization, as they cover the costs associated with Environmental Impact Assessments, Water Use Permits and other licensing fees. Small-scale miners under the CMS operate with tenure security and without fear of eviction or harassment from the military or the police. Proceeds from CMS earnings are to be shared as follows: 50% to the investor or titleholder, 20% to the workers, 10% to the community through the traditional authorities, 10% to the Minerals Commission and 10% to the district assembly. As of June 2020, nearly fifty-five CMSs had been launched across five regions in the country (Hilson, Bartels and Hu 2022).

Hilson, Bartels and Hu (2022) expressed optimism at the CMS, stating that the decentralization of ASM formalization and the involvement of the district assemblies would address the unprecedented bureaucracies, counteract the chronic rent-seeking of Minerals Commission officers in Accra and boost job creation in the local communities. A number of issues arise, however, from the operationalization of the CMS. First, the government's definition of the scheme places the availability of lands within the benevolence of large-scale mining companies and their relinquished lands, a situation that Hilson, Sauerwein and Owen (2020) have examined as highly unsustainable. Enthusiasm about the CMS notwithstanding, insights from the local communities tell a different story, as I will demonstrate in Chapter 6, where it will become clear how land allocation under the CMS largely works in favour of mining entrepreneurs, party favourites and other well-connected businessmen, at the expense of local communities and small-scale miners. In their study on the Chinese takeover of ASM in Ghana, Crawford and Botchwey (2017: 446) observed similar mechanisms of elite capture and 'clientelization' in the distribution of resources based on one's political party affiliation. This has not only deepened classed disparities but also raised doubts about the integrity and capacity of state institutions to address ASM's challenges.

Another notable observation I made throughout the scholarly legal and policy recommendations for ASM reform is the assumption of state law orthodoxy. Within the different schools of thought on formalization, the structuralists may deplore the legalists' fixation on legalization and find them deficient in suggesting a clear direction towards actual transformation of ASM. This notwithstanding, they all share a consensus towards state exclusivism in reforming the informal sector. Geenen (2012) rightly noted that ASM formalization embodied a minerals reform policy and regulatory apparatus that placed ASM within a standardized legal framework registered in, and governed by, a central state system. This state-centric property system lies in juxtaposition with the non-state system, which de Soto (2000: 59) referred to as a state of 'legal anarchy' where the poor are locked up in a 'legal apartheid' and unable to access the tools to create wealth.

As Lochery (2022) has pointed out, mining projects do not work in isolation but are integral to wider political assemblages – projects of statehood, empire-building, national and subnational economies and transnational relationships of trade, finance and migration. Lochery builds on scholarship showing how past and present processes of expropriation, dispossession, oppression and 'inclusionary control' enable capitalist extraction. It is within this complex interconnection between empire, statehood and the ongoing colonialities of legal imperialism that I present my critiques against ASM formalization. For this reason, I interrupt the scholarship's fixation on formalization with the following questions: why formalization? Why state laws? What further justifications can reasonably be postulated for the insistence on state-centric formalization in the face of nearly four decades of its overwhelming failures? And finally, why not an alternative framework in the form of the living customary laws? Admittedly, ASM represents a versatile mining venture made up of variegated site specificities and a diversity of individuals who work within a fluid, socially, legally and culturally heterogeneous context. To that extent, I share the literature's position that laws and policies need to be tailored to the different types of mining communities in order to meet the specific needs, skills and motivations of small-scale miners (Marshall and Veiga 2017). My point of departure, however, is the fixation on colonially inherited, state-centric formalization in pursuit of liberatory changes in the ASM sector. I argue that state-imposed norms and policies are part of the solution, but should not be upheld as the sole solution. Salo et al. (2016: 1066) share this view that the bureaucratic processes of ASM formalization must come under review, and that the success of mainstream formalization should not be seen as a prerequisite to, much less a synonym for, dealing with ASM's impacts.

Furthermore, I confront how state law is taken for granted as the normative regulatory framework despite the overwhelming evidence of customary laws within ASM. I argue that the state-centric legal framework of ASM formalization loses sight of a major feature of property rights, namely, that rights are socially constructed and that any property laws imposed without reference to the existing social contracts and customary laws would fail for lack of legitimacy. In advancing ASM reform, I delve deeper to question informality, the homogeneous conception of law and the dominant notion of legality/

illegality that sustains the prevailing concept of formalization. In other words, I present the position that the oversight of the pluralities of the Ghanaian legal system – particularly land tenure systems and the living customary law in ASM reform – underscores a huge failing of the prevailing formalization efforts. This, I will argue, forms a historical continuity of disconnection between what constitutes ASM law by the state and what is pertinent in the target local communities. This argument builds on Benton's (1994) critique of structural notions of legal pluralism, where the distinction between 'legal' and 'illegal' spheres within the framework of laws that stack the formal atop the informal sector may not always act to support the dominant relationship of one economic practice over another. This is because participants often engage in reinterpreting their positions within the legal order and the meaning of that order, seeking to alter or improve subordinate economic positions by using to their advantage what may appear to be highly prejudicial legal constructs. Ultimately, I will demonstrate that there are locally designed mechanisms, informed by the living customary law and Indigenous knowledges, that hold much more potential for ASM reform.

Conclusion

Over the past decades, there has emerged a burgeoning body of research pointing to ASM's indispensability and potential for economic development in Africa. The manifestation of this huge potential is, however, biased towards formalization, which is positioned as the surest pathway for control and mitigation of the adverse impacts of ASM as well as for harnessing the positive contributions of the sector. Nearly four decades of unsuccessful ASM formalization in Ghana, however, demonstrates an apparent shortage of ideas within the state-centric mechanisms on how to establish concrete ties between ASM regulatory reform and the realities on the ground. In reviewing the challenges of ASM, I have shown in this chapter the literature's interest in untangling the conflicts between imposed formalization measures and the pre-existing customary practices, lived realities and cultures of ASM operations. This, I believe, holds the key to ASM legal reform, which I shall pursue in the next chapter through a decolonizing approach to researching ASM law.

Notes

1. See Mary Esther Kropp Dakubu. 2012. 'The Portuguese Language on the Gold Coast, 1471–1807', *Ghana Journal of Linguistics* 1(1): 15–33, where the author postulates that *galamsey* may have been a derivation from *galimpeiro*, the Portuguese word for independent gold winners, which survived into the nineteenth century from the Portuguese encounter with the people of the Gold Coast.
2. See also Chapter 6, where I explain that Hardin's (1968) 'tragedy of the commons', which postulated that freedom in the commons brings ruin to all, has rightfully been debunked by economists like Ostrom (1990) and by other studies on collaborative resource-management systems.
3. The theory of intersectionality was coined by Crenshaw (1991) and describes a similar phenomenon, which Collins (2000) referred to as the 'matrix of domination'. It emphasizes the complexity of overlapping oppressions faced by Black women on account of race, class and gender. See Kimberlé Crenshaw (1991), 'Mapping the Margins: Intersectionality, Identity Politics, and Violence against Women of Color', *Stanford Law Review* 43(6): 1241–99; Patricia Hill Collins (2000), *Black Feminist Thought: Knowledge, Consciousness, and the Politics of Empowerment*, London: Routledge.
4. Ghana is in the process of reviewing its 2014 Minerals and Mining Policy and the Minerals and Mining Act, respectively, to reflect substantive changes in the government's response to *galamsey*. While the full policy document is currently unavailable for public scrutiny, information from ongoing consultative discussions points to intensifying measures aimed at, among other things, ending *galamsey* and sanitizing the sector through formalization. It remains to be seen what changes will emanate from this emerging ASM formalization system.
5. This is in accordance with Regulations 496 to 506 of the Minerals and Mining (Health, Safety and Technical) Regulations, 2012 (LI 2182).
6. Section 89 of the Minerals and Mining Act provides that where the minister, after consultation with the Minerals Commission, considers that it is in the public interest to encourage small-scale mining in an area, the minister may, by notice in the Gazette, designate the area for small-scale mining operations and specify the mineral to be mined. The tributer system generally involves an arrangement where portions of large-scale mining concessions are leased to ASM operators.
7. Section 38 of the Minerals and Mining Act provides for a compulsory reduction of prospecting licence, where the holder is required to surrender not less than half of the number of blocks of the prospecting area prior to, or at the expiration of, the initial term, so long as a minimum of 125 blocks remain.
8. This amount is at the exchange rate as of January 2025 and is subject to review by the government.

CHAPTER 2

Decolonizing Methodologies in ASM Research

Introduction

> Tomorrow comes.
>
> 'Now', says he, 'I shall see the King today! What time think you', he inquires of an official who has come to pay to him the compliments of the morning and see what he is about.
>
> 'At what hour shall I go to the Palace?'
>
> 'Oh', answers the official, 'You cannot see the King today; this is his birthday.'
>
> 'Birthday!', exclaims the sufferer, 'Why I should have thought that a very proper occasion. Why should His Majesty not kindly honour me by allowing me to pay him my first private visit on such an auspicious day, a day which only comes once in a year.'
>
> 'It comes once a week; it is every Wednesday', answers the officer, 'and on that day, the King keeps quiet and sees nobody.'[1]

The above exchange, between the Reverend Thomas Birch Freeman (the third Wesleyan missionary to arrive in the Gold Coast in 1838, and the first to journey into Asante) and a court official of the *Asantehene* (King of the Asante nation), illustrates one of the many differences between Western and African worldviews, as captured through the distinct conceptualizations of time. Here, impatiently craving audience before the Asantehene, the newly arrived Western missionary jumped excitedly at an opportunity to meet the King on his birthday, which he assumed was acknowledged and celebrated once every year, – only to be met with new information about a different concept in the culture he has visited.

Such assumptions of Western knowledges were a constitutive element of the process of colonization, where patriarchal, capitalist, Christian-centric and formalist–positivist ideologies were presented as natural and universal. The claim to know differently therefore presented a critique of this universalist pretension of Western traditions, and has been the position of decolonial and other critical methodologies where different cultural positions are considered epistemologically salient (Alcoff 1991–92: 5).[2] Despite recent calls for decolonizing the Eurocentrism embedded in modern academic knowledge production, not much attention has been paid to decolonization in ASM scholarship. This is despite the field's extensive focus on the extractive industry in formerly colonized, Indigenous societies of the Global South. This lacuna is prevalent even within the emerging scholarship that focuses on customary laws in ASM. Colonization and its Western universalisms manifested differently in the ways in which colonialists imposed their values and legal systems in mineral-rich communities (Youe 2010). Despite political independence, these colonially imposed and influenced values and legal systems persist in many mineral-producing African countries, hence substantiating the need for decolonizing the ways in which knowledges on mining and its legal framework in such communities are generated.

In this chapter, in an overt departure from the prevailing epistemic universalizations, I present decoloniality as my contribution towards constructing counterhegemonic narratives in ASM law and policy formulation. The literature I explored in Chapter 1 affirms the need for an alternative legal framework that, I argue, must begin with a decolonizing methodology that scrutinizes the way legality is constructed in ASM. This is underscored by the position that no radical transformation can emerge from the Western epistemologies that underpin the prevailing legal regime. A decolonial approach is imperative, not only because situated knowledges and Indigenous epistemologies have for a long time been disregarded in formulating ASM legal frameworks, but also because of its potential to shift normative attitudes and behaviours towards a more culturally appropriate and sustainable regulatory framework.

The questions that arise, then, are as follows: how do we move beyond the hegemony of colonial epistemology within ASM research, towards a decolonially grounded, theoretically rich and intersectionally nuanced understanding of law in ASM? What would our attitude to the ASM legal system be if we understood formalization in its broader historical context? What would the legal framework of ASM look like if we moved the locus of enunciation from its prevailing state-centric viewpoint to the local small-scale miners themselves? And more importantly, what methods are we deploying to gather information about subjugated knowledges in ASM towards a reconstruction of the notion of law in ASM? In this chapter, I approach these questions by drawing on critical reflections of my experiences of doing interdisciplinary research combining legal and historical approaches to demonstrate the impact that decoloniality can have in shaping debates on ASM formalization.

This methodological intervention is under the direction of the Akan philosophy of *Sankɔfa*, through which I combine archival research and data from interviews to weave a unique tapestry of research that engages a retreat into the past, reflection on the present and a reimagination of liberatory futures for ASM in Ghana. In the first section, I begin with a brief exposition on *Sankɔfa* as the overarching methodological framework for this book. In the second section, I provide an overview of decolonizing methodologies and explain the relevance of their historical approach to contemporary and context-specific analysis of ASM law. I proceed in the third section with a more specific discussion on decolonizing ASM legal research; in that section, I also reflect extensively on my initial methodological engagement with sociolegal ethnography as a departure from the doctrinal analysis of ASM law. This sets the background for the fourth section, where I explore my dissatisfactions with the methodological conceptualization of formalization, and dive deeper into decoloniality.

In the fifth and sixth sections, I shed light on my initial methodological setbacks and the comebacks I made through repurposing my research methods to gather knowledge remotely in an ethical and respectful manner in the case study area, Obuasi. Ultimately, these sections engage in critical reflection on the linkages between law and history, and on how data from remote interviews and the archives complement each other towards an understanding of contemporary neoliberal policy and legal formulations on ASM. In the final section, I address key ethical considerations in researching small-scale miners and their local mining communities, drawing on ethics of reflexivity, empathy, positionality and Indigenous knowledge coproduction as crucial for the methodological design of research involving Indigenous, vulnerable and formerly colonized societies.

Sankɔfa as Radical Methodology: Retreat, Reflect, Retrieve

Sankɔfa is an Akan principle philosophizing that in order to move forward and build a future, one must first reach into the past to retrieve that which is at risk of being left behind or forgotten (Osei 2020). *Sankɔfa* remains one of the most popular of the *Adinkra* symbols, which are a collection of centuries-old Akan visual symbols embedded with historical and philosophical significance. According to Owusu-Sampah (2014), these *Adinkra* symbols are credited to the Asante people and form part of their shared history with Akans in present-day Côte d'Ivoire. *Sankɔfa* is pictorially represented as a heart-shaped design with some appendages; the most popular rendition of it depicts a bird moving forward with its head turned backwards to pick up an egg. The egg represents precious wisdom gained from past experiences, which benefits future generations (Quan-Baffour 2012).

This pictorial representation originates from a classic didactic oral folktale about the value of traditional customs and practices. The protagonist of the tale is a bird who left her village after committing an act of disrespect to communal values, but returns to the village after facing certain obstacles in the forest. Upon her return, she is helped by her community to regain her confidence; with this renewed sense of self-worth, she is able to overcome the antagonisms that had previously defeated her (Opoku-Agyemang 2017).

Sankɔfa literally means 'to return' (*san*), 'to go' (*kɔ*) and 'to retrieve' (*fa*). The cultural significance of the *Adinkra* symbols lies in their iconological, symbiotic relationship with proverbs. For instance, *Sankɔfa* derives its philosophy and visual imagery from the Akan proverb '*sɛ ɛtɔ w'akyi a fa, na sankɔfa wɔ hɔ yi, yɛn nkyi*' ('if it falls behind you, retrieve it, for it is not taboo to return to history to reclaim the past

Figure 2.1. The *Adinkra* symbols of *Sankɔfa*. Wikimedia Commons, public domain.

in order to move forward'). Another related Akan maxim is '*tete wɔ bi ka, tete wɔ bi kyerɛ, nti sankɔfa yɛnnkyi*' ('the past has a lot to say, the past has a lot to teach, going back for something of the past is thus a virtue') (Owusu 2019).

Like the Southern African philosophy of *Ubuntu, Sankɔfa* hinges on communality, with the added emphasis on retrospection for the sake of future development. *Sankɔfa* intersects with Afrocentrism in their shared principles of communality, reflexivity and emphasis on the importance of contextualizing and grounding research in the history and present of our communities (Mohammed 2022). Afrocentric methodology emphasizes a shift from dominant research methods to ones that are responsive to the African worldview (Mkabela 2005). This involves the centring of Indigenous knowledges, which Dei (2000a, 2000b) describes as deriving from people's direct experiences with nature and its symbiotic relationship with the surrounding environments, and as being crucial for community survival. Indigenous knowledges are ancient, living, constant experiences proven and based on cognitive understandings and interpretations of social, physical and spiritual worlds, encompassing concepts, beliefs and perceptions of local peoples in their natural and human-built environments. They are transmitted orally and experientially within holistic parameters that are nonlinear and reflect a qualitative and intuitive mode of thinking that does not rely on explicit hypotheses, theories and laws (Wane 2011). The Asante culture – from which I undertake my research – typifies such Indigenous societies, where knowledges are transmitted through proverbs, songs, arts, craft, dance, rituals, chants and folktales in the everyday sociocultural expressions of life. Afrocentric methods are culturally sensitive, meaning that they acknowledge and are accommodating of other forms of knowing, other value systems and other ways of understanding reality (Ntseane 2011).

As an Afrocentric theory, *Sankɔfa* is decolonial and challenges imperial historiographies and Eurocentric accounts of Africa that mark colonialism as the beginning of the continent's history (Ogot 1992; Mafundikwa 2017). Thus, its call for retreating into the past implies a historical exercise far beyond the histories, assumptions and misconceptions imposed by colonizers. It is reflexive and self-critical, in that it draws on the past as a useful guide for planning the future through rectifying any wrongs and drawing relevant lessons from the experience (Matemba 2020). *Sankɔfa* encapsulates a quest for traditional knowledges and systems based on critical reasoning, as well as an intelligent and patient investigation of the past that will serve as a blueprint for a stronger and more positive future (Slater 2019).

Sankɔfa's call for imagining a future through the legacies of an uncolonized society is one that Africa-focused scholars can respond to by assuming the role of the *Sankɔfa* bird in retrieving important cultural elements from the past and successfully reimagining them to fit into a futuristic space. In their recent theorization of the informal social and environmental responsibility of artisanal miners, Vasquez-Brust, Arthur-Holmes and Yakovleva (2024) deployed aspects of Akan philosophy to address how informal miners' practices are deeply informed by principles of commonality, solidarity, tradition and human–nature interdependencies. In particular, their use of *Sankɔfa* emphasized the interlinkages between post-mining land reclamation exercises and the Indigenous notions of caring for Mother Earth. In the rest of this chapter and throughout the remainder of this book, I demonstrate how I also utilized *Sankɔfa*, not as a means to co-opt Indigenous Akan philosophies to transform ASM in service of classed and corporatist extractivism, but as the overarching decolonial methodological framework through which I trace the past, contemplate the present and devise more sustainable and culturally situated legal possibilities for ASM reform.

Decolonizing Methodologies: An Overview

There may have been a reinvigorated interest in conversations around decolonization in the academy following the 2020 global Black Lives Matter protests against racialized police brutalities. However, as Tamale (2020) put it, the struggle for decolonization is as old as colonization, and has been in existence since colonizers set foot on the lands of Indigenous Peoples. The term 'decolonization' was defined by Modiri (2019) as an insatiable reparatory demand that entails nothing less than an endless fracturing of the world colonialism created. As a preliminary step, decolonization therefore requires an understanding of the world colonialism created and the colonial legacies that are deeply rooted in current global systems.

Describing this world for the African, Fanon (1963: 185) wrote that: 'In the case of the African especially, white society has smashed his old world without giving him a new one. It has destroyed the traditional tribal foundations of his existence and it blocks the road of the future after having closed the road of the past'. Abraham (1962) noted that the future of Africa rests on the present, and the present is an outcome of the past. Repairing the present and unblocking the road to the future requires a thorough examination of the past and the complex structural, institutional and psychological wounds left behind by our colonial encounter (Tamale 2020: 18). It is only after uprooting these colonialist structures that the next stage in the struggle for decoloniality can be embarked upon, namely, reclaiming our broken traditions, restoring our fetishized spiritualities, embracing our Indigenous philosophies and rebuilding our own liberatory futures (Wane 2005).

History is therefore pivotal to decolonization, and it is for this reason that archival research forms a crucial part of this book's decolonial approach to ASM law. Wynter (2006: 107) has noted that early decolonization movements failed to impact knowledge production due in part to the imperviousness of disciplines to phenomena that fell outside their predefined scope, as well as their reluctance in theorizing from a relationship between the epistemology of knowledge and the liberation of the people. The interdisciplinarity of my research ensured that my decolonial approach was well grounded in the history and the present of law, with capacity for reimagining emancipatory futures for local miners.

In his interview with Jerome Brooks (1994), Nigerian novelist Chinua Achebe emphasized that until the lions have their own historians, the history of the hunt will always glorify the hunter. Africa has long been the subject of what Benyera (2018) refers to as a 'mishistoricization', where the history of the continent has largely revolved around accounts from the perspective of colonialists and Western writers who sanitized the evils of colonialism and embellished their narratives with untruths about how the continent received civilization through the benevolence of colonialism. These enduring stereotypical images pervade even some of the most progressive and liberal Western research institutions, where the annihilation of Indigenous African histories and knowledges continues through zero-sum, linear colonial knowledge production, silencing, erasure, amnesia and innocence (Rutazibwa 2020).

The universalization of Western knowledges was in keeping with the expansion of Western capitalism, and can be explained through Gramsci's theory of hegemony, which denotes how systems of power are constructed through knowledge by the creation of an order in which certain ways of life and thought are diffused throughout society as dominant, natural and universal (Hoare and Smith 1971). The result of this hegemony has been the silencing and epistemicide of Indigenous knowledges, which sadly persists in Africa's Westernized education systems, where students are taught about the 'advantages' of colonialism, European 'discoveries' on the continent and foreign theorizations of ourselves and our environment (Dladla 2017).

These distorted narratives were particularly prevalent in Western accounts of the continent's mineral resources. According to *The Gold Coast Chronicle* (30 July 1898: 3), during the early colonial days of present-day Ghana, the Western-educated locals contested casual Western references to the 'discovery' of gold deposits and trade in the Gold Coast from the fourteenth century, a timeline informed by the first recorded accounts of European contact. Even more recent publications reinforce this Indigenous erasure with their attribution of British-sponsored French miner Pierre Bonnat, who was once a prisoner in Asante, as the 'father' of gold mining in Ghana, despite oral-historical accounts and material evidence of Indigenous gold mining prior to European encounter (Hilson 2002b: 13). This thinking is extrapolated into the treatment of Indigenous mining and ASM as a footnote to the extractive industry, normatively viewed through the prism of large-scale mining corporations.

The call for deconstructing the universalization of Western knowledges in ASM knowledge production is vital to dismantling the prevailing capitalist neoliberal system in which many local small-scale miners continue to suffer. Drawing from the above, this book is grounded in an archival and oral-historical exploration of the colonial legacies of ASM's current policy and regulatory framework. This was informed by how absent the historicization of ASM law was within the mainstream literature and undertaken with the understanding that we cannot resolve the problems of ASM without tackling the root causes of coloniality that persist within the sector's legal framework.

Before I continue, I wish to interject here by addressing the timely relevance and urgency of this decolonizing approach, lest I am accused of derailing the ASM discourse with talks of history and colonialism. As Tamale (2020: 3) has pointed out, such retorts remain a pastime of some diplomats and scholars who are quick to urge African researchers to get over colonialism and to stop blaming external factors for the woes on the continent. Clapham (2020: 137), for instance, referred to an ideology of victimhood that consigned African researchers to a form of learned helplessness that, according to him, provided a comforting explanation for failure in the form of blaming someone else. This is reminiscent of Mbembe's (2002) accusation of Afroradicalist and Marxist thinkers as being preoccupied with a 'neurosis of victimhood' linked to the triple events of slavery, colonialism and apartheid.

Ndlovu-Gatsheni (2013: 46), however, reminds us that while we may be tired of talking about colonialism, the reality is that coloniality is not yet tired of dominating, exploiting and oppressing Africans. Colonialism, according to Grosfoguel (2007), refers to the colonial situations enforced by the presence of a colonial administration. The era of classical colonialism was characterized by territorial appropriation, direct control of social structures and exploitation of natural environment and human labour (Mohamed et al. 2020). While for many African states this period ended nearly sixty years ago, the multiple global structures put in place by colonialism did not instantly evaporate with juridical–political decolonization. Colonial forms of domination, which Quijano (2000) refers to as coloniality or the colonial power matrix, persist in ongoing cultural, economic, political, spiritual and epistemic oppressions. The racialized, capitalist and extractivist global economy established under colonialism remains profoundly entrenched in Africa's mining landscape, where mineral rights and its governance continue to be subordinated to Eurocentric liberalisms.

This is evinced by the persistence of resource extractivism, which relates to the longstanding colonialist fascination with the accumulation of wealth through the exploitation of large amounts of mineral resources from colonized societies to satisfy growing demands in the metropoles (Pereira and Tsikata 2021). Despite its predatory nature, resource extractivism continues to dictate the policy and regulatory framework of mining in many African countries, thus perpetuating inequalities and causing damage to the environment and cultures in these materially overexploited countries (Acosta 2011). For instance, more than one hundred mostly British corporations listed on the London Stock Exchange are said to have mining interests in thirty-seven African countries and, together, they control over $1 trillion of Africa's most valuable mineral resources (Curtis 2016). Ghana's first president, Dr Kwame Nkrumah expressed concerns about this phenomenon in *Neocolonialism: The Last Stage of Imperialism*, where he detailed the persistent colonial stranglehold on the extractive industry in vulnerable, newly independent African states, maintained by an intricate web of exploitative monopolies, conglomerates, agreements and foreign aid interventions.[3]

This is all happening at a time when local small-scale miners are constantly denied access to geologically productive lands and are forced to navigate deepening fractures, inequalities and state criminalization under the prevailing 'large-scale mining bias' (Hilson 2019: 852). Ghanaian feminist poet Ama Ata Aidoo (2017) described this ongoing coloniality as the:

> ...canonized Stability for
> just another neo-colonial phase
> of our post-colonial era?
> ...and there are fresh twin gods in town, they say, called
> Privatization and Divestiture...

As postcolonial, mineral-producing African governments continue to pay homage to the twin gods of 'Privatization and Divestiture', they end up sacrificing ASM on the altar of coloniality. Elsewhere, Cunha and Casimiro (2021: 71) described this new kind of colonialism as not based on political occupation but operating via the same kind of economic, cultural and political impositions, subjugations and exploitation carried out by transnational corporations and their Indigenous comprador elites. Critiquing the complicity of Indigenous elites who sustain and are constitutive of global oppressive structures signals a critical reflexive decoloniality that does not only rationalize and blame the political neglect of ordinary Africans on colonialism. Rather, it also takes cognizance of local sources of domination, unravelling their connections with colonial exploitation and its continuation in the postcoloniality (Fosu 2025).

For local small-scale miners, coloniality is not a distant phenomenon or an abstract ideology, but an ongoing reality that continues to: disrupt their access to mineral-rich lands; create, classify and criminalize them as 'illegals'; subjugate their Indigenous knowledges; and extricate them from aspirations for a reimagined society. Contemporary neoliberal discourses approach the present with a structural amnesia where they treat it ahistorically (Carpi and Owusu 2022). Such epistemic amnesia manifests in the ASM formalization discourse when scholars gloss over the colonialist roots of the modern state's intrusion into mineral rights governance. This attitude contributes to the pervasive coloniality that continues to shape the construction of state laws and how local miners who do not operate by them are perceived. This book aims to serve as a reminder of the persistence of coloniality in ASM and to admonish researchers on how imperative it is to not obscure the dire need for decolonization in the ASM discourse. Decolonization in ASM is crucial to the very survival and pursuit of justice for local small-scale miners, and it can make all the difference between their remaining shackled to or breaking free from the chains of an imposed 'othering' characterized by marginality and illegality. The process of othering, according to Indian feminist theorist Gayatri C. Spivak (1985), is a colonialist creation that juxtaposes the colonizer's definition of Self with the inferior, stigmatized Other in order to justify and rationalize imperialist objectives.

The notion of coloniality stresses that matters of epistemology, knowledge systems and worldviews play an important role in shaping global inequalities (Kerner 2013). Thus, in her *Decolonising Methodologies*, Smith (1999) urges that an important aspect of decolonization is to delve into the history of knowledges in our respective disciplines to understand how deeply imbricated they are with the colonial project. On her part, Nnaemeka (1994: 301) charges us to listen to the silences imposed by theory and to interrogate the histories of theoretical frameworks that are employed in canonical knowledge production. This, as I will show in the next section, informs the important first step I took in interrogating the history of ASM laws and the methods of legal research in ASM.

Decolonization and the Search for ASM Law

Historically, legal scholarship has followed two broad traditions. The first, referred to as the 'black-letter law', focuses heavily if not exclusively on the law as a self-sustaining set of principles accessed through reading court judgments and statutes with little or no reference to the outside world (McConville and Chui 2007). In other words, this disciplinary orientation assumes the character of legal scholarship as derived from law itself, conceived here as the formalist and centralist notion of rules located in codes, courts and constables, and premised on the state's exclusive authority to write and enforce them (Tamanaha 1997). Through this approach, Western law strives to enhance its autonomy and maximize its efficacy as a social system by freeing its institutions and practices from the societal context out of which they have emerged historically, and upon which they continue to rely socioculturally (Banakar 2011: 487). This decontextualization can be traced back to the intellectual and institutional separation of humans from nature, facts from values and reasons from beliefs during the Enlightenment (Norrie 2005). Accordingly, this traditional legal scholarship is centred on the derivation of principles and values from statutes and decided cases, and their reassembly into a coherent framework in the search for order, rationality and theoretical cohesion (Hutchinson 2013).

There is, however, a second tradition, with a different approach towards legal research. Law and Society, a primarily American movement established after the Second World War, accommodates insights from social-science disciplines to legal research as a way of challenging what it views as the mechanical, intellectually rigid, artificial and inward-looking legal formalism that had dominated American legal thought. In the UK, 'sociolegal studies' refers to policy-oriented or applied empirical research about law, and it grew out of law schools' interest to promote interdisciplinary studies of law. Sociolegal studies, as defined in the UK context, contrasts with the sociology of law, which, according to Banakar (2015), refers to more theoretically oriented studies. Sociolegal studies is often viewed in the light of its relationship to, and oppositional role within, law; it should therefore not be confused with the legal sociology of western European countries or the Law and Society scholarship in America that fosters much stronger disciplinary ties with social sciences. However, the term 'sociolegal studies' is often used to refer to all social-scientific studies of law, including legal sociology, sociological jurisprudence, legal anthropology and the Law and Society movement (Geoffrey 2009: 431).

Earlier European scholars like Ehrlich (1936) had deployed similar approaches in challenging the underlying ideology of legal positivism. Ehrlich argued for an empirically based concept of law that was broader than state law and existed independently of any outside authority. This approach urged lawyers to recognize the vital role of the informal and unofficial mechanisms of social control in creating legal institutions and moulding legal behaviour. With this approach, the starting point of legal research became the experiences and social realities of those at the receiving end of legal regulation whose perspectives and experiences were often overlooked in the legal system and theoretical discourses (Davies 2017a; Menkel-Meadow 2020). This departure from the focus on normative assumptions of policymakers and the attitudes and behaviours of state officials opened a new commitment to social justice that had many legal scholars questioning the hegemony of state law and the belief in the objectivity of its legal reasoning. This further led to a critical engagement with the relationship between law and issues of gender, race, class, ethnicity and other social relations of power (Feenan 2013).

A fundamental aspect of this approach was its interest in the 'gap' problem, namely an examination of the disparity between the 'law in the books' and the 'law in action' (Sarat 2004). According to Banakar (2015: 50), the law in action here often referred to what the courts actually did and how lawyers and laymen reasoned using the law. Many inquiries into the notion of the gap were conducted against the backdrop of an omnipotent nation state and usually started by exploring the gap between the intentions behind state law and its empirical manifestations in society. Banakar's (2015: 54) critique of this top-down approach was that it often neglected the historical dimensions of the gap as it is generated by conflicts that are built into modernity in general and modern law in particular, and which reveal themselves as dualities, antinomies and dichotomies.

This is akin to Davies's (2020) critique of the doctrinal approach, which, according to him, proceeded on the basis that law can be found without an inquiry into the meaning or origins of things. By failing to address law's origins, both the doctrinal and the top-down approach to researching the gap obscure law's historical role as a central organizing factor in the colonialist project. Starr and Collier (1989) have pointed out that historically, law has never been neutral, and its objectivity has only fitted with an ahistorical, functionalist view of a timeless, classless, custom-ridden Third World. According to the authors, this positivist, objective view of law was used to mask how colonized societies were restructured upon their contact with European imperialism. This view is further heralded by emergent Third World Approaches to International Law (TWAIL) that address the silences of law by thematizing its history, structure and processes from the perspectives of so-called Third World states. This approach brings to light the (in)visible histories of violence, coercion and exploitative inequalities framed by law, its relations of power and its creation and maintenance of invisibility regarding certain topics, subjects and sites (Frisso 2019: 479).

Sarat and Silbey (1988: 97) identified that, unsurprisingly, policymakers traditionally preferred to promote the top-down approach of bridging the gap, which equates law with state law and regulations. I noted in Chapter 1 how this phenomenon is evident in ASM law and policymaking, where state law is the starting point for addressing the disjuncture between formalization and the actual lived realities of local miners. However, there is another approach to the search for the gap, which focuses on bottom-up studies on how law is deployed and experienced within a given sociocultural space. In this model, there is a distinction between state law and what Ehrlich conceptualized as the 'living law'. Ehrlich's position was that a norm did not have to be laid down by the state to acquire a sense of legality. Instead, a norm gained legal authority when it dominated 'life itself even though it had not been posited in legal propositions' (Ehrlich 1936: 496).

This bottom-up model generates grounded theories that portray law not as an autonomous system consisting of rules and formal procedures, but as an integral and constitutive element of the cultural life of society and how ordinary people organize their daily lives. This underscores my decolonial sociolegal inquiry as a suitable approach that affords the theoretical, conceptual and methodological tools to not just understand but also validate the lived experiences of marginalized small-scale miners as a useful paradigm for theorizing law in their communities.

As a lawyer who had primarily been trained in the black-letter law tradition throughout my legal education, the sociolegal approach of researching the legal framework of ASM strongly appealed to my objective of unearthing alternative legal frameworks from below. My six-year legal education in Ghana was one of stark knowledge hierarchies where Eurocentric ideologies of law reigned supreme. The fact that my very first encounter with decolonial theories and sociolegal research only occurred at the doctoral level – despite the fact that I had previously conducted research on ASM as part of my undergraduate law degree – left me with profound embarrassment and a conscious awareness of the depth of coloniality within Ghanaian legal education. I therefore welcomed the opportunity to undertake interdisciplinary research comprising law and history, through which I aimed to contribute new conceptual and methodological insights to the Ghanaian ASM legal discourse. This choice was further guided by Nader's (1972) recommendation to 'allow the questions to lead the methodology, rather than vice-versa'. Clearly, the answers to the questions I pose about formalization, as outlined in the Introduction, could not be found through a doctrinal analysis, as the very logic of positivism that created the gaping injustices could not be entirely relied on for addressing the same.

By deploying sociolegal approaches, researchers like myself – who were raised exclusively in the black-letter law and the canonized texts of mainly Western writers – are able to stand at law's margins and move in and out of the confines of its traditional parameters in order to gain a sense of its politics, origins, meanings and distinctive institutional forms. In focusing on a bottom-up approach, I was able to place ASM law in its broader sociocultural and historical context, escape the intellectual constraints of doctrinal analysis and uncover valuable insights otherwise not discernible from a top-down approach.

I began this exercise by conceptualizing ASM as a social field with knowledge in situ, drawing from the notion of the semiautonomous social field conceived by legal anthropologist Sally Falk Moore. Moore (1978: 55) articulated the semiautonomous social field as a social locale capable of generating its own laws internally but whose autonomy was not complete due to its vulnerability to decisions and external forces beyond it. The social field is a classic anthropological concept in which the behaviour of the members of a unit, society or community is studied in terms of a series of interlocking institutions, norms and values (Mitchell 1966).

Evidence of small-scale miners operating with their own internally generated rules and customary law challenges the normative singularity of positivist law pushed by some proponents of formalization. It exposes the view of codified laws as a *fait accompli* that must be obeyed (regardless of the realities on the ground) as being merely a tool for the state to maintain its hegemony and marginalize elements that do not fit into its state-centric formalization mechanisms. This crumbling hold of positivism as the authoritative thesis underscores Davies's (2017b: 2) description of law as 'polyphonic, multisited and consisting not only of a variety of voices and perspectives but also located in a variety of places'. Furthermore, it foregrounds the sociolegal analysis of law as a proven social fact existing within a messy, interactional, plural and relational context that needs to be studied empirically to gain knowledge about how daily interactions inform legal processes (Tamanaha 2000). With this approach, every social field is conceived as possessing what Cover (1983) terms as 'jurisgenesis', which is the ability to construct legal meaning in their site of association.

Accordingly, the starting point to understanding ASM law will be to study it as part of the social organization of small-scale miners. To that end, ASM is conceived as a sociolegal field that represents an enduring, densely interconnected nexus of workers from diverse gendered, ethnic and classed backgrounds operating by their own endogenously generated rules. Here, law is not something local miners wait to be imprinted with, but consists of the many practices, patterns and networks through which they create their own legal meanings. This social field further operates within a wider community governed by customary laws administered by local traditional authorities. While the ASM social field has the capacity to create legal meaning to legitimate its activities, this is rendered semiautonomous due to its vulnerability to state hegemony. Consequently, any examination of this social field must take into consideration the wider matrix of the dominant state law, which introduces further complications through its binary notion of formality–legality and informality–illegality.

My choice of sociolegal research as a methodological approach seemed congruent with the wider ASM research due to the scholarship's heavy reliance on empirical analysis drawn from months – in some cases years – of fieldwork. However, there was a striking epistemological blindness to the broader historical, social and cultural context of ASM formalization. Added to this was the ongoing debate about the colonial roots of ethnographic research methods within contemporary discourse on decolonizing methodologies. This, as I will show in the next section, greatly informed how I manoeuvred my sociolegal approach and archival research.

From Fieldwork to Eurocentrism: A Decolonial Critique of Conceptualizing Formalization

Considering the use of bottom-up sociolegal and fieldwork approaches as a decolonial researcher comes with the inevitable moments of grappling with the propensity for perpetuating epistemic coloniality through these research methods. This issue has been addressed by earlier poststructuralist, decolonial, feminist and other critical theorists who interrogated ethnographic texts and the methodological processes that produced them (Skeggs 2001; Lather 2001). Methods of observing and collecting, analysing and presenting information from formerly colonized contexts have been criticized for being deeply intertwined with the colonialist project of intrusion, extraction, claiming and subjugation of Indigenous knowledges and subjectivities. For instance, although the assumption that law and the state are coterminous had been dominant in the West since the early nineteenth century, early anthropologists found it difficult to accept that colonized peoples, particularly those in the acephalous societies they observed, behaved as if they had law. This response was born out of parochial assumptions about African legal systems being less evolved versions of theirs, and the distorted representation of African religious and metaphysical beliefs as poor scientific speculations (von Benda-Beckmann 2009). This accounts for local peoples' distrust of anthropology (and its ethnographic methods), which Odanga (2022) referred to as 'that most irretrievably colonial of disciplines in the view of its history in Africa'.

This problematic nexus between colonialism and anthropological knowledge in sociolegal fieldwork needs to be juxtaposed with the reorientation where new work renounces the colonialist methods and practices of the discipline. For instance, White (2019) speaks of the abandonment of the 'savage slot' accorded to Indigenous Peoples as an embarrassing disciplinary anachronism. While not all anthropologists agree on the necessity of reflexive critique, many of them, according to Rose (2001), have for decades been critically examining their own practices and are researching from a place of ethical sensitivity to their topics and communities of study, with an awareness of power relations and a practice of decolonizing their data-gathering through ways in which human beings are not used as mere specimens for hypothesis and theory building.

Smith (2021) reminds us that in the academic sense, research methods are hardly neutral; they are tightly connected to the way the world is viewed and to how knowledges are generated and validated. This is seen in the ASM discourse, where research outcomes still favour quasicolonial assumptions and Eurocentric lens about small-scale miners despite concerns about the absence of consideration for the actual lived realities of these miners in state policy formulations. I problematize this methodological oversight as a product of colonial epistemology, which, as Grosfoguel (2007: 213) mentioned, involved studying subjects in the Global South using theories and methodological concepts deriving from the Global North. Such a paradigm ignores or greatly underestimates Indigenous knowledges, while privileging Western thinkers and neoliberal policies as the central theoretical apparatus. This colonial epistemology was one of my foremost observations and greatest dissatisfactions regarding the utilization of fieldwork and other bottom-up research methods in the ASM scholarship.

Unsurprisingly, this colonial epistemology tracked with how the concept of formalization itself was propounded. Fieldwork was pivotal to de Soto's (2000) examination of the challenges facing informal businesses in the developing world. He took his own advice to lawyers to 'step out of their law libraries so they can understand the people's law' by engaging with small-scale business owners in the streets of Peru. Through this approach, de Soto gained insight into the significant economic losses these businesses suffered due to their peripheral positioning outside of the formal legal economy. He shared the sociolegal position that law grew upwards from the structures and customs of society as it did from the state. He even argued against the posturing of states who, in their attempt to address the poverty facing the extra-legality, often responded by approaching these spaces as nothing more than a passive legal vacuum wherein state laws and policies could be imposed. In what seemed like a decolonial approach, de Soto cautioned legal researchers from emerging economies against their preoccupation with Western legal ideologies and the tendency to view their own local laws as not being genuine enough. He further exhorted lawyers to critique the Western legal traditions they had been taught. For Home and Lim (2004: 5), de Soto's focus on the voices of the poor amounted to a postcolonial theory that sought to fill the gaps and silences in narratives where a dominant culture and language spoke for subordinated voices.

This resonated with Moore's (1978: 4) suggestion that clarity in the workings of the legal system required a study of the social realities in the fringes to gain insights into how marginalized peoples use, abandon, bend, reinterpret, sidestep or manipulate the dominant rules. Moore's semiautonomous social field, which I referenced earlier on, was developed to explain why new laws or other attempts to direct change did not always produce the anticipated results or brought unplanned or unexpected consequences. She explained that this was partly because new laws were usually thrust upon ongoing social arrangements that were often effectively stronger than the new laws. According to Moore, adopting legal meanings within ongoing social arrangements was a much more effective exercise than the often-taken approach of drafting more stringent and loophole-free legislations.

Interestingly, however, de Soto's conceptual formulations fell into the same trap of Eurocentrism that he fiercely cautioned against. His conceptual approach may have deployed a bottom-up approach and championed customary practices as relevant for reform; his conclusive proposition, however, subjected these customary practices to the Eurocentric notion of a sole (Western) epistemic tradition from which to achieve truth and universality. Like many contemporary proponents of ASM formalization, de Soto's empirical research identified the bureaucratic constraints faced by extra-legals in registering their businesses under the formal legal economy, thereby acknowledging the state's complicity in the creation and perpetuation of the extra-legality and the poverty they faced. However, in answering the question of why capitalism succeeds in the West and fails everywhere else, de Soto ultimately positioned Western legal and capitalist ideologies as the ultimate pathway for poverty alleviation, uncritically neglecting the colonial histories of developing countries.

Elsewhere, Egyptian economist Samir Amin – who coined the term '*Eurocentrism*' as the title of his seminal book – exposed the flaws in claims about how capitalism developed in Europe. For Amin (2009), the narrative of capitalism's emergence from the endogenous European traits of rationality and triumph that continue to dominate social theory is a distorting one that disguises the true nature of the capitalist system, including its historical imperialism and racism. By placing capitalism within its historical context, Amin asserted the logical impossibility of any assumption that capitalism can develop in the periphery in the same way it allegedly did in Europe.

Colonial epistemology is, however, so deeply entrenched that our institutions of research continue to reflect it through colonialist axiomatic binaries of law that place the majority of nonformalized local miners at the periphery of a legitimacy defined through the lens of state law. In maintaining this framework, ASM research continues to generate knowledges *about*, rather than *with* and *from* the epistemic locations of local small-scale miners, despite its lengthy periods of fieldwork engagement with these small-scale miners. Moreover, while the emerging ASM scholarship's focus on customary land tenures and traditional governance may seem like an epistemic centring of customary and other non-state laws, it does not necessarily decentre the Western, colonialist experiences of customary law; as a result, it fails to engage with Indigenous epistemologies and the living customary law. Kenyan feminist scholar Achola Pala (1977: 9) described such push for integration into systems still nestled within the Eurocentric, capitalist and extractivist frameworks as, in fact, colonial.

While researching the nexus between ASM, law and the archives, I found myself constantly asking, 'Where are the African voices, and from which epistemologies are they speaking?' Many of the insightful readings suggested to me from well-meaning avenues reinforced the dearth of a decolonial approach to researching ASM, and prompted an appreciation of how uniquely positioned my decolonizing approach was from the extant literature. By addressing questions such as who is at the centre and who is at the margin of our discourse, decoloniality serves as an urgent admonition for researchers to look critically at where we are located and the position from which we enunciate our work. In addressing the colonial epistemology within ASM scholarship and its associated absences and epistemic erasures, I sought to heavily rely on the established intellectual labour of decolonial and Afrocentric scholars. Such epistemic prioritization, according to Fúnez-Flores (2022), represents an ethicopolitical move towards thinking with others and from other places of understanding, rather than assigning a naturally privileged epistemic vantage point that would reproduce an essentialist epistemic position. Decolonial feminist scholars, in particular, have expressed the urgent need for genuine alternatives to the prevailing colonialities surrounding mineral resource governance, which they urge should emerge from local communities and based on the lived realities, practices and aspirations of local people (Pereira and Tsikata 2021; UAF-LAC 2021). This resonates with Fanon's (1963: 201) metaphor of the law as a bridge, which he argued should not be parachuted down from above nor imposed by a *deus ex machina* upon the social scene, but, instead, must be built from the muscles and brains of the people, 'or else they are better off swimming across the river'. It was therefore only right that in researching the law of local small-scale miners, I would use theories that emanated from and were familiar to them.

Initial Reflections on the Methods of Researching ASM through a Pandemic

Before I delve into the specific archival methods and remote data-gathering approaches that I deployed in grounding my research in the history and present of the local mining community, it is important to point out here that this book emerged from research conducted during the COVID-19 pandemic. Both the personal readings and institutional training I undertook in preparation for my fieldwork made me acutely aware of the unpredictability of sociolegal ethnography and of the field of study as an uncontrolled environment often involving a myriad of unanticipated events that required constant reflexivity between theory, methodology and ethics (Starr and Goodale 2002). I was therefore prepared to make continual adjustments and reassessments during my time in the field. What I was not prepared for, however, was a complete overhaul of my fieldwork owing to the emergence of a global pandemic. I was reminded of Flood's (2005: 33) comment that with ethnography, it is not always possible to set up absolute prior theoretical frameworks no matter how precise one tries to be, because the researcher cannot always know what the outcome will be.

A new and deadly coronavirus had been detected in Wuhan, China, and was speedily raging across the rest of the world (Taylor 2020). This news came right about the time when I was celebrating the success of my Socio-Legal Studies Association (SLSA) grant application and frantically looking forward to travelling to Ghana for my fieldwork. I had also obtained ethics approval in what I shall reflect on later as a rather painful, lengthy and bureaucratic institutional ethics application process. At the time, my entire methodology entailed securing access to selected ASM sites in Obuasi and examining how the men and women perceived, conceptualized and used law. The lockdowns and flight cancellations following the spread of COVID-19, however, meant that travelling to Ghana for this in-situ ethnography was impossible. To say this was a difficult period would be an understatement. It felt like I had lost an entire year of valuable research mapping out a unique, decolonial sociolegal research project that was not going to happen.

The pandemic further highlighted some of the issues on coloniality, hierarchy and the blatant inequalities of the neoliberal global system that I was reflecting on in my research. Many African communities had to battle the pandemic without any social safety nets from their governments; they were rendered even more vulnerable by the unfolding vaccine inequality. Chen's report (2020) on the devastating impacts of COVID-19 on the informal economy underscored how lockdowns destroyed the livelihoods of informal workers (such as small-scale miners) who usually only earned on a hand-to-mouth basis. Within the ASM context, a study in Ghana, Liberia and Mali by Hilson et al. (2021b) showed how the vulnerabilities of local small-scale miners were triggered and exacerbated by the onset of the pandemic.

Under these circumstances, I contemplated not just the uncertain state of my research but also the wellbeing of the local mining community in which the study was to take place. I sat with intense discomfort upon encountering vaccinated (and sometimes unvaccinated) Global North-based researchers who were only concerned with the impacts of the pandemic on their research in the Global South, without much thought on its implications for these already vulnerable local communities. Dupuis (2022) explored the complexities of navigating feminist research ethics in the context of such a global health crisis, where one's physical presence as a researcher from the Global North posed a threat to research participants from the Global South. Here, she problematized the idea of risk in research as it generally related to geographical places or contexts such as war, rather than the risks introduced by the researcher to the place, the people and the relationship between the two. The absence of principles of mutuality and the academic propensity to function in temporalities not always compatible with human lives should therefore serve as a caution to researchers working with vulnerable communities.

Given the setbacks resulting from the onset of the pandemic, I mourned the in-situ ethnography that never was, and deemed it appropriate to repurpose my decolonial research. This involved the use of multiaccess tools such as online applications, which, as Liu (2022) indicated, have become even more relevant in the post-pandemic era where researchers adapt by deploying alternative points to renegotiate blocked access and re-establish relationships with participants. The multiaccess concept, according to Liu, suggests that access is not a one-time gain but a continuous negotiation over what activities researchers are involved in, which helps to overcome the shortcomings of a single-realm ethnography. I explain all of this to show that the changes in my methodology were not born out of a whim, but emerged from long moments of recovery from painful loss, reflexivity and a creative restrategizing towards maximizing rigour and accuracy in my data collection. It was a further demonstration of the resilience and epistemological flexibility of the decolonizing approach, which enables researchers not only to be guided by their research data when interpreting them, but also to break away from the canons and conventions around theories and methods (Mohammed 2022). Furthermore, it was a testament to how research premised on an ethics of care can be inclusive not just for the communities involved but also for researchers who have to conduct empirical research during such unprecedented times while being disabled, chronically ill, carers or vulnerable in other ways.

On the Methods of Researching ASM Law from Below

Data-gathering for this study entailed, first, a qualitative, multiaccess, remote approach involving interviews via Zoom and telephone calls. Participants were mostly invited through snowball sampling, which, as Parker, Scott and Geddes (2019) have explained, is a popular sampling method in qualitative research in which initial contacts known as 'seeds' make referrals to other respondents who fit the research criteria and who might be willing research participants. For qualitative researchers, snowballing serves as a form of nonrandom sampling where researchers use their social networks to establish initial links that develop momentum and capture an increasing chain of participants. Here, sampling is usually finished once either a target sample size or a saturation point has been reached.

This snowballing method is how I negotiated my relationships in Obuasi in establishing contacts and gaining access to relevant gatekeepers for my research. For instance, I initially sought partnership with an Obuasi-based civil society organization, the Centre for Social Impact Studies (CeSIS), known for its extensive research and engagement with local small-scale miners. This organization is what you will call a crucial knowledge broker between (inter)national organizations and local small-scale mining groups, serving as a valuable entry point into the community for many researchers. Our shared interests in ASM in Obuasi and as locals helped us forge a trusting relationship. Thus, even when the fieldwork was cancelled, I continued to receive support from CeSIS in conducting remote interviews.

Through this initial contact, I was able to gain access to other participants, including a leading member of the local small-scale mining association in Obuasi who served as a focal authority on the social practices of small-scale miners in the community. I also interviewed one Obuasi-based media personnel, three Ghanaian private legal practitioners and one state prosecuting attorney. As already established, the role of civil society in the ASM discourse profoundly informed government policy, particularly in the wake of media campaigns against the alarming rate of water pollution from ASM activities in the country. For my decolonizing approach, I chose to focus on civil societies that operated from, and had situated knowledges about, the local communities. Consequently, I interviewed two Obuasi-based civil society personnel with extensive knowledge of grassroots mobilization and engagement with local small-scale miners. In addition to their individual professional capacities, the Obuasi-based participants also provided insightful information on ASM from the perspective of the directly affected local communities.

The inclusion of non-miner participants was in keeping with Nader's (1972) admonition for studying up, which involves making connections between different sources of authority at all levels. This approach, according to Banakar (2011: 499), offered a social theoretical framework for conceptualizing and exploring the distinctive character of law in pluralistic communities. These interviews ensured that while I theorized from the subaltern ASM experience, I also actively pursued an interest in the wider community with which the ASM social field intersected to make sure that the law conceptualized from the research reflected the actual legal pluralities of the community. Further to this, I engaged two Obuasi-based research assistants who conducted interviews with six selected chiefs in the Obuasi area. These interviews focused on the linkages between the chieftaincy institution and ASM. They elicited oral histories of gold mining and of the role of chiefs as grantors of customarily held mineral-rich lands, settlors of disputes and enforcers of Indigenous knowledges in ASM.

The interviews were conducted around a set of open-ended questions designed to explore a variety of themes including sociocultural perceptions of state creation and criminalization of ASM informality, the land struggles of local small-scale miners, the sociocultural practices of Indigenous mining and customary land tenures in ASM. There was, however, room for flexibility, which allowed for more relaxed and engaging conversations that made use of storytelling and life histories. In particular, the interview with the chiefs served as a great source of oral history about gold mining, placing in clear context the religious, political, sociocultural and economic role gold plays in the local community.

A notable trait of decolonizing methodologies is that their knowledge production transcends scholarly texts. Here, thoughts are widely communicated through visual culture, Indigenous languages, proverbs, folktales, songs, storytelling, poems, cultural artefacts, philosophies and everyday behaviours (Elabor-Idemudia 2000). Storytelling in particular serves as a tool for critical participatory and socially transformative praxis, offering those typically silenced an opportunity to share their collective social experiences and thereby illuminate how the interpretation of past events in official colonial records and other written texts may be analysed to formulate certain hypotheses and identify certain attributes about their world (Sonn, Stevens and Duncan 2013). Ki-Zerbo (1981) highlights the place of oral traditions as a real, living museum, a conserver and transmitter of social and cultural creations stored up by people said to have no written records.

For Indigenous societies, law as a social phenomenon concerned with narratives serves as a vehicle to contest formal legal reasoning and argumentation, particularly as mainstream law-making treats oral traditions as antiquated and lacking in claims to authenticity, objectivity and continuity (Vermeylen 2013). Small-scale miners, whom I conceptualize as subaltern due to their historically subjugated marginality, continue to resort to Indigenous law-making processes transmitted from oral histories to negotiate access to land and navigate their site operations, profit-sharing and environmental management. Accordingly, my theorization of ASM law was embedded in these oral Indigenous epistemologies in an attempt to render visible the distinct cultural, social, political, aesthetic and linguistic systems long muted by centuries of colonialism, cultural imperialism and neocolonial politics surrounding knowledge production.

The choice of Obuasi as a case study for this research rested in its relevance in highlighting historic developments of ASM law and policy in Ghana. As already established, Obuasi also has a unique cultural position as an Akan community governed by Asante customary laws and practices and Indigenous spiritualities. Additionally, Obuasi holds a distinctive position within the Ghanaian gold-mining scene due to its history of tensioned relationships between ASM and corporate large-scale mining. The story of ASM in Obuasi is intricately intertwined with colonially enabled large-scale land grabs, Indigenous dispossessions, state politico-military protection of privatized property, the erasure and subjugation of Indigenous gold mining and the undermining of traditional regulatory systems. Obuasi stands at the crossroads of recovery from colonialism and the legacies of an ongoing coloniality that still militate against the community and its local small-scale miners. This intersectional paradigm makes Obuasi a perfect case study for research on decolonization in ASM.

Notwithstanding my own caution against imperialist generalizations of culture and the uncritical universalization of laws and policy frameworks, the frictions between state formalization and informal ASM in Obuasi, coupled with the longstanding history of resource contestations between large-scale mining and ASM operators, represent an ongoing reality that is symptomatic of many other ASM communities in the Global South. Barbosa (2022: 620) has explained that despite the heterogeneities and complexities of Latin American, African, Caribbean and Asian societies, there is a shared historical experience with violent territorial expropriation, epistemicide and other expressions of oppression. This enables the identification of commonalities and key learning points from each region, which, in this ASM context, renders the Obuasi case study a potential site for the excavation of knowledge relevant for governments, researchers, donors and policymakers working on ASM formalization in other highly contested mining terrains in formerly colonized countries of the Global South.

Finally, data from the remote interviews was analysed after transcription to generate a list of emerging themes that further informed the archival research subsequently conducted. Reliability and validity of the study was attained through triangulation of the data from the archives and the interviews. Thematically, I identified unifying topics on land dispossessions, state usurpation of control over mineral rights, the complexities of chiefly management of customarily held mineralized lands, the modification of Indigenous laws and state criminalization of Indigenous mining activities.

Community as a Decolonial Praxis in ASM Research

A fundamental aspect of decolonizing methodologies is the deliberate, conscious effort in building community as a research practice. Smith (2021) urges that in decolonial research, the single-white-saviour approach is no longer satisfactory, and our methodologies must always reflect how we are building community as a way of disrupting established norms. This contrasts with neoliberal globalization, which creates isolation and competition that does not just extract from the land, the body and the community, but also deploys a politics of care shot through asymmetrical power relations to perpetuate unequal arrangements propelled by injustice, anxiety, indignation, disenfranchisement and frustration (Martin, Myers and Viseu 2015).

Ethics of care and community as a decolonial research practice is embedded in the adaptation of Indigenous values such as the Southern African philosophy of *Ubuntu*, which prioritizes solidarity and community welfare without diminishing or disregarding individualist interests (Anofuechi 2022). Among the Asante people, proverbs such as '*wo nyɔnko da ne wo da*' ('your friend's dwelling is your dwelling') and '*bɛnkum dware nifa, na nifa nso adware bɛnkum*' ('the left hand cleanses the right, and the right hand also cleanses the left') capture this spirit of reciprocity and communality of care as vital for collective survival. This existence-in-relation and being-for-self-and-others, as Oyěwùmi (1998) called it, sums up the African conception of life and reality. It represents an ethical framework that emphasizes the responsibility of researchers as transformative healers, working with and actively involved in healing, building community and promoting harmony (Chilisa and Ntseane 2010).

In addition to working with the local mining community, my approach to building community as a decolonial research praxis involved a peer interview process in my qualitative data-gathering. Once again, I utilized snowball sampling by establishing initial access through my contacts. Here, I interviewed four African doctoral students whose research intersected with ASM from diverse disciplines including history, gender, development studies, agriculture, land economy and economics. In addition to forging collaborations in the field, these interviews elicited views about epistemologies in ASM research and Africa's extractive industries in general. I designed this peer interview process as a safe space for participants to share ideas and receive relevant feedback about their research projects and methodologies. Participants expressed curiosity and interest in my decolonial approach, hence foregrounding its uniqueness and providing an opportunity for me to expound on the potential of decolonizing methodologies in producing rigorous and meaningful interventions in ASM.

The peer interview process also served as an avenue to discuss the recent trend in Global North universities towards decolonization, and the need for Global South researchers to collaborate in spearheading these conversations. An intersectional reflexivity compels a revision of assumptions about shared experience, which, in the case of this peer interview process, was highlighted by the emergence of classed, gendered and spatial perspectives in our ASM analysis. For instance, I observed differentiated perspectives between participants who were indigenes of mining towns and those who were not. Additionally, different class positionalities revealed further differentiations in knowledges and perceptions about local small-scale miners even amongst those who hailed from mining communities.

Researching ASM Law from the Archives

The decolonial approach to researching ASM was bolstered by archival research and its exposition on Indigenous challenges to the assumed state monopoly over law-making in land and mineral resource governance. I began the archival research by entering various key terms – such as 'mining', 'gold', 'Gold Coast', 'Ashanti', 'chiefs', 'land' and 'Obuasi' – into the search engine of the online African Newspapers Archive. This generated a collection of newspapers encompassing the different views held by local people regarding colonial legal impositions. These newspapers, published by Western-educated Indigenous professionals and dating from 1897 to 1922, included *The Gold Coast Leader, The Gold Coast Aborigines* and *The Gold Coast Chronicle*. Akurang-Parry (2006) mentioned the use of the Indigenous press as a space for protesting colonial indirect rule. As Ward (1991: 96) observed, these newspapers may have had only a small circulation, but their contents were discussed by thousands of people who heard them at second hand. They carried not only the views of those whom British colonialists referred to as the 'troublemaking scholars' and the intelligentsia, but also the sentiments of the general population. In doing so, these newspapers provided a counterpoint to the legislative intentions and motivations of colonial administrators as captured in official colonial correspondence and missionary records, which I subsequently reviewed over a three-week period at the British National Archives and the Wesleyan Missionary Archives in London. This was supplemented by further archival research undertaken by a locally based archivist whom I engaged from Ghana's Public Records and Archives Department.

In decolonizing methodologies, greater attention is paid to oral sources of historical knowledge. According to Johnson (2008), 'listening to documents' and interpreting the 'written-oral as oral' are ways of overcoming some of the assumptions embedded in the dichotomy of written versus oral. In this regard, the Indigenous stories from the African newspapers complemented the oral histories from the interviews, all of which served as important tools for disrupting the dominant narratives on state construction of ASM laws. Together, they revealed that what ultimately became crystallized in the mining codes were not merely one-sided, objective laws, but the product of local resistances and longstanding negotiations.

As the different perspectives from the archives are put in dialogue with the oral histories from the interviews and the contemporary legal issues in ASM, they enhance an understanding of the historical tensions surrounding the construction of mineral and land rights, the assertion of Indigenous agency, colonial domination and how colonial legacies continue to direct and influence the lived experiences of Indigenous miners and local mining communities. This draws from Fuentes's (2016) engagement with Black feminist epistemologies in her archival research on enslaved women's experiences in Barbados. Here, Fuentes detailed how such multilevel examination of the archives and the different perspectives they present does not only shape the meanings produced about them in their own time and in current historical practices, but is also relevant for decolonizing and destabilizing colonial discourses invested in the construction of legal phenomena in formerly colonized societies.

This new way of reading the archive thus does not merely experiment with its silences but reflects on it in an epistemological sense. Addressing the archive as a source that must be read against the grain, this approach searches for bottom-up histories of resistance so as to locate human agency in small gestures of refusal and silences among the colonized. Stoler (2002) criticizes this approach as extractive, and instead recommends reading the archive as much along the fault lines as against the grain, so that we do not brush up against its received categories but read it for its regularities, logic of recall, densities and distributions, consistencies of misinformation, omission and error. In doing so, the archive becomes as much a source as a subject of study, a site of state ethnography where one can study the epistemological and political anxieties that constitute the colonial common sense on which it was built. By reading Indigenous perspectives from the local newspapers against the grain of colonial motivations for constructing new legal ideologies on land and mining, I am, like Buchanan (2007), able to analyse the archival documents in new ways and hunt out the silences, biases, oversights and even lies that infuse the written evidence that informs contemporary ASM laws. Additionally, reading along the grain grounds my decolonial approach to the archives as a space of ethnographic research where I am able to critically examine the colonial state as a crucial subject in law-making on land and mineral rights.

From the archives, official colonial correspondence, personal notes of colonial administrators, colonial maps, mining policies and legislations attest to the deployment of state laws in the usurpation of chiefly authority, the undermining of existing customary land tenures, the disruption of Indigenous spatiality and the imposition of the doctrine of eminent domain. This historical exercise accentuated the central role of law in legitimizing the imperialist project of dispossessing mineral-rich Indigenous lands and suppressing existing customary laws and practices on mining. Consequently, law is conceptualized as a historical product constitutive of this hierarchical order, rather than a universal category of fact.

Moreover, the ways in which the colonial state itself emerged to assert control over mining demonstrated a refusal to fully accept the colonized people's own understanding of law. Instead, they showed how colonial administrators made several concerted efforts to conform local mining practices and Indigenous legal systems to state impositions. These historical facts are masked by a doctrinal, top-down analysis of law, a reminder of Ake's exposition on Western development paradigms (1996) and their negative view of local cultures that prevents a full acceptance of local people on their own terms. In the ASM context, this situation has left behind the legacy of an uncritical, one-dimensional perspective of local small-scale miners as poor, powerless 'problems' to be solved, 'menaces' to be flushed out and 'criminals' to be dealt with.

A notable observation from the archives was whose voices were included and whose were left out. The volumes of archival materials on European gold-mining interests, as opposed to the muted voices of Indigenous gold miners, indicated what Jenks (2022) has referred to as the archive's central role as a colonial, Eurocentric and androcentric information system that renders certain histories legible while reinforcing the voicelessness of the marginalized in a manipulation of social memory. Archival research into the development of Ghanaian mining laws uncovers a hypervisibility of colonial administrators, local elites and foreign concessionaires, and a stark relegation of Indigenous miners into obscurity. Fuentes (2016: 29) observed that such archival (in)visibilities rely on the logics of colonial and capitalist functions, demonstrating how material power moves through the archives in the historical production of the subaltern.

In the next section, I continue to unpack how I navigated these structural powers in knowledge production by deploying decolonial ethics in achieving my research objective of upending coloniality in the ASM regulatory framework.

Decolonization and the Ethics of Researching ASM

According to *The Gold Coast Leader* (22 August 1914: 5), British academic F. W. H. Migeod arrived in Kumasi following the British annexation to research the abundance of gold in Asante. One afternoon, to confirm his hypothesis about how randomly available gold was in the land, Migeod picked up a shovel and began digging and panning vigorously with a colleague until they found an appreciable amount of gold in the garden of his lodgement. This incident would later form part of his lecture at a meeting of the African Society in the UK on 15 May 1914, titled 'The Gold Coast: Its Physical Features, Flora, Fauna and Ethnology'. Interestingly, this happened at a time when Indigenous gold miners themselves could not easily mine on their own lands due to stringent colonial legislative restrictions and licensing requirements.

In order to avoid the complicity of research in perpetuating these kinds of colonialist inequalities and extractivist practices, several research councils have drawn up new guidelines that highlight the need for consultation, negotiation, informed consent, involvement of Indigenous researchers, as well as respect for Indigenous knowledges, protocols and cultural and intellectual property rights (Igwe, Madichie and Rugara 2022). For instance, the National Ethics Guidelines in Australia and the San Code of Research Ethics have respectively adopted core values of reciprocity, respect and responsibility in research concerning Indigenous Peoples.

Over the past decades, there have been tremendous changes in academic norms with regard to procedures for institutional ethics approval and the ethics of researching vulnerable communities. The dehumanization of Black people in the unethical research practices on African American men in Tuskegee, Alabama between 1932 and 1972, for instance, prompted the establishment of the Institutional Review Board for American universities to ensure that their research adhered to principles of respect for autonomy, beneficence and non-maleficence (Walker 2009). These institutional ethical guidelines, however, do not necessarily emphasize the importance of learning the cultures of communities, following social rules in recruiting research participants and maintaining long-term relationships with participants, even though these may be the expectation of some communities (Mohammed 2022; Campbell 2010). Elsewhere, these biomedically derived ethics directives have been criticized for being overly prescriptive, more concerned with institutional risks and reputation, and woefully inadequate in addressing the situational ethics that arise from the unpredictability of doing research in cross-cultural contexts (Israel 2017). To an extent, these shortcomings encapsulated my experience with the institutional ethics application process, where I encountered back-and-forth queries about my local knowledge, my cultural awareness and the appropriateness of my action research approach.

On Relationship, Trust and Intersubjectivity in Decolonial Research

Research in Indigenous communities entails more than the rigid institutional ethics requirements for printed consent forms and Participant Information Sheets (PIS). Smith (1999) writes that, for the Indigenous world, the word *research* is one of the dirtiest words in the dictionary, hinting at the various reasons why local communities may be distrustful of researchers and our standardized ethics prescriptions. These suspicions are even more pertinent in the case of local small-scale miners, amongst whom there is widespread illiteracy in English. Requests for signatures or thumbprints from heavily criminalized small-scale miners is impractical and, to a large extent, insensitive. State criminalization has also rendered small-scale miners extremely guarded and protective of their space. While translation into local languages may be helpful under such circumstances, it still does not detract from how intimidating standardized ethics requirements can be within these spaces. This is in addition to the possibility of such documentation being easily manipulated to reinforce hierarchical power dynamics that subordinate the interests of the researched to those of the researcher (Wynn and Israel 2018). Respectfully tailoring ethical practices to cultural norms and developing interpersonal relationships built on trust have proven a more effective means of securing access and cooperation in local communities, although these are not practices that sit easily with university ethics guidelines (Vermeylen and Clark 2017).

As a member of the community, I knew firsthand the importance of building relationships and developing trust in navigating cultural conventions from a place of openness and honesty about my research objectives, its expected outcomes and its implications for the community. This trust is constantly negotiated and is built on the assumption that it will be reciprocated and not abused (Liamputtong 2008). Decolonial African feminist scholars draw on dialogue as a humanizing approach to working out new knowledge claims collectively with community members. Nnaemeka (2004) attributes this to the fact that conciliatory dispositions and strategies are highly valued and encouraged in an array of African cultures as a way of embracing diverse viewpoints. For instance, the Asante saying '*tekyerema bedeɛ ɛfa adie ɛsene ahoɔdenfoɔ*' ('a woman's tongue gets things more surely than a strong man') encapsulates the cultural value attached to utilizing dialogue, rather than force or violence, in articulating demands. This approach contrasts with the antidialogical actions of positivism typified by an oppressor who has monopoly over the interpretation of law (Vermette 2009).

Drawing from this dialogic approach, I followed the Asante tradition of *ammaneɛbɔ*, which is an interactional practice that involves conviviality and respect between a host and their guest. I also ensured that due protocol was followed in approaching local chiefs through the elders, and with the presentation of the customary *aseda* (offering of thanks, in this case in the form of money) to the chiefs. By custom, it is considered disrespectful, even a grave offence, to approach chiefs directly (Rattray 1929: 93). My observance of this cultural norm further ensured that the elders were able to vet my research for relevance to the community.

This dialogical and trust-building approach also involved introducing myself to my participants as Obuasi-born, and in the particular case of the chiefs, declaring my proximity to the chieftaincy institution through my maternal and paternal relations – a maternal uncle who sat on the council of the *Adansehene* as a representative of our hometown, and a paternal uncle who was chief of Akatakyieso, a bustling ASM community near Obuasi. In some of the interviews, these introductions were more straightforward due to my familiarity with the participants either as neighbours, former colleagues or schoolmates. This mode of self-introduction is typical of practices of introduction within Indigenous societies, and for those of us who are 'researchers-in-relation to the community', this becomes crucial to building trust because the significance of all our relations is always apparent to the community (Peltier 2018). The interviews proceeded with informal conversations about family, health and recovery from the lockdown, and bonding over shared memories of Obuasi. Participants had the opportunity to hear in my own words the information about my research that was contained in the institutionally mandated PIS and consent forms that I had already emailed or had delivered to them. I maintained flexibility and allowed for oral consent for those who declined formalized signatures to the printed consent forms. I was also conscious of the period of my empirical research; this was a time when the world was slowly recovering from a global pandemic that had taken an immense mental, social and economic toll on vulnerable local communities.

To ensure that my research did not inflict any financial or other material harm, the interviews were arranged at such times as were suitably convenient for participants. Ultimately, I maintained a responsiveness to their needs, with the recognition that they were the custodians of information which they had the right to decide whether to share with me or not. To safeguard the integrity of the qualitative research, I did not give research participants money in exchange for their information. Nevertheless, I recognized that accessing the internet to participate in the remote interviews was expensive in Ghana; I therefore provided an honorarium to some of the participants towards the purchase of internet data. Additionally, I made a conscious effort to pay the research assistants a reasonable, agreed-upon wage reflective of their labour.

Ethical concerns about protecting participants from harm do not only relate to physical or socioeconomic harm, but include protecting them from psychological harm and retraumatization, particularly in over-researched communities where participants have to recount narratives that open up psychological, racial, social and economic wounds (Warikandwa, Nhemachena and Mpofu 2017). In Obuasi, ASM and Indigenous land dispossession for corporate large-scale mining is a complex issue that, over the years, has seen the community become one of the hotspots of violent clashes in the country (Okoh 2014). Often, when the issues are raised, factions are quickly drawn and deep-seated resentment against chiefs, politicians and corporations alike rears its head. The intersection of colonialism, decolonization and law being broached within this historic gold-mining town required that I approached this qualitative data-gathering ethically, sensitively and carefully. Thankfully, ethics of care, reflexivity, trust, empathy, respect, humility and cordiality were useful in guiding me through this exercise.

(Re)Memory and Embodied Experience in Decolonial Research

The hegemonic Eurocentric paradigms that have informed Western philosophy and sciences assume a neutral, objective point of view. This idea of objectivity sprung from the treatment of knowledge as an object existing independently of human agents and being produced by a methodology that guarantees truth by setting aside personal, irrational, artistic, emotional and other vested interests (Anker 2016: 19). This canonical postulation discourages researchers from theorizing their lived experiences or inserting themselves into their work, in order to maintain objectivity and generate rigorous research (Dutta and Pal 2020). This has, however, been debunked as a socially constructed façade because a scholar's research ultimately gets filtered through their perspective or positionality, whether or not they are actively detaching themselves from their work (Bourke et al. 2009). For instance, in their study of Indigenous legal systems, early legal anthropologists were confronted with the reality that perceptions of unifying characteristics of law across cultures depended on the perspective of the observer. Exposition of Indigenous law from their ethnographic accounts unavoidably implicated what the researcher already thought law was, but also what the Indigenous informant understood the researcher to mean by law (Anker 2016: 9).

Decolonial epistemologists have shown that knowledge does not operate in a social or political vacuum, but within stratified power relations that shape which questions are deemed worthy of study and whose views count as 'knowledge' (Harding 1987; Haraway 1988). For researchers from the subalternized cultures of the Global South, the intersectionality of racial, class, spiritual, linguistic and geographical oppressions is difficult to escape. We are unable to participate in delinking the ethnicized, racialized and gendered epistemic locations from the subject that speaks, because participating in such decoupling reinforces the very silences we aim to dismantle. Decolonial ethics urges us to approach our research with an awareness of power dynamics, positionality, privilege, knowledge, reflexivity, and subjectivity (Bennett 2009).

Following from the above, I approached my research not as an objective observer but as someone immersed in a proximate connection to the subject and community of my research. I drew from my embodied experience and from what African American novelist Toni Morrison (2007) conceived as 'rememory'. Rememory serves as a means to recount and pass on events from collective memory from generation to generation. Soko-de Jong (2022) employed rememory in her reflection on her academic journey and as a tool for decolonization, which, as she emphasized, aligns with the Akan philosophy of *Sankɔfa* and how past wisdom can illuminate present experiences for liberatory futures. Consequently, I pursued accuracy and methodological integrity while embracing my positionality as an indigene of Obuasi, with the recognition that the two are not mutually exclusive. As an Adanse woman of the *Ɛkoɔna* clan, I hold the belief that my life, learning and research are connected to my relationship with my community, ancestors and cultural beliefs. Ntseane (2011) notes that in many African societies, the totemic symbolizations of our families are sacred to us and define our being and interconnectedness to the earth and to our ancestors. This forms part of the Afrocentric paradigm that defines and influences learning in our cultures. Accordingly, throughout this research, I invoked my insider status as a daughter of an Obuasi mine worker, and as a friend, schoolmate, family member and neighbour to many in Obuasi who have been or are still involved in ASM.

It is for this reason that I write from a first-person perspective. In so doing, I am able to lay bare the embodied experiences of my spiritual, social and academic relations, which greatly informed my search for alternative paradigms for ASM and its local mining communities. I use this narrative approach not to centre myself, but as a useful lens through which I convey the thematic arguments as issues that affect me and a community I care deeply about. On this, I draw on feminist empathy, which Eze (2015: 310) described as the ability to feel oneself into the experiences of undeserved suffering, unfairness, injustice or oppression. In employing Nigerian novelist Lola Shoneyin's *The Secret Lives of Baba Segi's Wives*, Eze emphasized the richness of empathy as a social, liberatory virtue that, in this context, helps to shed light on the pains of ordinary Africans, as well as to provide an introspective framework to enhance human flourishing in African communities that are still recovering from colonial violence and socioeconomic downturns.

Reflexivity in decolonial research also requires a recognition of positionality not only in terms of experiences of oppression, but also of privilege (Hamilton 2020). To that end, I was equally aware of my current privilege as a lawyer researching from a Global North institution, which placed me as an outsider to the community in some respects. The boundaries between insider and outsider identities are complicated and often not clearly delineated. Even for insider researchers, perceived financial standing, social status and distance (particularly for Global South researchers based in Global North institutions) can present as alienating factors. There is often the risk that our education in the core forcibly socializes and separates us from our African ways of knowing and being, thereby rendering us out of touch with the realities of the local communities (Ademolu 2023).

While contemplating this, I was reminded of the words of Dillard and Neal (2020): to be a student of *Ubuntu* is to recognize that belonging is not only determined by physical proximity; while we may move out of the continent, we carry our families and neighbourhoods inside of us. Indeed, one can study a culture even as an outsider, but as Nnaemeka (1994: 306) advised, that must come with a reflexive appreciation of our positionality and a large dose of humility. Consequently, I approached my research with the utmost humility and the recognition that I was, to a large extent, an outsider to the more intricate and detailed social field of ASM. After all, being a member of the community does not excuse one from being reflexive and asking the same questions about personal motivations (Few 2007). This is because the demand for reflexivity goes beyond essentializations enforced through hegemonic oppressions and self-descriptions. Rather, it involves the deeper task of epistemological self-reflexivity that explores the consequences of mobile subjectivity and efficacy for the political direction of our research (Bennet 2009).

Understandably, overidentification with one's culture can lead to the type of romanticization that produces other levels of distortion. It is for this reason that Afro-oriented decolonial scholars celebrate Indigenous knowledges through a critical lens, where they are immersed in the cultural and social milieu but simultaneously able to identify its flaws in order to reimagine liberatory futures (Nnaemeka 1994: 308). This critical reflexivity was manifest in how I grappled with my first experience with the archive. The archival research proved to be one of the most fulfilling and liberating experiences of this research project. My ethnocultural lived experiences and the oral histories I had gathered directed my search for archival materials. Some of the information I encountered and the themes I engaged with bore heavy emotional weight. As a member of the community, I was plunged into agony as a result of the accounts of struggles, erasures, silencing, dehumanization, conquest, dispossessions and defeat; I navigated this agony through journalling and writing poems, one of which I included as the epigraph to this book. The meticulous theoretical notes I kept, in which I recorded my ideas, thoughts, feelings and insights, served as great outlets and enriched my reflexivity. Indeed, Few, Stephens and Rouse-Arnett (2003) suggested such exercises as being helpful in introducing one's reactions and insights to the dynamics of the researcher–data relationship, and in providing tangible evidence of identifying personal biases.

I was often left disenchanted when my 'rememorying' clashed with the narratives I was being confronted with in the archives. One such occasion was the discovery of how embedded Reverend Thomas Birch Freeman was in the colonialist infrastructure, owing to his close association with, support and work for the colonial administration. These were facts I was unaware of, even though I was born and raised in the Wesleyan Methodist tradition in Obuasi, where many present-day adherents still travel to attend prayer sessions at the site in Fomena where the venerated missionary was said to have rested during his journey to Kumasi around 1839. On the other end of this archival journey was the joy of looking at archived photographs that gave me a deep sense of connection to my ancestors – the look in their eyes, their well-coiffed hair and *kente* clothing, the works of the goldsmiths in all their artistry. Moreover, the accounts of unrelenting local resistance to imperialism served as great motivation for the decolonial approach to my ASM research. Andrew and Neath (2018) have stated that while Indigenous Peoples may have originally been photographed for the documentation of a so-called primitive race or culture, the meanings of these pictures shift once they become accessible to descendants. We are struck by the anonymity of the portraits, but in these legacy images, we are able to see the blind spots of the past and the beauty of their present.

Indigenous Expertise and the Ethics of Knowledge Coproduction

Decolonizing methodologies involve the unlearning of notions of knowledge production and how we situate expertise in the academy, including practices that consciously privilege scholarship on Africa by Euro-Americans over that by Africans and African-descended scholars (Medie and Kang 2018). In other words, knowledge can only be decolonized if we re-examine who is considered a knowledge producer and what has conventionally been presented as valid and legitimate ways of knowing. Knowledge, they say, is power, but throughout the history of many formerly colonized societies, knowledge has mostly been attributed to the powerful, the settler and the colonizer (Dei and Imoka 2018). The academy upholds this parochial approach through its capitalist, exploitative and extractive politics of knowledge production that valorizes the heroic ambitions of the individual scholar, while downplaying and even erasing the collective, communal efforts of Indigenous communities who are reduced to being mere 'native informants' (Odanga 2022: 7).

For many Indigenous Peoples, knowledge is intimately related to the land, and as Rose (1996a; 1996b) has mentioned, the fact of localized knowledge is itself law. For this reason, decolonial scholars situate expertise in the local communities, thereby seeing participants as coproducers of knowledge rather than as mere objects of study (Mohammed 2022: 12). Drawing from this, I consider all my research participants to be scholars due to their situated knowledges.

The demand for constant reflexivity in decolonial research requires interrogating the power dynamics of research and our qualification to speak *for* others, so that we do not end up speaking *over* them and reinforcing the very epistemic violence we aim to be addressing

(Chiweshe 2018). Fanon (1963: 188) admonished that the very idea that local people do not have a perfect understanding of the complexities of their problems or are incapable of governing themselves is a very Western, bourgeois and contemptuous attitude that must be expunged from research. On her part, Smith (1999) urged researchers not to approach local communities flaunting our knowledge, as it would be presumptuous to assume that local communities are not themselves a repository of knowledge. After all, so many local communities are held hostage to expert knowledge that ends up negating Indigenous knowledges and reinforcing ethnocentric assumptions and stereotypes. This was very much evident in the archives, where I became acutely aware of how missionaries and colonial administrators with Christian and Western worldviews fetishized local customs and spiritualities, and how their accounts contributed to the colonialist suppression of Indigenous customs and practices.

I acknowledged Indigenous expertise in my preliminary meetings with the locally based research assistants, during which we discussed my decolonial approach, draft interview questions, the institutional requirements for meeting ethical guidelines and other ethical concerns that had not been considered at the institutional level. The research participants were also able to self-represent by conducting the interviews in a language that they were comfortable with. This way, some participants freely shared their ideas in Asante Twi, which I then transcribed and translated into English. As will become evident in subsequent chapters, I continued to acknowledge cocreation of knowledge in my writing by actively presenting quotations from my conversations with participants and referencing their knowledges to demonstrate how the data shaped my analysis. In doing so, my objective of seeking an alternative legal framework for ASM was achieved by capturing knowledge sourced from the expertise of the very people whose lived experiences render credibility and legitimacy to their non-state legal systems.

In challenging the passivity that is ever so often imputed to participants in ASM research, I avoided any pretension of speaking *for* local small-scale miners, or of viewing my study as something being done *to* them, rather than a collaborative project of knowledge coproduction. Knowledge coproduction highlights how suggestions for formalization have not worked because its underlying conceptualization has not been based on local knowledges, capacities, priorities and needs. What I aimed to do, therefore, was to speak *with* local miners and the community and to shift the paradigms from which knowledge production in the ASM discourse is conducted. Through this, I demonstrated that the subaltern ASM speaks as a site of knowledge production and legal theory from which hegemonic Eurocentric knowledges can be contested. As a social field, ASM is not merely a site for the extraction of data; researchers and policymakers who wish to address the issues within the sector must therefore do so with deep respect for the knowledges, needs and priorities of the small-scale miners.

A major dilemma that emerges from Indigenous knowledge coproduction is how to balance it with the default assumption of anonymity to satisfy the ethical requirement for non-maleficence. Here, we contend with how anonymizing can operate as a form of silencing (Chilisa 2005; Moore 2012). In amplifying historically silenced voices, there is an added responsibility to consider whether attributing expertise to named individuals will be in their best interests. A community-focused ethics of research teaches that certain silences are not ours to break, and that certain stories entrusted to us may not need to be shared no matter how well-intentioned we may be, especially if doing so would expose the vulnerabilities of participants and exacerbate the plight of our coproducers of knowledge (Boesten and Henry 2018). Considering the criminalization of ASM and its highly politicized nature in Ghana, I only shared the stories that I was explicitly permitted to. I also employed pseudonyms for all the research participants except the local chiefs, whose traditionally elite positionality accorded them more power and safety from harm.

Ultimately, local communities are always concerned about the long-term benefits of research in their communities. In pursuing coproduction of knowledge, decoloniality actively places the needs of local communities at the forefront by representing what they deem as important and beneficial to them. As a member of the community, I was acutely concerned about the prospect of my work ending up as another stockpile of data that offered nothing more than the illusion of positive change. Although they represent one of the most widely researched groups in Africa, small-scale miners and local mining communities continue to have some of the highest indicators of poverty and other social disadvantages. Ghanaian small-scale miners are no strangers to the gaze of researchers from all disciplines who traverse their mine sites digging for data. They are also all too familiar with the frustration and emptiness that comes with not having the supposed 'benefit' of research trickling into their communities.

During my institutional ethics application, I recall being queried whether it was necessary for my research to push for social change in ASM. My position on this was clear: the action-oriented approach of my decolonial sociolegal research compelled an engagement with notions of the social utility of research. Decoloniality is ultimately about transformation; it is about challenging what 'is', not just justifying and legitimizing existing practice. As Pereira (2002: 9) puts it, there is no way of creating knowledge that is not circumscribed by the oppressions of our times if we cannot imagine a better future, if we cannot dream of a way of life that does away with the domination that is part of our everyday realities, if we cannot envision other ways of being that transcend our divided realities. Here, the popular feminist-adopted slogan 'the personal is political' resonates, as theory-building is related to our experiences and engagement with real-world problems of development and state formation that our communities face (Hanisch 1970).

Reflexivity as an ethical notion ensures that researchers are accountable to the people with whom they cocreate knowledge, both during the research process and in the final research report (Guillemin and Gillam 2004). Part of decolonizing methodologies is the act of dismantling the extractive dynamic where research participants are viewed as sources of data that, once released, ends the relationship between the participant and the researcher (Pickering and Kara 2017). Besides, as researchers who are locally engaged and committed to local struggles, we are held by our communities and immediate families to a degree of accountability, involvement and responsibility greater than visiting or expatriate researchers will ever face (Mama 2011: 4; Peltier 2018; Mohammed 2022).

Every time I encounter the words of my participants in my writing, I am reminded of their complaints, their needs and their priorities. As with Dery's (2020) experience in his home region in the northern part of Ghana, the appeal for interventions continues to haunt us as researchers-in-relation even when our research is done and published. Not only did I endeavour to amplify the Indigenous voices from the interviews, but, like Fuentes (2016), I used the archives to locate the community's needs, to resist the authority of colonial systems that legitimate structures built on Indigenous subjugation, and to draw different conclusions interpolated by local perspectives.

Conclusion

Advancing a legal framework that addresses the prevailing challenges of ASM requires a critical methodology that not only describes the issues, but also involves assertive question-shifting, redefinition of issues, sharp attention to the power of dominant values, and vigilant monitoring of how research is used in generating knowledges. My decolonial approach aimed to reframe the ASM narrative and to ensure that its colonial legacies are not tucked away as part of some receding distant history but viewed as a living reality of small-scale miners in the local community. In this chapter, I have presented critical reflections on my deployment of decolonizing methodologies to counter the colonialist logics of knowledge production and law-making in ASM towards renaming the experiences of small-scale miners from their standpoints.

I map out how this journey upended the typical linearity of research and reveal the methodological dilemmas that I faced during one of the most unprecedented moments of recent history. As the ASM sociolegal field comes even more alive in the empirical analysis, I will further explore strategies for decolonizing knowledges in ASM. This, I hope, will contribute new perspectives to knowledge production and encourage researchers to diverge from the rigid binaries of state-centric legalism by delving into the rich tapestry of Indigenous epistemologies in their analysis of the legal framework of ASM in Ghana.

Notes

1. MMS/Special Series/Biographical/West Africa/597B; Extract of typescript manuscript of the journals of Reverend Freeman's visits to the Kingdoms of Asante and Dahomey, and to Abeokuta, Lagos and Bagadry between 1840 and 1843. Wesleyan Missionary Archives, SOAS, London.
2. Even on the stage where universal facts play out, universalised knowledges such as the linear time and space coordinates as assumed by the missionary above have been brought into question by scholars who have argued that time and space are cultural products. See Henri Lefebvre. 1991. *The Production of Space*. Oxford: Blackwell; Jack Goody. 2009. *The Theft of History*. Cambridge: Cambridge University Press. See also an exposition of Akan conceptualization of time and calendar in Kwasi Konadu. 2012. 'The Calendrical Factor in Akan History', *International Journal of African Historical Studies* 45(2): 217–46.
3. The publication of this book is said to have sparked controversy and led to strained diplomatic relations between Ghana and some Western countries, notably Britain and the United States of America. June Milne, Dr Nkrumah's editorial assistant, revealed in conversation with Zagba Oyortey, Director of the Ghana Museums and Monuments Board, that this publication, which exposed the workings of international finance capital in Africa and its extractive industry, was responsible for the CIA-backed coup against Nkrumah. The interview is available in this YouTube video: https://www.youtube.com/watch?v=rjUc_9Nmr_M.

CHAPTER 3

Decolonial Legal Pluralism and Informal Miners' Trajectories in ASM

Introduction

> Ordinance! Ordinance!! And yet another Ordinance!!!
>
> Here on the Gold Coast, the making of Ordinances is like the making of books, there is no end. Every Pharaoh must build his pyramid, and so every Gold Coast Governor must necessarily memorialise his administration by some ordinance or other. Today, it is an ordinance about pigs and sheep, tomorrow it is an ordinance to imprison at her Majesty's pleasure, or to deport some King or Chief… and so it goes on, ordinance to the right of us and ordinance to the left. We must be a peculiar race indeed to necessitate the making of so many ordinances to put us straight!

The above quotation is taken from the 11 March 1899 editorial in *The Gold Coast Aborigines*, titled 'Gold Coast – the Land of Ordinances'. It captured the frustrations of the people of the Gold Coast, whose unwritten laws and ways of life were being overturned, right before their eyes, by an overwhelming number of newly imposed written laws. About half a century later, Busia's (1951: 194) ethnography of Asante would reveal similar sentiments amongst a people who felt that their heads were essentially 'breaking' under the weight of many 'masters' in the form of their local chiefs, the *Asantehene* and colonial District Commissioners, all of whom were enacting different types of laws to regulate their lives. Over two decades ago, officials of the International Labour Organization (ILO 1999: 87) sounded the alarm about ASM being 'bedevilled with too many regulations that are mostly designed to constrain it'. As I have already established in the preceding chapters, current formalization measures are largely underpinned by a state centralism that many local miners find alienating, expensive, disruptive and unwelcome in their spaces, hence the persistent informality of ASM in the local mining communities. One of the objectives of this book is to show that the legal claims of local miners will be best achieved through a 'living' customary law rather than the prevailing state-centric legal framework. In this chapter, I demonstrate this further by introducing decolonial legal pluralism as the theoretical basis for the claims I make in this book.

Following this introduction, the next section opens with an overview of the theory of legal pluralism and its challenge to legal positivism. I demonstrate how legal positivism under colonialism was wielded to undermine and suppress Indigenous legal systems, particularly in mineral-rich communities. I explore how the dominant legal-centralist system reproduced colonial monist-pluralism, which paves the way for my argument for a paradigmatic shift towards a decolonial pluralism that is a more accurate and realistic reflection of the construction of ASM law in Ghana. In the subsequent section, I focus specifically on customary laws, and explore how the concept was absorbed, or even created, under the logics of colonial pluralism as a counterpoint to the living customary law. Following this, I make the case for a decolonial analysis of ASM law that accounts for the living customary law as a more suitable regulatory framework. In the fifth section, I outline and address possible concerns that may arise from the use of decolonial legal pluralism in reforming ASM law and policy on formalization. The sixth section concludes the chapter, with an emphasis on the fact that the strength of the legal analysis in this book is not only based on theoretical and conceptual debates, but is also enriched by empirical studies grounded in qualitative and archival research that I pursue in the chapters to come.

Decolonizing Legal Pluralism

Legal pluralism is generally defined as the coexistence of multiple legal systems within one geographical space or the same social field (Merry 1988: 869). As a first premise, legal pluralism challenges the positivist view that positions the state as the sole progenitor of rule creation and enforcement. Kelsen, whose works greatly influenced early ideas of legal positivism, saw law as a pyramid of norms in which the validity of each norm was ensured by a superior norm that was dictated by a sovereign centre – the so-called unity of laws (Kelsen

1967; Davies 2017b: 410; Cotterell 2006). This resonates with what Griffiths (1986) termed as legal centralism: the idea that law is and should be the law of the state, uniform for all persons, exclusive of all other laws and administered by a single set of state institutions. In contrast, legal pluralism viewed law as consisting of competing and sometimes contradictory orders outside of state law (von Benda-Beckmann and Turner 2018).

As I explained in the last chapter, early sociologists and legal anthropologists employed techniques and analysis from the social sciences to shift the gaze of legal research from the corridors of state institutions towards the concrete world of everyday social life, thereby proving an understanding of law as a social phenomenon (Anker 2016: 8). In so doing, they challenged the idea of law as a nonpolitical concept separate from social life and demonstrated that there are multiple forms of social control governed by other legal orders that can coexist alongside state laws (Davies 2005: 87). This was the pivot of the arguments of Eugen Ehrlich, the law professor from Chernivtsi, Bukovina, who is often considered as the father of legal pluralism. His central contribution to the sociology of law was his descriptive theory of law, which he propounded in response to normative legal positivism. Ehrlich did not confine law to the state but viewed it as being present in social life and everyday patterns of existence. According to him, 'it is not an essential element of the concept of law that it be created by the state, nor that it constitutes the basis of the decisions of the courts or other tribunals, nor that it be the basis of a legal compulsion consequent upon such a decision' (Ehrlich 1936: 24).

Ehrlich conceived actual social patterns, relationships and usages as part of a 'living law'. His classic depiction of the living law in rural Austria documented the ways in which local customary law continued its influence or even dominated despite sweeping claims of state monopoly on law. Ehrlich argued that laws encompassed a broader range of binding obligations and rules followed by people in their social lives and could be found in the 'inner order of the associations of human beings', which included but was not confined to the state. Legislation, regulations and judicial pronouncements were thus only one narrow form of law. Ehrlich's theories included a historical approach by which he argued that there has always been and will always be a great deal of law that is not part of the formalized system of law. His conclusion was that 'the centre of gravity of legal development therefore from time immemorial has not lain in the activity of the state, but in society itself and must be sought there at the present time' (Ehrlich 1936: 390).

For many formerly colonized societies, legal pluralism serves as an enduring testament to the dominance of state-centric conceptions of law and the suppression of Indigenous laws. Nursoo (2018: 56) described this as 'monist-pluralism', where there is an acknowledgement of multiple legal orders, but from the standpoint of a hierarchical legal order where the legal authority of the state, as it exists alongside other legal and political authorities, is singularly upheld at the top of the hierarchy. This hierarchization further manifests with state law being considered as 'official', 'formal' law, and all others as 'unofficial', 'informal' law, subordinate and extinguishable (Benton 2009). Monist-pluralism, according to Nursoo (2018: 65), is not genuinely pluralism for a cross-cultural, postcolonial context, because the monist element upon which its statist legal orders are predicated provides and only recognizes law developed in relation to the state. The monist-pluralist displacement of competing Indigenous legal traditions echoes Robert Cover's (1983: 40) notion of the 'jurispathic', which characterizes the functionality of the courts in the suppression of law. This jurispathy was a key element in the legal, economic, cultural and social changes introduced by colonialism. Newly imposed Western laws became, as Chanock (1985) puts it, the 'cutting edge of colonialism' that paved the way for imperialism. With their ordinances, courts and political administrative systems, newly introduced legal systems reshaped existing Indigenous laws in what Merry (1988: 872) referred to as the era of classic legal pluralism. Its ongoing colonialities continue to have profound influences on how formerly colonized societies access rights and benefits, particularly from their natural resources such as land and minerals.

Nursoo (2018: 65) proposed a second conception of pluralism, which she described as 'pluralist-pluralism'. Pluralist-pluralism departs from the hierarchized orientation by not presuming the primacy of one model of legal order or its ability to recognize other legal orders. Expressed differently, pluralist-pluralism does not privilege a statist or institutionalist perspective in determining what counts as 'law'. Rather, the multiplicity of laws and legal orders are placed on an equal footing. On her part, Araújo (2025)'s cartographic metaphor of law as a map offered a way to 'disobey' and 'turn upside down' modern epistemological hierarchies in decolonizing legal pluralism. This approach was based on the recognition of legal centralism as not only a fiction but also a Eurocentric instrument that limited political imagination. According to Araújo (2025), a decolonial approach to legal pluralism is imperative because it is attentive to the colonialist and imperialist foundations of the rule of law and the role of modern law in the legitimization of capitalist exploitation. A decolonial approach to legal pluralism does not seek to bend Indigenous laws to the validation of the modern canon. Rather, it paves the way to embrace subalternized Indigenous legal systems on their own terms and not through a system of forced assimilation. This approach to decolonization, as Nursoo (2018: 62) had earlier expressed, involves destabilizing the authority of law and enabling an analysis of the relationship between power and knowledge in revealing law's plurality of truths.

Within the bifurcated state in many African countries (Mamdani 1996) lies an abyssal line (Santos 2014) where there is an established hierarchy between modern law and customary law. This abyssal line draws a distinction between the formal and the informal, which, in the ASM context, has been used to legitimize the social struggles of informal small-scale miners and those who resist elite capture in the ASM sector. In the rest of this book, I advance a decolonial pluralist approach to ASM beyond Nursoo's pluralist-pluralism, and in the spirit of Araújo's (2025) approach to decolonizing legal pluralism. This decolonial pluralism argues that ASM's illegality does not necessarily emanate from the sector's informality, but from a longstanding history of calculated deployment of state law and elite traditional apparatus in the formulation of informality as an instrument of dispossession, classed consolidation and blame-shifting in the politics of environmental pollution. I advance the living customary law as a more sustainable regulatory framework for ASM governance, demonstrating that beyond recognizing its existence or placing it on an equal footing with state law, there should be scope for the living customary law to, in some cases, transcend state law as the dominant, normative legal framework in the design of transformative legal and policy measures for the sector. In the next section, I begin the process towards my decolonial pluralist conception of ASM law by examining the concept of the living customary law in juxtaposition to the official customary law.

A Tale of Two Laws: 'Living' Customary Laws and the Invention of the Official Customary Law

Despite its popular appeal to legalist thoughts on formalization within the mainstream ASM literature and policymaking circles, articulating the needs of small-scale miners through an integration into the dominant positivist legal system has, as I have already established, so far proven largely futile, hence the need for reimagined legal possibilities such as the living customary law. The concept of the living customary law as used in the African context became mainstream following the Women and Law in Southern Africa (WLSA) Project in the 1980s. The WLSA Project influenced scholarly distinctions between 'official' and 'living' customary law, and provided empirical evidence to show that women's legal claims were best served by deconstructing customary laws rather than by pursuing formal equality claims (Diala 2017). Mainstream scholarly conceptualizations often conflated the official customary law with the living customary law, a situation that Diala (2017: 147) attributed to the failure to provide a comprehensive explanation for the historical emergence of the official customary law.

The official, state-recognized customary law is identified as the product of a colonial and postcolonial distortion and the continued effort to pigeonhole Indigenous laws into Western legal systems (Bennet 2009). This category of customary law is often located within executive directives, codifications, judicial pronouncements and academic textbooks. Subjecting customary laws to standardized state procedures produced what is referred to as the 'created, invented or lawyer's customary law' (Woodman 1987; Crook 2008). Under colonialism, existing Indigenous laws were perceived as exotic and categorized as 'customs' or 'customary' mostly because they were unwritten. The positivistic theoretical model that governed colonial monist-pluralism was highly averse to this unwritten nature because it made Indigenous legal systems difficult to pin down. This othering of Indigenous laws led to their subordination as part of the colonial agenda of consolidating imperial power through newly imposed Western laws (Merry 1988; Nursoo 2018; Tamale 2020).

Colonial administrators learnt the laws and customs of the colonized societies, often relying on versions of customary law given to them by interpreters, European merchants, anthropologists, educated indigenes and other locals with capital and access to the colonial administration. Said's *Orientalism* (1978) teaches that such colonial pursuit of knowledge about the laws of the colonized was not motivated by a genuine desire for the truth, but rather for purposes of dominance and imperialism. This reckons with how state recognition of existing customary laws has not always been about achieving the best results for local people and their communities. For instance, under the British government's indirect rule system, state recognition was used as an effective strategy to lull the people into a false sense of security and acceptance, while the government strategically manipulated and altered the very nature of their customary laws through codifications, judicial pronouncements and even academic scholarship. The indirect rule system, which Mamdani (1999) described as one of the most profound assertions of colonial power, was one of the many elaborate systems by which colonial rule and its day-to-day violence was mediated through designated Native Authorities headed by local chiefs. In the Gold Coast Colony, for instance, the Native Jurisdiction Ordinance of 1878 presented the first public statement of the British government's jurisdiction vis-à-vis the chiefs. Section 5 provided that:

> It shall be lawful for the Head Chief of every division brought within the operation of this Ordinance, with the concurrence of the Chiefs, Captains, Headmen, and others who by Native customary law are the Councillors of his Stool to make such Bye-laws consistent with the laws of the Gold Coast Colony, and subject to the provisions of this Ordinance, as he may deem expedient for promoting the peace, good order, and welfare of the people of his division...[1]

Section 6 of the aforementioned Native Jurisdiction Ordinance further provided that:

> The Bye-laws so prepared shall be forthwith reported to the Governor for the approval or disallowance thereof by the Governor in Council and such of the Bye-laws as shall be so approved shall be published in the Gazette, and shall thereupon become as valid and effectual as if the same had been enacted in this Ordinance. No Bye-law which the Governor in Council disallows shall have any force or effect whatsoever.

Under section 10, head chiefs were authorized to form Native Tribunals to try breaches of byelaws and to 'exercise Civil and Criminal jurisdiction in the causes and matters aforementioned in which all the parties are natives, or in which any party not a native consent[s] in writing to his case being tried by the Native Tribunal'. These Native Tribunals were established for chiefs to apply Indigenous laws with the assistance of courtiers and court clerks under the supervision of the British District Commissioners.

Section 9 further provided that customary laws existing prior to the enactment of the Ordinance could have effect only if they were not repugnant to natural justice, equity or good conscience, nor incompatible either directly or by necessary implication with any enactment of the Colonial Legislature. Ultimately, customary laws were established as those existing Indigenous laws that were sanctioned by the colonial government. This was reinforced under section 2(1)(a) of the Native Authority (Colony) Ordinance, 1944, which officially defined native customary law as:

> ...a rule or body of rules regulating rights and imposing correlative duties being a rule or body of rules which obtains and is fortified by established native

usage and which is appropriate and applicable to any particular cause, action, suit, matter, dispute, issue or question, and includes also any native customary law recorded or modified in accordance with the provisions of sections 30 and 31 respectively.[2]

Sections 30 and 31 of the Native Authority (Colony) Ordinance essentially gave supervening powers to the Governor, who had the power to declare Indigenous customs and laws as compatible with or otherwise repugnant to English legal systems. Any challenge Indigenous laws held to the authority of the colonial state law was adjudicated in the newly established British-style courts and in native courts where judges assessed customary laws through a positivist orientation (Woodman 2012a). Many of these judges were not familiar with the customary laws of the areas they presided over, and they often lacked full awareness of the social relations and ramifications of the matters in dispute. Furthermore, their training in the English legal system carried legalistic imperatives that weakened their capacity to satisfy the requirements of the local communities (Tamanaha 2021). Consequently, local elders who gave evidence as witnesses in court often found that their opinions were divorced from the local contexts. Where there appeared to be contrasting accounts of customary law, what won the stamp of approval was often not the customary law in the sense of the lived social relations, but selective formulations that suited existing powers (Woodman 2011). Land and mining were particularly tensioned sites of legal contestations where customary laws were invented to suit the interests of the government, foreign concessionaires and their local allies (Snyder 1981).

This notwithstanding, the fact that customary law has undergone significant transformation does not detract from the legitimacy of the living customary law. The living customary law is the version of customary law from the perspective of those within the community in which the relevant norms are observed. According to Diala (2017: 156), many who observe the living customary law do not have a formalistic understanding of legality, nor any significant interest in legal theories. Under the living customary law, knowledge of the law is acquired through living, storytelling and other social interactions. Watson (2015) explained that such living laws are instilled with a relational philosophy in which humans, animals, plants and ancestors are interconnected in relation to the law and to the past, which is lived in the present and recreated in the future. Based on values, mores and traditions, the living customary law dwells in the memories of the people who practise it, and it is passed on from generation to generation. This stands in contrast to the philosophy underpinning Western law and its invention of the official customary law, which is rather aimed at a hierarchical, anthropocentric legal system structured by linear time and oriented towards ownership and control.

The soul of the living customary law is its adaptability to sociopolitical, cultural and economic changes. This flexibility is founded upon traditional values, including humaneness, family continuity, the duty of care owed to family members by the family head, the nonindividual nature of marriage and the preservation of ancestral homes, among others. From her study of the Chagga in Tanzania, Moore (1978) defined customary law as a cultural construct with political implications, a set of ideas embedded in a relationship that is historically shifting. She found that legal orders were neither static nor distinct; rather, they were involved in a constant process of creating norms and developing discourses that borrow from and react to other norms and discourses. People's attitudes to their communal values enable them to determine when customs outlive their usefulness or need to be readjusted due to their unsuitability to modern conditions (Diala 2017: 153). Tamale (2020: 139) reached a similar conclusion with her decolonial understanding of the living customary law. She identified the living customary law as not limited to an individual's interaction with their community based on horizontal relationships of consultation, participation and reciprocity, but also involving vertical interactions between an individual and outsiders such as the state, values occasioned by globalization and other external agents. It is the interplay between these levels of relationships that informs the flexibility of customary law.

One of the major strategies of colonialism was to attack the inherent flexibility of customary law. This was often achieved through codifications, which, as the South African Constitutional Court in *Shilubana and Others v Nwamitwa* noted, denied customary law the necessary space to evolve, rendering it stonewalled and distorting its mutable nature. According to Ranger (1983), the notion of traditional, precolonial African societies being ruled by unchanging, long-established customs was a myth established under colonial legal structures of the early twentieth century in an effort to restore some order after the chaotic years of the nineteenth century. Historical accounts of intense local resistances in the wake of the imposition of colonial monist-pluralism help to challenge the notion that customary law in African traditional societies was static (Merry 1988; Woodman 1996). While customary law by its very nature has always been in a state of adaptation and development, the combined impacts of increased mobility, migration, urbanization, commercialization, technology, modern systems of administration, religions and cultural worldviews have prompted social change to occur more swiftly.

Furthermore, while legal positivism boasts of the objectivity and fairness of state law, the works of poststructuralist philosophers, critical legal scholars, critical race theorists and decolonial scholars have shown that the law is not always neutral. For many in formerly colonized countries, the symbolic consequences of Western legal positivism are manifested in sanctioned distortions of their Indigenous knowledges and living customary laws in service of empire's land dispossessions and classed accumulations. Official customary laws were deliberately crafted and rationalized by the paternalism of civilization, where the existence of multiple legal and normative orders were typically regarded as principal constraints to directing 'native' societies and economies onto the trajectory of development (Porter 2012; Tweneboah 2020). Colonial monist-pluralism persists in the postcoloniality as a potent tool for the 'law and development' policies of foreign donor agencies, under whose directives many formerly colonized societies have been formulating measures to formalize their customary laws and land tenure systems (Woodman 2012b: 129).

Formalization and other policies that advocate for a unitary property system under state law derive from this worldview, which considers multiple legal systems to be a stumbling block to modernizing and transforming the ASM sector. This positivist rationality characterizes the operation of informal miners within anything other than state law as an illegality, even when there is an established system of informality that has a far more enduring appeal to small-scale miners and the local mining communities.

Beyond Recognition: Adopting Living Customary Laws in ASM Governance in Ghana

Woodman (2001: 28) explained recognition in the context of legal pluralism as comprising two main forms: institutional recognition, where customary law becomes incorporated under the state legal system; and normative recognition, where norms of customary law are integrated into the body of norms of state law and enforced by state institutions. While such explicit recognition of customary law may appear as the state abandoning its claim to monopoly of law, the reality shows a monist-pluralism where state law retains the dominant authority in determining the legitimacy of other normative orders.

This, as Tweneboah (2020) explained, pertains to the Ghanaian legal system, where there is a plurality of state laws coexisting hierarchically with customary laws and ancestor-based political institutions. In Ghana, the 1992 Constitution officially recognizes customary law as a source of law, which it defines under article 11(2)(3) as 'rules of law which by custom are applicable to particular communities in Ghana'. Additionally, articles 267 and 270 of the Constitution recognize customary institutions such as chieftaincy and customary land tenure systems. Similar provisions can be found under the Land Act, 2020 (Act 1036), and the Chieftaincy Act, 2008 (Act 759). A further complication to this monist-pluralism is the doctrine of eminent domain, by which the state recognizes the absolute rights of customary landowners but reserves to itself the exclusive authority in allocating the rights to any minerals found in the land. Under the Constitution, the state can compulsorily appropriate lands from customary landowners for public purposes, which include mineral extraction. This is carried in the spirit of article 20(1)(a), which provides that 'No property of any description, or interest in or right over any property shall be compulsorily taken possession of or acquired by the State unless the taking of possession or acquisition is necessary in the interest of defence, public safety, public order, public morality, public health, town and country planning or the development or utilisation of property in such a manner as to promote the public benefit'.

In recognizing customary laws, the Ghanaian Constitution, under article 1(2), establishes a hierarchy by which it ranks itself supreme, such that any other laws found to be inconsistent with the Constitution shall, to the extent of the inconsistency, be null and void. This constitutional dispensation forms part of the received legal systems by which all laws founded in legislation, religion and custom are subordinated to the premier law, namely, the Constitution. In addition to placing customary laws below the Constitution and statutory enactments, the Constitution also embeds customary law within the 'common law', a term that derives from the English common law. Article 11(2) defines the common law to comprise 'the rules of law generally known as the common law, the rules generally known as doctrines of equity and the rules of customary law including those determined by the Superior Court of Judicature'. These constitutional provisions demonstrate how entrenched the Ghanaian legal system is within its colonial legacies, where customary laws are still viewed through the lens of the colonially inherited common law, with slight modifications to suit modern circumstances.

In the mining context, state law recognizes customary law, and article 20(2) of the Constitution particularly requires all mining ventures, both large-scale and ASM, to acknowledge the rights of prior customary landowners and pay appropriate compensation for the use of their lands. The payment of compensation to customary landowners is also provided for under the 2006 Minerals and Mining Act. Beyond that, state law crowds out customary law and takes absolute control over all other matters relating to the administration of mineral rights. This monist-pluralism evokes a 'superior state approach to legal pluralism', or 'weak legal pluralism', which involves constitutional recognition of customary law so long as the latter does not conflict with state law (Griffiths 1986: 8; Tamanaha 2001; Pimentel 2011; von Benda-Beckmann 2021). Accordingly, while ASM and customary laws are duly recognized under the respective state laws, an ASM operation that derives exclusively from customary claims to mineral rights is deemed a constitutional contravention. Systems theory offers further insights into this framework, where there is a recognition of the interdependence of different subsystems, legal actors, institutions and processes in a legal system, with emphasis on invalidating and delegitimizing any acts or processes that are not recognized by the system (Macarthy and Uhumuavbi 2025). By this principle, formalization under the prevailing monist-pluralism works as a tool of repressive exclusion where, despite ASM's formal recognition, state law still struggles to accept its predominantly customary underpinnings and miners' negotiations for mineral rights under customary law. Ultimately, the state's monist-pluralist approach to ASM admits certain customary rights while maintaining the prerogative to define the parameters for recognition of any other recourse to mineral rights.

For the foreseeable future, the state is bound to retain its position as a central political figure in the modern capitalist world (Santos 2020). However, this position of power lies in contestation with other non-state forms of governance, and in many cases, the state may not be as relevant or as powerful as these other legitimating institutions. Ehrlich's submission (1936: 63–64) on this point is that 'A man conducts himself according to law chiefly because this is made imperative by his social relations. The state is not the only association that exercises coercion; there is an untold number of associations in society that exercise it much more fully than the state'. In ASM, this is observable in how local miners continue to resort to customary laws, traditional institutions and their own social organizations to access mineral rights, despite the state's positioning of itself as the sole arbiter of mineral rights through the institutionalization of constitutional and statutory prohibitions.

Informal ASM exists as a typical representation of Moore's semi-autonomous social field, where customary laws, Indigenous spiritualities and state laws intersect to generate the systems upon which the various actors conduct their business, such as negotiating for access to land, allocating labour and profit, marketing their produce and engaging with their local communities. In Ghana, political administrative boundaries often overlap with those of traditional administrations. Thus, within the same geographical area, there is often a combined jurisdiction of local government authorities (assemblymen, Unit Committee members, district chief executives and municipal chief executives, members of Parliament) and traditional authorities (local chiefs, regents, the Council of Elders, heads of clans and families). Informal miners also belong to social associations where they possess 'jurisgenesis', namely, the capacity to internally generate legal meaning from within their own established organizational structures (Cover 1983: 4). This speaks to an 'interlegality' (Santos 1977: 5) where local miners draw on various normative and symbolic resources to frame their reality without losing their peculiar informality and flexibility.

Based on the above, it is only reasonable that the state gives focused attention to the existing plural legal orders in designing ASM laws and policies. In doing so, states can examine the limits of the ideological power of their laws, that is, the areas where it does not penetrate or where alternative forms of ordering persist. Ignoring this plurality creates what Benjamin (2008) described as sterile dualism, where inconsistencies and unresolved tensions at the intersection between statutory and customary legal mechanisms undermine both the state's formalist resource-governance mechanism as well as the livelihood security of local resource users. Following de Soto's theory of extra-legality, Siegel and Veiga (2009: 53) suggested that the most effective way to achieve ASM formalization was to 'absorb the customary practices of informal artisanal miners into the mainstream legal economy'. This has generated an emerging interest in the study of customary laws, where researchers are drawing on empirical evidence from different mining communities to map out the best strategies for absorbing existing customary law into ASM formalization mechanisms. Verbrugge, Cuvelier and Van Bockstael (2015), for instance, found customarily negotiated arrangements between informal miners and local communities in the Philippines, Congo and Liberia, where a system of benefit-sharing agreements has become institutionalized.

Speaking of a similar dynamic in the Ivorian small-scale diamond-mining sector, De Jong and Sauerwein (2021) noted the recognition of customary institutions and the establishment of a collaborative arrangement between a parastatal mining company – La Société pour le Développement Minier de la Côte D'Ivoire (SODEMI) – and local chiefs of villages, organized in the form of cooperatives. This agreement provided a level of shared control and benefit-sharing, where SODEMI determined the locations of the mines and the communities received 12% of all proceeds. Under this arrangement, mining licences were granted to villages and not individual mine sites. In Senegal, Persaud et al. (2017) found a system where power is shared between the *Diourakountiqui* (mine site chiefs) and the *Tombouloma* (persons responsible for the security of the ASM site and the village). The traditional authority of local chiefs in the mining villages is respected in all negotiations, and there is room for the *Tombouloma* and the *Diourakountiqui* to account for lands given for operations, provide technical assistance, resolve conflicts, exact taxes and generally maintain order and control at the mining sites.

In Ghana, what could have passed as a remotely similar comanagement system was the Community Mining Scheme (CMS). I mention it here briefly as an illustration of a monist-pluralist governance system that falls short of the decolonial pluralist framework I advance in this book. As I already established, the CMS was ostensibly launched by the government to enable a more decentralized and localized autonomy in the management and operation of ASM with oversight and technical and financial support from the state. However, as will become clear in Chapter 6, this supposedly decentralized governance system has been co-opted by persons with proximity to the state, while local miners continue to struggle with access to mineralized lands.

Moreover, while scholars in favour of customary law in ASM formalization may find the hybrid state–traditional governance system a more welcoming approach than the strictly state-centric format currently in play, there is nevertheless the need to be cautious of the asymmetries of power and the colonialist dynamics that are also generated by this hybridity. The ultimate focus of many of these so-called decentralized ASM governance systems remains the attainment of a monist-pluralism where the state maintains dominance and yields very limited concessions to local miners in key decision-making. This reflects a weak legal pluralism that only serves as fertile ground for rentier politics and collusion between political and traditional elites for their own material gains (Van Bockstael 2014; De Jong and Sauerwein 2021). Omeje's (2008) exploration of rentier politics in the extractive economies of the Global South traced it to the colonial manipulation of the political economy; here, the corporatization of public law, along with the instrumental value of lawlessness at the top echelon of the state, facilitated capitalist accumulation at the expense of underprivileged and marginalized social groups. In this instance, the rentier state is defined as one that is largely dependent on rents, taxes and royalties relating to extractive resources; these, in turn, are controlled by the governing elite, who are often in collusion with exploitative agents of international capital, and who mainly expend these revenue profits to their own benefit rather than for the general welfare of society. In the Ghanaian ASM context, Ayelazuno and Mawuko-Yevugah (2021) have drawn attention to the relationship between the international and domestic in the exercise of agency by African states, as well as to the class dynamics that perpetuate neopatrimonial practices and thereby contribute to the government's failure to implement its ASM policies.

The lesson here is that state recognition is not a magic wand that, by itself, can invoke equality and justice. Formal recognition hardly involves the state entering any given space of customary law and submitting itself to what Anker (2016: 3) described as the potentially disruptive process of asking, 'What place is there for me in your universe?' Rather, the state enters and takes over those spaces as though they were legal voids, with no regard to the ongoing social arrangements. Moore (1978) explained that the social space between legislator and subject is not a normative vacuum. Similarly, between the well-lit, air-conditioned edifices where ASM enactments and policies are produced and the dark, rocky, scorching pits of informal miners, there is an embodiment of living customary laws that needs to be fully embraced to foster a more socially and environmentally responsible governance of ASM. Such non-state laws, according to Teubner (1997: 3), have legitimating capacity in their own right and do not need to be measured against the state legal system to attain legitimacy. Besides, state recognition, or any other form of incorporation or validation for that matter, is not a prerequisite to the empirical existence of other legal orders (Griffiths 1986). Araújo (2025) has stressed that merely acknowledging the existence of multiple legal orders without being open to learning from their epistemological diversity neither challenges the centralist view of the modern constitutional paradigm nor decolonizes the hegemonic Eurocentric canon and the hierarchies it entails. In other words, the recognition of legal pluralism must dispense with the consolidation of subalternity, the reinforcement of otherness and the re-creation of colonial forms of neo-indirect rule.

The decolonial legal pluralism I advance here affirms the living customary laws of ASM not from a position of state power, dominance and control, but from the perspective of mutually coexisting laws. Drawing from a combination of Ehrlich's living law (1936) and the African conceptualization of the living customary law, I posit the living customary law of ASM as a legitimate legal framework that truly reflects informal miners' engagement with existing customs, practices and Indigenous knowledges in a way that encompasses horizontal and vertical normative interactions. The living customary law of informal ASM is a fully fledged legal system capable of legitimating the informal operations of local miners, and it should be recognized as such. Conflating ASM informality with illegality because of its reliance on the living customary law is a positivist conceptualization of law that is not only colonialist and ethnocentric, but also disregards the overwhelming empirical evidence that points to the legitimating authority of the living customary law. In considering this empirical evidence as well as the history of the contested emergence of the prevailing monist-pluralism and its licensing regime, I am able to interrogate the state's pronouncement of illegality on informal miners' dependence on customary law in accessing mineral rights.

Decolonial legal pluralism provides the theoretical framework for uncovering why a historical, state-sanctioned policy intervention like ASM formalization is simply not gaining the envisioned traction at the local level. This is achieved by 'looking in', as suggested by Anker (2016: 5), which involves a critical examination of the very nature of the state laws upon which such policies are predicated, so as to open up a space of engagement with alternative legal possibilities. Without this approach, one risks missing the intricate ways in which Western law is tied up in the colonially transplanted orthodoxy of formalization. Decolonial legal pluralism enables us to ceaselessly ask questions about power, positionality and agency, which are necessary to unearth the prejudices and assumptions inherent in the legal materials produced by the state. Some of these relevant questions include: who are the makers of ASM law considered to be? To whom is this law targeted, and how are their voices represented in the process of law-making? ASM researchers and policymakers cannot meaningfully speak of addressing the environmental hazards of ASM without first asking these crucial questions about the construction of the laws that underpin formalization, unlearning the colonial monist-pluralist approach to law and ensuring that local miners and the mining communities are placed at the centre of law-making.

Without this approach, the absorption of customary law into ASM formalization will merely result in an infiltration of state law in a way that will strip local miners of their flexibility and gradually restructure the informal system to formally resemble the alienating, legalistic state law. By embracing a decolonial pluralism, states can begin to finally accept the reality that the answers to the social and environmental challenges in ASM do not lie in more stringent state laws and criminalization, as these only work to weaponize poverty and create further difficulties for vulnerable miners. In a decolonial pluralist framework, attempts at ossifying the living customary law through stifling codifications will be restrained, since the focus of governance will be shifted from forced assimilation towards the creation of a decentralized system grounded in a nonhierarchical legal structure where local miners can work in an environmentally responsible and nonexploitative environment.

Addressing Critiques of Legal Pluralism in ASM

Envisioning an ASM legal framework grounded in decolonial legal pluralism is not without its concerns. One of the foremost issues with legal pluralism in Global South contexts is about its colonialist roots. Legal pluralism is predominantly regarded as having emerged as a field of anthropological enquiry where early researchers like Malinowski (1926) examined the interactions of normative cultures in colonized territories. The question that then arises is 'How can a concept with such strong ties to colonialism and that is embedded in relations of unequal power (between imperial legal systems and the laws of the colonized) be useful in decolonizing ASM governance in the postcoloniality?'

While it is certainly true that colonial impositions of European legal systems significantly reshaped the legal landscape of many African societies, Diala and Rautenbach (2024) remind us that legal pluralism in Africa is not solely a product of colonialism but is also reflective of precolonial and postcolonial African realities. African societies were hardly insulated from each other and, as evidenced by historical accounts of societal encounters through trade, marriage, nomadic settlements, migration and conquest (Macarthy and Uhumuavbi 2025), legal pluralism existed in Africa long before the continent's interaction with foreign legal systems through colonialism.

Again, beginning in the late 1970s, sociolegal scholars shifted the application of legal pluralism from colonized societies to the more industrialized countries of Europe and the United States. This era of 'new legal pluralism' also shed the fixation on colonized societies and expanded into researching legal relations between dominant and subordinate groups as well as the interaction between state and other unofficial forms of ordering (Merry 1988). With this paradigmatic shift, the concept of legal pluralism becomes relevant even in decolonial contexts, as it facilitates the study and critique of law in plural normative orders, demonstrating how laws are historically derived and usually intertwined in the varying social microprocesses (Griffiths 1986). In the same way, the relation between customary laws and state laws in the Ghanaian ASM regime is very complicated and involves a long history of contestations, depicted by outright rejections (where, for example, the state bans informal mining, or informal miners reject the imposition of formalization) and acceptances (where, subject to certain prescribed processes, the state accepts informal mining). Accordingly, an understanding of both classic monist-pluralism and decolonial legal pluralism is relevant for the study of a field such as ASM, whose legal system is at the intersection of historically constructed colonial laws, modern state-centric laws and the living customary law. Moreover, as earlier discussed, the works of Nursoo (2018) and Araújo (2025) point to a decolonial legal pluralism that offers a theory of resistance to the prevailing hegemonic and colonially inherited legal systems that govern ASM.

Another recurring critique of legal pluralism is that it widens the definition of law even to the extent of including any social practices, hence rendering the idea of law very vague and unspecific. Merry (1988) puzzled over this when she asked, 'Where do we stop speaking of law and find ourselves simply describing social life?' This concern arises in the ASM discourse, with questions such as 'Should all the social practices that informal miners observe in their daily lives be included as law?', 'What counts as "the living customary law" and what should be left out?', 'Who/what determines the criteria of such inclusions and exclusions of legality?' and 'How practical is an ASM law and policy framework governed by living customary law?'

First, Diala (2017) offers a response to these questions by making use of Hart's argument, which is that a sense of obligation is what distinguishes customs that are mere social habits from customs that are regarded as law. Davies (2017b: 40), however, clarifies that Hart's recognition of law was relevant to 'legal officials', and so its customary practice at the foundation of a legal system was extremely limited and intrinsically undemocratic. According to Davies, the assumption that it is possible to find a conceptual distinction between things that are law and things that are not is characteristic of legal positivism. Consequently, Merry's anxiety (1988) over where law ends and social normativity begins unduly limits legal theory to questions of definition and prevents an expansive and experimental approach to understanding law's multiplicity. This, by Davies's (2017b: 40) exposition, begs the question of why the recognition of law should be exclusive to officials, when everybody in a political community and beyond it has a stake in the identity and nature of law. While it may be necessary in some contexts and for certain purposes to adopt a provisional definition of law, such provisional and practical definitions do not exhaust the idea of law, and there should be opportunity to explore law's other possibilities. Moreover, as I have already established, the fact that alternative knowledges of law are not officially sanctioned does not make them any less real or valid.

Like Araújo (2025), Berman (2009) found the whole debate about law versus non-law largely irrelevant in a legally pluralist context. According to Berman (2009), the key questions should involve the normative commitments of a community and the interactions among normative orders that give rise to such commitments, and not their formal status. He noted that official laws that were contrary to prevailing customary or community norms often had little or no real-world effect, at least not without the willingness or capacity of coercive bodies to exercise sustained force to impose such rules. Accordingly, the focus should not be on who has the formal authority to articulate norms or the coercive power to enforce them, but on empirically studying which statements of authority tend to be treated as binding in actual practice, and by whom. This echoed Kleinhans and Macdonald's critical legal pluralism (1997), which focused on the individuals who follow, use and interpret law as the productive site for its symbolism, sense and normativity, and thus provided a departure from the reification of law and communities in the social-science approach to legal pluralism. Critical legal pluralism argues that the whole idea that diverse forms of law could be identified based on functional and other criteria is suggestive of a universal understanding of law that possesses imperial overtones for non-Western understandings of law. This approach endows legal subjects with a responsibility to participate in the multiple normative communities by which they recognize and create their own legal subjectivity.

Another concern in the context of natural-resources scholarship is that the application of legal pluralism creates knowledge uncertainties. The argument here is that state law affords a certain level of certainty and predictability that will be eroded once multiple legal orders are made to apply. Customary laws are viewed as being in a constant state of flux, with different versions that are often conflicting, vague or elusive. According to Tamanaha (2021: 177), this makes it difficult, even impossible, to precisely identify customary norms, since the assortment of contingencies can vary so much from one case to another. This concern is what drives policymakers, development practitioners and proponents of ASM formalization towards the consolidation of all property rights under a unitary system governed by the rule of state law.

In the ASM context, this particular critique arises with concerns that recognizing multiple legal frameworks would lead to a complex, incoherent and messy governance framework. However, as I argued in Mensah (2021), such concerns typify a Eurocentric ontological and epistemological framing of law that projects the idea of a homogenized legal positivism as the standard of law. They are based on the myth that legal meanings are stable and of coherent foundation, which denies the human element of law – of relation, interpretation, symbolism and its embodied practices. According to Griffiths (1986), lawyers and social scientists often suffer from a chronic inability to see that the legal reality of modern society is not that of a tidy, consistent and organized ideal, but rather an unsystematic collage of inconsistent and overlapping parts. Legal pluralism offers a critique to this presumed objectivity of law by challenging the view of law as coming from 'nowhere', rendering law subjective, indeterminate and therefore open to contestation. As Tweneboah (2020: 5) rightly argued, legal pluralism offers a discursive, analytical and normative lens for addressing the tensions between the different normative systems in Ghana, and helps us to avoid assumptions about a unitary, simple, postcolonial legal history that accounts for the competing normative claims in Ghanaian society. Homogenized assumptions about the ASM sector have been proven to be erroneous and to only lead to impractical policymaking (Verbrugge and Besmanos 2016; Hilson 2010). For informal miners, it is the seemingly complex, heterogenous legal system that has sustained their operations for centuries. This goes to show that a formalization scheme that attempts to impose homogenous conceptions of law on such a heterogenous group who work within a fluid, legal and culturally heterogenous context is bound to fail due to its disconnect with the actual lived realities of the target community.

Meinzen-Dick and Pradhan (2001) have indicated that while knowledge uncertainties may be inherent in legal pluralism, they are not necessarily obstacles to equitable and sustainable natural resource management. The flexibility of legal pluralism affords local resource users an important coping mechanism and responsiveness in dealing with sociopolitical uncertainties such as those relating to their livelihoods or the environment. Like most natural resource users, informal miners face unpredictable fluctuations in natural resource availability, which call for different sets of rules to deal with varying situations. Recognizing the multiple and often overlapping bases of claims for natural resources leads to a more accurate understanding of the situations that resource users face, as well as greater flexibility to adapt to the changes and uncertainties. In her ethnographic work with the San peoples of Namibia, Vermeylen (2010: 53) identified that rigid assimilationist policies that disregard Indigenous Peoples or seek to strip them of their customary laws or their unique characteristics end up totalizing their communities and creating a dichotomization that subjugates and opens them up for exclusion rather than inclusion. Policies like formalization, which seek to integrate all property rights under statutory law in such legally plural contexts, only lead to cumbersome and culturally inappropriate results that sacrifice adaptability for uniformity. It is more useful to recognize and negotiate, than to ignore the tensions that exist or to create a myth of a legal homogeneity that provides an easier narrative in the short term but fails to address the long-term contestations and inequities. The perceived indeterminacy of the living customary laws of ASM is not a deficiency or a characteristic that takes away from its legitimacy or potency as an independent form of legal regulation. Rather, the indeterminacy is a strength, in that it makes the living customary law more flexible and adaptive and better suited to the ever-changing circumstances of informal ASM operations.

Embracing this complexity of ASM law will involve addressing the passive dismissiveness of the plural legal context within which ASM operates. In their study on the gulf between donors/policymakers and ASM researchers in the theorization of ASM informality, Hilson and Maconachie (2017) argued against what they described as an increasing misdiagnosis of plural tenure regimes and customary rights within the ASM discourse. While the authors admitted that there were legitimate concerns about the plurality of subsurface and surface rights in several mineral-producing countries, they believed that little attention should be paid to such discussions given that the purpose of many mining sector reforms was to facilitate large-scale mining access and legitimize host governments' control of mineral rights solely for economic gain. In critiquing discussions about pluralist systems in the ASM discourse, Hilson and Maconachie (2017) indicated that the unique and superior mining titles enjoyed by large-scale mining were more directly a result of the state's political commitment in prioritizing large-scale extraction; in effect, that the competing claims of other resource users such as small-scale miners were a product of ASM's low level of policy treatment, as opposed to a genuine overlapping of claims.

While I would agree with the authors about the disconnections regarding the theorizations of ASM informality, I am unable to fully share their view on the plurality of land claims in ASM. As Berman (2009: 225) has noted, the world is plural, and scholars would do well to study the multiplicity and engage in the conversation rather than succumb to a top-down, universalist framework that only distorts the astonishing variety of law and legal claims on the ground. The prevailing mining political economy and its superior policy treatment of large-scale mining claims are a legacy of colonial resource extractivism and its monist-pluralism, where state oversight and licensing systems are used as instruments of dispossession, exclusion and materialist accumulation. If we are to sanitize the ASM sector and rid it of its environmental and social cankers, there needs to be a thorough interrogation of this history and the question of the plurality of land claims in the extractive industry.

There is also the question of the sufficiency of customary laws in addressing the challenges fostered by the dominant state-centric legal system. Ghanaian scholar Kojo Amanor (2009a: 97) pushed such a critique with his argument about the oversimplicity of frameworks that present customary relations as representative of subaltern rural interests in opposition to a corrupt state. The implication here is that customary laws are not necessarily superior in terms of equity, efficiency or sustainability (von Benda-Beckmann, von Benda-Beckmann and Spiertz 1997). Following her ethnographic study of the chieftaincy institution and land tenure in southern Ghana, Ubink (2008) cautioned against the idealization of customary land tenures and the assumption that customary laws would be a more equitable alternative to state formalization. Admittedly, traditional institutions like chieftaincy have been noted to be embedded in structures of oppression and inequality in their administration of customary land tenures. However, the evidence suggests that rentier politics and abuse of power are not peculiar to customary law administration. While Ubink (2008) viewed the breakdown in traditional values and systems of accountability in customary land administration as a failing that required increased state intervention, scholars like Ruffin (2019: 104) have noted that such an approach only illustrated how Western scholars employed legal pluralism to valorize state centralism while devaluing the epistemological foundations of the living customary law. Ruffin argued that conceptualizations of legal pluralism, such as Twining's legal pluralism of social fact (2010), promoted individualism (individual rights as opposed to collective duties and rights), dualism (the separation of doctrinal law from its sociocultural context) and materialism (the distinguishing of individual materials based on categories of winners or losers). This stands in contrast to the living customary law, which pursues *Ubuntu* and holistically promotes restorative justice, relationship-building and acknowledgement of the ancestors. This version of legal pluralism, however, does not appear to be a favourite among many experts of customary law who perceive legal pluralism in the African context as nothing more than a species of normative pluralism.

Araújo (2025) has cautioned that legal pluralism should not be seen as an alternative for when the state fails, but should instead be recognized as promising in its own right as a foremost framework for recognizing the coexistence of plural normative orders and subverting colonial and neocolonial hierarchizations of law. As I will demonstrate in Chapter 6, increased state interferences, whether of the colonial or postcolonial kind, have not always been a useful intervention in addressing the challenges within ASM. Traditional authorities may have, over the years, demonstrated their penchant for colluding with political elites and the well-connected in subverting customary rights for their personal gain. However, the state has also not shown itself to be an entirely trustworthy agent in maintaining values of communality and care for the land and the people. Moreover, Ubink's position (2008) leans towards a saviourism that overlooks the violence, intimidation and suppression that was employed in what she described as the colonial government holding local chiefs to account. The state has not always had the best interests of the local people at heart, and as the empirical evidence will confirm, it has often been more attuned to projecting its own understanding of law and governance onto pre-existing dispositions in ways that have proven harmful to the most vulnerable in society. Instead of using legal pluralism to advocate for more state interventions in informal spaces like ASM, the focus should rather be on how customary systems of accountability, communality and care, which have been weakened by colonial and postcolonial state interventions, could be rehabilitated to benefit the people. In resolving the tensioned conflicts between formalization and the persistent informality of ASM, the answer offered by legal pluralism, as Berman (2007) has posited, does not lie in providing an authoritative metric for determining which norms prevail in this messy legal hybridity. Indeed, legal pluralism fundamentally challenges both the positivist and natural-rights-based assumptions that there can ever be an answer to such questions. Tsing's (2005) notion of friction, which she conceptualized as the awkward, unequal, unstable and creative qualities of interconnection across difference in the coproduction of cultures, provides further clarification to this argument. Friction reminds us that heterogenous and unequal encounters can lead to new arrangements of culture and power that open up the possibility of an ethnographic account of global interconnections. Here, universals are local knowledges in the sense that they cannot be understood without the benefit of historically specific cultural assumptions. This insight embraces a departure from uncritical universalist applications of state-centric ASM formalization and advances the need for micro-level empirical studies to contextualize, theorize and unearth problem-solving methods that address the specific issues on the ground.

Diala and Rautenbach (2024) offer adaptive legal pluralism as a theoretical framework that emphasizes how dialogue, negotiation and mutual adaptation between state and Indigenous laws can harmonize to find practical solutions to the normative challenges brought on by overlapping legal orders. Between an adaptive legal pluralism and a decolonial approach that confronts the colonial legacies of the criminalization of ASM informality, governments and other stakeholders can creatively chart out culturally relevant regulatory mechanisms for a more sustainable ASM. How such an adaptive, decolonial, pluralist approach to ASM governance will look in practice will depend on the commitment of states, traditional authorities, small-scale miners and other key actors to redirect themselves away from the prevailing extractive and environmentally destructive system, towards a more inclusive, transparent and communally beneficial arrangement. Policymakers need to step outside of parliamentary laws and into the muddy pits of informal ASM spaces. There, they will be confronted with the realities of sociocultural, economic and political complexities that will, hopefully, provide them with a deeper understanding of law and the need to embrace the living customary law in devising new regulatory frameworks for ASM governance. This also means that any critique of or claim to expertise in customary law in the ASM context should be subjected to a test of its epistemological foundations. To that end, any conclusions derived exclusively from Western legal thinking, or solutions that are not grounded in Indigenous ethics and epistemologies, should be thoroughly dissected and confronted.

Conclusion

This chapter provided an overview of legal pluralism, which forms the theoretical framework through which I conceptualized the living customary law of ASM. I demonstrated that despite its critiques and limitations, legal pluralism – and, in particular, decolonial legal pluralism – is the most suitable conceptual framework for disrupting the hegemony of state law and its formalization policies. I employed decolonial legal pluralism to hold up the mirror of the past to the prevailing legal system, which I dissected as a flawed, colonial-oriented, rigid legal orthodoxy that is impractical for local ASM realities. The living customary law is offered not as an abstract, far-fetched theory, but as a better fitting, present body of legitimate normative orders coexisting with other legal orders in the semiautonomous social field of informal ASM. In the next chapter, I continue to demonstrate this conceptual possibility as I draw on a wealth of empirical evidence to further discuss legal pluralism in the ASM context.

Notes

1. CO 97/2; Gold Coast Acts 1865–1883: The Gold Coast Native Jurisdiction Ordinance, 1878, section 5. The same provision was repeated in a subsequent amendment under the 1883 Native Jurisdiction Ordinance.
2. CO96/775/14; Native Authority (Colony) Legislation.

CHAPTER 4

'Native' Lands, State's Gold

Mapping the History of Monist-Pluralism in ASM in Ghana

Introduction

> The stage opens with the appearance of missionaries and anthropologists, traders and concessionaires, and administrators. While the 'missionaries' with 'Christianity' perverted implore the colonial subject to lay up 'his treasures in Heaven where neither moth nor rust doth corrupt', the traders and concessionaires and administrators acquire his mineral and land resources, destroy his art, crafts and home industries.
>
> —Dr Kwame Nkrumah, speech at the Conference of Independent African States, 15 April 1958

Of the major issues that drive ASM scholarship, access to mineral-bearing lands is a subject of great concern for small-scale miners, governments, researchers, policymakers and international donor agencies. While there has been considerable attention directed to formalization as an orthodoxy, until more recently there was little attention paid to the intersection between customary land tenure systems and ASM formalization (Nyame and Blocher 2010; De Jong and Sauerwein 2021; Mensah 2021). More importantly, references to the history of gold mining in Ghana fail to emphasize the linkage between colonialism and the emergence of modern state law in the fragmented regulation of ASM in the country. To address this conceptual blindness, I present in this chapter an empirical analysis that probes into the history and legacies of colonialism in the construction of rights, access, power and resistances at the intersection of ASM, land, mining and customary law in Ghana. I deploy a combination of oral histories and archival materials to trace the emergence of the centralized absorption of resource governance as a long-term colonial mechanism that needs to be deconstructed towards reforming the ASM sector.

In the first section, I begin this exercise by providing a descriptive and interpretative account of the emergence of the modern Ghanaian state and of the fundamental role of colonial monist-pluralism in this development. In the second section, I centre Indigenous accounts of the histories of gold mining and its interconnections with customary land tenures. Next, I outline a brief history of key European jurisdiction in the gold-mining sector, beginning with the centuries-old pursuit of gold towards the gradual and unsteady first phase of politico-economic colonization. Here, I emphasize the transplantation of the Crown Lands Bill of 1894 and the 1897 Lands Bill, respectively, as well as the concepts that laid the foundation for the appropriation of Indigenous ecological and mineral spaces. This chapter derives its impetus to recover Indigenous knowledges and memories of gold mining from narratives of how local people interpreted their encounters with colonial legal intrusions in their gold-mining spaces. As a result, this section will highlight not only how European pursuit of Indigenous sources of gold altered the commercial and legal landscape, particularly in the invention of new forms of customary land tenure, but also the Indigenous resistance to what was deemed to be an attempted annexation of their ancestral lands and mineral rights.

I deploy the archives and the historical literature to demonstrate how the objectification of mineral-bearing lands allowed colonial authorities to reduce them to items to be traded, to be used to produce profit and to be governed by the colonial state. In doing so, I show how official state recognition, licensing requirements and formalization operated within the categories of force, violence and coloniality to enforce state control over mineral rights. This is particularly highlighted in the examination of the 1900 Concessions Ordinance in the second section, where I show how monist-pluralism bolstered new notions of resource distribution, mineral-rights governance and the regulation of Indigenous mining. In the final section, I focus specifically on Obuasi, tracing how the interplay of British militarism, mercantilism and missionary work engendered a violent corporatist hegemony and suppression of Indigenous gold mining within one of Ghana's oldest and most profitable gold-mining communities. Taylor's seminal monograph (2006) on Ashanti Goldfields Corporation (AGC) has already expansively explored the corporation's evolution from a nineteenth-century British mining firm in precolonial Asante, into a twenty-first-century multinational African company. In focusing on Obuasi, this section builds upon Taylor's work by specifically examining how state law facilitated AGC's frontier expansionism in Obuasi and its impacts on Indigenous, small-scale gold mining in the area. This historical exercise is a vital first step in the decolonial approach to analysing ASM formalization, offering key insights into the mechanisms and relics of colonial entanglement in Ghana's mining industry.

Monist-Pluralism and the 'Making' of the Gold Coast

British colonialism came with the institutionalization of a monist-pluralist legal system by which colonial administrators allowed existing Indigenous laws to apply alongside and subject to the legitimization of the newly established colonial state and the English laws it introduced (Mamdani 1996). In present-day Ghana, colonial positivist law was extended in piecemeal fashion, from the time of the first British trading forts and settlements to the British government's formal usurpation of control over the council of merchants and the quasi-state functions it eventually assumed. It is noteworthy to mention, as will become clearer later in this chapter, that these trade and political manoeuvres were all in pursuit of gold.

To put it briefly, the introduction of British colonial monist-pluralism and its usurpation of power and jurisdiction in the Gold Coast Colony can be traced back to the time of George Maclean. As Boahen (1975: 34) noted, Maclean was appointed not by the British government but by a committee of British merchants trading in the region, and he was never a Governor of the Gold Coast. Indeed, had it been left to the British government alone, British contact with the Gold Coast would have ended in 1828 with the decision to withdraw from the region altogether, due to the decline in trade and the costly wars with Asante between 1807 and 1826. Upon the government's withdrawal in 1828, the British merchants insisted on taking over the administration of the forts, an arrangement to which the government agreed by retaining the forts as nominal dependencies of Sierra Leone. In the usual alliance between empire and mercantilism, the responsibilities of the British Crown were transferred to the merchants on certain terms, including the understanding that they were to administer only the forts of Cape Coast and Accra, appoint a committee of three merchants to London and establish a council of five in Cape Coast. The council of merchants was to confine its jurisdiction only to the people living within the two forts, and it was not to interfere with the affairs of the local states. Maclean assumed office as president of this

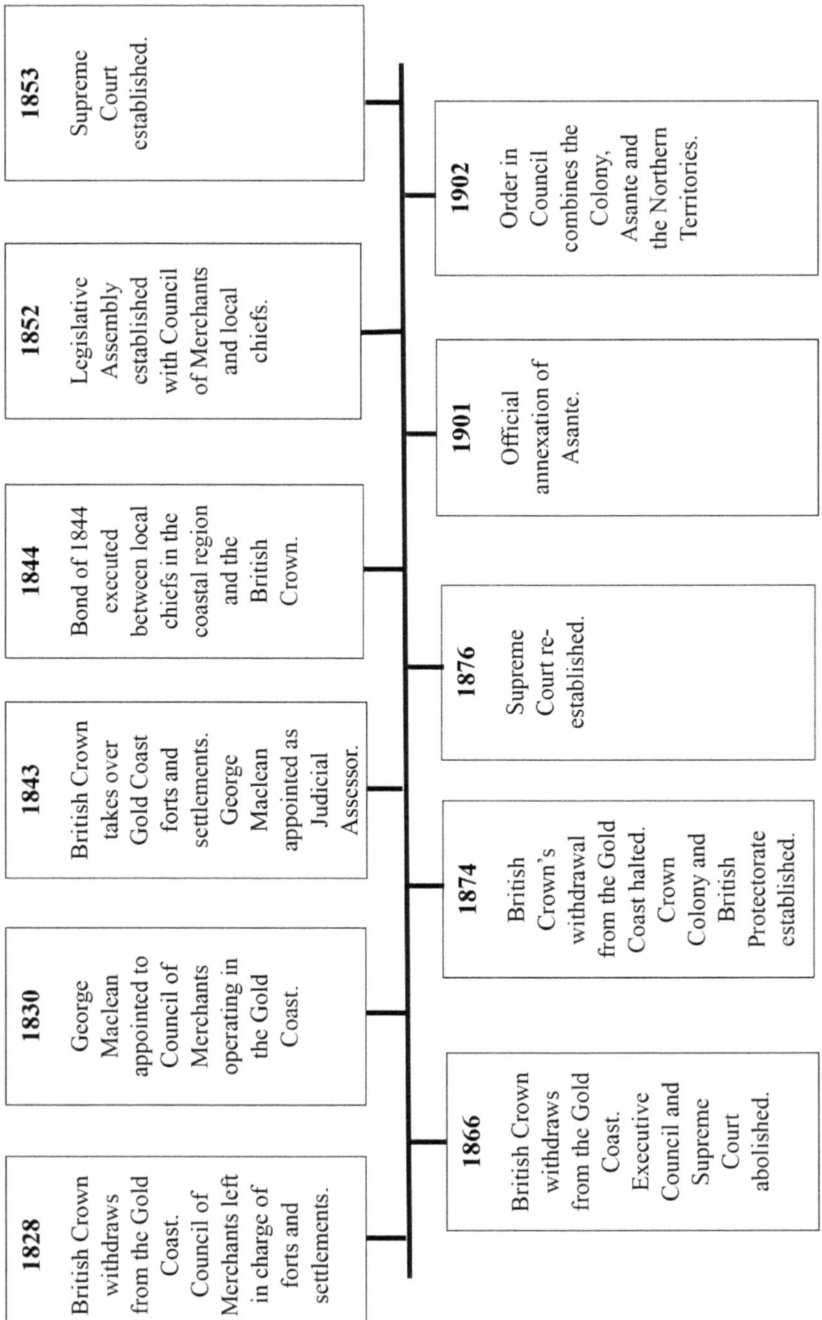

Figure 4.1. Timeline of British jurisdiction in the Gold Coast, Asante and the Northern Territories. © Linda Mensah.

council in February 1830, and subsequently as Judicial Assessor from 1843 till his death in 1847. The council of merchants administered the forts under the directive that their magistrates and officers had no jurisdiction, either civil or criminal, nor any power of trial over the local people (Kimble 1963: 193).

This, however, changed under Maclean's presidency of the council, as he flagrantly ignored the instructions about noninterference in local politics. Maclean inserted himself into peace negotiations between Asante and Fante, and cases from the surrounding communities were increasingly brought to the Cape Coast Castle where his judgements became generally accepted, although not strictly enforceable (Kimble 1963). Additionally, Maclean stationed magistrates and local militia as policemen in some of the coastal states, toured and occasionally deployed some of his council members to attend the local chiefs' courts to ensure what they deemed as the 'proper administration of justice' (Boahen 1975: 39). While Maclean's overreach of juridical powers caused a scandal for which he was subsequently investigated and reprimanded, the British Crown eventually formalized the system Maclean had initiated by resuming direct control of the forts and settlements in 1843. In the same year, the Foreign Jurisdiction Act was passed by the British parliament to 'remove Doubts as to the Exercise of Powers and Jurisdiction by Her Majesty's Dominions' (Kimble 1963: 194). Maclean was then appointed as Judicial Assessor to the local chiefs in 1843, with express instructions to maintain the exercise of jurisdiction in the case of crimes and misdemeanours committed among the neighbouring Indigenous communities.

Shortly after this, the Bond of 1844 was executed, under which certain local chiefs were said to have acknowledged the power and jurisdiction of the Crown and given their formal consent to the trial of criminal cases before the Queen's judicial officers. This Bond referred to the local territories as a British protectorate, although no such jurisdiction had been formally defined. In addressing misconceptions about this Bond as some sort of 'Magna Carta of Ghana', Boahen (1975: 41) forcefully argued that the Bond of 1844 was a mere declaration on the part of the local Fante chiefs and could therefore not be construed as a treaty legitimizing the annexation of the region as a protectorate under British rule. Indeed, the local leaders never ceded land to the British, and the understanding was that they were aligning themselves to the British government not as subjects, but as independent nations in a relationship based on equality and open dialogue. In examining the contested nature of the formal existence of this so-called British protectorate, Shumway (2014) indicated that

British records themselves stated clearly that such a protectorate was never established by any written document and that its boundaries were never determined. These records, however, imply that the Gold Coast was under some kind of British governing authority after the Peace Treaty of 1831, signed between the Fantes, Asantes and Maclean in the Adanse capital of Fomena to establish peace in the territory following the Second Anglo-Ashanti War of 1826. The British, however, used the rhetorical invention of a protectorate as a precedent of guardianship and, subsequently, as justification for the declaration of colonial rule in 1874 (Shumway 2014).

The Bond of 1844 kickstarted the establishment of a legal framework by which an Order in Council was enacted to authorize judges, magistrates, assessors and other officers to extend their jurisdiction outside the forts and to observe local customs that were compatible with the laws of England (Kimble 1963: 195). This caveat was the hallmark of the repugnancy rule, by which Indigenous laws were subjected to the standards of English natural justice, equity and good conscience (Bentsi-Enchill 1969). This repugnancy test would, throughout the era of colonial pluralism and beyond, be wielded as an assimilationist tool to subject Indigenous laws to Western legal standards.

Colonial legal pluralism continued to gain ground with its uncoordinated yet steady incursions into the political, judicial and legal authority of local chiefs. In April 1852, a meeting at the Cape Coast Castle was convened by Governor Hill and attended by his Council together with the chiefs of the communities under British protection. This meeting constituted itself into a Legislative Assembly legally recognized by the British government, with full powers to enact laws to govern the local communities (Kimble 1963: 172). A Supreme Court was established in 1853, with jurisdiction inside the forts and settlements and an appeal therefrom to the Governor and Council of the Gold Coast. As the power and prestige of this transplanted British judicial system increased, the authority of the local chiefs and their courts began to wane considerably (Kimble 1963: 195).

There was a temporary halt to the growth of British power following the renewal of Asante invasion of the southern districts in 1863, which led to recommendations from a select committee for British withdrawal from the whole of West Africa. Accordingly, the British abolished the Executive Council and the Supreme Court in 1866 and joined all the British settlements under one government based in Freetown, Sierra Leone. Once again, these withdrawal efforts were short-lived, as the British eventually made a formal declaration through Letters Patent issued on 24 July 1874, converting all

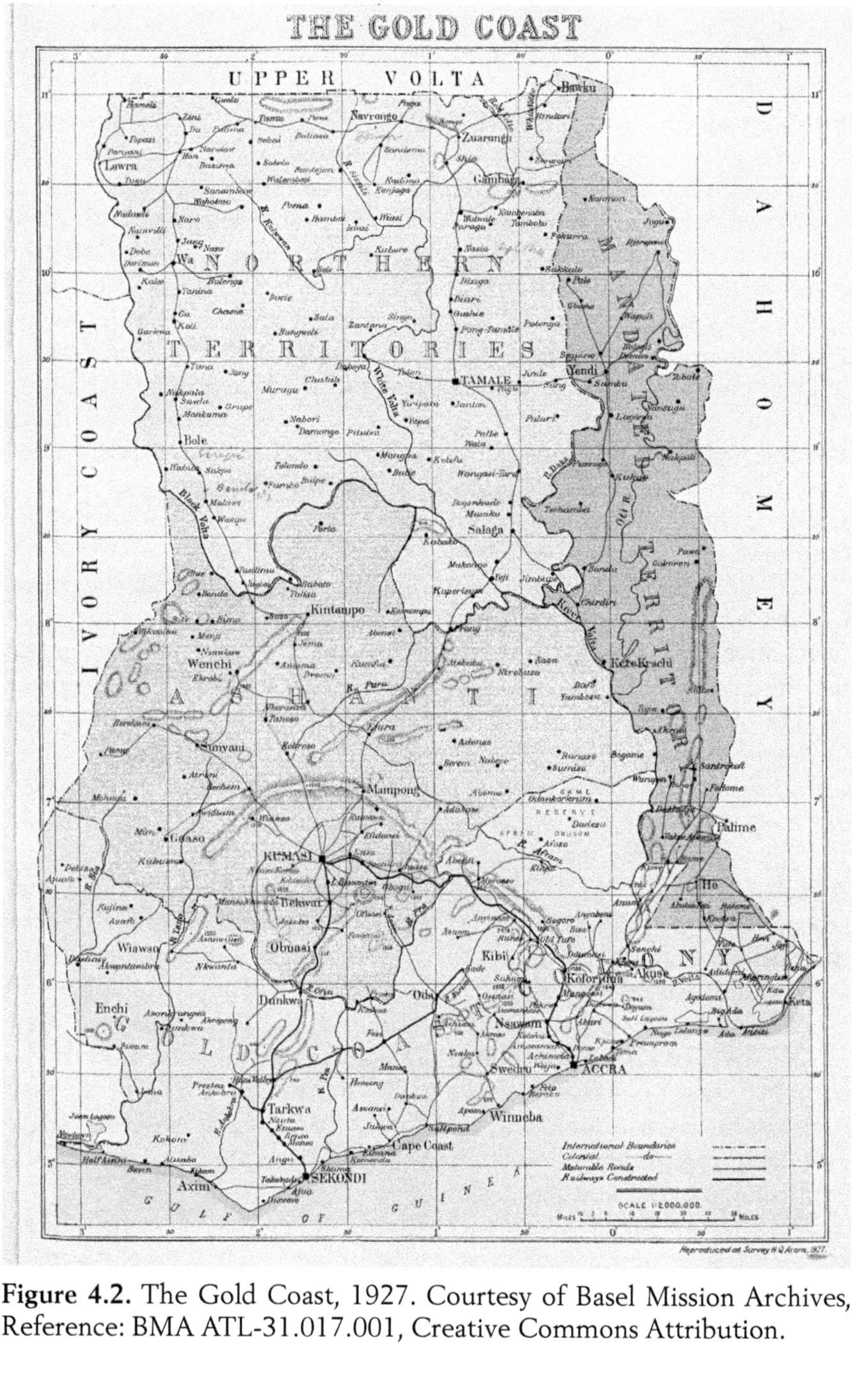

Figure 4.2. The Gold Coast, 1927. Courtesy of Basel Mission Archives, Reference: BMA ATL-31.017.001, Creative Commons Attribution.

their settlements into the Crown colony and the southern states into a British protectorate (Boahen 1975: 43; Shumway 2014: 166).

In the first few years of their new colony and protectorate, the British introduced a series of measures calculated to ensure effective authority and jurisdiction, one of which was the re-establishment of the Executive Council that had been abolished in 1866 (Boahen 1975: 57). On 6 August 1874, an Order in Council for the first time authorized the Legislative Council of the Gold Coast to legislate, with a further declaration of the Queen's powers and jurisdiction to include the preservation of peace; the administration of both civil and criminal justice; the establishment and regulation of courts of justice, including so-called native courts; the enactment of laws framed with due regard to local laws and customs subject to the repugnancy test; the hearing of appeals from native tribunals; the establishment of municipalities and the raising of revenue, among others. By this time, certain rights were said to have been acquired by usage, by sufferance and by tacit assent of the inhabitants over and above those specifically granted by the Bond of 1844 (Kimble 1963: 302).

The Supreme Court was re-established by the 1876 Supreme Court Ordinance, which, together with the 1876 Criminal Procedure Ordinance, abolished both the court of civil and criminal justice and the office of the Judicial Assessor, vesting the latter's appellate jurisdiction over native courts in the Chief Justice. The Supreme Court Ordinance provided for the application of the common law, doctrines of equity and statutes of general application as they existed in England in 1874, except where specifically modified by local ordinances. In 1877, provision was made for appeal to the Privy Council in London. African lawyers who were professionally trained in England and grounded in the principles of English law began to be admitted before the Supreme Court, hastening the process of assimilation and adding to the political and legislative changes that widened the sphere of English law in the colony (Kimble 1963: 305). According to Tamale (2020: 134), such institutionalization and professionalization of the administration of justice caused many elite Africans to accept the positivist orientation of colonial state law as natural and, in doing so, to associate progress and access to justice with such a judicial system and its formal, modern statutory laws.

The Supreme Court Ordinance empowered District Commissioners to be *ex-officio* commissioners of the Supreme Court, with the authority to exercise the powers of a judge of the Supreme Court within their districts. One of the first District Commissioners was appointed in Tarkwa in 1880, consolidating British power in the gold-mining areas (Boahen 1975: 59). In further pursuit of colonial monist-pluralism, the Supreme Court Ordinance provided for the observation of Indigenous laws in all cases between locals, and in most cases between Africans and Europeans unless excluded by a contract (Kimble 1963: 305). As monist-pluralism goes, the intention with this arrangement was not to have Indigenous laws coexist on an equal footing with the newly introduced English legal system. English laws were viewed as more advanced, and proponents of empire considered its imposition to be a great gift to the colonized peoples, substituting 'civilized' law for anarchy and freeing them from the scourges of war, witchcraft and tyranny (Ranger 1983). As was commented in *The Gold Coast Aborigines* (24 July 1898: 3), it was thought that in being accorded the 'right' of the English legal system, the Africans would be protected from the heathenism of their 'fetish' priests and 'savage' kings, resulting in the evolution of the black race.

By Letters Patent of 13 January 1886, the Office of Governor of the Gold Coast was officially constituted. As the Queen's representative, the Governor acted alongside an Executive Council, a Legislative Council and a judiciary composed of British officials. Even when subsequent reorganizations led to the inclusion of a handful of indigenes in the Legislative Council, the Governor retained the power to permit the official majority to push any bills through. In effect, the local people had no share in devising laws and could only resist or criticize, such critiques often being invited afterwards by the government (Ward 1991: 81).

In 1899, technical difficulties regarding the definition of a protectorate re-emerged when it became necessary to determine the legal position of the newly conquered Asante Kingdom and to conclude whether its capital, Kumasi, fell within the jurisdiction of the Supreme Court (Kimble 1963: 316). Following the defeat of Asante in the Fifth Anglo-Ashanti War (also known as the Yaa Asantewaa War, or the War of the Golden Stool) in 1900, Asante was annexed by Imperial Order in Council on 26 September 1901. The Governor of Gold Coast was given full powers and jurisdiction to provide for peace, order and good government having regard to Indigenous laws and subject to their compatibility with the powers and jurisdiction of the Crown and the welfare of the local people (Kimble 1963: 323). This was subsequently legislated under the 1902 Ashanti Administration Ordinance. From 1 January 1902, the different Orders in Council governing the various territories were combined and the Gold Coast was established as comprising three separate but related territories: the colony, Ashanti, and the Northern Territories (Kimble 1963: 325).[1]

Administratively, the colony was divided into three main provinces, each ruled by a Provincial Commissioner. The same system existed in Ashanti and the Northern Territories, but whereas the three Provincial Commissioners of the colony were directly responsible to the Governor, there was a Chief Commissioner in charge of Ashanti and another in charge of the Northern Territories. The provinces were further divided into districts headed by District Commissioners, many of whom were British barristers who were required to familiarize themselves with the local law and customs of their districts before taking office. The District Commissioners' courts exercised both civil and criminal jurisdictions, and occasionally heard appeals from the local chiefs' courts (Ward 1991: 68). A disproportionate amount of the District Commissioners' time was taken up by disputes over land, which – as I will later show – prompted the establishment of a special Concessions Court to handle matters specifically relating to mining and timber concessions. These ad hoc yet persistent consolidations of colonial monist-pluralism, which had all begun with a mercantilist pursuit of gold, demonstrate both the materialist underpinnings of the emergent legal system and the need to reimagine alternative legal frameworks if we are committed to reforming the ASM sector in a nonexploitative and culturally situated manner for the benefit of small-scale miners and the local communities.

Indigenous Gold Mining and Customary Land Tenures in Present-Day Ghana

According to Dumett's (1998) historical exposition of gold mining in present-day Ghana, Indigenous gold miners – known in Asante Twi as *sikadifo* – occupied an extremely important place in the economic history and culture of the Akan people. Gold mining was one of the central occupations of Akan people, and it involved a seamless seasonal complementarity with hunting, farming and mining. Traditionally, *sika futuro* (gold dust) was the major currency of practically all the Akan states, and *sika* (gold) was a marker of status and influence, the touchstone for judging both personal and institutional wealth. In Asante, for instance, revenue from gold mining served as one of the most important building blocks for state formation and the consolidation of the kingdom in the seventeenth and eighteenth centuries.

The oral and written historical accounts of the technical expertise of Indigenous gold miners and the sophistication with which they operated and remained alert to new challenges and opportunities in their trade led Dumett (1998) to conclude that the foreign traders and colonial administrators who regarded Indigenous gold mining as primitive were rather jaundiced in their views. Indigenous miners pursued their craft with different tools such as hoes, short-handled hammers, long-handled chisels and shovels. Mining methods ranged from the 'fire-setting' method, to panning (alluvial gold mining), shallow-pit surface mining and deep-shaft mining for reef gold. Over time, European-made pickaxes and heavy equipment were also adopted. Taylor (2006) confirms that towards the end of the nineteenth century, some of the royal mines in Asante, such as the King Prempeh Mines, were known to have adopted more modern forms of mining in their operations.

In Obuasi, British mining engineers and concessionaires who arrived in the nineteenth century were met with the deep-level type of gold mining locally known as the *amenapeaa* or *nkron amena,* where gold was extracted from crumbled reefs using shafts that were about twenty feet in depth and spaced approximately six feet apart. To light up the dark shafts, Indigenous miners used candles or lamps made of clay and cotton wicks soaked in palm oil, which were held in place and prevented from caving in through the use of long bamboo poles and heavy timber (Dumett 1998: 57). Oral accounts are additionally informative about Indigenous mining methods such as *saaboa,* which involved the crushing of rocks and the extraction of gold from reef sediments.[2] There is also the popular *anweaseɛ* method, where local miners sweep and gather sand sediments to be washed and panned.[3]

Mining was usually carried out in family- or kin-based modes of production with clear-cut divisions of labour along gender lines. While there were distinct variations from one community to another, mining was generally intertwined with the local customary land tenures.

Apoh et al. (2017) define customary land tenures as the legitimate ownership of specific lands in connection to which members of an Indigenous group held cultural connections and authority. Lands amongst the Akan were held communally under paramount titles, subparamount titles, determinable estate (otherwise known as possessory or usufructuary titles) and tenancies that included the *abunu, abusa* and the annual crop tenancies and licences (Ollenu 1962: 2). The *abusa* involved an owner of uncultivated land granting it to another person (usually a stranger) for cultivation, the two then sharing the produce in the ratio of 1:2. With *abunu,* the landowner transferred an already cultivated farm to another person (stranger or not) for maintenance, the two then sharing the proceeds in moieties (Danquah 1928: 220–21). In many parts of southern Ghana, the paramount title is referred to as 'stool land', where 'stool' refers to the carved wooden stool symbolizing chieftaincy (Ollenu 1962: 9). The stool holds traditional significance as the embodiment of the soul and spirit of the family as well as their collective authority. The stool constitutes a corporate entity, with its occupant (the head of the community) and his trustees (his elders and councillors) holding the lands for the use of the community (Kasanga and Kotey 2001). Stool lands are therefore held not as individually vested properties, but in trust for, and on behalf of, the larger community by titular holders such as chiefs, queen-mothers, priests, regents and heads of clans and families (Ollenu 1962: 10).

The usufructuary titles ensured that subjects of the stools enjoyed rights of allocation to portions of the stool land for cultivation, building a house, mining and other relevant purposes. Such a title became the highest estate that a subject or individual member of a family could hold in stool or family land. Ollenu (1962: 46) preferred the term 'determinable interest', which to him highlighted the fact that it was a type of absolute, inheritable and alienable ownership that might be determined under certain conditions without affecting the community ownership. However, this right did not extend over land that had lawfully been enclosed, worked or reduced into possession by another. In the context of mining, this ensured that the extraction of gold from pits already dug by others was duly prohibited. Individuals or groups could mine for gold almost anywhere they chose, within the limits of their own lineage or stool lands. Those who were the first to find a lucrative area usually brought their family members with them to the location, leaving latecomers obligated to respect the exclusive rights of the discovering family or group to their already excavated pits (Dumett 1998: 67).

Having regard to the superior nature of the determinable title, customary law prohibited an allodial titleholder from alienating a usufruct land or dealing with it in any way without the prior consent of the subject-owner (Ollenu 1962: 56). It was reported in *The Gold Coast Chronicle* (15 February 1898: 2) that land could be obtained by purchase under customary law, although what the purchaser acquired was not an absolute ownership free from liability to the community. Most communities required the performance of customary observances, such as the pouring of libations and the provision of gifts – including sheep, rum and a small sum of money – to the priest on behalf of the gods. This practice was known as 'drink money' or 'customary drinks', and it formed an acknowledgement of the chief's titular ownership of the land, a show of allegiance and a request for the gods to bless the transaction (Ubink and Quan 2008).

Strangers – that is, persons who were not subjects of the stool – were required to first obtain permission to mine by paying a token fee and performing the necessary rituals prior to commencing their mining operations. These rules of access were much tighter for lands under the direct control of a king's own lineage (so-called royal lands). In those cases, the king or chief might only permit his own family or retainers to mine, excluding strangers altogether. Though pathways of state appropriation varied considerably in practice, it became established for local miners to retain one-third of their proceeds and turn over one-third to the local chief or stool, leaving the remaining one-third for the paramount ruler or king (Ofosu-Mensah 2011). According to Cape Coast lawyer John Mensah Sarbah in *The Gold Coast Aborigines* (5 November 1898: 3), some stool authorities claimed an absolute right to all nuggets found within their custodial lands. *The Gold Coast Aborigines* (12 November 1898: 3) further reported lawyer John Mensah Sarbah confirming that 'It has not, I think, been common amongst the natives to make allotments of metalliferous lands. They generally have the rights to win gold, out of which a certain proportion goes to the stool-holder'. In some usufruct relationships, an *abunu* share distribution of halves was arranged. In Asante, tax administration evolved to include one-tenth of an ounce of gold per man and a luxury tax on any chief who increased the amount of his gold jewellery or ornaments. This was based on the rationale that the *Asantehene* was the heir to the gold of every individual. These state claims over proceeds from gold mining helped, among other things, to strengthen the central resource base of the Asante Kingdom. This hold of the centralized Akan states over mineral rights was, however, weakened by the accelerated intrusion of alien capitalism, coupled with steady colonial control over gold-mining governance.

A Brief History of European Jurisdiction in Gold Mining in Ghana

According to Howard French's account (2021: 2–3) of European expeditions to West Africa from the mid-fifteenth century, these voyages were entirely motivated by a search for the source of West Africa's prodigious wealth in gold. In modern-day Ghana, this Atlantic trade began with the arrival of the Portuguese from 1470 and largely redirected gold trading from the northern Sahara regions towards the coastal south (Boahen 1975: 17). This extensive gold trade, established by the Portuguese and secured by the building of the fort at Elmina in 1482, would later go on to fund other expeditions to Asia and the New World. Elmina, which the Portuguese named 'La Costa da Mina' (Coast of the Mine), served as an important trading post for other European nations in their bid to procure and secure gold in the region. While the trafficking of enslaved persons formed part of Portuguese activities from the outset, it was only much later in the 1640s that the region became a major source of enslaved people (French 2021: 95). Dumett (1998: 43) noted that even at the height of the slave trade in the eighteenth century, European interests beyond the coastal areas continued to centre mainly on gold, with an unceasing aim of keeping trade paths open.

Although gold was the earliest and most enduring attraction for European commerce in the Gold Coast, it was not until the late nineteenth century that overseas firms were able to undertake direct mining on a permanent basis. The Portuguese twice attempted and failed to operate a mine in the coastal region – the first, in 1622, had poorly shored tunnels; the other, in 1636, coincided with an earthquake. As a result, for the next two hundred years, European merchants would obtain gold solely produced by local miners through barter trade (French 2021: 15). Indeed, one of the very first attempts at modern, industrialized mining began in 1860 with Thomas Hughes, an educated Indigenous man from Cape Coast who imported heavy machinery to start mining operations in Western Wassa. However, Hughes's efforts were frustrated by the local chief, who ordered his operations to cease, and his machinery destroyed. It was not until 1877 that a subsequent attempt – this time by the British-sponsored French trader Pierre Bonnat and his African Gold Coast Company – would succeed in the Tarkwa district (Boahen 1975: 93).

The mid-seventeenth century also saw the rise of the powerful and dominant Asante empire, a polity made up of speakers of the Asante Twi language who had extricated themselves from their former Denkyira overlords.[4] Boahen (1975: 15) described the centralized Asante empire as consisting of two parts – metropolitan Asante (also known as the Asante Confederacy), which was made up of twelve core states, including Adanse; and provincial Asante, comprising conquered states to the north and south of metropolitan Asante. Through military victories against other groups within the subregion, Asante came to dominate the entire gold trade of the Gold Coast by the 1750s. Around 1850, when Gold Coast forts and settlements were separated from Sierra Leone, gold dust was the second main export for the British, their supply coming mainly from Asante (Kimble 1963: 4). While the *Asantehene* was in power, European gold prospectors were not welcome in the territory. According to Taylor (2006), Asante's foreign policy towards Europeans was generally underpinned by caution and suspicion, particularly with regard to its gold production, and the chiefs kept the locations of their gold mines secret from prying foreign concessionaires.

The pursuit of gold precipitated many wars between Asante and the coastal Fante groups, and subsequently between Asante and the British. For instance, the year 1874 was marked by the Fourth Anglo-Ashanti War, a military campaign where Asante's desire to continue its monopoly over the interior gold trade with Europeans on the coast was challenged by the penetration of British mercantilism and militarism (Kimble 1963: 264). Public interest in Europe was sparked by reports of soldiers returning from the war with unanimous proclamations about the abundance of gold in Asante. As was reported in *The Gold Coast Chronicle* (22 April 1899: 3), Sir John Glover's address at the Liverpool Town Hall recounted the abundance of gold from the Volta River to Kumasi, and described seeing at first hand people 'mining for gold as they would dig for potatoes'.

Asante had not yet been annexed under British jurisdiction at this point, despite its decisive defeat in the 1874 Anglo-Ashanti War. The British government's refusal to annex Asante was eventually overturned by intense pressure from British merchants in the region. According to *The Gold Coast Chronicle* (16 October 1897: 2), the colonial government was anxious to strengthen its political position within the territory, while private merchants and concessionaires were equally eager to capitalize on the abundant and now freely available resources, especially given the factions, dissension and chieftaincy disputes resulting from the weakening of Asante in the war. Intense pressure emerged from Glasgow, Liverpool, London and Manchester merchants who wanted the colonial government to intervene in Asante and to secure the interests of mining investors in the profitable gold mines. In March 1892, the West African section of the London Chamber of Commerce pressured the government about the necessity to safeguard the region from encroachment by foreign governments (Boahen 1975: 72). This was in response to fears of French colonial ambitions and attempted penetration into Asante, which eventually resulted in Governor Brandon Griffith's insistence to quickly bring Asante under British jurisdiction (Ward 1991: 279).

By 1895, Asante's foreign policy had shifted towards a more welcoming approach to investment from foreign concessionaires in its gold-mining sector. The Asante embassy in the UK sought to conclude a wide-ranging agreement that would have allowed the development and modernization of Asante's goldfields in a manner centrally controlled by the *Asantehene* (Taylor 2006). These efforts, however, did not bear any fruit. In 1897, Sir William Maxwell, who had then succeeded Griffith, delivered a message to the Legislative Council on the same day as the introduction of the infamous 1897 Lands Bill, which read almost like an open invitation to traders and prospectors to extend their operations to Asante (Kimble 1963: 23). This Lands Bill, as I shall discuss in the next section, set the course for the exclusive state oversight of mineral resource governance as remains the case today. With the defeat of Asante in the Fifth Anglo-Ashanti War in 1900, the road to the interior was opened, possibilities seemed boundless and there was a great influx of mining and commercial enterprises into Asante (Ward 1991: 23). *The Gold Coast Chronicle* (29 April 1899: 3) reported that the colony grew in importance within several years of the annexation of Asante, with more industrialized enterprises moving into the newly conquered territory. There was, for instance, a total of 25,415 oz of gold exported at a value of £91,497 within the first few months of the conquest of Asante. Whereas trade in the colony was valued at £736,131 in 1887, in ten years this increased by 130% to £1,641,981. Much of this enormous increase was attributed to the collaborative efforts of British-based gold merchants and the military advancement into Asante.

At this time, the foundation for the prevailing dual-mining economy was perfectly established. According to *The Gold Coast Aborigines* (19 March 1898: 4), several privately funded prospecting expeditions saw European engineers, geologists, geographers and other researchers travelling to the colony. A report in *The Gold Coast Aborigines* (17 December 1898: 4) projected that once the entire mining region was opened up with the necessary capital investment and railway and infrastructural development, the large gold deposits in the interior gold belts '[would] put South Africa in the shade'. As I mentioned in Chapter 1, this projection became a reality in 2018, when Ghana overtook South Africa as the leading gold producer in Africa. Jackson (1992), Dumett (1998), Hilson (2002b) and Mark-Thiesen (2018) have written extensively on the colonial-era infrastructural developments in Ghana, particularly the construction of railway lines running exclusively through mining and port areas as one of the many ways in which empire and mercantilism worked closely together to further frontier expansionism and resource extractivism. As Ye et al. (2020) have highlighted, the key features of extractivist systems do not only involve monopoly control by an operational centre over the resources to be extracted and the close interlinkages between state and private capital groups, but also include the creation of infrastructure – roads, waterways and the like – to enable the removal of extracted resources for export. Railway construction began in earnest in 1898 with the first line running from the port city of Sekondi to the mining district of Tarkwa, and it reached the gold-mining town of Obuasi in 1902 (Boahen 1975: 99). AGC was instrumental in this railway extension to Obuasi, guaranteeing revenue for the colonial government that enabled the construction to proceed (Taylor 2006). As *The Gold Coast Chronicle* (22 April 1899: 3) reported, the Secretary of State for the Colonies worked closely with mining corporations on behalf of the British government, prioritizing their protection, meeting deputations, developing infrastructure and extending a fostering hand towards the welfare and promotion of their mercantile interests.

Christian missionaries, whom Tamale (2020: 6) referred to as the handmaidens of colonialism, also saw the British military advancements in Asante as a welcome development. These missionaries aided the colonial project through their Christianization, which they viewed as essential for awakening the energies of the local people towards the speedy development of their natural resources.[5] In Obuasi, the mining corporation and missionaries worked hand in hand and saw themselves as pioneers of civilization amongst a people who, as *The Gold Coast Aborigines* (28 January 1899: 4) reported, were deemed to be living under 'conditions of the greatest barbarity'. The proselytizing agenda of Christian missionaries worked to undermine Indigenous belief systems and was supported by funding from the mining corporation, which went towards the construction of the first Wesleyan Methodist church building in Obuasi, among other things.[6]

Eventually, the mining industry in the Gold Coast gradually became an enclave of European mining corporations, with limited opportunities for Indigenous gold miners. In a 1946 Memorandum on Mining Policy in the Gold Coast, the colonial government justified this European incursion into the mining sector with the argument that the sector's multiplicity of owners – as was the case under the customary system, where each person could mine for gold on their own land – was an obstacle to the organization of efficient units of economic operation. The colonial government felt that prospecting and mining operations were better left to the larger companies under state oversight to ensure the implementation of a better organizational structure.[7]

While the government welcomed the idea of new fields for European mining enterprises, it also had to consider the issue of land and customary mineral rights governance within the region (French 2021: 262). As more foreign gold-mining firms entered the Gold Coast mining scene in the 1880s, it became common practice for them to obtain concessions from lands already being worked by Indigenous miners. The advancement of British mercantilism into the gold-mining areas set new precedents for customary land tenures, one of which was the practice where foreign concessionaires negotiated land transactions solely with chiefs. According to *The Gold Coast Aborigines* (12 November 1898: 3), as demand for land grew and more foreign concessionaires sought large tracts of land, the absolute sale of stool lands became more common. Chiefs and their councillors frequently parted with stool lands in long leases under English form, mostly for their personal benefit. Since the transfer of land rights and even the sale of land was already established under customary law, the alienation of land to Europeans by means of mining concessions could hardly be said to have raised a new principle or contravened customary law. These large-scale land transactions raised many problems, however, one of which was the question of the rightful authority to grant concessions under customary law, namely, whether that was the subordinate stools or the paramount stools (Ollenu 1962: 25).

Gold Coast Indigenous scholar J. E. Casely Hayford (1903: 45) argued that paramount chiefs only had powers of ratification and confirmation, which, according to him, were not absolutely essential to make the transactions valid, even when such practices were becoming more common. This argument was rooted in the customary law principle that ownership of land by a substool was a condition precedent to ownership by a head or paramount stool. This principle is figuratively expressed by the Akan proverb '*brɔdeɛ ase wɔ Odikro*' ('the root of the plantain belongs to the *Odikro*'), which underscores the fact that the head stool could not become the owner of any land unless the land was first owned by the *Odikro* (the local headman) or, in some cases, by a representative of the substool (Ollenu 1962: 27). Consequently, the sale of stool lands exclusively by head chiefs was an invented tradition, but one that subsequently received the blessing of the colonial government and became institutionalized under the 1897 Lands Bill and the 1900 Concessions Ordinance.

While there were different customs pertaining to the various ethnic groups, the established practice was that a subchief who wished to dispose of land was required to inform the paramount chief in what was merely a formality, since the paramount chief was in no position to exercise any power of prohibition. The problem with the colonialist interpretation of this principle was that it strategically ignored the intricate customary differences between the various communities and succeeded in generating from it a homogenous customary system that treated the paramount chiefs as the primary and often sole point of contact for customary land transactions. In Asante, for instance, the colonial government realized that many subchiefs were refusing to execute leases with foreign concessionaires. Colonial administrators therefore instituted a system where they would bypass such chiefs by asking only the head chiefs to sign the leases.[8] Amanor (2008: 102) explained that this practice of transacting lands with only paramount chiefs demonstrated the state's absorption of the customary realm as a colonial strategy to constrain the development of free land markets and speculation in land, thereby preventing land users, usually the holders of usufruct, from selling lands. Hirons (2014: 23), on his part, noted that many of the head chiefs were spurred on by the refusal of local miners to pay tributes to them; as such, they expedited agreements with European mining companies for the latter to take over existing concessions.

This invented tradition ignored the prominence of usufructuary titles held by ordinary citizens that, as I already established, could not be unilaterally disposed of even by head chiefs. Granted that since the concessionaires were mostly foreign and not subjects of the stool, the permission of the chiefs was a requirement under customary law. However, the exclusion of usufruct titleholders (and, in some cases, family heads who held the allodial title) in such transactions was an absolute deviation from the existing customary norms. This exclusion of usufruct titleholders and the substitution of local head chiefs in concessionary grants might also have been facilitated by the false notion that individual ownership of land was foreign to customary law. According to Ollenu (1962: 29), this could not be further from the truth. Under customary law, whatever property an individual acquired by their own personal exertion was recognized as their self-acquired or individual property, and nobody could interfere with their right to the enjoyment thereof.

Moreover, the practice of dealing exclusively with chiefly allodial titleholders reinforced a deeply classed and gendered hierarchy in customary land tenure arrangements in mineral-rich communities, wherein only the mostly male traditional elite were consulted in land negotiations. As Ghanaian feminist scholars Awumbila and Tsikata (2010: 98) observed, the socioeconomic and political dimensions of colonial extractivism became evident in the deepening gendered inequalities and the complex changes in social relations. Certainly, it is important to acknowledge here that some of these changes were brought about by local chiefs on the back of fear of retaliation from the colonial government and threats of destoolment and violence.

With time, European concessionaires began to feel that the Indigenous legal system was not adaptable to the changes brought on by the increased land commodification and the vast wealth from industrialized gold mining (Kimble 1963: 20). The colonial government became increasingly concerned about what it deemed to be the uncontrolled acquisition of land from chiefs by speculators, which it aimed to rein in through legislative interventions. The development of modern gold mining therefore represented the first serious impact of Western economic forces upon Indigenous mining systems and customary mineral rights governance. These attempts at formal legislative intervention first came in the form of the Crown Lands Bill.

Gold Mining, the 1894 Crown Lands Bill and the 1897 Lands Bill

The growing demand for concessions came with an increase in land disputes, fraudulent land deals and general exploitation of local landowners. Due to limited local knowledge of European measuring standards (which had become the standard for boundary measurement), it happened that, occasionally, two or more European concessionaires would receive the same – or overlapping – concessions from the same chief or from two or more chiefs. *The Gold Coast Leader* (18 April 1914: 6) also reported that some educated locals used their knowledge of the changing circumstances to dupe their uneducated fellow countrymen by obtaining lands at ridiculously low prices and reselling these to European concessionaires at a huge profit.

Following a mining land dispute in 1889, Governor Sir William Brandford Griffith proposed a sovereign remedy by which the whole country would be taken over as Crown land and administered at what he considered would be a greater advantage than the inhabitants could achieve for themselves. This, he believed, was necessary for enabling the government to control the territory and supervise the granting of mining concessions to Europeans. In 1891, this matter was carefully considered by the Chief Justice J. T. Hutchinson, who rejected the Governor's proposal, particularly with regard to its introduction of the concept of waste lands, noting that all lands in the colony had an owner according to the existing customary land tenure system. As Ollenu (1962: 4) rightly argued, one of the first basic principles of customary land tenures was that there is no land without an owner. It may be vested in more than one person at the same time, but the right title or interest vested in the one may be materially different from that of the other.

Hutchinson cautioned the colonial government about the possibility of local hostility should a policy on Crown land expropriation be implemented. Instead, he suggested, the legislation should be limited to minerals and forests rather than all waste lands (Omosini 1972: 453). This concept of waste lands was given the same meaning as 'unoccupied lands' under the already enacted Public Lands Ordinance, 1876 (Adu-Gyamfi et al. 2020: 163). Under this Public Lands Ordinance, the British Crown was given an absolute and indefeasible right to lands determined as public lands, free from all adverse or competing rights, titles, interests, trusts, claims and demands. Provision was made for the payment of compensation to prior owners. Section 7(6), however, stated that no such compensation was to be paid in respect of 'unoccupied lands', which it defined as follows: 'Any Lands shall be deemed unoccupied where it is not proved that beneficial use thereof for cultivation or inhabitation or for collecting or storing water or for any industrial purpose, is or has been had during the lives of any person claiming interest therein or of the last immediate Ancestor or predecessor of such person'.

Hutchinson's advice was not fully accepted by Governor Griffith, who consulted his son, a former chief justice of the colony then in Jamaica. The crux of the son's advice was to replace the existing land tenures with a system of land registration, with the aim of respecting and recognizing Indigenous rights under the trusteeship of the government. Registration would mean that all land holdings would be deemed as deriving from the Crown, and where there was non-payment of the prescribed tax, the land would automatically revert to it. Ultimately, all unoccupied lands would come under government control. This scheme, which was underpinned by a gross misinterpretation of the customary system of fallow and shifting cultivation, was first attempted in the coastal areas where quasi-English titles were already established, but it was rejected as impracticable for a colony with limited surveys or boundaries (Omosini 1972: 456).

In August 1891, a circular was sent out to District Commissioners instructing them to oversee and tender advice on the grant of all concessions. According to *The Gold Coast Chronicle* (5 November 1897: 2), this was sold as imperative for putting the local landowners and the chiefs on guard, and to protect them from being taken in by dishonest land speculators. The exchange rate at the time was reportedly mineral-rich concessions 'for the paltry sum of a bottle of rum, a bale of cloth or a case of gin' (Kimble 1963: 333).

Eventually, a legislative intervention came in the form of the 1894 Crown Lands Bill. One of the most contested provisions under this Bill, according to *The Gold Coast Aborigines* (5 February 1898: 3), was the attempt to 'vest waste lands, forest lands and minerals in the Queen … to protect the forests from injury by the reckless felling of timber and to prevent waste and forest lands and minerals from being improvidently dealt with'. Under this legislation, all future transactions in concessions were to be made subject to the Governor's approval, and royalties were to be paid by concessionaires directly to the government. However, protection was given to all traditional rights on occupied lands and those used for shifting cultivation. This draft was approved by the Colonial Office with minor amendments and given its first reading in the Legislative Council in November 1894. This Bill immediately came under intense scrutiny from the chiefs and educated indigenes who rejected its premise of waste lands and reiterated that under customary law, there was not an inch of land in the country without an owner (Omosini 1972: 458). Vesting all waste lands to the Crown was seen by the local people as an attempt to take away their Indigenous lands and deprive them of the benefit of their gold and other natural resources. Sir William Maxwell, who succeeded Governor Griffith in April 1895, was pressured by the mounting local opposition to abandon the draft Bill altogether in October 1895, although he also had plans in the offing to introduce an entirely new Bill (Kimble 1963: 339).

A new Lands Bill was formally introduced into the Legislative Council on 10 March 1897. This Bill was framed to give the Crown rights of administration but not of ownership, as the intention of vesting waste and forest lands in the Queen was said to have been abandoned (Kimble 1963: 340). As *The Gold Coast Chronicle* (16 October 1897: 3) reported, section 25 of the proposed Bill made provisions for local landowners to exchange their titles for land certificates that were to be transmitted exclusively in accordance with English law. Governor Maxwell's disdain for the existing customary land tenure system was seen in his insistence that customary laws were unknown and could therefore not constitute the basis of any secure form of land title. If there was anything useful in traditional land custom, he wanted it incorporated and enacted in written form in an Ordinance (Omosini 1972: 459). This spoke to the longstanding Western tradition of rationalizing the binary relationship of orality and literacy, where written accounts were associated with truth, reliability, stability and trustworthiness (Vermeylen 2010: 192). In this sense, the written English property law system was deemed to be more civilized (and too advanced for the 'unevolved mind of the native' to comprehend), while the unwritten customary laws were considered primitive and unable to facilitate honest transactions in mining concessions.

The Lands Bill therefore represented one of many ways by which British colonizers enacted laws based on their limited understanding of existing customary laws, and on the assumption that the unwritten normative orderings did not have the capacity to provide the needed protection to transacting parties.

Under this new Bill, the government could declare that any piece of land had no owner and subsequently authorize its occupation. This provision was based on the same wrongful assumption of 'unoccupied lands' as was the erstwhile 1894 Crown Lands Bill. Local people were allowed to make grants and concessions to other indigenes, but not to Europeans except by express permission of the Governor. In practice, most concessions would be granted directly by the government, using its powers of administration. This was designed to ensure that concessionaires would get a firm title and would not be subject to varying local uncertainties (Kimble 1963: 340). However, the colonial government's supposed intention of protecting locals from swindling concession-mongers was not well received by the local people, nor were Maxwell's assurances of distinction between ownership and administration under the new 1897 Lands Bill. The indigenes still felt that the Lands Bill was merely a cover for illegal usurpation of their ancestral lands, as well as a betrayal of the government's earlier position not to interfere in their territory and customary land administration. Local opposition to the Lands Bill birthed the Gold Coast Aborigines' Rights Protection Society (ARPS) in 1897; this was arguably the first nationally organized protest group in the Gold Coast to galvanize support from chiefs and other local people (Kimble 1963: 341). *The Gold Coast Aborigines* (11 June 1898: 3) reported that the ARPS was partly motivated to oppose the Lands Bill for fear that the Gold Coast would face the same fate of settler colonialism as had befallen other Indigenous Peoples like the Māori of New Zealand.

As Rutazibwa (2020: 231) argued, the invocation of *terra nullius* and principles of waste or unoccupied lands involved the deliberate erasure of existing land claims and the violent projection of lands and people as blank slates for the taking. The Western, colonial tradition paternalistically justifies dispossessing Indigenous Peoples of their lands by claiming the absence of legible property legislation, portraying these communities as uncivilized and incapable of establishing the necessary protections. Through use of their own legal concepts, British colonial administrators sought to impose upon the local people their system of property registration and their Lockean notion of possessive individualism and private property rights free of overriding communal interests (Home and Lim 2004: 3).

According to *The Gold Coast Aborigines* (12 March 1898: 4), a deputation organized by ARPS members, which included E. Peterson, Jacob Wilson Sey (president of the ARPS), Thomas Freeman Jones, George Hughes, J. W. De-Graft Johnson and some local chiefs, was sent to England following the first reading of the Bill in order to petition against it. Part of this petition was a non-negotiable demand for the colonial government not to interfere with Indigenous customary land tenures. According to *The Gold Coast Aborigines* (11 February 1899: 2), the deputation also raised an issue with the nonparticipatory nature of the legislative process, especially as neither the people nor the chiefs had been consulted and included in the drafting and preparation of a Bill that was purported to protect their interests.

Following the deputation, a compromise was achieved when the colonial government agreed to a juristic legal pluralism under which customary land tenures would prevail where the indigenes were concerned. However, as *The Gold Coast Aborigines* (21 May 1898: 2) reported, the decision as to whether or not a matter was an Indigenous issue was to be determined by the British-style courts and not the traditional dispute resolution systems or the Native Administrations headed by the chiefs and their elders. This offer was rejected by the chiefs, who mobilized another protestation in the form of counsel representations before the Legislative Council. Indigenous lawyers John Mensah Sarbah and P. Awoonor Renner made representations on behalf of the local people during the second reading of the Bill, where they argued vehemently against what they viewed as the Bill's attempts to alter the local people's natural right of absolute ownership and turn them into mere holders (Kimble 1963: 345).

As usual, the main objections to the Lands Bill centred on the concept of waste lands and the proposed procedure for the administration of mineralized lands. Sarbah described the new Lands Bill as an elaborate expansion of the abandoned 1894 Crown Lands Bill. During the representations before the Legislative Council, he reminded the colonial government that every piece of land in the Gold Coast had an owner whether or not it was described as waste. Another objection related to the introduction of the Gazette, which was the official system for recording all new government legislations and notices. Sarbah argued that notices in the Gazette were insufficient warning to those who would be affected by the grant of concessions, and that it would be more appropriate for the government to personally deliver notices to the chiefs through a qualified interpreter (Kimble 1963: 353). Sarbah also highlighted a crucial deficiency in the colonial interpretation of customary land tenures, which was the imperialist tendency to homogenize Indigenous customs and practices. As was reported in *The Gold Coast Aborigines* (12 November 1898: 3), Sarbah pointed out that Governor Maxwell's introduction of the Lands Bill had been premised on his wrongful assumption that the *Asantehene* owned all the lands of the coastal areas, and that by defeating the said king, the British government could rightfully assume his paramount powers and justifiably take control over all the lands in the region. In other words, Maxwell believed that by the government's automatic assumption of Asante paramountcy, the practice of chiefs granting concessions to foreigners without his sanction was illegal under customary law. Sarbah then took the opportunity to provide an overview of the different customary land tenures pertaining to the various ethnic groups, emphasizing that the *Asantehene* did not have any sovereign or paramount title to any lands along the coast to which the colonial government could lay claim.

In that regard, Sarbah also argued against the colonial government's attempt to impose a semblance of English feudalism on the existing customary land tenures, stating that even in the centralized Asante Kingdom, there was an established hierarchy of chiefs where the *Asantehene*'s sovereign title was mostly administrative. The local chiefs had direct control of their lands and could lease or transact them as they wished for the communal benefit of their people. On this, Sarbah cited the example of the chief of Bekwai (the *Bekwaihene*, a divisional chief of the Bekwai state holding allegiance to the sovereign *Asantehene*), who had leased a large concession within his territory to AGC of his own accord in the early 1890s. As *The Gold Coast Aborigines* (5 February 1898: 2) noted, neither the Bond of 1844, the 1874 Proclamation defining British jurisdiction nor the Superior Court of Judicature Act of 24 July 1874 gave the British government authority over Indigenous lands.

Ultimately, the colonial government ascribed the opposition to the Lands Bill to local land speculators who were said to dislike the idea of the government's sanction as a requirement for validating concessions. These accusations of wilful misrepresentation by interested parties aroused much resentment, especially when the government singled out the educated locals (Kimble 1963: 343). British historians like Kimble argued that the new legislation was not primarily intended as the insidious attack upon local land ownership and mineral rights administration that its opponents made it out to be, but rather was a well-intentioned attempt to address the increasing number of land disputes in transacting mining concessions (Kimble 1963: 333). On his part, Ward (1991: 250) also explained that there was no deliberately planned system of alienation under the Lands Bill as the word 'colonialism' suggested – that it was an oversimplification to speak of a British colonial policy, since the empirical evidence pointed to an improvisatory British system working mostly out of necessity in a spasmodic and often incomplete way. Rather, the British government merely wanted to maintain law and order in land administration in the colony.

Chanock (1991), however, contended that in West and Central Africa, the plural legal model of colonialism that included the invention of customary land rights was a strategy that benefitted colonialists by protecting their privileged access to English-style courts and giving them the power to oversee land transactions. This legal system, according to Chanock, was central to facilitating the extraction and export of resources. In *Pollution Is Colonialism*, Liboiron (2021: 9) set out the direct linkages between colonialism and the land, indicating that whereas colonialism is often understood as a monolithic structure with roots exclusively in bad action, in reality it can often involve a set of contemporary and evolving land relations that are maintained by so-called good intentions and good deeds. Drawing on Foucault's articulation of power as regimes of truth (that allow certain things – but not others – to make sense and to circulate as truth), Liboiron described how colonial state formation is characterized by the use of conquest and genocide to secure control over Indigenous lands. In other words, the act of making plans for land in ways that align with colonial goals amounts to colonialism, however well-intentioned these goals may be. Consequently, routinized state access advocating for the governance of rivers, lands, minerals and other resources remains an act of colonialism – whether motivated by profit, growth, development or environmental conservation – as long as it assumes entitlement to Indigenous lands (Liboiron 2021).

Moreover, missing from the British colonialist concept of waste land and attempt to conform customary land tenures and mineral rights governance to British laws was an appreciation of the place of the land within Indigenous law and society. Speaking from a North American Indigenous context, Liboiron (2021: 43) argued that the concept of land extends beyond a fixed, material space. Rather, it includes the notion of a spiritually infused place grounded in interconnected and interdependent relationships and cultural positionings. It refers to a unique entity that is the combined living spirit of plants, animals, air, water, humans, histories and other events recognized by Indigenous communities. Adding to this, Black (2011) postulated that the land is law and is therefore an important part of understanding the survival of Indigenous legal systems. Whereas Western law is anthropocentric, Indigenous law originates in the land and considers it, rather than any human being or human systems, to be the source of life and health. Nti (2012: 3) related this principle to the Gold Coast resistance to the Lands Bill, postulating that while the colonial government viewed land as a component of economic and political power, the Indigenous people considered their lands to be a cultural and religious resource that gave them necessary connection with their ancestors in their everyday lives. To the people of the Gold Coast, resistance to the Lands Bill meant not merely protection of their lands, but preservation of their heritage, spiritualities and customary laws.

The Lands Bill would eventually fail once more due to increased local resistance. Nevertheless, the colonial government was insistent on finding some means of protecting unscrupulous prospectors and concession-mongering chiefs from one another, as well as to ensure the development of mining and commerce in the colony (Kimble 1963: 356). However, as Ward (1991: 97) put it, the government never fully recovered the public confidence that it lost in 1897 during the entire Lands Bill debacle. While the idea of a Lands Bill was aborted, the Gold Coast government from that time onwards was always under suspicion of wanting to steal the people's land. In 1930, for instance, two Gold Coast indigenes wrote a letter to *The Times* newspaper objecting to the government's legislations regarding forest reserves – according to them, the repeated statements about stopping land erosion and protecting the catchment areas of rivers were nothing but a cover for the government's real intention of using established forest reserves for mineral exploitation and keeping the profits away from the rightful African owners (Ward 1991). Briefly put, further resistance was ignited by the Forest Bill that the government sought to introduce in 1910, since its provision to place all unused forests under the government's management for posterity was regarded as an attempt to reintroduce the Lands Bill through the back door (Amanor 2008: 59). When an amended version of the Forest Bill was passed in November 1911 by the Legislative Council, the ARPS once again sent a petition to England, followed by a four-man deputation made up of J. E. Casely Hayford, E. J. P. Brown, T. F. E. Jones and Dr B. W. Quartey-Papafio. This deputation gave evidence before the West African Lands Committee, following which the 1911 Forest Ordinance remained a dead letter (Boahen 1975: 119). These tensions persisted into the enactment of the Concessions Ordinance of 1900, which finished laying the foundation for the consolidation of the eminent domain in mineral rights governance in the colony.

The Concessions Ordinance

By 1900, British authority had effectively been established, and the chiefs had all been deprived of the main elements supporting their status (Boahen 1975: 62). The conditions were therefore perfectly in place for establishing colonial control over the Indigenous mineral governance system. In 1900 a Concessions Bill was drafted, in which all references to public lands were omitted; this was essentially an amended version of Part III of the 1897 Lands Bill, which contained provisions on state absorption of mineral rights governance. In particular, sections 19(1)(a) and (2) provided that there was to be no interference with the rights of local landowners to make grants, as long as they could establish their title. Under this Concessions Bill, prospective European concessionaires were required to approach the chiefs to bargain for lands. A survey of the land would then be undertaken and, in the absence of any opposition from any other party, a certificate of validity would be issued. The rent for the transaction was to be paid to the government, who would transfer the proceeds to the chief. The chiefs were required to keep one-third of the proceeds for themselves, one-third for the stool and one-third for the elders (Kimble 1963: 70). A Concessions Court was established and authorized to adjudicate over concession transactions and to determine whether boundaries of concessions were properly surveyed. The Concessions Court was also to determine whether the proper persons were the parties to the transaction, whether there was mutual understanding and whether the terms were reasonable.

Lawyer John Mensah Sarbah had earlier argued against the Concessions Court, specifically the provisions that allowed for the state to be a party to all proceedings before the court. As was reported in *The Gold Coast Aborigines* (21 May 1898: 3), Sarbah was sceptical of the possibility of an impartial outcome from the Concessions Court following the state's involvement as a party. Sarbah viewed the Concessions Court as unnecessary, owing to the existence of the already established Supreme Court. By establishing an additional Concessions Court and setting itself as a party to every matter before the said court, the government was unduly complicating the already complex plural legal system and intentionally rendering the judicial system alienating to the local people.

The Concessions Ordinance was eventually passed into law in 1900 despite a minority objection from the ARPS who, according to *The Gold Coast Aborigines* (17 March 1900), viewed the Ordinance as nothing more than the 'despicable Lands Bill clothed in fine, smooth words'. Ultimately, the Concessions Ordinance became the official, statutory enunciation of the doctrine of eminent domain whereby the government institutionalized a monist-pluralist system of mineral rights governance. Under this system, the rights of customary landowners to mineral-bearing lands were recognized but subjected to state legitimization, oversight and authorization for validity. Despite controlling all aspects of mineral resource governance, the colonial government still maintained that by way of policy, the mineral resources in the Gold Coast were, unlike other colonial territories, not the property of the Crown but that of the Native Authorities or the stools; this was their position as far back as the late 1950s.[9] It is worth noting that it was overt resistance to ideas of absolute ownership that fuelled the oppositions that delayed the state's assumption of control over mineral rights under the previous Lands Bills. However, a strategic shift in the legal language reframed the matter in terms of administration and mediation, rather than ownership; this softened the local stance and saw to the passage of the Concessions Bill, although it effectively also made the government the ultimate arbiter over mineral rights even when the government did not overtly claim ownership over mineralized lands.

In Asante, special arrangements prevailed prior to the promulgation of the 1903 Ashanti Concessions Ordinance. In accordance with the existing colonial monist-pluralism, the government required the Resident of Kumasi (representative of the Governor) to be notified of applications for concessions. The Resident would instruct the chiefs to appear before him, ascertaining from them in the presence of the applicant whether they were willing to grant the concession applied for and willing to cooperate in the supply of labour for the mine. In the presence of the chiefs, the Resident would then arrange with the applicant the sum that they would receive annually as consideration for the concession. The terms of the agreement would be drafted in a deed to be signed by the interested parties in the presence of the Resident. Additionally, the chiefs were to be advised that the remuneration would be paid to them directly by the Resident.[10] These arrangements were made with the understanding that chiefs in Asante could not grant lands to foreigners without the paramount king, and that since the government had assumed the position of paramount following the annexation of Asante after the 1900 Yaa Asantewaa War, all concessionary grants should be made with the prior consent and sanction of the Governor. All chiefs in Asante were warned not to grant any mineral rights without the Governor's authority, or else the government would not recognize the concession.

The interconnection between the unyielding colonial attempts at legislating forest reserves and mineral resources governance and the consequent Indigenous resistance led the colonial government to establish a special Commission under the chairmanship of H. C. Belfield, with a mandate to study the land question with special reference to concessions (Kimble 1963: 366). *The Gold Coast Leader* (25 January 1913: 5) reported this commissioned inquiry as being necessitated by the mining corporations and their incessant push for the government to review the customary laws in their interests. Belfield's inquiry involved a two-month period of research where he engaged with forty-four witnesses, including chiefs, elders, lawyers, a judge, mining managers, European lawyers representing mining corporations operating in the colony, five Indigenous lawyers and some other educated locals. Published on 12 July 1912, the findings revealed, among other things, that too many concessions had been granted on terms unfavourable to the inhabitants, mostly because the chiefs had little idea of area measurements and were usually unaware of the extent of land being signed away. Belfield reiterated that the Crown had no vested rights of ownership in any lands save the forts on the coast, and any endeavour to extend those rights would amount to a breach of faith with the local people (Kimble 1963: 367). As was reported in *The Gold Coast Leader* (25 January 1913: 5), Belfield advised the government not to lose sight of the fact that the land was the property of the people, and that a concession was a contract between the landowners and the concessionaires to which the government was no party.

Belfield, however, approved of state oversight in the granting of mining concessions. He suggested that the policy whereby the local chiefs were made the grantors and payees of concessions should be maintained, subject to state supervision, to ensure that improvident alienations might be prevented. The Concessions Ordinance and the conclusions from Belfield's inquiry demonstrated the persistence of the colonial government in subjecting Indigenous mineral rights systems to the language accepted by the dominant colonial state law and to policymaking favourable to European large-scale mineral exploitation.

They further illustrated Stoler's (2002: 107) position that colonial commissions of enquiry largely acted in response to crises and as a way for the colonial state to invoke 'outside experts' to verify and attest to the state's ability to act towards what it deemed as public interest. From the Lands Bills to the official stamping of the Concessions Ordinance by the Belfield Commission, the trajectory of the doctrine of eminent domain revealed a systematic incursion into the Indigenous administration of mineral rights through the state-commissioned organization of knowledge towards the prescription of what state officials were charged to know and enforce. In the next section, I examine how the practicalities of this newly instituted administrative system impacted Indigenous mining.

The Concessions Ordinance, Formalization and the Regulation of Indigenous Mining

One pertinent development from the colonial government's usurpation of control over mineral rights governance was the introduction of licensing requirements and formalist regulation of Indigenous gold mining. The first official recognition of what was termed as native mining methods was introduced under section 16 of the withdrawn Lands Bill, later to be reincorporated under the 1900 Concessions Ordinance and its subsequent amendments. The definition of concession under the 1900 Concessions Ordinance excluded Indigenous landowners who mined on their own customarily held lands or operated on lands smaller than 25 acres in area. Indigenes who wanted to mine by modern methods, whether on their own lands or on government-validated concessions, were required to take out a mining licence as prescribed under section 34 of the 1900 Concessions Ordinance. This requirement for licensing also applied to the Native Authorities, the colonial administrative territorial divisions headed by local head chiefs. Order in Council No. 9 of 1926 exempted certain classes of concessions from the operation of the 1900 Concessions Ordinance, including exemptions from taking out a prospecting licence where the mining area was restricted to a concession smaller than 25 acres in area.[11]

Section 25(1)(b) of the 1901 Concessions (Amendment) Ordinance further exempted 'mining according to native customs' from the requirement for a mining licence. Mining according to native customs was defined as 'washing gravel taken from riverbeds or from pits and does not include crushing or smelting'. Section 36(1)(a) and (b) of the 1939 Concessions Ordinance provided that 'no person shall carry on mining in the Gold Coast without a mining licence from the Chief Inspector of Mines; and without being the holder of a concession granting the right to do so from the native having the power to grant such right, unless he is the owner of the land on which such mining is carried on'. Again, section 36(2) provided that section 1 did not apply to native mining methods that did not entail the use of machinery or methods commonly employed in modern mining practice. Thus, while Indigenous miners were permitted to mine using these strictly defined mining methods, they were prohibited from carrying out mining operations by modern methods on a concession validated under state law, unless they were licensed to do so.[12]

This official, legislative recognition was premised on an acknowledgement by the colonial government that the Indigenous populations had received enlightenment under colonial rule, and should be encouraged to participate directly in the mineral wealth being exploited by European firms. According to the acting Commissioner for Lands, the pursuit of mining by the indigenes was a:

> ...reasonable desire which requires control but not prohibition and I think it would be eminently desirable from a policy point of view to relax the existing restrictions sufficiently to permit such mining, for Government would be embarrassed if called upon to reply to a criticism suggesting that foreigners had virtually been given a monopoly of the right to extract minerals.[13]

Accordingly, the decision to make provision for locals to mine by modern methods was deemed necessary for fostering responsibility in them and encouraging them to develop their own resources, to show initiative and to thereby demonstrate their capacity for self-government in due time.[14]

To a person without knowledge of the colony and its Indigenous institutions, these provisions of the Concessions Ordinance seemed like a fair and plausible demonstration of the government's commitment to officially accommodate Indigenous miners and their mining methods. However, as John Mensah Sarbah argued when the 1897 Lands Bill was introduced, the entire legislative approach to defining native mining methods was misleading and enunciated mechanisms that could only end up stultifying the development and flexibility of Indigenous mining systems. The statutory definition ossified native mining within a rigid circumscription of subsistence beyond which local miners were not lawfully permitted to advance. This action by the colonial government limited Indigenous miners' production, which was further used to justify their confinement to 'small-scale' status and exclusion from large-scale land acquisitions and technological expansions. As was commented on in *The Gold Coast Chronicles* (20 September 1897: 3), a strict interpretation of the law rendered it unlawful for Indigenous miners to saw timber for use in their mining pits since the saw machines were imported from Birmingham, and their use could therefore not be considered as part of the prescribed 'native mining methods'.

With this legislative definition, the British government betrayed its understanding of the essential characteristics of Indigenous mining and its underpinning customary law, namely, its flexibility and adaptability to changing times and circumstances. With its official recognition, the colonial government set the definition of 'native mining' in stone and created the myth of an unchanging method of Indigenous mining. As Nekam (1967: 45) rightly cautioned, there is a danger in codifications formulating wrong or incomplete customary laws due to the differences within the various ethnic groups, as well as the tendency for such codifications to transform customary law by rendering it inflexible.

With time, colonial administrators concluded that the Concessions Ordinance did not exempt Indigenous miners holding 25-acre concessions from the requirement of a prospecting licence. It followed that, with the exception of section 33(1) of the Concessions Ordinance, all prospectors, Indigenous or foreign, were required to take out a prospecting licence whether they were operating within a concession or on their own lands.[15] Another important aspect of the legislative recognition and regulation of Indigenous gold mining was its imposed tax obligations. For instance, Indigenous miners were subjected to the payment of a £30 stamp duty tax.[16] Colonial administrators further agreed for Part 5 of the Concessions Ordinance, which related to the payment of profit tax, to apply to Indigenous miners seeking to mine using modern mining methods.[17] This led to the prohibition of the sale and purchase of minerals from local owner-miners who defaulted in the prompt payment of profit and other taxes. Some colonial administrators anticipated objection to the introduction of this new system, which they viewed as contradictory to the established policy of not taxing local people who mined on their own lands.[18]

Other colonial administrators, however, felt that there was no reason to exempt Indigenous landowners who mined using modern methods, whether by themselves or through an incorporated company, from the same tax liability as the large-scale mining corporations operating under the Concessions Ordinance.[19] In their view, customary landowners who desired to mine on their own lands in accordance with 'modern' mining methods should equally be prepared to abide by 'modern' standards of tax assessment and comply with all relevant state laws. Additionally, it was suggested that section 41(1) of the Concessions Ordinance should be amended to permit the employment of a firm of chartered accountants to draw up the necessary statements and balance sheets for Indigenous miners. Colonial administrators even suggested a firm of auditors and chartered accountants in Accra whose services they believed could be of use to local miners in that regard. There were also recommendations for the employment of government auditors who would be specifically assigned to scrutinize the tax returns of Indigenous miners.[20] The colonial government further insisted on the services of competent assayers to appraise the gold won by Indigenous miners, in order to provide effective monitoring of operations and an accurate declaration for assessment of tax.[21]

Notwithstanding the encroachment of these regulatory processes on Indigenous mining, the general attitude of the government towards Indigenous miners was mostly that of neglect, apathy and, in some cases, disapproval. Colonial administrators were neither optimistic nor supportive of Indigenous mining operations, as most believed that local landowners would be better off renting their lands to large-scale mining corporations rather than pursuing mining by themselves. The main argument was that the mining companies were proven to be competent and trustworthy, making them better suited to undertake and supervise mining operations.[22] It was expected that local landowners would seek assistance from their District Commissioners before entering into any negotiations for the services of mining agents. Beyond that, the colonial government kept a hands-off approach and was reluctant to probe into the intricate details of any contractual arrangements between local miners and their mining engineers or contractors.

Colonial administrators felt that it was impossible to protect local owner-miners from any unscrupulous mining engineers or contractors unless the parties brought the agreement for validation under the Concessions Ordinance. Beyond recognizing the rights of Indigenous landowners to mine on their lands and rendering invalid any contractual obligations between landowners and agents that had not been submitted to the District Commissioners or the Secretary for Mines for advice, colonial administrators did not see any other support they could offer to Indigenous miners.[23] Interestingly, this was not their attitude during the boom in European concessionaires, nor was it their general approach towards large-scale mining corporations – the colonial government was deeply invested in validating all the land transactions of these parties, and ensuring the success of their operations in the colony. Moreover, this apathetic attitude seemed inconsistent with the increased supervisory role that the colonial government consistently appropriated for itself in the Indigenous mining sector through its licensing demands and formalization schemes.

Another major outcome of state control over mining was the enactment of criminalizing legislations such as the Mercury Ordinance of 1932. While the purpose of this Ordinance was stated as the control of the importation and possession of mercury, colonial reports indicate that it was promoted and passed under the aegis of large-scale mining corporations who were anxious about protecting their gold from being stolen and processed with mercury by indigenes. Although there is no indication that this Mercury Ordinance had any bearing on a reduction in the alleged theft of gold from the mining corporations, what the evidence suggests is that this piece of legislation was less about limiting mercury use for environmental protection than it was about safeguarding the interests of foreign industrialized mines against competition from Indigenous miners (Tschakert and Singha 2007; Aryee, Ntibery and Atorkui 2013; Yankson and Gough 2019).[24] While the colonial reports did not register the objections of local people to this Ordinance, it is clear that even some colonial administrators were sceptical about its objective and explicitly indicated that they were 'not quite satisfied as to the necessity for this legislation'.[25]

These colonial-era legislative impositions on Indigenous mining reveal a clear distinction made by colonial administrators between Indigenous mining – categorized as small-scale – and foreign large-scale mining, which was seen as the epitome of the mining industry. This distinction is tied to the current dual-mining political economy and the formal/informal binary in ASM. It also aligns with historical discourse of the formality/informality binary within the context of dualism, a framework originating from the concept of the 'dual economy' as introduced by Dutch colonial administrator and academic Julius Herman Boeke. In his work on the Dutch East Indies, Boeke wrote about a dualism featuring the colonially regulated, highly capitalist economy on one side, and the 'native' economy on the other (Guha-Khasnobis, Kanbur and Ostrom 2006).

Development economists crystallized Boeke's idea into a two-sector model of development, in which a modern/capitalist/industrial/urban/formal sector occurred alongside a traditional/rural/informal one. A further notion of dualism appears in the work of Keith Hart (1973: 61), the anthropologist who is credited with having coined the term 'informal' in contradistinction to 'formal' during his study of a slum area in Accra. This colonial divide between formal and informal persists as an enduring legacy of how laws and regulations in ASM are constructed, and it is particularly evident in historic gold-mining communities like Obuasi.

Obuasi and the Ashanti Goldfields Corporation: State-Sanctioned Land Grabs and the Colonial Market Economy

According to Dumett (1998: 47), mining history turns on local history; in the case of Obuasi, this has mostly revolved around a history of being known as the first enclave of modern European capitalist penetration into the Indigenous mining sector in Asante. Taylor's detailed account (2006) of AGC in Obuasi showed how this community became the spot where one of the most lucrative mining bargains in the world was struck by British prospector Edwin A. Cade. Cade's concession was secured from a group of Indigenous concessionaires including J. P. Brown, J. E. Ellis and J. E. Biney, through a written agreement leasing 100 square miles of land from the chiefs of Adanse and Bekwai.

Initially, the colonial government was unable to recognize or disallow Cade's negotiations, since they took place in Asante two years prior to the extension of colonial jurisdiction into the territory. In 1897, however, Cade established AGC in England, after which a fresh agreement was drawn up with the government as a third party who received a royalty and forwarded the original sums promised to the chiefs. The chiefs of Adanse and Bekwai were to receive £100 and £600 annually, while the government received a royalty of 3% on profits plus a commuted royalty of £500 for each of the first five years. This agreement remained unaffected by the 1900 Concessions Ordinance and the 1903 Ashanti Concessions Ordinance. Section 50 of the 1900 Concessions Ordinance and section 55 of the 1903 Ashanti Concessions Ordinance respectively provided that 'The provisions of the Ordinance shall not apply to the rights which were the subject of an agreement between Sir W. E. Maxwell and the Ashanti Goldfields Corporation Limited, and other parties dated the 3rd day of June 1897'. Additionally, AGC secured the right to undertake mining, trading, rubber and timber extraction, roadmaking and town-building. As was reported by *The Gold Coast Aborigines* (14 May 1898: 3), the Governor's representative opened the company's first mine in Obuasi on 2 May 1898, at a ceremony also attended by the *Bekwaihene* and a nephew of the *Adansehene*.

In the town of Anyinam, one of AGC's most productive Obuasi mine sites, the story of Cade's acquisition includes local recollections of a certain white man who arrived and was warmly received by the chief with some gold in exchange for a piece of cloth. According to the story, this white man's visits increased in frequency until one day, the chief and the people noticed numerous white men arriving with heavy machinery to commence mining on their land.[26] This local 'rememorying' further points to longstanding contestations about the validity of AGC's claim to mineral rights under the Obuasi lease and its impacts on traditional rights, including those held by local miners. Taylor (2006) described AGC's lease as a rather unprecedented and legally peculiar concessionary agreement that essentially ratified the colonial government's right to grant concessions, a position that was vehemently opposed in the Gold Coast by the ARPS. Questions surrounding the validity of AGC's concession agreement mainly related to whether the colonial government could grant concessions in Asante or simply recognize those obtained from the Indigenous Fante entrepreneurs. Taylor (2006) was of the view that the original transaction between the Fante entrepreneurs and the *Bekwaihene* at the time, Nana Yaw Boakye, was not the transfer of an inalienable title to the land but built on the traditional sharing system known as *abusa*.[27]

According to *The Gold Coast Aborigines* (8 October 1898: 4), AGC, like most foreign mining ventures in the colony, set up its first shafts in areas with already existing Indigenous gold operations. Indeed, the pervasive quality of the royalty system throughout Akan culture is highlighted by the fact that when the first European mining companies arrived in the late 1890s in mining communities like Obuasi, they found it difficult to recruit locals to their capitalistic system of wage labour, and consequently maintained the *abusa* method of payment where tribute workers were allowed to continue their traditional mining methods on AGC's newly acquired concessions.[28] Thus began the spatial overlaps between AGC's concessions and Indigenous mining sites, as well as the ensuing sharp social tensions that persist today. While AGC used the locations of existing native pits to commence its surface mining operations, the corporation managed to drive away the inhabitants of Obuasi from their lands, including the rich goldfields of Anyinam that were initially left to private local miners, about a thousand of whom were eventually forced out to make way for AGC's operations. By using its 1897 lease agreement, AGC further managed to impose control over local miners and goldsmiths in Obuasi, mostly through the issuance of licences. For instance, local goldsmiths had to apply for an AGC licence in addition to a government licence, a requirement that was not applicable to goldsmiths operating in the other gold-mining areas. AGC justified this extra bureaucracy as a way to stop illicit gold trading (Taylor 2006). This history reveals that licensing requirements – imposed on a mining community that had long operated without them – were not merely regulatory measures, but tools of corporate control over Indigenous mining. They served to mask the true objective: facilitating frontier expansion, displacing the Indigenous people and enabling materialist accumulation.

The monopoly held by AGC in Obuasi was not only limited to its acquisition of virtually the entire community as its concession; there were also massive efforts to exert control over the social, economic, cultural and political aspects of the lives of the indigenes. Through its Ashanti-Obuasi Trading Company, the mining corporation wielded a monopoly over trading across the entire community.[29] On 14 September 1905, the Ashanti-Obuasi Trading Company entered into a Memorandum of Agreement with the colonial government for the exclusive rights to sell spirits within the areas bounded by the corporation's concessions. According to *The Gold Coast Leader* (24 May 1913), the corporation then sought to extend this agreement to include all trade within the Obuasi area, and succeeded in keeping both Indigenous and European traders from operating in the community.[30] For Li (2014: 589), this phenomenon exemplifies how large-scale extractive industries are built upon economic enclaves characterized by exclusions, restrictions and complex capitalist infrastructure involving markets that are often harder for local people to access.

Cade was deeply appreciative of the colonial government's facilitation of AGC's acquisition of the Obuasi mining concession; according to *The Gold Coast Aborigines* (8 October 1898: 4), he referred to it as 'a useful field for British enterprise [that] has been discovered in this last addition to the British Empire'. This alliance between empire and mercantilist extractivism remained the bedrock of AGC's operations in Obuasi, where in many instances, the corporation used threats of force or retaliation by the government against the chiefs and people in securing its concessions. For instance, when the *Bekwaihene* contested the corporation's mining operations in Sansu, Anyinam and Korkoteasua (communities in the Obuasi area) on the grounds that those areas were outside the confines of the lease granted to AGC, officers of the mine responded with threats of having the chief arrested by the government. The colonial government sent surveyors and declared the lands to be part of the corporation's concessions. However, in the case of Sansu, it became apparent to the government that the local chiefs had not been fully cognisant of the enormous extent of the concessions they had granted to the corporation. Nevertheless, using threats of force, this government intervention eventually led the local chief to concede on the matter.[31] These tensions, according to Taylor (2006), were reinforced by the disinterest of the colonial government and AGC in seeking a conclusive legal ruling on the validity of the corporation's lease agreement. Indeed, some within the colonial establishment believed AGC's agreement to be illegal, although this was never formally communicated to the local chiefs. The government and the corporation continued to operate under the assumption that the agreement was valid and not open to challenge by way of petition.

Evidently, this collaboration between empire and AGC in Obuasi was a mutually beneficial and profitable endeavour. AGC's operations

Figure 4.3. Photograph of Native village, Ashanti Obuassi Gold Mines, 31 May 1906. Courtesy of National Archives, Kew, COPY 1/498/30, used with permission.

served as a significant source of tax revenue for the colonial government, which in turn protected the corporation and legitimized its large-scale land grab and mining activities in the local community. For instance, in addition to the general gold duty paid by all the other mining firms in the colony, AGC paid an additional royalty of 5% (5% *ad valorem* Concessions Duty) under a separate agreement reached with the government in 1896.[32]

Moreover, while nearly all the mining corporations were allowed to employ their own Mines Police within their mining areas to keep internal theft in check, many of these corporations also requested and were granted additional state policing to address what they alleged to be an increase in illicit mining within their enclaves.[33] In Obuasi, more armed state police were deployed in the community as a result of AGC's constant complaints to the colonial government about being threatened by the chiefs and people of Adanse. The colonial government also considered a proposal for an additional volunteer corps made up of European mine employees, who would be provided with uniforms, arms and ammunition at the expense of the mines.[34]

As questionable as it was, and despite its constraints on the potentiality of Indigenous gold mining in Obuasi, AGC's mining lease remained the legal basis of the corporation's operations in the community until its renewal on 1 January 1969. The gold-mining town of Obuasi stands as a textbook illustration of the intricate interconnections between colonial resource extractivism, Indigenous dispossession, the undermining of traditional authority and the subjugation of Indigenous miners in formerly colonized mineral-producing societies. We cannot fully address the environmental negativities and social tensions within ASM in mining communities like Obuasi without confronting this history and the underlying colonialist legacies within the current licensing framework of ASM formalization. While the colonial government's superintendence of the extractive industry was rationalized in the name of development and the interests of the local people, the evidence rather suggests the imposition of a legal and policy framework that worked to limit the advancement of Indigenous mining operations. This underscores the scepticism of decolonial scholars towards intervention policies and, more often than not, their predatory paternalisms of local development (Arnfred and Ampofo 2009: 5). Just like the colonial government, the modern state continues to negotiate concessions at an ever-increasing pace, a phenomenon that has led to disruptive effects such as negative environmental consequences, social volatility and scarcity of land for local communities (Feintrenie 2013).

Conclusion

The appeal to history that examines contexts and subjective positioning in addition to isolated facts and events forms a crucial part of the process of validating and legitimizing claims. Nigerian feminist scholar Oyèrónkẹ́ Oyěwùmi (1997) implored that historical explorations involve looking not only at mere individual and isolated events, but also at the unique framing and shaping of discourse. This historicization helps to situate events within their specific and unique cultural and political contexts. The misreading and misrepresentation of African histories has engendered a failure to critically interrogate social phenomena on the continent. As Oyěwùmi (1997) has argued, this has led to the uncritical adoption of imposed Western constructs without a fundamental questioning of their origins and sociolegal formations, resulting in flawed and problematic replication of Western systems.

As traced in this chapter, the history of uncoordinated colonial attempts at monopolizing mineral resource governance, local resistance and large-scale land grabs in Obuasi demonstrates a mining regime whose foundations are underlaid by violent legal impositions, dispossessions and exclusions. It shows a colonial regime that assumed centralized oversight over mineral resource governance through the principle of the eminent domain, which was crystallized into law following years of local resistance and negotiations. A pattern of uneven governance between large-scale mining and Indigenous mining became institutionalized under this centralized absorption of mining governance. While the colonial state and (in some circumstances) mining corporations introduced licensing requirements for Indigenous miners, they simultaneously showed a lack of commitment to resourcefully supporting Indigenous mining. This support was rather channelled to the more industrialized, foreign large-scale mining. The uniqueness of Obuasi within this colonial–mercantilist matrix demonstrates what is established today as the contested dualism between large-scale mining and ASM in Ghana. As the next chapter will confirm, this differentiation between Indigenous and large-scale mining remains the underlying principle of law and policy in Ghana's contemporary extractive industry, as well as its unsuccessful attempts at formalizing its local small-scale mining sector.

Notes

1. It is important to note here that 'Ashanti' was the British rendering of 'Asante'.
2. Nana Kwadwo Asamoah, chief of Adaase. Interview with the author, Adaase, 22 July 2021.
3. Nana Gyamerah Kwabena Oyiakwan II, chief of Kwapia. Interview with the author, Kwapia, 7 September 2021.
4. The name Asante comes from the Twi phrase 'ɔsa nti' ('because of war'). Over the first half of the eighteenth century, the victories of this kingdom stitched together a territory roughly congruent with modern Ghana.
5. See the works of Reverend J. Delaney Russel in 'Coomassie – the City of Blood', *The Foreign Field of the Wesleyan Methodist Church* 79(VII) (March 1911). See also Reverend Thomas Birch Freeman's description of the British expansion into Asante as 'an important acquisition calculated to materially extend British commerce, enlarge the local revenue and increase the beneficial prestige of England on the Gold and Slave Coasts'. MMS/Special Series/Biographical/West Africa/597B; Extract of typescript manuscript of the journals of Reverend Freeman's visits to the Kingdoms of Asante and Dahomey, and to Abeokuta, Lagos and Bagadry between 1840 and 1843. Wesleyan Missionary Archives, SOAS, London.
6. Handwritten note on the history of the Methodist Church in Obuasi; this was part of a compilation of church history for the centenary celebration of the Wesleyan Missionary Society in Ghana. Wesleyan Missionary Archives, SOAS, London.
7. CO 852/1220/6; WAF 34/2/01: Memorandum on Colonial Mining Policy, 1946.
8. Letter from Acting Resident to the Colonial Secretary, dated 31 January 1900.
9. Minerals Duty Ordinance 1952 – Explanatory Statement on the Minerals Duty Bill Dealing with Gold Coast Mining Taxation.
10. Concessions in Ashanti – Rules to be observed by persons desirous of obtaining mining rights or other rights in Ashanti from Governor Hodgson, dated 7 August 1899. This legislative arrangement was reiterated in subsequent amendments, such as under section 11(3) of the 1939 Concessions Ordinance, which provided for local chiefs to be summoned before the Chief Commissioner in respect of land and mineral rights transactions.
11. CSO 19/614; Letter from the Secretary for Mines, Mines Department – Tarkwa, to the Colonial Secretary, dated 9 March 1933.
12. CSO 19/614; Minerals Winning of, by Natives; Letter from the Acting Attorney-General, dated 17 May 1934. See also CO96/754/8.
13. CSO 19/614; Letter from the Acting Commissioner for Lands, Gold Coast Department, to the Acting Colonial Secretary, dated 15 June 1934.
14. CSO 19/614; Letter from the Acting Secretary for Mines, Gold Coast Mines Department, to the Colonial Secretary, dated 5 June 1934.
15. CSO 19/614; Memo from the Colonial Secretary's Office, dated 27 May 1933. Remnants of these colonial licensing requirements and the 25-acre limitation for Indigenous mining concessions persist under the prevailing ASM formalization scheme. See also sections 89 and 111 respectively of the Minerals and Mining Act, 2006 (Act 703).
16. CSO 19/614; Letter from the Acting Attorney-General, dated 17 May 1934.
17. CSO 19/614; Memo from the Acting Treasurer to the Colonial Secretary's Office, dated 22 August 1934.
18. CSO 19/614; Memo from the Treasurer to the Colonial Secretary's Office, dated 18 September 1934.

19. CSO 19/614; Memo from the Acting Secretary for Native Affairs, dated 1 October 1934.
20. CSO 19/614; Letter from the Acting Secretary for Mines to the Colonial Secretary, dated 14 July 1934.
21. CSO 19/614; Letter from the Acting Colonial Sectary to the Acting Secretary for Mines, dated 13 August 1934.
22. CSO 19/614; Letter from the Acting Secretary for Mines, Mines Department – Tarkwa, to the Colonial Secretary, dated 16 August 1934.
23. CSO 19/614; Letter from the Acting Secretary for Mines, Mines Department – Tarkwa, to the Colonial Secretary, dated 16 August 1934.
24. CO 96/704: Letter from Sir Phillip Cunliffe-Lister, Acting Governor – Government House, Accra, Gold Coast, dated 15 July 1932. This letter indicated that between 1925 and 1932, there were a total of 180 cases of gold theft reported to the police, out of which 148 were prosecuted in court, with a total of 145 persons being convicted from these cases.
25. CO 96/704; Letter from Sir Phillip Cunliffe-Lister, dated 7 May 1932.
26. Local chief who opted for anonymity. Interview with the author, 14 July 2021.
27. Taylor (2006) further explained that the reason for the *Bekwaihene*'s inclusion in the lease agreement was that the *Adansehene*, Nana Nkansah, who was the actual paramount overlord over Obuasi at the time, had sought to secede from Asante to join the British protectorate in 1879. This was seen as an act of grave disloyalty to Asante and led to the invasion of Adanse by the *Bekwaihene*, who assumed control over parts of Adanse, including Obuasi. As already established, Governor Maxwell's posturing during his facilitation of AGC's lease was driven by his wrongful belief that he had personally replaced the *Asantehene* as paramount chief, and was therefore granted direct dominion and the power to validate concessions in any part of Asante.
28. Letter from Messrs Ashurt to Colonial Office, dated 28 April 1900. Enclosure No. 239A: 31 March 1900. This evolved into the tributer system that persists today, albeit in limited circumstances.
29. CO96/674/1; Letter from A. J. Dawe to the Under-Secretary of State for the Colonies regarding the Ashanti-Obuasi Trading Company Spirit Licence, dated 15 June 1927.
30. CO96/684/4.
31. CO 96/356/11; Further correspondence (15 December 1898 to 31 December 1900) relating to Land Concessions and Regulations; Letter from Governor Hodgson, dated 28 October 1899; Enclosure 2 in No. 171; Letter from Ashanti Goldfields Corporation Limited, dated 9 June 1899; Letter from Yaw Borkey, King of Bekwai, to Ashanti Goldfields Corporation, dated 7 June 1899; Letter from Mr Daw to King of Bekwai, dated 8 June 1899.
32. CO 852/1236; Minerals Duty Ordinance 1952: Explanatory Statement on the Minerals Duty Bill Dealing with Gold Coast Mining Taxation.
33. CO 5542/222.WAF34/2/01. Sutherland, D.A. *Memorandum on Mining in the Gold Coast*. Colonial Office 1951.
34. CO 96/741/10; Mining Matters: Despatch 73 Protection for mining companies: Police force increases, dated 26 February 1900; Letter from Governor Hodgson to Honourable Chamberlain, dated 6 February 1900; CO 96/361/18; Letter from Governor Hodgson to Honourable Chamberlain, dated 20 July 1900.

CHAPTER 5

Navigating Colonial Legacies and the Living Customary Law in ASM Formalization in Ghana

Introduction

This chapter forms the second part of the empirical analysis in this book, in which I draw parallels between the history of colonial monist-pluralism in land and mining governance and the prevailing ASM regime in Ghana. This is aimed at highlighting how colonialism has reconfigured itself in contemporary state visions of ASM law and policy governance. In the first section following this introduction, I demonstrate how the doctrine of eminent domain introduced under the different Lands Bills and the 1900 Concessions Ordinance persists within the current constitutional democracy in Ghana, despite several postcolonial mining law reforms. Following from my discussion of the historical Indigenous perceptions of, and resistance to, colonial land laws, the second section examines the contemporary local view that ASM formalization functions as a mechanism by which the state absorbs control over mineral resource governance. The contrast between local perspectives on ASM informality and the dominant state notions of formalization helps to shed light on how local communities view law and legitimacy within ASM. In the third section, I situate the discussion within the context of ASM in Obuasi, examining how local miners navigate the living customary law and land contestations amidst state-protected corporatist interests. This context specificity enables better understanding of the colonial-era alienation of Obuasi by Ashanti Goldfields Corporation (AGC), now AngloGold Ashanti (AGA), and its implications for contemporary ASM in the local mining community.

Surviving Empire: The Eminent Domain and Neocolonial Extractivism in Ghana

While direct colonization symbolically ended with 'flag independence', the exploitation, oppression and violent extractivism it engendered continued in what Wynter (2006: 107) described as the achievement of 'map emancipation' without 'territorial emancipation'. According to Tamale (2020: 34), many African countries have, since gaining political independence, entered into 'eco-colonial pacts' in which multinational corporations take over large tracts of Indigenous land. In the

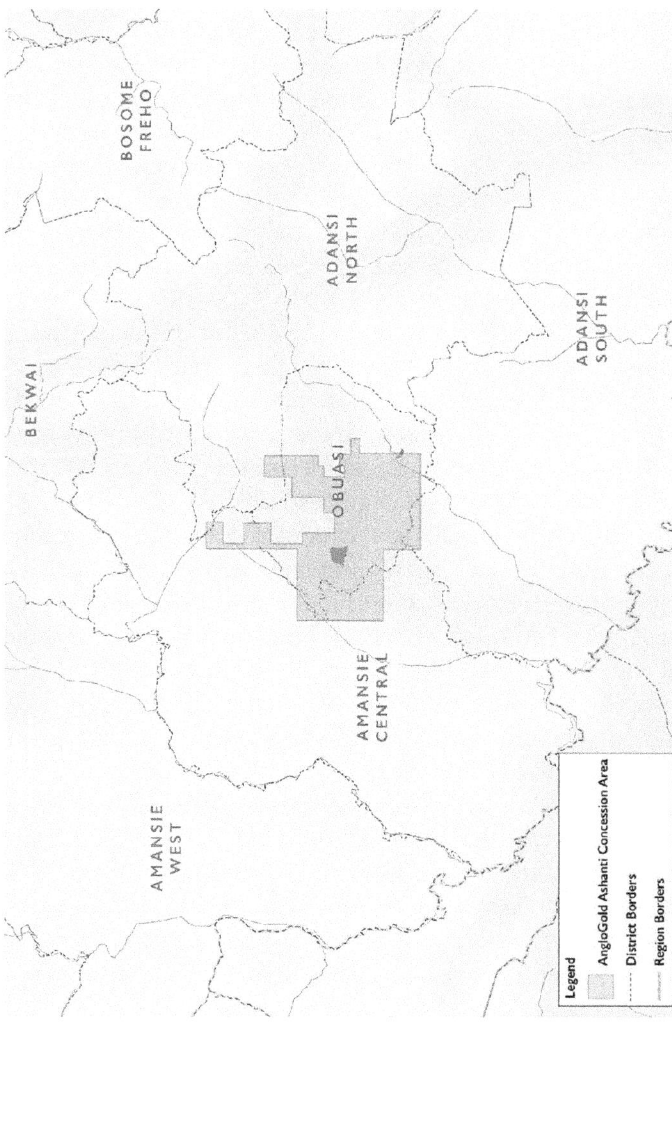

Figure 5.1. A map of Ghana showing the extent of AGA's concessions. © Linda Mensah.

context of ASM, this has resulted in a scarcity of areas for which local small-scale miners can obtain legal mining titles, because so much land is 'frozen' under exploration concessions by mining companies who may not actively use them for years. This happens to be the case with AGA, whose concessions currently cover five administrative districts in Ghana, including Obuasi Municipal, Bekwai Municipal, Amansie Central, Adansi North and Adansi South; most of this land has not yet been developed, and is projected not to be for a very long time to come.

Since Ghana attained political independence in 1957, there have been a number of attempts at reforming its land and mining administration. These notwithstanding, there are still many implicit and explicit legal and policy commitments attached to the colonially constructed structures. As postcolonial governments worked on dismantling the colonial government's mineral resource governance system, they became increasingly focused on gaining control over existing foreign-owned mining corporations, largely neglecting to consider Indigenous, small-scale mining as a result. During the first three years of independence, for instance, all seven major gold mines in the country were owned by foreign mining companies, and Nkrumah was said to have ignored calls for the introduction of measures that would enable Ghanaians to enter the mining field (Boahen 1975: 196). Instead, his government went out of its way to give grants and interests to expatriate mining companies that were not making much profit then, ostensibly in order to keep them in operation and thus prevent unemployment arising from the closure of the mines (Boahen 1975: 197).

By March 1961, Nkrumah had established the State Mining Corporation, through which he nationalized the entire mining industry, except for AGC's Obuasi mine and another one in Konongo. These mining sector reforms were facilitated by the introduction of the Mining Act of 1962, under which Nkrumah vested ownership of all mineral resources in the Presidency, for and on behalf of the people. By 1966, the Konongo mine was also nationalized. AGC's Obuasi mine remained privately owned, with the government taking a majority in the shareholding (Elbra 2017).

Nkrumah's move towards resource nationalism did not come as a surprise to anyone who had closely followed the events in the Gold Coast leading to political independence. Nkrumah strongly believed in a pan-African socialist society, and his resource nationalism was heavily informed by his distrust of the capitalist extractivism of foreign mining corporations, which he described as a betrayal of the personality and conscience of Africa (Nkrumah 1962: 74). Mining corporations maintained a close alliance with imperial expansionist projects and, later, showed strong opposition to independence and a desire to preserve their entrenched control over mineral resources in the colony. For instance, during his tenure as chairman of AGC, Major-General Edward Spears – who was known for his racist opinions and resistance to nationalism – referred to Nkrumah's Convention People's Party (CPP) as an extremist group and accused Nkrumah of trying to disrupt the country with his calls for immediate freedom from colonial rule.[1]

Despite his socialist leanings and policy of self-reliance, Nkrumah was unable to completely undo the colonial corporatist capture of the mining sector. Rather, Nkrumah ended up maintaining close ties with foreign mining interests and reinforcing the monist-pluralism of the eminent domain, whereby state sovereignty over mineral rights remained in service of capital (Taylor 2006). In effect, not only did Nkrumah's postcolonial government fail to address the inequities and ambiguities of AGC's 1897 agreement, but there was also no serious policy engagement with Indigenous, small-scale mining.

Ultimately, AGC was granted a new, fifty-year lease from 1 January 1969, with the government of Ghana, AGC and Lonrho Limited as parties to the lease. Following Nkrumah's deposition, a subsequent military government issued a National Redemption Council Decree (NRCD 132) to presumably capture the commanding heights of the economy, including the extractive industries dominated by large foreign enterprises. As with the previous government, these efforts did not aim to address the issues with Indigenous mining, but to forestall government ownership of the large-scale mines. NRCD 132 led to the cancellation of Lonrho's mining lease and the transfer of the company's assets to a new Ghanaian entity known as AGC (Ghana) Ltd, of which the state owned 55%, with the remaining 45% owned by Lonrho. In 1993, a mining licence was obtained for an additional 65 square miles, bringing AGC's total concession area to 190 square miles. NRCD 132 would eventually be repealed under Rawling's National Democratic Congress (NDC) government, who further granted AGC a new, thirty-year mining lease from 5 March 1994, for the original 1897 concession area and the contiguous plots that the corporation later acquired (Taylor 2006).

While these new lease agreements did not explicitly include the local chiefs as parties, there were arrangements for rent to be paid to the Adanse stool for ownership of the AGC concession in Obuasi, in acknowledgement of the precolonial customary land tenures. In contemporary times, customary lands remain an integral part of land ownership in Africa, where over 75% of land is covered by customary land tenures (Chirayath, Sage and Woolcock 2005). In Ghana, customary land tenures constitute the dominant form of land ownership, with over 80% of all land in the country falling under customary law (USAID 2012; Ghebru and Lambrecht 2017). Under the current legal pluralism, articles 36(8) and 267(1) of the 1992 Constitution provide constitutional recognition to customary land tenures by vesting all customary lands in the appropriate stool, skin or family, with the mandate for such lands to be managed in accordance with the fiduciary duty of the traditional authorities towards their people. This is further acknowledged under the new Land Act of 2020 (Act 1036).

In the spirit of the colonially inherited legal system, the Constitution makes room for state and public lands, which, as I established, emerged from the colonial government's legal impositions and experimentation with Indigenous territoriality. The eminent domain enables the government to compulsorily acquire all mineral-bearing lands as public lands to be administered under state-sanctioned orthodoxy. This has generated liberalized mining codes specifically designed to facilitate the attraction of foreign investment in the mining industry through large-scale concession grants, tax breaks and low-revenue payments (Campbell 2010). For instance, attempts to attract foreign investment into the mining industry led to the passage of the Minerals and Mining Law, 1986 (PNDCL 153), a result of numerous deliberations and policy amendments carried out shortly after the implementation of the country's 1983 Economic Recovery Programme, which was backed by the World Bank and the International Monetary Fund (Hilson 2013).

Despite these neoliberal structural adjustment policies and their emphasis on rolling back the state, the stronghold of state centralism in the extractive industry remained. This reflected the legitimation of state presence and its associated activities, which was based in no small part on historical experiences in colonized countries that established the association between formality and superiority (Banks, Lombard and Mitlin 2020: 230). Consequently, while local small-scale miners struggle to gain access to geologically productive lands for their operations, large-scale mining companies, by contrast, are able to almost effortlessly navigate this system in negotiating claims to large tracts of geologically productive land, with the help of both the state and traditional authorities. This is unsurprising, considering the fact that the legal and policy infrastructure of the entire mining industry was strategically established to cater to large-scale mining under the centralized oversight of a colonial government that inserted itself as the ultimate arbiter of mineral resource governance. However, these dominant circumstances do not go uncontested, as was the case with local resistance to the Lands Bills. In the next section, I explore these persistent resistances and consider local perceptions of ASM informality in contrast to the dominant narrative of the ASM legal framework.

ASM Formalization in Ghana: State Law as Inequality, and Local Perceptions of Legitimacy

The historical trajectory of monist-pluralism in Ghana's mining industry shows that state law hardly facilitated a level playing field for local small-scale miners. As demand for mineral-bearing lands soared, the state prioritized large-scale mines in land allocations, exacerbating inequalities in access to mineral-bearing lands. Over the past decades, this has been compounded by developments where neoliberalization and increased land commodification have birthed a 'new African land tenure' with significant impact for agriculture and the extractive industry (Chimhowu 2019: 897).

ASM formalization has turned out to be an exclusionary mechanism that has driven many small-scale miners into poverty, criminality and marginality. This follows from the colonial licensing of so-called 'native mining', which merely imposed more restrictive requirements and tax obligations on Indigenous, small-scale miners, without the commensurate state support in land and logistical advancement.

Challenging the rigid formal/informal binary is crucial to my interrogation of how the postcolonial state perpetuates this colonial legacy by using criminalization to regulate informal mining. It also highlights how local elites – motivated by class interests – encroach upon informal ASM spaces, blocking access to mineral rights for more marginalized and disadvantaged groups. This is apparent with the increasing number of Chinese mining firms in the Ghanaian ASM scene, a development widely known to be enabled by local politicians and other well-connected individuals who facilitate land acquisition and licences for their Chinese associates. These local actors are also known to assist their Chinese counterparts in evading the legal repercussions of their involvement in informal ASM, an opportunity that is hardly afforded to the low-waged, local small-scale miners.[2]

Furthermore, local ASM operators are left to navigate a prohibitively expensive and highly frustrating registration and licensing procedure. Take, for instance, the initial processing fee, which is said to cost about GHS 1,500 (approximately £80.82) for each concession. By the time the final licences are issued, applicants would have spent not less than a total of about GHS 5,000 (approximately £269.40). These figures do not even take into account the other unofficial fees and bribes that applicants are forced to pay to government officials to facilitate the registration process.[3] This is because, although applicants are not formally required to follow up their applications in Accra, many of them are forced to incur extra costs to do so due to the stagnating delays, stifling bureaucracies and corruption associated with Minerals Commission officials in Accra.[4] Thus, in addition to the huge costs, local miners also have to contend with a slow registration process that usually takes between six months and two years to complete.

It is this absorption of resource governance by the state and its concomitant bureaucracies, coupled with a lack of enthusiasm and political commitment in supporting local small-scale miners, that is believed to have given rise to informality in the ASM sector. According to a local small-scale miner:

> It is these same bureaucracies that have birthed the *galamsey*. If somebody is living in the community, working, planting his cocoa, and after digging the earth he finds a rock that contains gold, now he says, 'I don't want to do illegal mining, so I am going to go through the process'. But the money he has to pay, every process he passes through, and then the thing gets to Accra and after one year [the licence] has not returned. There's no way he will sit by the gold and go hungry. So that is precisely what birthed the *galamsey*.[5]

Hilson (2013: 54) remarked upon this phenomenon when he described ASM informality as a creation of state bureaucracy. Roy (2009: 819), too, had earlier concluded that informality did not lie beyond planning; rather, it was planning (by colonial and postcolonial state mechanisms) that led to informality.

For many in the local mining communities, ASM is the only means of surviving the harsh economic realities. Accordingly, the imposition of an expensive and bureaucratic formalization process in legitimating this livelihood opportunity is not perceived to be as empowering or liberating as the government and proponents of formalization make it out to be. Local miners do not view the system as offering any incentive for formalization, especially as they are forced to wait up to two years and pay huge registration costs to register their ASM operations, while simultaneously having to endure poverty that the government fails to address in their local communities. In one of my interviews, a local resident likened the perceived absurdity of formalization to the government asking people living by the riverside to refrain from drinking the waters on their own lands.[6] This was reiterated by another Obuasi resident, who quoted an Asante adage: 'One does not sit by the riverside and wash one's face with spittle'.[7] As the historical evidence has established, centuries of socioeconomically exclusionary policies and large-scale land grabs in Obuasi have left many without lands to farm or mine. As with the local resistance to the colonial Lands Bills, the perception that the government's legal requirements are merely means to deny locals access to benefits from ancestral lands only fuels resentment and opposition, even against well-intentioned state laws and intervention policies. This phenomenon further highlights the differences in local perspectives regarding law and legitimacy in the context of ASM.

While state bureaucrats and city-based environmentalist groups associate ASM informality with illegality, and denigrate informal small-scale miners as the source of all the environmental hazards associated with ASM, there are others in the local communities who view these miners as young men and women who are only trying to make a decent living. As Hilson (2013: 59) observed, Ghana's policymakers depict licensed small-scale gold miners in a very different light from *galamsey*. While policymakers commend the former, they generally hold a deeply negative – and often baseless – view of *galamsey* as being comparable to armed robbers and rapists; they even go so far as to use the media to associate *galamsey* operators with unrelated offences such as petty theft, racketeering and prostitution.

Granted, small-scale miners have long been locally stereotyped as environmentally irresponsible, womanizers, alcoholics, financially inept spendthrifts living hand-to-mouth, and susceptible to exploitative labour practices – especially during periods of low gold yields.[8] Some of the negative perceptions about small-scale miners also stem from their involvement in Indigenous spiritualities and their general physical appearance, particularly those who keep dreadlocked hairstyles that are usually associated with drug use, especially marijuana.[9] It is safe to say that this phenomenon is not restricted to ASM – contemporary discourse on the politics of black hair shows a deeply entrenched colonial legacy of disapproval for certain Afro and natural hairstyles that are deemed untidy in missionary/secondary schools and other professional settings.[10]

Notwithstanding these negative associations, there is a deep sense of acknowledgement regarding the contributions made by small-scale miners to the local economy. Many small-scale miners have built homes, sent their children and other family members to quality schools and provided for their families – all through their earnings from ASM.[11] In Obuasi, the recent ASM boom in the Akatakyieso village alone is said to have created job opportunities for over two thousand miners, some of whom are students working to pay their tuition fees.[12] Apart from making a living for themselves, small-scale miners in the Obuasi area are also known to contribute to the local communities by providing communal labour towards infrastructural developments such as the construction of CHPS (community health clinic) compounds, roads and schools.[13] Many of these small-scale miners have lived in the community for years and are regarded as respectable members of society. They are viewed as industrious people who wake up at the crack of dawn and trek long distances to undertake physically laborious duties, just to make ends meet. As a local chief put it, these are not people whose work should be associated with laziness or criminality.[14]

Accordingly, the general perception is that as long as small-scale miners are not resorting to stealing, violence, disturbing the peace and other socially disruptive behaviours, the community does not have any problems with their operations. Local small-scale miners are also content, as long as they have lands to work on. Their main grievance is when the government tries to 'knock their food out of their mouths', that is, to obstruct their means of livelihood by tagging them as 'illegal' and using the military to harass and evict them.[15] In summary, while there is acknowledgement and condemnation of the widespread environmental negativities surrounding ASM, there is also an understanding that it is a viable livelihood. One local chief quoted the Akan saying '*Efie biara Mensa wɔ mu*' ('In every household, there is a Mensa'), with the implication that every community or association has its own social deviants. This is to say that criminality is not exceptional to ASM, and while it cannot be denied that some small-scale miners may also be involved in socially deviant activities, it is unfair to generally criminalize the entire ASM sector and its participants.[16]

This further explains local dissatisfaction with state criminalization of ASM and militarized interventions against small-scale miners. The general consensus is that in absorbing ASM governance through formalization and emphasizing the negative environmental impact of the sector, the state is too far removed from the motivating factors and complex dynamics of ASM on the ground. As one Obuasi resident put it:

> Parliament sits and passes these laws without knowing what *galamsey* is all about. Our people in Accra don't understand what *galamsey* is about. They only speak big English and then pass big laws. Eventually the laws don't even work and then we are back to square one. They think it is just some greedy young men in the community destroying the environment. It goes beyond that. There are people whose livelihoods depend on it, so let's acknowledge these people. Let us find a way of giving them a livelihood, a livelihood that they themselves

can determine and will be happy with. There are also those who want to do the mining. Whether we like it or not, they still want to do mining.[17]

Poverty has long been cited by researchers as a central driving factor in ASM, a fact that governments continuously fail to consider in their law and policy directives. As a practising Ghanaian lawyer reiterated during our interview, until the underlying economic issues driving people into ASM are recognized and addressed, state law and its criminalization will continue to have little impact in deterring *galamsey*.[18] To that end, mining laws and policies need to be designed to address the gaping inequalities faced by local small-scale miners, instead of only serving the interests of large-scale mining companies and the political and traditional elites in the minority.[19]

The gaps and inconsistencies within the government's ASM laws and policies deepen the community's distrust of state absorption of ASM governance and its rationalization of criminalization. During an interview with me, a Ghanaian state prosecuting attorney revealed that the government had gone to great lengths to ensure the prosecution of informal miners, including assigning specific state attorneys to various regions to focus exclusively on prosecuting *galamsey* cases.[20] Even so, there were situations where cases involving *galamsey* operators with government ties ended up being 'foolish cases', as Ghanaians put it – cases that end in unfair acquittals, or are discontinued owing to prolonged court delays or the prosecution's disinterest in pursuing proceedings.[21]

Indeed, the general perception is that the state's criminalization of informal ASM and its use of militarized interventions amount to nothing more than a waste of national resources and a way for the government to create jobs for its affiliates through the establishment of multiple uncoordinated committees.[22] The Inter-Ministerial Committee on Small-Scale Mining, for instance, was established in 2017 to coordinate militarized evictions, and it comprised representatives from across the security agencies, ministries and regional security councils (Hilson 2017: 109). Disbanded in early 2021, this committee was distinct from the government committee established to coordinate the forfeiture and burning of excavators used by informal small-scale miners. When some of the seized excavators mysteriously disappeared from the government's outfits, yet another separate committee was established to investigate the matter (Donkor 2023). This multiplicity in state governance echoes the colonial monist-pluralism of the multiple ordinances that provoked public outcry during the Lands Bills debacle.

In addition to the widely publicized allegations of the extortion of small-scale miners by military personnel, the evidence further revealed instances of military personnel actively protecting *galamsey* operations run by persons affiliated with the ruling government – even exempting these operations from raids, arrests and forfeiture of equipment.[23] This is compounded by the fact that the military personnel were deployed without much consideration of, or consultation with, the people in the local communities. In Obuasi, residents spoke of their apprehensions at seeing heavily armed military personnel parading the streets, a traumatic reminder of the town's history of state violence, which has long been tied to corporate interests, and of periodic violent confrontations between small-scale miners and the security forces of the mining corporation.[24] I personally recall witnessing military personnel chasing *galamsey* operators and hearing gunshots in the background while I was driving through AGA's now-defunct Pompora Treatment Plant (PTP) on my way to visit family in Moinsi Valley, an AGA housing suburb in Obuasi. Local civil society organizations who raised objections to the militarized evictions were accused by government officials of causing fear and panic.[25] In Obuasi, members of the military's Operation Vanguard only attempted to engage with local media and civil society organizations after public reports emerged about their extortion activities and involvement in ASM, leading many locals to describe these attempts as mere face-saving publicity stunts.[26]

These exclusionary tactics remain a predominant feature of state absorption of ASM governance, especially for local miners who have consistently expressed to the government the futility of its militarized interventions. For local small-scale miners, any semblance of inclusion in state policy deliberations is often marred by the harsh reality of a lack of serious consideration of their input. As one local miner put it: 'As for engagement, they engage us. But your input – whether they will implement it or not, that is another question. As for the engagement, yes, but as for our input, no, they don't take it into consideration'.[27]

This accentuates the argument that the study of ASM informality is not just a study of poor or subaltern small-scale miners. As Banks, Lombard and Mitlin (2020: 232) put it, the poverty narrative of informality is deeply intertwined with inequalities in political power, economic opportunity and access to spatial resources, factors that determine who can speak, negotiate and be heard. It is therefore important for me to draw upon theories of intersectionality in examining the issues of ASM in their classed and racialized complexity.

Moreover, claims of ever-increasing environmental degradation from formal ASM operations reportedly owned by politicians and well-connected businessmen have led to further dissatisfaction with the state's criminalization of informal ASM as an environmental protection policy. As already established, there is a longstanding history of local scepticism regarding routinized state control over Indigenous lands under the aegis of environmental protection. In Obuasi, it does not help that many view the military deployments as not truly about protecting the environment, but a means for AGA to protect its concessions from small-scale miners. This is especially so given small-scale miners' argument that their operations involve hard-rock mining and not alluvial mining, which is arguably the main source of water pollution from ASM.[28] Indeed, local miners consider hard-rock gold mining to be less environmentally destructive compared to alluvial gold mining, for many reasons. While alluvial gold miners may exhaust their 25-acre concessions within just two months of operation, hard-rock miners are said to be able to operate on the same land size for nearly two to three years before moving on to the next concession. In Obuasi, small-scale miners divide each mining site into about two to three hundred different pits, with each pit being worked by around thirty people.[29]

The rigid state-imposed distinction between formalized (legal) and informal (illegal) ASM is accepted by formalized small-scale miners who are quick to dissociate themselves from the *galamsey* due to the stigma associated with the term, choosing rather to refer to themselves as 'small-scale miners'.[30] Formalized ASM operators pride themselves on being law-abiding citizens who comply with standard environmental protection measures in their mining activities. They distance themselves from the *galamsey*, whom they describe as 'nation-wreckers' responsible for all the water pollution, land degradation and other environmental hazards associated with ASM.[31]

Local perceptions of formalized miners, however, tell a different story. To begin with, there were complaints that some formalized ASM operators commenced their activities in the local communities without any prior consultation or engagement with the chiefs and the local people. Furthermore, most formalized ASM operators were seen as worse perpetrators of environmental havoc than the informal *galamsey* operators. The protection afforded to formalized ASM operators by state licences often meant that the chiefs and local people had no power or authority in confronting them over their blatant impunity in committing environmental harm. This was compounded by the fact that state agencies like the Environmental Protection Authority (EPA) and the Minerals Commission were seen as turning a blind eye to these environmental improprieties.[32] These factors account for the resistance displayed by some communities, who have actively organized to drive formalized ASM operators away from their areas. Some residents admitted to preferring the *galamsey* over formalized ASM operators, mostly because the latter were seen as extractive and detached from the community, whereas the *galamsey* were often locals or migrant workers with stronger ties to the local community.[33]

The evidence further suggests that the eminent domain – the principle by which the state vests all mineral rights in itself – is generally viewed as a problematic colonial legacy and the singular source of conflict in the Ghanaian mining sector. The prevailing legal framework recognizes the customary authority of chiefs with respect to stool lands, but does not allow them power to grant mineral rights in the land; this plurality of authority is considered to be a controversial, bureaucratic principle that needs to be deconstructed.[34] Indeed, some chiefs found it absurd that the state had sole authority in administering mineral rights and their associated revenue, while they and their people were left to bear the brunt of poverty and food insecurity, as well as the cultural, social and environmental repercussions of the mining activities in their local communities.[35]

The gap between local perceptions of ASM informality and the dominant state narrative of ASM illegality is further understood when one considers that much of the mainstream depiction of *galamsey* is propagated by media houses based in the major cities of Accra and Kumasi. Certainly, local communities are concerned about the alarming environmental pollution arising from highly mechanized ASM operations in their communities; in some cases, they do also support deterrence in the form of militarized raids and criminalization.[36] Of even greater concern to them, however, is the media's fixation on the negative environmental impact of ASM – for example, Citi TV's #StopGalamseyNow campaign – and its comparative silence regarding the environmental hazards perpetuated by large-scale mining corporations. As one local media personnel put it:

> We have legal mining companies carrying out illegal activities in Ghana here. AGA is causing harm to some people. Where I am you cannot even drink the water here. Has Citi TV come to campaign again? Now there's a dam just behind my house. There's an AGA dam there. Anytime it rains it floods the school, which is just below where the dam is. What have you heard about it? What have they done about it?[37]

In Obuasi, a local chief gave an account of polluted waters, houses being wrecked by cracks resulting from AGA's rock-blasting, and injuries sustained by local people due to boulders falling from the blasted hills, none of which make mainstream news.[38] While local small-scale miners struggle to find lands to operate, some large-scale mining companies and formalized ASM operators are able to disregard local customs and cause severe environmental damage without any significant state intervention. Waterbodies that hold spiritual significance for local communities are often entirely redirected or heavily polluted during the mining process; such desecration of the rivers forces the communities to stop performing their rituals. Consequently, the local mining communities do not only lose access to their rivers as a source of drinking water, but are also denied access to the cultural essence and ritual value of these rivers. This, according to Schmidt (2014), has significant implications for the fundamental human, cultural and religious rights of these communities. As I have demonstrated, the politics of mining pollution in Ghana reflects a pattern where the *galamsey* are disproportionately blamed for environmental harm, while that caused by large-scale mining and formalized ASM remains overlooked in mainstream media and by state bureaucrats.

Another reason for the local distrust of ASM formalization involves its consultative methods. The participatory processes by which local communities are required to be informed of prospective ASM operations only make provisions for notices (drafted in the English language) to be circulated in the Gazette, in newspapers and at the offices of local government authorities. These are of little practical relevance to communities who are predominantly illiterate in the English language, and where residents do not typically visit local assembly and municipal buildings simply to read notices. As an Obuasi resident commented, 'When it comes to the concessions, [the law] says that the notice has to be posted at the district assembly for about twenty-one working days. Ask yourself: how many people go to the district assembly to read what's on the noticeboard?'[39]

In contrast to these methods, local information systems – such as community information centres, local radio stations and traditional mechanisms used by local chiefs – offer wider coverage and constitute more realistic and effective mediums through which the government could engage with local miners and mining communities.[40] This lack of consideration in the state's communication of intentions and ideologies to local communities does not only violate the local people's right to relevant environmental information, but is also reminiscent of the colonial government's policy of notification through the use of gazettes, despite its inaccessibility to a large Indigenous population. As was noted in *The Gold Coast Chronicle* (16 October 1897: 4), the Aborigines' Rights Protection Society (ARPS), which was integral to local resistance against the colonial Lands Bills, was particularly critical of the colonial government's publication of notices and legislations in the Gazette. This explains why the ARPS took it upon themselves to study, interpret and explain gazetted laws to the local people.[41]

Just like in colonial times, state-sanctioned resource extractivism continues to function not as a regenerative system, but as a culturally, socially and economically exploitative field that prioritizes the market profit of a few classed people over communal interests. This phenomenon presents a classic reminder of Audre Lorde's (1984) statement that 'the master's tools will never dismantle the master's house'. This underscores the need to critically examine state-centric control over mineral rights governance as a system built on colonial violence, heightened policing, carcerality, Indigenous dispossession and restrictions on local miners, rather than an effective framework that redresses injustices and provides equal access and opportunities for mining communities that have been historically marginalized and exploited.

Navigating ASM Informality and Corporate Resource Extractivism in Obuasi

As a result of their empirical inquiry into the relationship between ASM and surface land tenure arrangements in the Philippines, Liberia and the Democratic Republic of Congo, Verbrugge, Cuvelier and Van Bockstael (2015) observed that environments characterized by fragmented state machinery and weak enforcement of formal tenurial regimes often gave rise to other forms of informal, shadow governance systems. While their empirical analysis was drawn from mostly post-war contexts, the situation in Ghana demonstrates that, post-conflict or not, many mineral-producing countries of the Global South have proven themselves unable – and, in some cases, unwilling – to effectively wield their hegemonic power over mineral resources in addressing the issues associated with ASM (Rosen 2020).

Under these circumstances, small-scale miners resort to acquiring lands through informal negotiations with customary landowners. The rights acquired are usually leases, as the customary landowners do not grant absolute alienation but retain the reversionary interest as soon as the ASM operation is completed (Verbrugge, Cuvelier and Van Bockstael 2015; Nyame and Blocher 2010). These negotiations and subsequent agreements are usually conducted without the involvement of lawyers or written contracts. Under this informal system, conveyance is completed by a transfer of interest in the land once the parties have verbally agreed on key terms, including the land involved, the price, the date for full payment of rent, the date of transfer, the period of occupation, as well as other matters relating to the reversion of interests to the transferor. The parties do not follow any statutory timelines for the completion of the transaction; rather, they set their own, and may agree on a reasonable timeline for completion of the transaction. There is therefore more room to frame the agreement to suit their convenience (Lodoh 2002).

Earlier ethnographic analysis from other African countries has noted that in order for informal miners to be able to mine peacefully within a particular community, it is necessary for them to obtain the permission of the landowner, or that of at least one influential community member who can provide assurance to the community at large (Jong and Sauerwein 2021). This reflects the practice of small-scale miners in Obuasi, who typically initiate land negotiations by approaching the local chiefs or other customary landowners. The parties generally show respect for the chieftaincy hierarchy by notifying the relevant subchiefs and divisional chiefs who have direct jurisdiction over the land in question.[42] All relevant local chiefs are involved as customary witnesses, ensuring that in case of a dispute, the chiefs can rightfully intervene to settle the matter. Informal small-scale miners and local customary landowners may not have the opportunity to access justice in the formal court system when their constitutionally prohibited transactions end up in dispute. They do, however, have recourse to informal means of dispute resolution; these are more beneficial to them because they do not entail the legal technicalities, filings, payments and bureaucracies of the state court system. Often, such conflicts are resolved with the assistance of chiefs, elders and leaders of the informal miners' groups serving as mediators or arbitrators.[43]

Social practices are shaped by participants' perceptions of their legal context. Accordingly, although the Ghanaian Constitution and the Minerals and Mining Act prohibit the granting of mineral rights except through state-authorized agencies, many people in mining communities such as Obuasi regard their informal allocation of land for ASM as constituting definitive and legitimate transfers. In my interviews with them, some local chiefs admitted that prior to the government's ASM ban, they used to grant lands for ASM operations through verbally negotiated arrangements, despite their awareness of the doctrine of eminent domain and the state's monopoly over mineral rights grants.

While it offers flexibility and ease of transaction, the informal approach to customary land negotiation also renders contracting parties immensely vulnerable (Lodoh 2002). Customary landowners who negotiate for payment based on percentage of proceeds instead of upfront rents may find themselves without any remuneration in the event that the small-scale miners abscond and renege on their part of the bargain.[44] As already established, prospective ASM operators practically conduct their own prospecting, given the lack of technical or logistical support from the government. Faced with significant financial constraints, many informal miners are unable to undertake thorough investigation to ascertain the geological productivity of the land. This, in turn, translates into economic uncertainties, which can further result in little to no returns for local customary landowners who negotiate for payment based on percentage of proceeds.

For informal small-scale miners whose operations traverse state criminality, obtaining lands directly from customary landowners may be a great business risk. However, under the current circumstances, it is the only option for many of them. Most of these local miners do not possess customary interest in mineral-bearing lands even as indigenes; this, in addition to AGA's ownership of virtually all the geologically productive lands in Obuasi, has meant that local small-scale miners face extreme difficulties in securing access to mineral-bearing lands for their operations. Additionally, despite some of them having years of local knowledge in ASM, many of the youth are deemed unemployable by the mining corporation due to their lack of formal education. Consequently, it is not uncommon for local miners to negotiate access to lands with chiefs, local farmers and other customary landowners to commence their own mining operations.[45]

Through this informal approach, local miners and customary landowners are able to navigate a monist-pluralism where formality is inextricable from political and economic power in undermining customary systems and denying small-scale miners access to benefits from the land. Bryceson (2018: 31) described this as the frontier democracy in artisanal mining, wherein miners exercise agency independent of the state in the pursuit of mining, with scope for collective self-governance and political activity. Here, informality becomes a survival mechanism and a form of resistance, as local informal miners and customary landowners bypass the eminent domain, rather than succumb to its exclusions, in order to benefit from the abundant mineral resources in their local communities.

In Ghana, small-scale miners navigate the complex monist-pluralism of the mining regime through their own cooperatives and social organizations, including the Ghana National Association of Small-Scale Miners (GNASSM), which is organized in zones and districts across the country. Members in the Obuasi zone fall under the Dunkwa district, which encompasses six other zones: New Edubiase, Bekwai, Jacobu, Dunkwa, Duaso and Amansie West.[46] GNASSM is largely constituted of formalized ASM operators, and is run by duly elected executives and taskforces who work to oversee tax payments, the distribution of mine pits, the maintenance of health, safety and environmental standards, profit distribution and other relevant aspects of their operations.[47] There are also other small-scale miners who operate informally, either individually or in groups independent of the GNASSM. With the exception of state licensing, both formalized and informal ASM operators rely on virtually the same informal relations in their ASM activities. Financing is usually provided not by banks, but by private sponsors who facilitate the acquisition of lands and equipment, the payment of wages for hired workers and the negotiation of benefit-sharing arrangements (Nyame and Grant 2014).

Indigenous spiritualities also remain an important factor in ASM. As I mentioned in the Introduction, gold is believed to possess a sacred aura in Akan folklore; it is also a symbol of royal splendour and spiritual power. Within this belief system, gold has magical properties and is a living organism that can move through the ground and pop up anywhere like quicksilver (Dumett 1998: 60). These ideas were confirmed by local chiefs and community members, who reiterated the importance of obtaining the blessing of the gods prior to embarking on an ASM expedition – this is done by pouring libations and praying to the gods to release the gold, as well as to seek protection, health, safety and good fortune for all the miners involved. Customs are also strictly observed, with transgressions punishable by accident or injury. One such custom is the *dabɔne*, a sacred day when no mining or other form of work on the land is permitted – in Adanse communities, the *dabɔne* falls on Tuesdays. Furthermore, women in Obuasi are forbidden from approaching many of the mine pits because menstruation is associated with uncleanliness, and any shedding of blood near the pits would be considered a defilement of sacred soil.[48] According to Dumett (1998: 61), early European traders rationalized these taboos as mere attempts by local chiefs to deliberately scare off intruders and prevent European fortune seekers from learning the locations of their most valuable gold mines.

Despite its age-old history of gold mining, Obuasi continues to experience sporadic booms in ASM as more small-scale miners push the frontiers of their operations into rural communities where mining occurs in offshoot camps popularly known as 'ghettos'.[49] The *galamsey* in Obuasi are highly mobile, going wherever the gold is. For instance, at the time of this research, many of the *galamsey* were working in Akrokerri and Akatakyieso, where gold had recently been discovered by small-scale miners.[50] Informal ASM in Obuasi is mostly carried out using the hard-rock mining method, by a heterogenous mix of Indigenous and migrant miners.[51] In addition to negotiating access to mineralized lands through customary land tenures, *galamsey* operators in Obuasi are also widely known to operate on AGA's concessions. These occur at popular sites across Ahansonyewodea, Anwiam, Aduaneede, Akrokerri, Akatakyieso, Amamom and Anyankyerem. The *galamsey* operators are also known to operate from Kokoteasua, Abompekrom, defunct AGA treatment plants such as PTP, and a location known as Kodor, which the local miners refer to as their 'World Bank' due to the richness of the site.[52] The Kokoteasua site was one of AGA's oldest and richest concessions. When it was decommissioned several decades ago, local miners took over the site, only to be driven away by the corporation.

Several attempts by AGA to secure its propertied concessions – such as installing fencing, deploying guard dogs and private security and collaborating with state security agencies – have done little to keep away the *galamsey*.[53] The ongoing disputes over mineralized lands in Obuasi carry on a history of clashes, injuries and fatalities in the local community as resulting from a combination of factors including the market economy, violent state intervention and the displacement of Indigenous communities. Just like its colonial-era predecessor, which, as mentioned by *The Gold Coast Aborigines* (23 July 1898: 4), operated its own Mine Police and deployed arms in protecting its concessions and intimidating the local population, the AGA of today has been known to leverage its economic influence in obtaining both private security and state military forces to safeguard its concessions from the *galamsey*. In 2017, it was revealed that AGA was operating a clandestine private detention facility where trespassing *galamsey* operators were detained and tortured (Ellimah 2017: 172).[54] Many local chiefs in the Obuasi area are afraid to openly criticize these human-rights violations because of the corporation's colonial-era lease over large parts of Obuasi, and also because of their dependency on AGA for royalties and other amenities such as schools, roads and free electricity in their communities.[55] Enabled by the market economy, state indifference to local welfare and support from its politico-military apparatus, colonial forces continue to undermine local peoples' rights and their traditional authority.

A breakthrough in addressing this centuries-old land contestation seemed to have been achieved in 2016, following AGA's mine closure in 2014. The mine closure kickstarted conversations about the future of Obuasi and the need to refashion an economy that is not primarily centred around AGA's presence in the community. These discussions were spearheaded by local civil society organizations, with one of the outcomes being a proposal to support local industries such as ASM. A Movement Committee was formed as a result of stakeholder consultations organized with the support of the United Nations Development Programme (UNDP), Third World Network, AGA officials, small-scale miners' groups in Obuasi and government officials. This committee successfully negotiated for AGA to cede 60% of its concessions to local small-scale miners. A significant portion of these concessions had been unexploited, and it was anticipated that the mine would be unable to cover its extent for a long time to come.[56] Following this announcement, the local civil society organizations took the opportunity to organize the small-scale miners into more structured cooperatives in preparation for the new developments. Many small-scale miners received training in the safe use of mercury, health and safety measures and other technical skills through overseas courses and programmes offered by Ghana's University of Mines and Technology in Tarkwa.[57] In Obuasi, such cohabitation arrangements are not new, as colonial records point to several instances where AGA's predecessor, AGC, allowed local private miners to work the corporation's concessions and to be paid once successful results were achieved. According to Taylor (2006), the colonial government at one time allowed Indigenous miners to operate on the parts of AGC's concessions that were not actively being worked, with the condition that the mine could take over these areas at any time without providing compensation to the local miners.

Unfortunately, the small-scale miners discovered that large portions of the concessions ceded under the recent AGA arrangement were geologically unproductive.[58] Moreover, all the hard work came to nought following the 2016 general elections, when the newly elected New Patriotic Party (NPP) government put the entire negotiated arrangement on hold and rather launched its vicious war on *galamsey*, once again proving how state incursion into ASM governance often frustrates the interests of local miners on the ground.

Conclusion

In this chapter, I have traced the ongoing colonialities within Ghanaian ASM, with a specific focus on how informal miners in the historic gold-mining town of Obuasi navigate criminality and colonially inherited legal limitations. As Nkrumah (1963) rightly stated, colonialism and its attitudes die hard, and a colonial hangover still informs behaviour in certain parts of the Western hemisphere, with dire implications for formerly colonized societies. This chapter has built on the historical analysis in the previous chapter to demonstrate the enduring nature of colonial monist-pluralism and the implications of its capitalist processes on local miners. The difference in state and local perceptions of informal ASM also highlights the blurred distinction between formality/legality and informality/illegality. As the empirical evidence shows, this distinction is subject to negotiation and contestation in ways that challenge the state's tendency to uphold a rigid dichotomy between formality and informality. More importantly, in this chapter I have shown how ASM has survived and navigated these colonialities through its use of the living customary law, a fact that underscores the need to rethink the state's central and controlling role in administering claims to mineral rights.

Notes

1. CO/96/684/4; Address given by Major-General Edward L. Spears, board chairman of the Ashanti Goldfields Corporation, at the 53rd Ordinary General Meeting held in London on 12 May 1948. Published in the *Financial Times*, 15 May 1950.
2. Efe Blankson (alias), Ghanaian legal practitioner. Interview with the author, 5 April 2021.
3. The conversion was calculated based on the exchange rate as of January 2025.
4. Kofi Anokye (alias), Obuasi small-scale miner. Interview with the author, 4 February 2021.
5. Ibid.
6. Haruna Asana (alias), Obuasi resident and local media personnel. Interview with the author, 10 March 2021.
7. Kwame Ampem (alias), Obuasi resident and local civil society executive. Interview with the author, 19 March 2021.
8. Haruna Asana (alias), Obuasi resident and local media personnel. Interview with the author, 10 March 2021.
9. Local chief who opted for anonymity. Interview with the author, 14 July 2021.
10. For a recent case involving high-school students who were refused admission into Ghana's Achimota School on the grounds of their natural dreadlocked hair, see Justice Agbenorsi (2021), 'Achimota Ordered to Admit Rasta Students', *Graphic News*, 31 May. https://www.graphic.com.gh/news/general-news/rastafarian-student-wins-case-against-achimota-shs-school-ordered-to-admit-rasta-students.html accessed 4 January 2023.
11. Local chief who opted for anonymity. Interview with the author, 14 July 2021.
12. Nana Kofi Berkyi Ababio, chief of Akrokerri. Interview with the author, Akrokerri, 17 July 2021.
13. Nana Boaten, chief of Amamiriwa No. 2. Interview with the author, Amamiriwa No. 2, 4 July 2021.

14. Nana Gyamerah Kwabena Oyiakwan II, chief of Kwapia. Interview with the author, Kwapia, 7 September 2021.
15. Nii Obodai (alias), local civil society executive. Interview with the author, 16 April 2021.
16. Nana Boaten, chief of Amamiriwa No. 2. Interview with the author, Amamiriwa No. 2, 4 July 2021.
17. Nii Obodai (alias), local civil society executive. Interview with the author, 16 April 2021.
18. Kwabena Bentum (alias), Ghanaian lawyer. Interview with the author, 24 February 2021.
19. Ibid.
20. Ama Dede (alias), Ghanaian state prosecutor. Interview with the author, 8 April 2021.
21. Efe Blankson (alias), Ghanaian legal practitioner. Interview with the author, 5 April 2021.
22. Kwame Ampem (alias), Obuasi resident and local civil society executive. Interview with the author, 19 March 2021.
23. Nii Obodai (alias), local civil society executive. Interview with the author, 16 April 2021.
24. Ibid.
25. Ibid.
26. Ibid.
27. Kofi Anokye (alias), Obuasi small-scale miner. Interview with the author, 4 February 2021.
28. Kwame Ampem (alias), Obuasi resident and local civil society executive. Interview with the author, 19 March 2021. See also Chapter 1, where this point was confirmed by Hilson and Maconachie (2020c) in their extensive overview of militarized conservatism in the fight against ASM.
29. Kofi Anokye (alias), Obuasi small-scale miner. Interview with the author, 4 February 2021.
30. Ibid.
31. Ibid. As established in Chapter 1, this aligns with the depiction in ASM literature of the social and environmental ills of ASM as being 'expressions of informality'.
32. Nana Kofi Berkyi Ababio, chief of Akrokerri. Interview with the author, Akrokerri, 17 July 2021.
33. Dzifa Hormenu (alias), early-career ASM researcher. Interview with the author, 10 February 2021.
34. Nene Okwei (alias), early-career historian and extractive-industry researcher. Interview with the author, 11 February 2021.
35. Nana Kwadwo Asamoah, chief of Adaase. Interview with the author, Adaase, 22 July 2021.
36. Kwame Ampem (alias), Obuasi resident and local civil society executive. Interview with the author, 19 March 2021.
37. Haruna Asana (alias), Obuasi resident and local media personnel. Interview with the author, 10 March 2021.
38. Local chief who opted for anonymity. Interview with the author, 14 July 2021.
39. Haruna Asana (alias), Obuasi resident and local media personnel. Interview with the author, 10 March 2021.
40. Ibid.
41. In many African mineral-producing regions, this colonial-era, corporatized, detached model of community engagement remains common practice in community consultations conducted as part of regulations for the assessment of environmental impact. A recent example can be seen in the Shell Seismic Survey case (*Sustaining the Wild Coast*

NPC & 6 others v Minister of Mineral Resources and Energy & 4 others [High Court, Eastern Cape Division, Grahamstown Case No. 3491/2021]).

42. Nana Kwabena Nyame, chief of Amamiriwa No. 1. Interview with the author, Amamiriwa No. 1, 10 July 2021.
43. This was confirmed by all six local chiefs interviewed in Obuasi.
44. Kofi Anokye (alias), Obuasi small-scale miner. Interview with the author, 4 February 2021.
45. Nii Obodai (alias), local civil society executive. Interview with the author, 16 April 2021.
46. Kofi Anokye (alias), Obuasi small-scale miner. Interview with the author, 4 February 2021.
47. Ibid.
48. Ibid.
49. Nii Obodai (alias), local civil society executive. Interview with the author, 16 April 2021.
50. Nana Kofi Berkyi Ababio, chief of Akrokerri. Interview with the author, Akrokerri, 17 July 2021.
51. Nana Kwadwo Asamoah, chief of Adaase. Interview with the author, 22 July 2021.
52. Haruna Asana (alias), Obuasi resident and local media personnel. Interview with the author, 10 March 2021.
53. Local chief who opted for anonymity. Interview with the author, 14 July 2021.
54. This was further confirmed by Nii Obodai (alias), local civil society executive. Interview with the author, 16 April 2021.
55. Local chief who opted for anonymity. Interview with the author, 14 July 2021.
56. Nii Obodai (alias), local civil society executive. Interview with the author, 16 April 2021.
57. Kwame Ampem (alias), Obuasi resident and local civil society executive. Interview with the author, 19 March 2021.
58. Kofi Anokye (alias), Obuasi small-scale miner. Interview with the author, 4 February 2021.

CHAPTER 6

Reclaiming the Past

Chieftaincy, ASM and the Decolonial Reimagination of Indigenous Mineral Governance

Introduction

Ongoing debates over the involvement of chiefs in perpetuating ASM informality and its environmental hazards continue to inform local perceptions about customary institutions as well as key government policy responses to ASM. Having established the plurality of Ghana's legal system and the colonial legacies in ASM formalization, I now turn to the prevailing institutional pluralism, focusing on chieftaincy as a key feature of informal ASM. The chieftaincy system in Ghana has evolved over the years, as successive colonial and postcolonial governments have sought to sidestep the authority of chiefs and to divest them of their political and economic strength. This is further complicated by chiefs whose visibility was marked by their willing collaboration with empire.

In this chapter, I discuss growing concerns about the connections between chieftaincy, rentier politics and elite capture within customary land administration. These connections have huge implications for ASM, where informality thrives on lands facilitated by local chiefs and other customary landowners. I argue that ongoing discussions in the literature on chieftaincy reveal how scholarship on topics affecting Indigenous institutions is often Eurocentric, which highlights the need to move away from Northern epistemologies on these subjects. In addressing these issues, I argue that chieftaincy as an institution must prioritize Indigenous African epistemologies and knowledge systems. An Afrocentric perspective on chieftaincy is imperative, not only because of how the institution has been historically manipulated and criticized, but also because of its potential to address the unique challenges of ASM formalization.

It is for this reason that I once again propose *Sankɔfa* as a radical philosophy for decolonizing theorizations about chieftaincy, particularly as it is meaningfully extended to the ASM context. Given the historical association of *Adinkra* symbols with chiefly regalia, there is no better lens through which to examine the institution than the *Adinkra* symbol of *Sankɔfa* (Britwum 1974). In keeping with *Sankɔfa*'s principle of retreating into the past, the first section of this chapter will provide an overview of precolonial Asante chieftaincy and its accountability mechanisms. In the second to fifth sections, I address how colonial legal pluralism – particularly through its system of indirect rule and formalization of chieftaincy – undermined traditional sociopolitical structures, which ultimately weakened the chiefs' authority over mineral resource governance and institutionalized a form of social differentiation that foregrounded resource extractivism and new forms of customary land tenure.

In the sixth section, I reflect upon the enduring nature of chieftaincy in the present-day postcolonial nation-state, outlining the key position it currently occupies in ASM as a result of the vacuum created by Ghana's partisan politics and the institutional deficiencies of the state. This is followed by an examination, in the seventh section, of the debates surrounding the role of chiefs in customary land administration and ASM. In the eighth section, I address critiques of the chieftaincy system; in doing so, I highlight concerns about the abuse of power and the government's exclusionary policies, which reinforce colonial hierarchies by only granting authority to paramount chiefs despite the important role played by subchiefs and *adekurofo* (headmen) in the local mining communities.

This analytical framework will guide my focused examination of chieftaincy in the Adanse Traditional Area, where Obuasi is located, as well as of its implications for Indigenous mining and customary land administration in the mining community. With a view to both the past and the present, *Sankɔfa* inspires a reorientation and construction of a future suitably moulded by Africans for themselves. In the ninth section, I pursue this futuristic reimagination by first problematizing the critiques of chieftaincy from a decolonial perspective, particularly highlighting how colonialism created and exacerbated the complexities of the role of chiefs in land and ASM governance. This leads to my evaluation, in the tenth section, of the government's latest Community Mining Scheme (CMS), an institutional attempt to remedy the ailing regulatory and policy framework of ASM. Here, I dissect the shortcomings of this state initiative as yet another squandered opportunity to relinquish state hegemony for communality, traditional knowledges, chiefly inclusion and the living customary law – crucial components for transformational ASM governance. I thus call attention to the need for a paradigm shift in knowledge production surrounding chieftaincy, especially where Indigenous ventures like ASM are involved. In the final section, I establish my deployment of *Sankɔfa* as a decolonial lens through which I emphasize a reimagination of the institution of chieftaincy, with the ultimate goal of reclaiming Indigenous knowledges relevant for reforming institutional governance in ASM.

Chieftaincy in Asante: A Historical Overview

Historically, chieftaincy in Asante was determined by a lineage-based system, which understood human beings to be composed of two principles: the *mogya* (blood), which is inherited from one's mother, and the *ntorɔ* (spirit), which is derived from one's father. One's lineage comprises men and women who trace their descent through the matrilineal line to a common female ancestor. For many Akan people, this matrilineal bond is of great political and cultural significance because it determines succession to property and to political offices such as chiefship (Busia 1951).

Communal life was centred around this system of lineage. The broader Asante society was composed of individual villages, each comprising multiple lineages that constituted the local political unit. Chieftaincy was woven into the social and cultural fabric of the land, with the family head at the base of the traditional political hierarchy and the paramount chief at its apex. Generally, Asante society was politically categorized into three fundamental levels, namely, the village, the *Ɔmansin* (division) and the *Ɔman* (state), each with its respective governing council (Brempong 2001). Each village was overseen by an *odikuro* (local headman), who was selected from one of the lineages. The *odikuro* and the heads of the other lineages formed the council, which discussed and managed the affairs of the village. Within an established decentralized system of sociopolitical organization, the *adekurofo* (headmen) served as the official representatives or spokesmen through whom the chief communicated his orders (Busia 1951: 63). This decentralized system involved a hierarchy of divisional chiefs, subchiefs and *adekurofo*, all of whom were accountable to the paramount chief. In Asante, the *Asantehene* ruled as sovereign over individual states that each had their own paramount chief, divisional chiefs, subchiefs and *adekurofo* (Brobbey 2008).

As already established, land and gold were central to the office of Asante chiefs, who exercised judicial, political and military authority over these resources. During the historical period of recurrent intra- and interethnic conflict, chiefs fought wars to extend their frontiers and to defend the mineral wealth in their lands from external aggression (Seini 2006; Nukunya 2016). They also served as gatekeepers of the gold mines, working to prevent prying foreigners from learning their mine locations, overseeing the exaction of revenue from the mines, resolving conflicts, mobilizing mineral resources for community development and ensuring the maintenance of proper environmental standards through the use of established Indigenous knowledge systems (Acquah 2006; Boateng, Afranie and Amoah 2016).

These chiefly responsibilities regarding land and mineral resources were guided by several accountability mechanisms, the most significant of which was rooted in the Indigenous spirituality of the Asante people and their reverence for the ancestors. A chief's authority was based on the belief that he mediated between the community and the divine; his leadership was thus legitimized by its relationship with the spiritual realm. The political, judicial, military and administrative position held by a chief was considered sacred because he occupied the stool of the ancestors, who were believed to be constantly watching him, and to whom he would be accountable after his death. This served as a potent guarantor of morality and dutifulness in his office (Busia 1951: 25).[1] As occupants of the stool, chiefs were by custom charged with the responsibility of guardianship over the land and its mineral wealth for both the living and the dead. The sanctity of the office was emphasized by the rituals attached to the enstoolment proceedings, during which the observance of certain customs was obligatory to ensure that the reign of the incoming chief was not jeopardized (Akrong 2006). A chief who abused his power or failed to secure the wellbeing of the people and the land was divested of not only his position, but also his special connection with the ancestors as established during his enstoolment (Busia 1951: 37).

Other accountability measures ensured that levies, services, tributes and other revenue from stool lands and mineral resources were not used for the personal enrichment of the chief but deposited into the stool treasury to enable him to fulfil his official obligations. While chiefs were customarily expected to make use of stool property to maintain themselves in a manner befitting the dignity of the stool, they were also under strict obligation to avoid waste, and to use part of the property income to acquire additional property for the stool, towards the general welfare of the people. Relatedly, Asante people had a customary principle preventing chiefs from holding personal property while in office. This was an additional measure to ensure the accountability and total focus of the chief in preserving the lands and resources for the benefit of his people. Because chiefs could not own land in a private capacity, everything owned by an incoming chief became stool property upon their assumption of the position. According to Ollenu (1962: 43), some communities permitted their chiefs to hold personal property; however, this was conditional upon making a mandatory declaration of all self-acquired property to the elders upon election to the stool. Failure to do so resulted in the merging of all such property in the stool, where it would be subject to the same rules as any other stool property. Over time, further exceptions were made, permitting individuals to continue their own businesses – to the knowledge of the elders – and to retain said businesses and any consequent assets acquired as personal rather than stool property.

The established system of participatory governance was central to traditional accountability measures in the chiefly administration of land and minerals in Asante. A chief was bound by tradition to periodically consult with his council on all matters, and to act only upon their advice – although he was permitted on rare occasions, such as in an emergency, to act on his own initiative (Busia 1951). This strict constitutional injunction was so important that it was ingrained in the enstoolment process, where chiefs were made to swear their allegiance to this mandate. According to Busia (1951), the efficiency of Asante constitutionalism depended on chiefs acting with the concurrence and advice of their elders. The council of elders was also hereditary in nature, and together with the chief, it formed the government, who – along with the priests/priestesses – performed the necessary rituals and sacrifices for the welfare of the people, and ensured that law and order were maintained.

The persistent refusal of a chief to consult or act upon the advice of the elders was grounds for removal from office (destoolment). This consultative directive and the constitutional practice of destoolment constituted vital checks on chiefly authority ensuring that the will of the people was given utmost consideration by the occupant of the stool in the performance of his legislative, judicial and executive functions (Busia 1951: 21). These conditions were largely upheld in Asante until after 1896, when British annexation weakened the entire system of chieftaincy. Having witnessed snippets of precolonial chieftaincy in Asante, early British diplomats like Bowdich and missionaries like Freeman noted instances where all the chiefs from the various Asante states would be called to the capital, Kumasi, to consider important proposals affecting the entire kingdom – these concerned matters including festivals, community development and foreign policy, particularly diplomatic relations with the British.[2] At such meetings, each chief had an equal voice, and the weight of his opinion depended on his rank and status rather than on the size of his state (Busia 1951: 22, 90).

In this section, I have examined the historical nature of chieftaincy in Asante, outlining the various measures put in place to ensure that chiefs preserved the territorial integrity of the various communities, protected the gold mines, guaranteed respect for usufructuary rights and administered revenue from the mineral wealth in a transparent and accountable manner. This system of governance, however, experienced a significant change under colonialism and its indirect rule system, which undermined the chiefs' authority over gold mining in the country.

Figure 6.1. Photograph of King of Bekwai and retinue, 1901. Courtesy of National Archives, Kew, CO 1069/34/54, used with permission.

Figure 6.2. Photograph of an Asante priest, titled 'Fetish priest and child pupil, Ashanti', 1901. Courtesy of National Archives, Kew, CO 1069/34/63, used with permission.

Chieftaincy under Colonial Rule

Integral to the road to British imperialism in the Gold Coast was an uncoordinated yet resolute usurpation of chiefly authority by British merchants and, eventually, colonial administrators. As *The Gold Coast Aborigines* (2 April 1898: 4) reported, this was first seen in Cape Coast with the unauthorized hearing of appeals from decisions of the local chiefs' courts, and then with British administrators' overt attempts to disregard the customary norms in establishing persons without royal lineage to the stool.[3] According to *The Gold Coast Aborigines* (11 June 1898: 2), these blatant manoeuvres occurred despite the British government's initial assurance that it would 'not interfere with the election of native chiefs'. As colonial administrators made great strides in usurping chiefly roles, the impact of Christian missionaries further eroded the reverence for traditional authorities and other customs that had historically bound the people together. The indirect rule also played a key role in the disintegration of chiefly authority. Operating on a monist-pluralist hierarchy wherein traditional chieftaincy was subordinated to colonial state administration, it was fuelled by the notion that two contending forces could not coexist on an equal footing, and one had to overshadow the other in terms of power and influence (Boafo-Arthur 2003).

The colonialist invasion of Africa and the realization of its imperialist ambitions were therefore marked by the disruption of the continent's organic development of diverse sociopolitical institutions, in which power was originally held by chiefs, queen-mothers and elders (Tamale 2020: 147). Resistance from local chiefs responding to the usurpation of their authority was met with depositions, arrests and exiles. The message to the other chiefs was clear: with the might of British militarism, imperial subjugation was inevitable, and any resistance would cost them their stools (Boahen 1975: 46). Speaking on the exiling of anticolonial activists in her home country of Réunion, decolonial feminist writer Françoise Vergès (2021) articulated how colonialism spread fear as a disciplinary technique, and how this fear became one of the state's favourite weapons for inducing conformity and manufacturing consent.

Gold, Chiefs and the Pax Britannica in Asante

According to Obeng-Odoom (2016), the emergence of the central colonial state brought with it a delinking of property rights from economy and society in a manner contrary to its prior role in nourishing and expanding the social foundations of communities. Colonialism instituted a statist and bureaucratically managed system that transferred community benefits to private individuals and corporate entities seeking to profit from common resources, thus laying the foundation for the marketization of the commons in the colonies.[4] The Europeans' preoccupation with gold in the Gold Coast largely informed all aspects of their dealings with the local people, and while British military campaigns into Asante may have been initiated under the banner of protecting coastal communities from Asante's tyranny, the imperial pursuit of Asante's vast gold resources soon became very clear.[5] In one of his first public interactions with the defeated chiefs of Asante, Governor Hodgson declared the paramount authority of Asante, as vested in the Queen of England, to be exercised by the Resident of Kumasi acting under the Governor's authority. Accompanying this imposition of a Pax Britannica was a declaration of interest in the gold wealth of Asante. His exact words to the chiefs were:

> You have gold in great quantity[,] and you are all aware that the white man is coming to show you how that gold can be got to the best advantage not only to the white man himself but to you Kings and chiefs.[6]

As the foremost target of imperialism, chiefly authority was strategically undermined by British colonizers in the newly annexed Asante territory as a means of exerting control over its gold resources. Indeed, Governor Hodgson's initial proposal was for all lands in Asante – and if this was not possible, at least the lands of chiefs who withstood the British during the war – to be annexed to the Crown.[7] Further efforts to weaken chiefly rule in Asante included the exiling of the defeated *Asantehene* and some of his most prominent divisional chiefs and loyal court officials. According to *The Gold Coast Aborigines* (17 December 1898: 1), it was rumoured that one of the Asante subchiefs who was exiled alongside the *Asantehene* had offered information about the location of a rich goldfield in Kumasi in exchange for his freedom. Although his information proved profitable, in that gold was extracted from the location in question, he was still detained and punished for aligning with the *Asantehene* in the war. Among the exiled chiefs were the *Adansehene*, Nana Kwaku Nkansah, whose paramountcy extended to the Obuasi gold-mining community, and two of his linguists, as well as Nana Yaw Appiah, chief of Adanse Akrokerri, another prominent gold-mining town in the Adanse area.[8]

The vacuum created by the disruptions to chieftaincy in Asante did not only weaken the power of the institution, but also led to strife, political unrest and general confusion that was heavily exploited by the government and British mercantilists. Incidentally, it was during this period of unrest that the government assumed the authority to validate the concession obtained by Ashanti Goldfields Corporation (AGC) in Obuasi from the local chiefs, and to execute a lease between itself and the mining corporation to that effect (Taylor 2006). Additionally, owing to the disturbances in Asante, the British government took over the collection of rent and royalties from all mining ventures – including AGC's operations in Obuasi – transferring payments away from the chiefs while continuing to claim that it had no rights over land in Asante.[9]

The pursuit of gold further enhanced the establishment of new precedents in customary land transactions with local chiefs, where it became 'customary' for only head chiefs or kings to sign leases for concessions (Boafo-Arthur 2003). Accordingly, the existing accountability mechanisms within the chieftaincy system were replaced with a more hierarchical arrangement where chiefs who aligned themselves with the colonial administration – whether out of personal gain or fear of exile – were given more power and control. With the increased marketization of mineralized concessions, British colonialism systematically concentrated power within a class of chiefs who took advantage of the growing demand for mineral-bearing lands to abuse their power (Berry 2000). In Asante, incidences of bribery, corruption and misappropriation of stool revenue amongst chiefs became common, which led to much anxiety, distrust and suspicion. This even escalated into secession attempts by some chiefs from the Asante Confederacy (Busia 1951: 190).

Some Adanse chiefs became particularly notorious for selling large tracts of land to mining and timber concessionaires for their own personal gain.[10] Efforts to demand accountability were frequently frustrated by the technicalities of the new plural legal system and the colonial interpretation of customary law; this happened in 1949, for instance, when the *Adansehene*, Nana Adjei Bonsra, was publicly accused of misappropriation and was called upon by some community members to account for revenue from concessions.[11] Protests by the educated elite and the youth against chiefs, especially concerning the administration of mineral resources, were often swiftly and brutally suppressed by the state (Owusu-Mensah 2014).[12] Ultimately, the indirect rule functioned as a performative tool, showing support for traditional political institutions while simultaneously undermining their accountability to the people (Obeng-Odoom 2016: 399).

Furthermore, the Western logic of hierarchized dualisms undermined the cosmological foundation of the office of chiefs, which was understood to provide equilibrium among nature, the ancestors and the living. With the colonial secularization of chieftaincy, chiefs were forced to abandon their sacred duties and rather turned into 'decentralized despots' who acted as agents of colonialism in the plundering of mineral resources for corporate and private profit (Mamdani 1996). The traditional '*ka bi ma me nka bi*' ('speak and let me also speak') system of democracy also suffered serious maladjustment as many chiefs, especially those installed by the government, failed to consult with their elders and the people. With time, local sentiments towards the Asante Confederacy Council became mostly those of estrangement, suspicion and indifference, since many felt excluded from the deliberative process of key policies that affected their daily lives (Busia 1951).

Accompanying the erosion of the chiefs' military and political might was a further breakdown of their role in the administration of the gold mines. As already mentioned, the colonial government required all concessionary grants to be made with the prior consent of the Governor. Chiefs who dared to contravene this directive were immediately threatened, as happened to the queen-mother of Ejisu, Nana Yaa Asantewaa, who received a warning from the Resident of Kumasi for granting a mining concession without the consent and approval of the Governor.[13] Local chiefs were increasingly left with very little authority concerning the granting of concessions, as most foreign concessionaires found it more advantageous to deal with the government instead of the chiefs.[14]

With the colonial government's control over the transaction of mining concessions, Asante quickly became a hotspot for British elites – lords, captains, lawyers and academics, among others – who were backed by colonial administrators in intimidating chiefs into revealing secret mine locations in the local communities. The practice at the time was for foreign concessionaires to approach chiefs bearing introductory letters from the Resident of Kumasi, whose authority compelled the chiefs to grant the concessionaires access to mines in their communities. In one such instance where the chief refused access, he was reported to the Resident, who sternly responded thus: 'This is to tell you once again I want you to give him [Captain Campbell, the British concessionaire] every assistance and show him everything in the way of mines there are in your district. You are to keep nothing back but to tell him everything, or I shall be very displeased with your conduct'.[15]

Mining companies like AGC took advantage of these circumstances, and began lobbying the government to pressure local chiefs for access to mines previously owned and managed by the chiefs, such as the famous Prempeh Mines from which the *Asantehene* reportedly obtained much of his gold.[16] In the wake of the Third Anglo-Ashanti War, AGC pushed the narrative that there was no recognized king or chief governing over the lands, since many of the communities had been largely deserted – the government, in its position as the paramount authority, should therefore facilitate the corporation's access to gold mines in the area.[17]

The colonial government's interpretation of the customary law to justify and legitimate its control of mineral resources was a misapplication of British feudal principles to Asante. Contrary to interpretation by colonial administrators and anthropologists like Rattray (1929), the hierarchical structure of Asante chieftaincy was not a feudal system where the various divisional chiefs held their office or lands directly from the *Asantehene*.[18] Thus, even with the colonial dismantling of the Asante empire and the subsequent creation of the Ashanti Confederacy in 1935, lands in the respective Asante divisions still belonged to the individual stools (Busia 1951: 52). This misinterpretation of Asante customary law was one of many instances of invented tradition that served the colonial administration's imperialist agenda of centralized control over mineral exploitation.

Chieftaincy Formalization

The colonial encroachment on chieftaincy was ultimately concretized through legislative formalization of the institution. According to Oomen (2000), the history of recognition of chieftaincy and customary law teaches us some powerful lessons on the constituent effect of legal recognition. Recall the 1878 Native Jurisdiction Ordinance that set out to define, facilitate and regulate the exercise of certain powers and jurisdictions by established Native Authorities, including the explicit power given to the government to dismiss a chief (Kimble 1963: 460). A Native Affairs Department was also founded in 1902, to secure greater continuity in administration and to assist in providing information about Indigenous customs (Kimble 1963: 466). In 1904, the Chiefs Ordinance was enacted to ensure that the decision of the Governor would be final and unchallenged regarding any question on the election or deposition of a chief.

Colonial attempts to redesign chieftaincy in the likeness of British models were apparent in the invention of new traditions such as the creation of new paramount areas and the appointment, demotion and elevation of chiefs by the government. For instance, under a 1910 amendment to the Native Jurisdiction Ordinance of 1883, the Governor was authorized to suspend or depose chiefs who appeared to him to have abused their power, as well as chiefs who were considered unworthy or incapable of exercising their duties justly. Under section 3 of the 1932 Native Authority Ordinance, colonial administrators were authorized not only to delineate specific areas as Native Authorities, but also to appoint chiefs and declare one Native Authority subordinate to another. These incursive acts were premised on the wrongful assumption that chiefly power was not inherent but derived from the British Crown (Gocking 2005).

In 1927, the Native Administration Ordinance was passed after more than forty years of local resistance to the government's attempts to revise the 1883 Ordinance. The 1927 Ordinance marked a shift in focus, from the definition and restriction of the power of chiefs to the fortification of an institution that now seemed an essential adjunct to the central administration of the colonial government. The Provincial Councils that had initially appeared as simply a piece of electoral machinery were now given formal administrative and judicial powers, including the right to hear appeals in stool disputes. They were to adjudicate on the demands of subchiefs for independence, among other things, with the Governor as the final arbiter on all stool disputes and matters affecting Indigenous customs (Kimble 1963: 493). Local opposition to the Ordinance came primarily from the Aborigines' Rights Protection Society (ARPS), who contended with the chiefs for the power to codify customary laws. The educated local politicians felt that the chiefs were overstepping their constitutional authority at the expense of the people, and that ARPS alone should be free to assume leadership on a national scale. Additionally, the ARPS argued that the law placed head chiefs beyond the control of their subchiefs and people, contrary to Indigenous customs of accountability (Kimble 1963: 496). As Boahen (1975: 134) observed, the contest between the educated elites and the local chiefs raged on throughout the 1920s, with the colonial administration actively supporting the latter in the interest of their indirect system of government.

More specifically in Asante, the Ashanti Administration Ordinance of 1902 provided for persons only recognized by the Governor to exercise any powers as head chief. Exiled Asante chiefs were replaced by nominees deemed qualified based on their loyalty to the British government rather than by their connection with the stool family. Indeed, several of these new chiefs were alien to the communities they were called upon to rule (Kimble 1963: 479).[19] Ultimately, the chieftaincy selection process – a thoroughly participatory system involving consultations with the queen-mother, the adult men and senior women of the royal lineages and the people – was jettisoned and replaced by a colonialist and deeply patriarchal system where the will of the people was now subjected to the sanction of the government (Busia 1951: 9, 106).

The colonial government radically changed the chieftaincy and clan system, such that the exiled *Asantehene*, Nana Prempeh I, was initially only allowed to return as a private citizen, and was subsequently installed only as *Kumasihene* (chief of Kumasi, the capital city of Asante) on 11 November 1926.[20] This was further accompanied by the 1935 reconstitution of the Ashanti Confederacy, which was mandated to administer chiefly duties with oversight from the government (Busia 1951: 180).[21] This reorganization of the Asante Confederacy was not based on the historical rights of the chiefs under the erstwhile union of Asante states, rather, it served as a convenient governance system for colonial oversight. Additionally, the formation of the colonial state involved a remapping of territorial boundaries and the creation of new state institutions. Section 3 of the 1902 Ashanti Administration Ordinance authorized the division of Asante into districts, and further empowered the administration to alter any such divisions so made. These districts were headed by District Commissioners, who acted as magistrates, and principal executive officers with responsibility over the chiefs. The mining town of Obuasi fell under the Southern District. Under this new system, head chiefs of the various divisions acted as president of their respective Native Authorities. For instance, the Adanse Division formed part of the Ashanti Confederacy as a Native Authority with the *Adansehene* as president. While the government administered in terms of the larger territorial administrative units (districts), the chiefs were more interested in the ethnic groups they represented.

These territorial demarcations went through several reorganizations and were mostly at variance with the established political system in Asante (Busia 1951: 104). The colonial remapping of territory was considered a most humiliating affront to the authority of chiefs, whose very offices embodied their roles as custodians of the land and settlers of its boundaries (Valsecchi 2007).[22] Interference in the established spatiality was therefore a vital colonial tool for diminishing the influence of traditional institutions and curtailing their powers (Tamale

2020: 147). The territorial overlaps created by these colonial demarcations ignited intense land conflicts, such as the disputes between the *Adansehene* and other paramount chiefs following the designation of the Rivers Pra and Offin respectively as boundaries between the various tributary states. According to *The Gold Coast Leader* (18 April 1914: 3), a key issue in these land disputes was determining which chief was entitled to receive rents and royalties from gold-mining operations within the contested boundary areas. Further evidence from colonial reports revealed protracted and costly land and chieftaincy disputes in Adanse, most of which arose from colonial interference regarding the definition of boundaries, the amalgamation of states and the installation or demotion of paramount chiefs in the region following the Asante uprising against the British in 1900 (the Yaa Asantewaa War).[23] The legacy of these colonial interferences persists today in the form of disputes relating to boundaries and chieftaincy succession.

In rapidly developing communities like Obuasi, the influx of migrant mine workers dramatically changed the focus of political power, as many of the new settlers began to look to colonial administrators rather than the chiefs for leadership. In Obuasi, the local chiefs witnessed a sharp decline in their influence as colonial perceptions of customary law led to assumptions that migrant mine workers for AGC were not subject to the local chiefs and customs. This was compounded by section 2(1) of the Native Jurisdiction (Amendment) Ordinance of 1927, which enabled colonial administrators to appoint village headmen who were granted chiefly powers and jurisdiction. Mining corporations like Obuasi's AGC also established a system of appointing 'Native Headmen' as liaisons between their workers and management, a role that often rivalled that of the local chiefs in terms of leadership and influence.[24]

Judicially, Native Authorities administered the Native Courts, which in Asante were established under the Native Courts (Ashanti) Ordinance of 1935 (Cap 80). This Ordinance defined the civil and criminal jurisdiction of the courts, which were to be administered in accordance with the prevailing customary laws. Briefly put, the Native Courts were structured into four different grades, namely Courts A, B, C and D; Court A (the *Asantehene*'s Court) was the highest Native Court in Asante, and it had original jurisdiction (in certain constitutional cases) as well as appellate jurisdiction. Appeals from the Native Courts were heard by the Chief Commissioner's Court, from which a further appeal could lie to the West African Court of Appeal (WACA), and yet another to the Privy Council.[25] Under sections 3 and 4 of the Native Law and Custom (Ashanti Confederacy Council) Ordinance,

1940, local chiefs in the Confederacy Council could enact customary laws, subject to the repugnancy test as well as the approval and rights of modification afforded to colonial administrators. This repugnancy test, as already established, subjected Indigenous laws and customs to European constructions of natural justice, morality, good conscience and equity.

Ultimately, the political, judicial and social custodianship of chiefs over land and mineral wealth came under the oversight of a new cohort of British administrators and other technical agencies including treasury, lands, mining and forestry departments respectively (Busia 1951: 139). Like most colonial inventions of customary law, the system of indirect rule alienated the chiefs from their people and created feelings of distrust and apathy. For instance, while the Confederacy Council purported to legislate for the ordinary people, its powers did not derive from them, and many in Asante were generally unaware of the activities of their chiefs, most of whom only engaged with the people when enforcing byelaws enacted by the Council (Busia 1951: 194).

Retreating into the past reveals the significant regression that occurred when colonial monist-pluralism altered traditional governance systems through legislative formalization, state recognition and territorial usurpation. By undermining the authority of chiefs as gatekeepers of the mines, custodians of the land and settlers of the boundaries, colonial administrators were able to effectively undertake large-scale land grabs, the extraction of resources, the marginalization of Indigenous miners and the imposition of an eminent domain – all of which are colonial legacies that persist in today's ASM regime.

Chieftaincy and the Modern Ghanaian State

Chieftaincy survived the uncertainties it faced in the early days of independence, when opinions differed on its relevance in the postcoloniality. The wilful – and, in some cases, coerced – alliance of chiefs with the colonial government led many in the early post-independence nationalist movements to decry chieftaincy as an ally of empire and an inherently corrupt, anachronistic, undemocratic and antiprogressive institution with no relevance to modern society (Abotchie, Awedoba and Odotei 2006). This period of history further epitomized class struggles where revolutionaries within the grassroot organizations viewed local chiefs as embodying the arrogance associated with elite power. State antagonism towards chiefs re-emerged during the socialist revolution of the Provisional National Defence Council

(PNDC) in the early 1980s, where the military regime considered the integration of chiefs into structures of governance as an affront to the ethos of democracy (Aryee 2007).

This, and the fact that postcolonial governments considered chiefs to be their competitors, led to calls for the abolition of the institution (Boateng and Afranie 2020). These notwithstanding, early postcolonial governments were unsuccessful in dismantling chieftaincy, but rather succeeded in their own invention of tradition through legislations that enabled them to remove chiefs (especially those opposed to their government), declare new paramountcy and create new traditional states (Rathbone 2000). For instance, the first post-independence government under Nkrumah diluted the traditional structures of authority and replaced the colonially established Native Authorities with local councils (Taylor 2006). It was not until the National Liberation Council (NLC)'s coup against Nkrumah that chiefs who had been removed for their opposition to Nkrumah's CPP government were reinstated to their stools in 1966 (Boahen 1975: 231). With the return to democratic governance following periods of military rule, the 1992 Constitution recognized the historical relevance of chiefs to governance in the country and sought to resolve the earlier tensions by inscribing the legitimacy of chiefs as established by custom and usage. This constitutional recognition followed the definition of a chief, under article 277 of the 1992 Constitution and section 57 of the 2008 Chieftaincy Act (Act 759), as 'a person who, hailing from the appropriate family and lineage, has been validly nominated, elected or selected and enstooled, enskinned or installed as a chief or queenmother in accordance with the relevant customary law and usage'.

The 1992 Constitution finally put an end to early postcolonial legislations – such as the 1959 Chiefs (Recognition) Act (Act 11), the 1961 Chieftaincy Act (Act 81) and the 1985 Chieftaincy (Amendment) Law (PNDCL 107) – that continued the colonial legacy of requiring state recognition for the installation of a chief. Under article 270 of the 1992 Constitution, Parliament is explicitly prevented from having any power to enact any law that confers on any person or authority the right to accord or withdraw recognition to or from a chief for any purpose whatsoever. Additionally, the 1992 Constitution follows the established tradition of the 1969 Constitution by recognizing that Divisional Councils, Traditional Councils and Regional and National Houses of Chiefs are integral parts of state machinery. This recognition is further enhanced by the Chieftaincy Act, which mandates the Regional and National Houses of Chiefs with administering all chieftaincy matters in the country. The institution is overseen by a

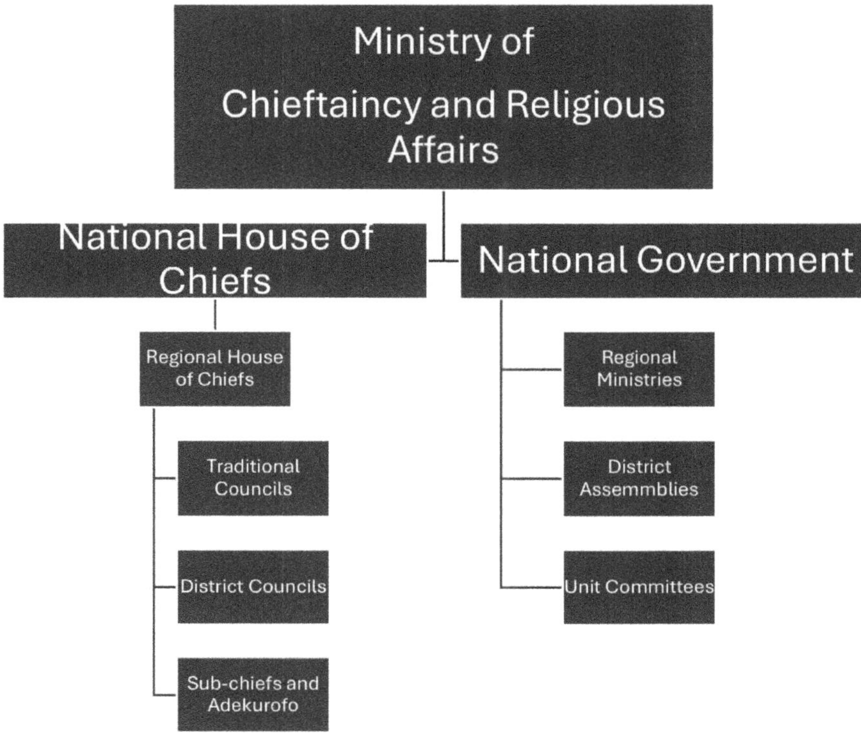

Figure 6.3. An organizational chart of Ghana's National House of Chiefs, 2021. © Linda Mensah.

Ministry (the Ministry of Chieftaincy and Religious Affairs) that was instituted in 2006 to represent the interests of chiefs at the executive level of government and to grant them direct representation at cabinet meetings (Abotchie, Awedoba and Odotei 2006).[26]

The current constitutional recognition of chieftaincy runs on the formal acknowledgement of a hierarchy that has been a major source of contention within the institution in contemporary times; it also retains key colonial legacies mostly related to customary land tenures and ASM.

Chiefs, Customary Lands and ASM

As was the case with the colonial government, control over land and mineral resources greatly informed the early state's subjugation of chiefly powers and authority. Nkrumah's postcolonial resource nationalism, for instance, was not only driven by a desire to reclaim the country's mineral resources from imperialist control, neocolonial corporate financialization and resource extractivism. It was also motivated by a resolve to diminish the role chiefs maintained in mining transactions under colonial indirect rule – particularly those he viewed as enabling colonial exploitation of mineral wealth at the people's expense. Stools controlling territories with vast mineral resources – such as the *Asantehene* and the Akim Abuakwa chiefs, for whom the colonial government established secretariats to facilitate formalized land allocations – became the primary targets of Nkrumah's legislative attrition (Quan, Ubink and Antwi 2008: 183). Key instances of legislation – including the 1958 Akim Abuakwa (Stool Revenue) Act (Act 8), the 1958 Ashanti Stool Act (Act 28) and the 1960 Stool Lands Control Act (Act 79) – brought the administration of revenue in these stools under strict government control. In addition, Nkrumah's CPP government substantially intervened in the chieftaincy system by separating the Bono-Ahafo area from Asante, designating the former a separate region with its own House of Chiefs and promoting a host of pro-CPP chiefs to paramountcy in the resource-rich latter region (Boahen 1975: 194).

A reformulation of the colonial legacy of eminent domain was instituted by the passage of the 1962 Concessions Act (Act 124), which provided for the colonial-era Concessions Ordinance to cease to apply to stool lands. More particularly, the 1962 Minerals Act (Act 126) abolished the colonial arrangement where mineral resources were acknowledged as vested in the stools, rather vesting them in the President for and on behalf of the Republic. Under the 1962 Administration of Lands Act (Act 123), the administration of stool lands was also to be closely monitored by the state. A new trajectory of monist-pluralism in mineral resource governance was therefore instituted, and is now currently enshrined under the 1992 Constitution and the 2006 Minerals and Mining Act (Act 703).

Nevertheless, local chiefs maintain immense control over land allocation, and mining is one of the many spheres in which their traditional authority over land becomes more visible. As Carolyn Logan's study of chieftaincy (2013) observed, many Ghanaians place considerable value on the role and leadership qualities of traditional authorities, as well as their accessibility to ordinary people. In the local mining communities, chiefs have been able to leverage their customary authority to serve as principal brokers of private investment, developmental aid and other socioeconomic projects. This is because issues of socioeconomic development continue to revolve arounds chiefs at the local level, despite the reduction of their political and economic powers (Ahwoi 2010).

In the rural communities, where the function of state institutions is mostly extractive (i.e. to collect resources and taxes), rather than restitutive (e.g. to facilitate infrastructural developments, provide access to land and alleviate poverty), the absence of the state creates an opportunity for chiefs to direct, guide and provide for their communities. The evidence suggests that despite the comparatively little nationwide publicity they receive, many sub-chiefs and *adekurofo* in the rural mining communities have been instrumental in securing infrastructural developments funded by ASM revenue, such as road construction, schools, CHPS (community health clinics) compounds, KVIPs (public toilets) and potable water. Chiefs have also been known to secure deposits from ASM operators for the purpose of enforcing proper environmental standards and ensuring that post-mining land-reclamation exercises are carried out. A recent study by Adu-Baffour et al. (2025) shed light on how local chiefs channelled their commanding authority to orchestrate connections among various public and private stakeholders towards a community-based ASM land-restoration project in Ghana. In the absence of effective state mechanisms, the local chiefs mobilized communal labour and leveraged their connections to secure funding and access machinery vital for the land rehabilitation, while simultaneously navigating complex, re-emergent challenges relating to customary land tenure and benefit-sharing arrangements.

A reflection on the present circumstances of chieftaincy's prominent position in customary land tenure shows a tensioned legal plurality underscored by a formal recognition shrouded in statutory limitations, as well as concerns about their chiefly authority in ASM. The involvement of chiefs in ASM has, however, also generated heated debates regarding state-centric formalization and the prevailing monist-pluralist governance of mineral rights.

Critiques of Chieftaincy in Land Tenure and ASM Governance

To use Oomen's analogy (2000: 71) of traditional institutions in South Africa, chieftaincy in Ghana is filled with remnants of colonialism – some are buried deep and some are starting to emerge, while others continue to be repainted and refurbished due to a lack of alternatives. There is nearly always debate within communities about the future of the chieftaincy system. This is reinforced by canonical theorizations that consciously or unconsciously regurgitate violent colonialist logic about the institution. According to Mawuko-Yevugah and

Attipoe (2021), the variance in attitudes towards chieftaincy is deeply rooted in a longstanding debate between modernity and tradition, in which chieftaincy is argued to be an anachronism that should not have survived the twentieth century, let alone the twenty-first century. Chinsinga (2006) had earlier described traditional institutions as instruments of social oppression devoid of progress in areas of political organization, women's rights, social mobility and economic rights.

In Ghana, critics of chieftaincy are usually armed with concerns over the perpetual succession conflicts, multiple sales of lands, elite capture, rentier politics, corruption, misappropriation of stool land revenue, lack of accountability and perceived undemocratic inclinations that continue to plague the institution (Amanor and Ubink 2008: 9). The resurgence of interest in customary land tenures has reignited concerns about integrating customary and formal land tenures towards a decentralized administration. Within this modernist framework is a focus on the chieftaincy system and its role in customary land administration in the twenty-first century. For instance, the recently enacted Land Act of 2020 legislates Customary Land Secretariats (CLSs) under chapter 1 of part two as a pathway for formalizing customary land tenure. The Land Administration Project (LAP), which birthed the CLSs, was introduced as part of the government's commitment to guaranteeing the title security of small landowners and protecting them against powerful chiefs and elders in the community (Ministry of Lands and Forestry 2003–2008: 67). However, the involvement of chiefs in land tenure administration under the CLS model has generated deep scepticism from scholars like Amanor (2008), who described the strengthening of customary land tenure administration under the CLS model as a misplaced approach. Amanor (2008: 9) emphasized that the much-touted flexibility and negotiability of customary land tenures seldom operated on a level playing field, but rather emerged from the interests of local elites who continually redefine customary tenure to create insecurity for local land users, thereby dispossessing them of their access to land and natural resources.

With increased land commodification, chiefs are said to have reduced their custodial function over customary lands, acting instead as purveyors who prefer to transfer lands to the highest bidders. Usufructuary landowners and local farmers with weak bargaining powers and low social capital are losing their lands and livelihoods to chiefs and local elites in mass rural land displacements, a situation that Kasanga and Kotey (2001) referred to as a national disease. Quan, Ubink and Antwi (2008: 197) argued that the LAP–CLS objectives of delivering accountable and equitable land administration run counter to those of established interest groups – such as chiefs – who are more inclined to redefine customary land relations to their own advantage. Amanor and Ubink (2008: 16), on their part, accused the LAP of choosing to work within the existing power structures of chieftaincy instead of attempting to create a more democratic framework for land management. Ubink (2009) further raised concerns that chiefs are resisting the introduction of more transparent and accountable means of administering stool land revenue, and would rather use the CLS model to gain further control over land.

The constitutional recognition of chiefly authority over stool lands is said to be shrouded in ambiguity, leaving room for misappropriation – especially considering the breakdown of traditional accountability measures and the failure of the Office of the Administrator of Stool Lands (OASL), the state-mandated agency for the collection and redistribution of stool revenue, to address these loopholes (Boamah 2014). Ubink and Quan (2008: 198) added that traditional authorities display little transparency in the use of stool land revenue, and most local communities realize little to no benefit from the land as they are rarely and inadequately compensated for land loss. These misappropriations are said to stem from the informality surrounding the negotiation of customary land tenures (Kasanga and Kotey 2001).

These concerns permeate into ASM, where the blame for the upsurge in informal ASM and its associated environmental impact is placed foremost at the doorstep of local chiefs. Due to the state-centric association of informal ASM with criminality and notoriety, local chiefs are accused of tarnishing the reputation of their stools by granting lands to informal small-scale miners (Boateng and Afranie 2020). In Obuasi, the evidence suggests deep resentment towards some chiefs on account of their lack of transparency in the management of revenues obtained from ASM. In one of my interviews, a resident described a well-known chief in a bustling ASM community as '*frakadam*' (treacherous and egotistical), owing to the chief's notoriety for granting encroached AGA lands for ASM and using the proceeds to amass personal wealth.[27] William Tsuma's research (2010) on Ghana's extractive industry highlighted the problematic position of chiefs in the management of stool land revenue, and singled out chieftaincy as the most corrupt institution hampering development in extractive communities. To distance themselves from this stigma, some chiefs outrightly deny involvement in, or knowledge of, informal ASM in their communities, while others pledge their support to the state in driving away informal miners.

As someone whose maternal and paternal families are affiliated with the respective stools in their communities, I approach chieftaincy with the utmost respect but also with critical reflexivity and acknowledgement of its tensioned complexities. My encounter with some chiefs from Obuasi in my professional capacity left me with some of the most conflicting and deeply uncomfortable experiences of my legal career. While practising in Accra, I witnessed first-hand the lavish lifestyles, plush mansions and luxury cars of chiefs from my community, who used their royal positions to broker huge foreign deals and other mining-related contracts for their privately incorporated companies, all against the backdrop of the endemic poverty, neglect and deprivation faced by our people back home in Obuasi. Rosen's ethnography of Obuasi (2020) highlighted such chieftaincy conundrums in the mining community of Sansu, where allegations of revenue misappropriation and involvement in corporate land grabs had been levelled against the local chief, resulting in one of the most fractious chieftaincies in the area.

In Obuasi, concerns have arisen over chiefs who have adopted landlord-like approaches in their granting of lands for informal ASM operations. Stories were recounted of local farmers who found their crops completely razed to the ground by Chinese ASM firms, to whom local chiefs had reallocated their farmlands without their knowledge or consent.[28] The increased demand for mineral-bearing lands has resulted in productive farmlands and even virgin forests being sacrificed for ASM operations – not for the benefit of the community or that of local small-scale miners, but for the personal gain of chiefs, political elites, local businessmen and foreign ASM firms (Batterbury and Ndi 2018). This further damages the reputation of chieftaincy, undermines communal property rights, fuels land conflicts and intensifies the already volatile tensions between local farmers and ASM operators in the local communities (Abudulai 2002).

Another issue raised against chieftaincy is its hierarchical structure, which in recent times has highlighted the institution's key role in the development of local communities. The codified system of hierarchy recognizes chiefs in descending order from the *Asantehene* to paramount chiefs, divisional chiefs, subdivisional chiefs, *adekurofo* and other chiefs recognized by the National House of Chiefs, as further provided under section 58 of the Chieftaincy Act. Under article 271(2) of the 1992 Constitution, the National House of Chiefs is established as the highest judicial body of chieftaincy, and like the Regional House of Chiefs, its membership is practically limited to paramount chiefs. Article 272(c) further mandates the Regional and

National Houses of Chiefs with codifying customary law, which implies that those who are not paramount chiefs are unable to participate in these Houses, and are therefore also unable to influence the nature of customary laws at the national level (Crook 2005). As the core consultative systems of traditional governance have collapsed, these chieftaincy hierarchies have, – mirroring the situation under colonial indirect rule, – created a classed collective of paramount chiefs who may not often engage with their people, subchiefs and *adekurofo*, with whom they may hardly share the same aspirations. This is particularly apparent in local mining communities where government policy initiatives often exclude lower chiefs and the *adekurofo*, despite their being the first to be blamed for the negative externalities of ASM in their communities.

Arguments against the LAP and the CLS place significant emphasis on the colonial state's redefinition of customary authority, and on the characterization of customary land relations as a product of the dominant interests of political alliances, rather than a historical fact (Amanor 2008: 79). Amanor (2004) had argued that the notion of the customary powers and rights of chiefs is loaded with political invention and should therefore not be treated as if it was a timeless principle of customary tenure. From this perspective, the LAP is viewed as an opportunity for traditional authorities to regain the official support and authority over land that they formerly enjoyed under British rule (Quan, Ubink and Antwi 2008: 191). For Crook (2008: 131), the ability of chiefs to profit from the market value of stool lands is a direct legacy of the law and institutions developed during the colonial period. This colonial legacy, he argued, is particularly strong in the Akan areas, where political jurisdiction has long been conflated with allodial land ownership or trusteeship and management rights. In the ASM context, a study conducted by Akafari et al. (2021) described the recent wave of chiefly involvement in the expropriation of land for gold mining as a reinvigoration of the long historical phenomenon of the colonial state's co-option of chiefs in the capitalist concentration of mineral resources.

In analysing how precolonial accountability measures were destroyed under colonialism and not subsequently rebuilt, Ubink (2009: 174) questioned whether the state was sufficiently capable of overseeing chieftaincy in the absence of these traditional accountability measures. Ubink and Quan (2008) attributed the mismanagement of the customary land tenure system to the government's policy of non-interference in chieftaincy matters and the unwillingness of the state to introduce effective checks and balances over traditional authorities.

Despite the constitutional moratorium under article 276 of the 1992 Constitution against chiefly involvement in partisan politics, it is commonly known that local politicians often solicit the endorsement of powerful paramount chiefs, believing their backing will translate into votes from the chiefs' subjects (Thompson 2016). Moreover, the allegiance of some government officials to their stools trumps their loyalty to the state, to the extent that they are often unwilling to pursue government policies that are not supported by their local chiefs.[29] These political alliances, coupled with the practice of appointing highly educated and politically affiliated professionals to chieftaincy positions, blur the line between governmental and traditional authority, making it difficult to ensure accountability at either end of the spectrum spanning state and customary administration (Ubink and Quan 2008: 204).

While the establishment of CLSs under the Lands Act reflects attempts by the state to address legal pluralism, the general scholarly consensus is that it has done little to resolve the legal uncertainties that often disadvantage marginalized and dispossessed actors in customary land acquisition. This has generated support for a formalization of customary land tenure that neither envisages nor backs the incorporation of chiefs as central to customary land administration (Abudulai 2002). Currently, these scholarly concerns have not done much in changing the government's clear political stance of maintaining the CLSs under traditional authorities. This hybrid system of governance is still in its early stages, and the impact of these ongoing debates on future reforms remains to be seen. Concerns about chiefly authority in land administration continue to permeate discourse surrounding the role of chiefs in ASM, where the issues are even more politicized and hotly contested. State criminalization, combined with the belief that chiefs who grant lands to informal miners are polluting the lands and desecrating their sacred oath of office, has led to intense agitation for increased state curtailment of chiefly involvement in ASM, including calls for the prosecution and destoolment of such chiefs. While a critical decolonial reflexivity enables us to acknowledge the power inequalities in chieftaincy and the institution's problematic association with ASM, the arguments against chiefs raise some very questionable analyses of colonial legacies in chiefly land administration that also need to be interrogated. In doing so, we can begin to reclaim the past and repair that which is broken in the institution of chieftaincy, instead of throwing the baby out with the bath water.

A Decolonial Turn to Addressing Critiques of Chieftaincy in Land and ASM Governance

Decolonial scholarship, as already established, advances the need to resist coloniality by retrieving our knowledge systems and institutions from the margins to which they have been displaced. Part of the process of decolonizing chieftaincy involves challenging the ideas and conventions that diminish the importance and legitimacy of its Indigenous epistemologies, particularly in the context of land and ASM management. To begin this decolonial enquiry, I problematize anti-chieftaincy sentiments by highlighting their failure to undertake an equally critical evaluation of the role of chiefs in customary land tenures and ASM. This serves as a caution to scholars whose critiques of chieftaincy are premised on concerns about equity in customary land tenure administration, without any recognition that colonialism itself employed similar justifications of equity, good conscience and natural justice as tools to discredit, subjugate and dismantle Indigenous laws and accountability mechanisms. As a re-memory tool, *Sankɔfa* demands such reflexivity and self-critique in dealing with formerly colonized societies; otherwise, we risk reproducing harmful historical practices that could restrict and suffocate future reform and progress (Abraham 1962).

Since colonization, European systems of governance have typically been seen as the epitome of civilization, whereas Indigenous chieftaincy systems are continuously discredited. Many racist descriptions of the continent stem from colonialist biases that led to the stereotype of Africans as savages lacking proper systems of culture, law and sociopolitical administration. These colonialities persist today and are particularly pervasive in scholarship that fixates on chiefly mishaps and ultimately projects European models of governance as the standard against which other traditional systems are measured.

Efforts at decolonizing chieftaincy therefore need to confront this violent history and its ongoing legacies while emphasizing the importance of valuing our Indigenous knowledge systems and celebrating their legitimacy in our communities. Scholars of chieftaincy like Ubink and Valsecchi, respectively, argue for increased state control over chiefs by citing colonial heavy-handedness as having curbed the chiefly abuse of power. However, such an argument needs to be situated within the context of the epistemic and materialist violence perpetuated by such colonial oversight. This requires a confrontation of the glaring historical evidence, as I have set out above, which clarifies how the supposed 'benefits' of colonial surveillance rather weakened traditional accountability measures, thus opening the floodgates for some chiefs to abuse their power in amassing personal wealth (Rathbone 2000). The absence of such a critical, decolonial lens often leads to conclusions that instrumentalize normative plurality while either ignoring or actively calling for the elimination of its realities when proposing ways to regulate socioeconomic, cultural and political systems (Porter 2012: 162).

Although chieftaincy was heavily modified and undermined by colonialist regimes, the role of chiefs as custodians of customary land tenure does not exist as a consequence of state recognition and appointment. On the contrary, chieftaincy is rooted in a history that precedes the colonial and modern nation state. It is backed by values of spirituality, communality and participatory governance, all of which are legitimated by the beliefs of the people as vital to the soul of their Indigenous communities (Busia 1951). As Oomen (2000: 80) explained, chieftaincy encompasses religion, tradition, governance and customs; the wrongs of chiefs hence cannot be a reason to do away with the institution altogether, but is rather an opportunity for empowering the institution and restoring its weakened systems of accountability.

Similarly, Asante chieftaincy is as much about the stool – which represents the institution – as it is about the occupant of the stool. One of Busia's (1951: 194) notable observations about chieftaincy in Asante was that despite the numerous colonial intrusions, sentiments of nationhood persisted and found expression in allegiance to the Golden Stool. Accordingly, despite their general disaffection with colonial alterations of chieftaincy, people continued to respect the stools and to look to the chiefs as not only their rulers and guides, but also the symbols of their unity, traditions and values (Busia 1951: 214). This has been contrary to the expectations of modernization theorists who were convinced that chieftaincy was an ancient relic that would become outmoded and wither into irrelevance, to be replaced by modern institutions of governance (Harneit-Sievers 1998). Decades into postcoloniality, chieftaincy remains strongly politically relevant, demonstrating that modernization theorists gravely misjudged the essential characteristics of customary laws and its institutions, namely, their resilience, fluidity and adaptability.

Moreover, framing elite capture, rentier politics and revenue misappropriation as primarily inherent flaws of chieftaincy, whose solution lies in increased state control, ignores the equally damning revelations of state incapacity and corruption. It also reproduces the exact colonialist logic underpinning the superimposition of English legal and administrative systems on traditional institutions deemed incapable of administering the indigenes and their resources. Quan, Ubink and Antwi (2008: 196) noted that proposals to replace chiefs in customary land management with supposedly more democratic systems under local government control implicitly assumed that the interests of key personnel in these state institutions aligned with those of land users, whereas the interests of chiefs did not. However, given the cavalier attitude with which some district chief executives reportedly handled district assembly finances, this assumption does not hold. As Kotey (1996) has noted, the incompetence of state land agencies, along with their rampant irregularities and mismanagement, undermines the state's moral authority to denigrate chiefly land administration.[30]

A decolonial examination of chieftaincy recognizes that the institution does not endorse the notion of chiefs as owners of stool lands, nor that of stool land revenue as being chiefs' personal property. Such a decolonizing approach to chieftaincy also involves extricating it from the hegemonic assumptions of neoliberal and neocolonial actors who suppose that its systemic challenges demand calls for its subjugation to their interests. Chieftaincy holds immense emancipatory potential for ASM, but this is often buried in the avalanche of literature and public discourse devoted to its weaknesses. Consequently, there is an acute lack of sensitivity and regard for the many grassroots initiatives undertaken by chiefs towards improving rural economies and supporting environmentally sound ASM operations in the local communities. An opportunity for the Ghanaian government to demonstrate such locally situated governance for ASM recently arrived in the form of the Community Mining Scheme, which has unfortunately fallen into the same traps as the failed system of formalization, due to the exclusionary and colonialist tactics employed by the state.

The Community Mining Scheme as a Remedial Response to Informal ASM

The Community Mining Scheme (CMS) was a policy initiative rolled out by the New Patriotic Party (NPP) government in 2019 as an alternative to *galamsey*, following widespread public pressure to address the alarming environmental harm associated with ASM. This project aimed to ensure decentralized governance, predictability and transparency in land acquisition; to that end, the state would not only issue licences but also provide relevant geodata, equipment, financial support and training to local small-scale miners. On their part, it was envisioned that large-scale mining companies would contribute to this endeavour by providing technical and safety-related logistical support. It was revealed in the Ghana News Agency (24 March 2022) that the CMS would be managed by an Oversight Committee and governed by a Small-Scale Miners' Code of Practice.

Initially, local chiefs were particularly interested, because they assumed the CMS would serve as an inclusive policy framework that would prioritize their involvement in managing the mineral wealth in their local communities for communal growth. As it stands, however, many chiefs have been left disillusioned by the design and policy implementation of the CMS, for many reasons. Foremost on the list of grievances is elite capture by local politicians, who are accused of exploiting the CMS to unfairly allocate demarcated lands to their political allies.[31] Even more concerning is the revelation that many CMS lands were allocated to Chinese ASM firms, while local small-scale miners remain unable to access lands for mining. Furthermore, the promises of job creation for local youth have been left unfulfilled, since CMS ventures frequently rely on already-hired workforces. Ironically, there is nothing more antithetical to the government's ASM formalization policy than the realities of the CMS, whose initiatives are marketed as 'community'-oriented programmes and linked to specific communities, but in practice entail no community involvement or benefit whatsoever, beyond being geographically situated in these communities. Some of these communities have received little to no compensation for the demarcation of their lands as CMS sites, and in one such locality, the chiefs had to resort to instituting a formal court action to register their grievances against the local government and the relevant mining venture. In confirming the lawsuit in his interview, the chief of Adaase emphasized that the legal action was part of fulfilling his traditional duty as custodian of the land. According to him, when there are environmental disasters resulting from ASM in the local communities, people hardly ever ask, 'Which district/municipal chief executive's lands are these?' Rather, the question is always 'Which chief's lands are these?'[32]

Many of the chiefs and *adekurofo* shared their grievances about their exclusion from key discussions leading to the formulation of the CMS. Throughout the entire project, the state adopted its usual position, treating chiefs as passive recipients of already-designed state policies that they were obligated to enforce in their local communities. Many of them were kept in the dark about the entire initiative, only to be informed days before they were expected to host durbars for the inaugural ceremony.[33] Beyond this, little to no consultation had been conducted with them regarding their role or the benefits that their communities would receive. Some of these chiefs registered their objection by refusing to host or attend their local CMS inauguration ceremonies.[34]

In cases of state engagement with chiefs, consultations were held with paramount chiefs, but subchiefs and *adekurofo* – who live in the local communities and are in direct contact with the people – were mostly excluded. Due to the failings of the traditional democratic system, information does not always trickle down from the paramount heads; when it does, there are often hesitations to abide by instructions due to a lack of shared interests.[35] Additionally, owing to the non-participatory nature of the CMS, local chiefs typically did not know which entity had been awarded lands in their communities, until the assigned ventures arrived with already-issued licences to commence operations. In several instances, sacred groves in the local communities were approved for the CMS because the Minerals Commission failed to undertake prior consultations with the chiefs.[36] This undermined the authority of local chiefs, who now face extreme difficulty in ensuring the compliance of CMS firms in the observance of customary rituals.

Furthermore, the heavy mechanization involved in the CMS has increased the rate of land degradation, which has in turn led to an astronomical increase in food insecurity in the local communities. While the government supposedly introduced the CMS to address the alarming environmental pollution from *galamsey*, the evidence on the ground indicates worsening conditions resulting from some of these state-backed CMS projects. In Obuasi, the general sentiment – as shared by certain national media personnel – is that the CMS is merely a rebranded form of *galamsey*, in which the government has capitalized on informal ASM's environmental notoriety to drive away local small-scale miners and replace them with party affiliates.[37]

Although the government touts the CMS as a novel mining model, a closer look shows significant overlaps with the prevailing ASM formalization. Legislatively, the CMS is still regulated by the existing Minerals and Mining Act, in addition to the tributer system under Regulations 493–506 of the Minerals and Mining (Health, Safety and Technical) Regulations, 2012 (LI 2182). Licensing is still very much centralized, and the application process virtually follows a markedly similar bureaucratic procedure involving the same government agencies as in the prevailing formalization process (Minerals Commission of Ghana 2021). The training aspect of the CMS bears similarities with the government's 'Youth in Mines' programme, where trainees were paid a monthly allowance to undergo relevant training to be licensed for ASM. As was reported by the *Ghanaian Times* (18 April 2007), the Youth in Mines project was part of the National Youth Employment Programme (NYEP) launched in 2007. There is, however, no mention of CMS trainees receiving a monthly training allowance. Considering the similarities in composition of the Community Mining Oversight Committee and the District Small-Scale Mining Committees established under section 92 of the Minerals and Mining Act, it remains unclear how different or coordinated their roles will be. Section 92 of the Minerals and Mining Act lists the members of the District Small-Scale Mining Committee as: the district chief executive (or her representative), the head of the district office of the Minerals Commission, one person nominated by the district assembly, one person nominated by the Traditional Council, an officer of the Inspectorate Division of the Minerals Commission and an officer from the Environmental Protection Authority (EPA). On the other hand, the Community Mining Oversight Committee under the CMS is constituted by the Divisional/District Police Commander, the chief of the relevant community, the Member of Parliament, members of the District Small-Scale Mining Committee, with additional members to be co-opted from the Water Resources Commission and the Forestry Commission (Minerals Commission of Ghana 2021).

The evidence from Obuasi demonstrates that the CMS, while sold as a decentralized, community-focused remediation policy for *galamsey*, has rather been reduced to a site of contestation between chiefs and state officials, characterized by open attacks, accusations of mismanagement, a lack of administrative knowledge, acts of exclusion and attempts at delegitimizing each other. Many chiefs have called for the CMS to be scrapped in its entirety, while others are still hopeful about its transformative potential. 'It is bent, but not broken', said one of the chiefs during his interview, as he spoke in anticipation of the CMS being rid of the elite capture perpetuated by local politicians and foreign ASM firms.[38] Siegal and Veiga (2009: 51) have advised that a policy of ASM formalization is only as effective as its implementation methodology. As I argued in Mensah (2021), government policy guidelines regarding the CMS must move beyond superficial political promises and clearly define the rights and responsibilities of all stakeholders, including local government officials, chiefs, small-scale miners, large-scale mining corporations and local communities. Beyond the fanfare of durbars, the state needs to instil trust and confidence in its commitment to inclusivity and transparency in implementing a more democratic and community-driven CMS. This would ensure that the programme functions effectively in achieving the ultimate goal of environmental sustainability in the ASM sector, instead of operating as a mere rebrand of the failed formalization schemes.

Chiefly Role in ASM and the Decolonial Reimagination

Decolonization in the spirit of *Sankɔfa* draws on African knowledge systems to conceptualize new frameworks for understanding various phenomena on the continent (Chilisa, Major and Khudu-Petersen 2017). For many marginalized and formerly colonized societies, Western theories tend to be grossly inadequate, and the sustainable solutions to our oppression, exploitation and subordination hardly lie in vague, alien legal rights and policies, but in a careful and creative deployment of more familiar cultural norms, values and institutions (Tamale 2008). This speaks to Gyekye's notion of cultural revivalism (1997), which addresses contemporary problems through the reclamation and revitalization of Indigenous traditions destroyed in the wake of colonialism.

Accordingly, in examining the institution of chieftaincy, I am guided by *Sankɔfa* to look inward for Indigenous knowledges and values that have the potential to address the failings of ASM formalization. This will first require an evaluation of the abuse of the hierarchy system, which currently manifests in the exclusion of the *adekurofo* and other subchiefs from key ASM policy deliberations. True to its adaptable and flexible nature, chieftaincy has successfully crafted an image that aligns with contemporary society by eclectically blending age-old customs and traditional attributes (van Rouveroy van Nieuwaal and van Dijk 1999). However, not all age-old customs are beneficial to contemporary circumstances. While decolonial scholars work within cultural specificities to realize goals requiring a departure from the dogmatic and rigid view of traditional institutions, our embrace of culture is not uncritical; this is particularly so in light of how traditional institutions like chieftaincy have historically been rife with power inequalities that found new manifestations during and after colonialism (Fosu 2025). Drawing on the work of Fanon, Tamale (2008) urged a critical awareness of the colonial constructions and reinterpretations within our traditional institutions, where, after centuries of colonial domination, we find a culture that is rigid in the extreme. This critical awareness enables us to reject ethnocentric and racist projections while also dutifully confronting the tensioned position of traditional institutions as sites where harmful past practices are heralded, in the name of culture, to perpetuate patriarchal, classed and ethnic violence (Ampofo 2009: 28).

Sankɔfa does not suggest a romanticization of precoloniality or a nostalgic return to the inefficiencies of the past. Rather, it presents an opportunity to understand the contested past in the ongoing evolution of traditional systems (Matemba 2014). Frempong (2006) encapsulated this with his observation that the political and social systems of precolonial Africa did not represent 'a golden age'. Nevertheless, they exhibited tenets of democracy and communalism within the context of their traditional values and cultures. Consequently, my argument is for embracing – not replacing – chieftaincy in ASM governance, while also recognizing the need to discard its oppressive aspects and accommodate its numerous liberatory aspects. The impetus for critiquing and reflecting upon chieftaincy's entanglements with coloniality and its political use of hierarchy needs to come from within the institution itself. Addressing these problems is not something that the government can undertake alone in its current state. Recall that early postcolonial governments bemoaned the colonial deployment of chieftaincy hierarchies, arguing that these hierarchies and their intrinsic emphasis on hereditary rights and privileges were patently inconsistent with postcolonial concepts of constitutional democracy. Their anti-chieftaincy radicalism, however, did not translate into a subversion of the deeply engrained hierarchies and nonegalitarian culture they vociferously opposed. On the contrary, they ended up manipulating this very system in their own invention of traditions (Rathbone 2000).

For this reason, my reimagining of chieftaincy within the context of ASM calls for shattering the heightened walls of hierarchy and reviving *Ubuntu*, the principle underpinning the communally oriented values of participatory governance and accountability that were once fundamental to the institution. This does not promise to be an easy feat, particularly since such a radical reconfiguration of chieftaincy will potentially be accompanied by a loss of the power, wealth and influence that some paramount chiefs have accumulated over the years. Here, *Sankɔfa* provides a useful paradigm in reminding stool occupants that chiefship is not an office to be associated merely with the flamboyance of power and personal wealth, but is one with an intrinsic cosmological significance, where service and stewardship to the people, the land and the environment is a legal, moral and spiritual responsibility. As Akyeampong and Obeng (2005) pointed out, power, as held by Asante chieftains, did not exist in a vacuum; it was constructed as interactive, taking cognisance of the rights, obligations and expectations of the ruler and the ruled. Environmental pollution resulting from unregulated ASM within local mining communities signals a failure of leadership that cannot be fully mitigated unless the rot of abuse of power, rentier politics and misappropriation of stool land revenue is purged from all spheres of mineral resource governance. If environmental sustainability is to be a reality within local mining communities, it will require the active contribution and participation of paramount chiefs, subchiefs, queen-mothers and *adekurofo* in the restructuration of their powers and corresponding obligations.

This will necessitate greater involvement by the *adekurofo*, the subchiefs, the women's and youth groups and the small-scale miners whose operations form an integral part of local communities. As I have shown, the marginalization of subchiefs and *adekurofo* has not prevented them from doing their work altogether, but it has affected the transmission of knowledge, the institutional development of chieftaincy and its potential for developing rural economic ventures like ASM for the benefit of the communities.

This is not to say that rethinking the role of chieftaincy in ASM is grounded in a hostility to the nation-state or a parochial allegiance to ethnic units of community (Abraham 1962: 39). Rather, it is about recognizing the traditional legacies of the institution and rebuilding its weakened systems for the benefit of local communities. As Fanon (1997) put it, the fight for national culture must start with the liberation of ethnic groups within the nation, as they form the material foundation upon which a culture is built. While state recognition is no longer a prerequisite for enstoolment and the performance of chiefly duties, chieftaincy as an institution is still very much dependent on, and mutually constitutive with, the state (Adotey 2019). Long gone are the autonomous chieftaincy systems of the past, which had their own political and military powers, and the emergence of the nation-state has brought on an enduring, plural legal and institutional regime whose existence must be duly acknowledged and effectively navigated. In this interconnection, chieftaincy continues to exert significant social and political power that often rivals that of the central government in legitimacy, recognition and loyalty by subjects. The evidence on the ground highlights the significant influence of chiefs in Ghanaian jurisprudence, for example, with recounted instances where litigating parties often accorded much more respect to chiefly declarations than to formal judicial decisions, despite the constitutional supremacy of formal courts over traditional courts in some of these cases.[39]

This brings home Hirons's argument (2014) for a more decentralized ASM governance system involving chiefs at the local level. The Local Administration Act of 1971, which gave chiefs two-thirds representation on local councils and one-third representation on district councils, was removed in the 1988 legal reforms. Currently, the argument is that the new local system of government, as it pertains under article 242(d) of the 1992 Constitution and the 2016 Local Governance Act (Act 936), fails to fully integrate chiefs – both structurally and functionally – into decision-making processes at the local level. I further pursue Hirons's proposals (2014) in calling for a more decolonized ASM governance system that is inclusive of local traditional authorities, particularly the subchiefs and *adekurofo*, beyond the singularity of membership on the committees of state regulatory agencies. This way, chiefs will play a valuable role in administering the living customary law alongside local informal small-scale miners. The sacred oath of office and the permanent nature (barring death or destoolment) of chieftaincy sit in contradistinction to the temporality of political office, giving chiefs a greater degree of responsibility as they step in to fill the void created by state incapacity in ASM formalization.

These proposed reforms can be carried out in tandem with the government's efforts at decentralizing the ASM formalization system. A good starting point for this collaborative, decentralized ASM governance would be to reframe the state's goal of 'driving away the menace of *galamsey*', such that the menace in question refers to the environmental harm posed by the sector, rather than its informal status. In doing so, culturally situated knowledges and the living customary law can be effectively harnessed to combat the bile of environmental pollution and used to restructure ASM as a viable source of livelihood for rural economic development. The evidence confirms that traditional authorities and local miners possess extensive knowledge of the local terrain, land acquisition processes and the day-to-day operations of ASM. They therefore have a lot to offer in terms of localized expertise relevant for transforming the sector. Traditional systems of democratic governance and accountability can be strengthened and incentivized to collaborate with the state in holding miners, politicians and the traditional elite accountable in the allocation of mineral-rich lands, as well as in the fiscal and environmental management of ASM.

Conclusion

Institutional monist-pluralism involving chieftaincy and the modern nation-state remains a key legacy of colonialism that impacts customary land tenures and ASM administration in Ghana. In this chapter, I examined the instrumentality of chieftaincy in ASM, drawing upon the Akan philosophy of *Sankɔfa* to demonstrate the potentiality of reflecting on contemporary situations, retreating into the past to examine the source of prevailing issues and weaknesses, and reclaiming relevant knowledges for a liberatory future. Despite having faced colonial manipulation and anachronistic, undemocratic labelling, chieftaincy has remained a crucial – albeit contested – element of the Ghanaian sociocultural fabric, particularly within the context of ASM. Using a decolonial framework, I established that since tradition is far from fixed, and is constantly debated at the local level, ASM governance can be reformed through a reimagining of the role of chiefs. It is only by taking cognisance of this that policymakers and the institution itself can begin to draw up legal and policy measures that will ensure sustainability in ASM and improve the lives of small-scale miners in mining-affected communities.

Notes

1. In some non-Akan states, this power was held by priests who combined their spiritual office with that of ruler, legislator, chief magistrate and administrator. A key feature of the colonial invention of customary law was the homogenization of chieftaincy, which ensured that Akan-style chieftaincy systems were instituted across the entire country. Consequently, various offices that were formerly centred around local priests were apportioned between the priests and colonially appointed chiefs. The priests retained only their religious and spiritual function, while the secular duties of office were vested in the chief as the head of the state. In the northern parts of Ghana, priests known as the *Tindana* retain strong control of the land, performing sacrifices for its fertility, the people and all things relating to it (Ollenu 1962).
2. MMS/Special Series/Biographical/West Africa/597B; Extract of typescript manuscript of the journals of Reverend Freeman's visits to the Kingdoms of Asante and Dahomey, and to Abeokuta, Lagos and Bagadry between 1840 and 1843. Wesleyan Missionary Archives, SOAS, London.
3. This publication reported of the attempt by British administrators to establish one Mr Coker on the Cape Coast stool, using threats of exile to intimidate local chiefs and the council of elders into supporting the government's objectives. During the Land Bill protests, it became common for British administrators to engineer chieftaincy succession disputes by supporting claimants whom the local people opposed, with the belief that chiefs loyal to the colonial government would help quell local resistance to state legal impositions. This had succeeded in Sierra Leone during the imposition of the hut tax, where chiefs who opposed the tax policy were removed, imprisoned and replaced by chiefs who encouraged their people to pay the tax.
4. The marketization of the commons proceeds from the perspective that markets are natural and the best institution to organize the commons. State intervention in privatizing the commons is seen as imperative for protecting the environment, which in turn ensures transferable property rights. This, as I stated in Chapter 1, proceeds from Hardin's

(1968) notion of the tragedy of the commons, which has rightfully been debunked by Ostrom (1990) and other institutional economists.

5. WO 106/286; Précis of the Ashanti Expedition Wolseley: Intelligence Department, Horse Guards, War Office, 13 April 1874.
6. CO 96/359/13; Notes taken at a public palaver of native kings and chiefs that was held in front of the Kumasi Fort at 4pm on Wednesday, 28 March 1900.
7. Letter from Governor Hodgson to Secretary of State for the Colonies, Joseph Chamberlain, dated 24 July 1900.
8. CO 96/362/80; The then *Asantehene*, King Prempeh I, was exiled to Sierra Leone and later removed to Seychelles, where it was believed he would not be able to encourage any further resistance against the British. The Ashanti Political Prisoners' Detention and Deportation Ordinance of 1901 was subsequently passed to retrospectively sanction the arrests, detentions and deportations of the named chiefs. Note also that amongst the Akan, custom does not permit a chief to speak directly to anyone on formal occasions; chosen for his wisdom and eloquence, his court official – the *ɔkyeame*, or spokesman – does this on behalf of the chief. According to Ward (1991: 53–54), the British commonly and wrongfully translated the word *ɔkyeame* to mean 'linguist', although the *ɔkyeame* was not necessarily supposed to speak any language but his mother tongue. The *ɔkyeame* also acted as a judge, delivering judgements in the chief's court, and occasionally as a diplomat.
9. CO 96/746/5; Lord Hailey's Notes on Adansi Division, Fomena, dated 11 February 1948.
10. CO 96/746/5; Lord Hailey's Notes on Adansi Division, Fomena, dated 11 February 1948.
11. CO 96/814/2; Petition to the Colonial Secretary by Dr J. B. Danquah on behalf of 'nine men of Adanse', dated 3 October 1949.
12. See, for instance, section 12(1) of the Native Authority Act, which provided for punishments for persons who undermined the authority of the chiefs.
13. CO 879/67; Letter from the Resident of Kumasi to the Colonial Secretary, dated 30 March 1899. Note that this is the very same queen-mother who assembled an insurrection against the British, which led to the Yaa Asantewaa War in 1900. Amongst the Akan, the queen-mother was usually the mother of the king. Her title, *ɔhemmaa*, derived from the king's title of *ɔhene*. Queen-mothers sat as members of the king's council and were influential in setting up the king as ruler of the community. See J. B. Danquah. 1952. 'The Culture of Akan', *Journal of the International African Institute* 22(4): 360–66.
14. CO 96/357; Letter from Captain Campbell to Colonial Office, received 11 August 1899.
15. Letter from Captain Stewart, Resident of Kumasi, to Chief of Nkwanta, dated 6 March 1899. Recall that in Chapter 2, I hinted at this practice of foreigners using state-authorized introductory letters to intimidate their way into accessing secret gold mines in Asante. It is therefore unsurprising that some local communities are distrustful of foreign researchers with institutionally authorized introductory letters and ethics approval who seek their consent for participation in research projects regarding their communities.
16. CO 879/67; Letter from Governor Hodgson to Secretary of State for the Colonies, Mr Chamberlain, received 10 October 1899.
17. CO 879/67; Letter from Ashanti Goldfields Corporation to Governor, dated 15 December 1898; No. 219, Letter from Edwin A. Cade, Managing Director of Ashanti Goldfields Corporation Limited, to Colonial Office, received 3 April 1900. See also Chapter 4, where I showed how AGC similarly used the government's military forces and political backing to threaten local chiefs who contested the corporation's encroachment beyond the originally granted boundaries, thereby entrenching its hold over its

concessions in Obuasi. This was supported by colonial administrators who deemed it axiomatic to extend the government's arm of protection to European mining corporations in the colonies. Letter from the Governor, dated 17 July 1900.

18. Minutes of Meeting at the Chief Commissioner's Residency, dated 10 February 1948.
19. Letter from Governor Hodgson, dated 17 July 1900.
20. CO 96/675; Ashanti Native Jurisdiction Amendment Ordinance Enclosure No. 3, Letter from Chief Commissioner's Office to the Colonial Secretary, dated 10 September 1927.
21. Membership of the Ashanti Confederacy Council consisted of the *Asantehene*, the head chiefs of the Divisions, the chiefs of each of the nine Kumasi clans and seven extraordinary members of the Kumasi Division. The inclusion of non-chiefs and the blend of literate and nonliterate members on the various committees of the Confederacy Council were a further demonstration of the changes made to chieftaincy administration under colonial rule.
22. Amongst the Akan, chiefs are referred to by the title of *ɔhene*. According to Valsecchi (2007), the word etymologically derives from *hyeɛ* ('boundary') and was coined in 1929, by Gold Coast intellectual J. de Graft Johnson, to mean 'one who decides boundaries'.
23. BW 90/251; Reports on Land Disputes in the Adansi Division, Obuasi District, Ashanti, May 1949, Enclosure in Gold Coast No. 62 of 24 March 1947. See also Busia (1951: 205).
24. CSO 19/9/39; Tribal Headmen in Mining Areas, Letter from the Governor to the Rt. Hon Malcolm MacDonald, dated 20 May 1939.
25. CO 1018/9.
26. Following the 2024 general elections, the newly elected National Democratic Congress (NDC) government scrapped this Ministry, placing it under the Ministry of Local Government, Chieftaincy and Religious Affairs.
27. Haruna Asana (alias), Obuasi resident and local media personnel. Interview with the author, 10 March 2021.
28. Nii Obodai (alias), local civil society executive. Interview with the author, 16 April 2021.
29. Kwabena Bentum (alias), Ghanaian legal practitioner. Interview with the author, 24 February 2021.
30. Following the death of a former chief executive of the Forestry Commission, he was revealed to have bequeathed portions of the Achimota Forest, a national forest reserve, to members of his family. This revelation has cast serious doubt on the commitment of the state and its appointees in their management of forests and lands in the country. See Manasseh Azure Awuni (2022), 'Full Details: Achimota Forest Lands, Gold Businesses and Guns in Sir John's Will', *The Fourth Estate,* 23 May. Retrieved 12 December 2022 from https://thefourthestategh.com/2022/05/23/full-details-achimota-forest-lands-gold-businesses-and-guns-in-sir-johns-will/.
31. Haruna Asana (alias), Obuasi resident and local media personnel. Interview with the author, 10 March 2021.
32. Nana Kwadwo Asamoah, chief of Adaase. Interview with the author, Adaase, 22 July 2021. See also the 2021 action instituted in the Obuasi High Court by the chief of Kwapia against Chinese ASM firms and their local partners, the Minerals Commission and the Environmental Protection Agency (now Environmental Protection Authority), in respect of the Adaase Community Mining Site: *Nana Gyamena Kwabena Oyiakwan II, Chief of Kwapia and Nana Anokye Ababio, Krontihene of Kwapia v Lan Haisong, Li Dehao, Huang Shen Gjun, Wen Shili, Obuasi Municipal Assembly, Asamoah Gate, Simon Kwadwo Antwi, Minerals Commission, Leap Palm Oil Company, Justice Ofori Ampofo and Environmental Protection Agency (EPA Obuasi)*.
33. Nana Kwabena Nyame, chief of Amamiriwa No. I. Interview with the author, Amamiriwa No. 1, 10 July 2021.

34. Ibid.
35. Nii Obodai (alias), local civil society executive. Interview with the author, 16 April 2021.
36. Nana Gyamerah Kwabena Oyiakwan II, chief of Kwapia. Interview with the author, Kwapia, 7 September 2021.
37. Haruna Asana (alias), Obuasi resident and local media personnel. Interview with the author, 10 March 2021. See also Neil Nii Kanarku (2021), 'Government's Community Mining Program a Disguised Galamsey – Okyenhene' *Citi Newsroom*, 5 April. Retrieved 12 December 2022 from https://citinewsroom.com/2021/04/governments-community-mining-program-a-disguised-galamsey-okyenhene//.
38. Nana Gyamerah Kwabena Oyiakwan II, chief of Kwapia. Interview with the author, 7 September 2021.
39. Kwabena Bentum (alias), Ghanaian legal practitioner. Interview with the author, 24 February 2021.

CONCLUSION

Moving Forward

Deconstructing ASM Informality and the Living Customary Law in Ghana

In the Wesleyan Missionary Archives located at the School of Oriental and African Studies (SOAS), a collection of photographs depicts Wesleyan missionary activities across the colonized world. One photograph, titled 'A Man and the Bible He Cannot Read', features a West African man dressed in a European suit and seated by a table upon which rests an open Bible. This photograph struck me as a perfect metaphor for the colonized African: draped in an entirely new regalia, rendered nameless, and propped up beside a book they say he cannot read!

The imposition of Western rationality, universality and legal systems has long been justified by the colonial construct of the savage as illiterate and lacking the civilized legal and administrative frameworks needed to manage their lives, lands and abundant resources. Such colonial paternalism permeated the mining economy as Europeans travelled to West Africa in pursuit of gold, subsequently establishing new legal systems there to facilitate its extraction. As such, my primary research objective was to question the origins of the formal/informal categories within the extractive industry and to examine how these categories are used by the state, the media, activists and researchers, to the detriment of informal small-scale miners. In problematizing the state's deployment of ASM informality, it was necessary to look beyond the commonly proposed solution of state-centric laws in formalization measures, and to instead embrace Indigenous epistemologies and the living customary law as a more liberatory framework.

Figure 7.1. 'A Man and the Bible He Cannot Read'. Courtesy of the Wesleyan Missionary Archives, SOAS, MMS/West Africa/Photographs/Box 1195A, File 28, used with permission.

I aimed to achieve this through a decolonial reimagination where the law is excavated from the situated knowledges, lived experiences, stories, practices, spiritualities and customs of the local community. As my overarching methodological framework, the Akan philosophy of *Sankɔfa* guided my central argument that the ongoing discourse surrounding ASM formalization needs to interrogate and transcend the integration of informal small-scale miners into colonially erected legal and institutional systems. The distinct nature, history, governance systems, sociocultural contexts and actors of ASM necessitate a critical re-evaluation of the origins of formalization and its criminalization of small-scale miners. McFarlane and Waibel (2012), for instance, have addressed the need to move away from binary approaches and to rethink the very notion of the formal/informal divide, as well as its implicit assumption of formality as norm and informality as deviation. In outlining critiques of de Soto's thesis on formalization (2000), Home and Lim (2004: 2) emphasized that de Soto evaded some difficult questions regarding the colonial sanctioning of pre-emption, the role of capitalism and land titles in perpetuating colonial power structures, and the inequalities faced by the poor who are pushed out by larger, wealthier and possibly foreign investors attracted by the latent capital in land. This, as I have highlighted, forms a major blind spot in the ASM formalization discourse, which – despite ongoing discussions on decolonization – has failed to confront the coloniality that underpins access to land titles and mineral rights in formerly colonized mineral-producing countries of the Global South.

By retreating into the past, I was able to reveal how positivist law and its colonial monist-pluralism was used to suppress local resistance, justify the violent dispossession of colonized communities and undermine their existing mining practices, land tenure systems and sociopolitical structures. These injustices, as I have shown, were compounded by the introduction of legislative formalization, as the state positioned itself as arbiter of mineral rights and administrator of Indigenous mining, without any commensurate commitment to – or apparatus for – supporting Indigenous miners. For Hilson and Gatsinzi (2014: 3), the challenges faced by African dual-mining economies can be traced to the heyday of the Structural Adjustment Programme, when a publication by the World Bank (1993) titled 'A Strategy for African Mining' called for host governments to prioritize opening up their large-scale mining to foreign investors in order to promote export-based mineral development. While the structural adjustments exacerbated a large-scale mining bias against local small-scale miners, closer historical analysis reveals that the bedrock of the dual-mining economy, the contemporary challenges it presents to local miners and its differentiated regulatory frameworks extend beyond the World Bank. Indeed, policy stratifications within the political economy of mining emerged under colonialism, when British mercantilism, militarism and missionary work coincided to lay the foundation of the formal/informal divide in the sector.

Despite much greater awareness among governments and international donor agencies of the dynamics and contributions of ASM, the sector continues to be relegated to the periphery in state mining policies and support programmes. Political independence has wrought little for epistemic and economic liberation, especially within the mining regime, where many African countries continue to cling to colonial legal infrastructure even as they recognize its limitations in addressing the problems on the continent. In the ASM context, postcolonial governments maintain the colonial strategy of accumulation by dispossession through the formulation of neoliberal mining laws and the imposition of bureaucratic formalization measures that local small-scale miners are unable to comply with, and for which they remain criminalized and deprived of access to mineralized lands for their operations.

I deployed a decolonial, pluralist framework to underscore the need to disengage formalization from a Eurocentric matrix that imposes a singular mode of organizing land relations around formalized and codified property rights. As Okrah (2008) has stated, policies that are built on imperialism and social injustice can never achieve any meaningful benefit to the local people, no matter how well intentioned they are. Accordingly, we can acknowledge the enduring colonial legacy of legal pluralism, while also recognizing the need to move beyond a fascination with its systems and ideologies – systems that are incapable of interrogating the power dynamics and injustices within the current legal framework. In pursuing a decolonial legal pluralism towards the reconstruction of ASM as a socially, economically and culturally emancipatory space, I advance the need to embrace pluralistic views of governance that are inclusive of local small-scale miners, chiefs and women's groups.

ASM formalization, even in the form of newly introduced policy interventions like the Community Mining Scheme (CMS), reflects a centralized bureaucratic system where classed capture, professionalization and mechanization work to alienate and marginalize small-scale miners while undermining traditional authority in the local mining communities.

Local small-scale miners may welcome state support in accessing geologically productive lands and environmentally safe logistics, but the evidence suggests that they are most certainly not enthusiastic about participating in the classed, restrictive and burdensome state-sanctioned licensing processes. In that regard, they would rather maintain the informality of their operations. This confirms an earlier study, conducted by Geenen (2012), which noted that many ASM operators were not necessarily interested in acquiring formal licences, as informality was better suited to their rudimentary, temporary and seasonal mining activities. This persistence of ASM informality stands, to an extent, in resistance to the dominant legal ideologies as rooted in colonial disenfranchisement, capitalist extractivism and other policy measures incompatible with the lived realities of small-scale miners.[1]

Furthermore, the empirical analysis contests the notion of informality as disorganized and lawless, rather depicting informal ASM as a social field organized by social associations operating under the living customary law. ASM groups, local mining communities and chiefs collectively offer a wealth of knowledge that can be tapped in reforming the sector. I reached this conclusion by considering Ehrlich's conceptualization of the living law (1936), which asserted that since norms are social practices, law cannot be reduced to the 'formal' laws of the state; rather, it must include 'informal' social codes that exist independently of the state. Tamale (2020: 140) has urged that if reality indicates that the living customary law plays a dominant role in the lives of African people, then our attention should be directed upon it. In probing the issues raised by the structuralist framework surrounding informality, Benton (1994) emphasized the need to recognize that under particularly well-defined conditions, the informal sector may even emerge to impel economic growth through various innovative strategies that are simply not possible in the more rigidly constrained formal sector. Indeed, the informal economy in Africa is said to account for 50–80% of the continent's GDP, 60–80% of its employment and 90% of its new jobs (Benjamin and Mbaye 2014). Informality, as I have demonstrated, represents the dominant and normatively preferable approach for small-scale miners, who, together with their local mining communities, maintain a perception of legality and legitimacy that differs from the state's formalization mechanisms. The government therefore needs to discard its policy of blanket criminalization and instead examine how it can speak the predominant language of informality in addressing the challenges associated with ASM.

And now, what do we do with formalization in the legal pluralist world of ASM?

To chart new pathways for ASM formalization within complex, legally plural contexts like Ghana, we must understand that legal pluralism is not merely the formal inclusion of various actors within a single system. Rather, it involves an interactive relationship between different legalities, each embedded in social, historical and cultural contexts that may not easily align with the logic of state law (Boccheni and Castaneda-Quintana 2024). This is particularly pertinent as policy reforms such as the Community Mining Scheme (CMS) are being rolled out. According to the Ghanaian government, the CMS was necessitated by, among other things, the aim of 'providing members of mining communities an opportunity to engage in small-scale mining as well as obtain direct benefit from mining operations' (Minerals Commission of Ghana 2021). While the inclusion of chiefs as co-opted members in the Community Mining Oversight Committee reflects an effort to integrate the complex configurations of customary law into state systems, the overall implementation of the CMS illustrates how disempowering and counterproductive the recognition of legal pluralism can be, especially when the dominant decision-makers fail to grasp the intricacies of the overlapping legal orders. The assumption that simply including the chiefs of the relevant mining communities in the Oversight Committee ensures equitable participation grossly overstates the government's understanding of the complex power dynamics and struggles for autonomy that underpin the persistence of informality in ASM. It further overlooks the lack of representation of local small-scale mining groups and the tendency for ASM formalization mechanisms to strategically position foreign and classed interests over those of the local mining communities.

A more suitable representation of decolonial pluralism in the operationalization of ASM formalization needs to transcend the tokenization of select chiefs in the centralized managerial systems, and revisit what 'community engagement' means to the people. Additionally, both chieftaincy and the state need to simultaneously grapple with internal reforms that will rid their respective institutions of structural incapacities, misappropriations, stifling bureaucracies, power inequalities and corruption that constrain access to mineral rights and environmental oversight of ASM operations in the local communities. An effective harmonization of the living customary law and state law in ASM formalization can be achieved through a participatory governance system that engages local institutions and draws upon the knowledges of chiefs (particularly subchiefs and *adekurofo*) and small-scale miners' groups. This would have further governance implications, such as a reconstitution of Community Mining Oversight Committees and the empowerment of chiefs and local ASM associations with greater responsibilities.

Globalization complicates the struggle for decolonization because it requires us to constantly address the marginality of African agency and knowledges by simultaneously emphasizing Africa's specificity and globality (Ndlovu-Gatsheni 2017; Fosu 2025). This raises the tantalizing question of how a decolonial and legal pluralist reformation of ASM formalization can be managed amidst neoliberal pressures and unprecedented socio-economic changes within the global extractive industry. Now, more than ever, collaborations involving foreign donors who finance ASM formalization projects, such as the UNEP's planetGOLD and the World Bank, must be grounded in epistemological decolonization,[2] recognizing local communities as sites of conceptual development and the production of theory. Furthermore, redirecting funding away from criminalization and carceral state responses, and towards supporting informal ASM with access to lands, geodata and logistics, will not only be a more beneficial use of resources, but will also constitute a radical departure from the colonial legacies of state apathy and punitive posturing towards local small-scale miners.

The living customary law has the potential to enrich state law in constructing a shared system of access to mineral rights and environmental sustainability. Here, capacity-building for key regulatory agencies would have to acknowledge the governance potential of local ASM groups and traditional authorities, recognizing their relevance for achieving proper environmental regulation and compliance monitoring. To this end, a decentralized hybrid system comprising local chiefs, ASM groups and local government agencies could be established and logistically supported in the local mining communities; such a system would facilitate the registration of small-scale miners, streamline ASM administration and mainstream local miners' access to land. In practice, this would mean that local mining associations, overseen by traditional authorities and local government agencies, would ensure transparency in access to lands, environmental protection, health and safety measures and land reclamation. Here, chiefs would not be granted merely ceremonial roles on oversight committees, but would instead hold definitive responsibilities that are subject to strengthened traditional accountability measures.

For the resolution of land contestations in ASM, large-scale mining corporations also need to have a more clearly defined role in the shaping of policy and negotiation of partnerships in ASM governance. In dealing with local small-scale miners, corporations like AGA must confront their violent colonial histories within the local mining communities and recognize the influence they hold in the global capitalist mining political economy. This could serve as the first of many steps in providing redress to the land struggles faced by local miners. In tackling the past, the corporate sector should design internal policy measures that are informed by the legal pluralist realities of their mining operations – these include the means by which they obtain concessions, particularly those already being worked by local miners, and how national mining regulations and the politics of environmental pollution are skewed in their favour. The current system, in which large-scale corporations permit ASM operators on their concessions, must be clarified and integrated into mainstream operations, with clear, transparent terms to address the volatile land conflicts that arise in local mining communities. A spatial and temporal awareness of large-scale mining can serve as a precursor to resolving longstanding contestations and ensuring that the prospecting capabilities of small-scale miners are not exploited by large-scale corporations.

On this note, I would like to conclude by briefly emphasizing that decolonizing legal education is essential for the overall achievement of a decolonized ASM formalization. In conceptualizing his theory of formalization, de Soto (2000: 209) was particularly critical of lawyers from the Global South for their resistance to change and their unwillingness to construct bridges that would enable the informal rules of the poor to be integrated within the realm of formal law. I have critiqued the Eurocentric framing of de Soto's call for integration into formal legal systems, highlighting the absence of any demand to dismantle the colonial underpinnings of such systems. Nevertheless, I share his concerns about the nature of the legal profession in developing countries, which, as I have experienced, continues to be shaped by colonial-era models of professionalization in its classism, hierarchization and subjugation of Indigenous legal systems.

In bemoaning de Soto's theory of formalization, Tanzanian scholar Issa Shivji (2006) criticized the legal intelligentsia for oiling a 'rule of law' rooted in the exigencies of 'the rule of capital' in the service of corporatocracy. According to Shivji, the Anglo-American law that is being globalized and localized essentially works to enable institutional frameworks in which corporate capital can exploit resources without let or hindrance. In all of this, lawyers fail to question what would become of the vulnerable once we heed de Soto's advice to 'breathe legal life into their dead assets'. Shivji closed his argument with an admonition to reflect on the past, since history demonstrates that the wealth accumulated in capitalist centres fixated on formalist approaches usually renders the vulnerable dead, mutilated, malnourished, divided, conflict-ridden and as the nameless wretched of the earth.

The reformation of ASM formalization in Ghana must entail a rethinking of the foundational pedagogies upon which future lawyers, judges and law enforcement personnel are trained. Ghana's legal education system needs to reignite the fervour of the country's anticolonial past and critically engage with the complex class solidarity of Indigenous colonial-era lawyers and their unceasing resistance against monist-pluralism and legal transplantations within the matrix of land and mining regulations. bell hooks's transformative pedagogy (1994) advocates for a knowledge system that is connected to the decolonial struggle and acts towards the practice of freedom. 'The law is the law' should not be a slogan regurgitated in justification of oppressive legal frameworks, but a wake-up call to question where our laws emanate from, whom they serve and how beneficial they are to the general welfare of the people. As Ruffin (2019: 106) has argued, there must be a change in the way law – particularly customary law – is taught in law schools, so as to reflect the ontological, epistemological and axiological perspectives of the living customary law. Additionally, according to Ruffin, African countries need to empower a new generation of customary land lawyers, court jurists and land governance experts who will be mindful of indigeneity, and who will argue and decide cases with an awareness of their sociocultural contexts, even if these cases are decided in venues upholding the rule of state law orthodoxy.

It is only within the wider paradigm shift of a decolonized legal system that there can be a meaningfully decolonial and pluralist system of ASM governance – where the living customary law is recognized as a legitimate overarching framework, where informality is decriminalized, where access to land is transparent and where small-scale miners and traditional authorities are included in decision-making. In order to achieve sustainable ASM and address its unique challenges in the country, the Ghanaian legal education system must be decolonized. This requires a common understanding – by lawyers, judges, researchers and activists – of law's duty to the principle of *Ubuntu* and to the liberation of the people from systemic inequality.

Notes

1. In making this point, however, I note Varley's cautions (2013) against ascribing a generalized resistance to informality. Varley argued that to dwell on informality as resistance or reverse colonialism is to romanticize it at the expense of a more prosaic assessment of the material constraints facing the urban poor and the resources they use to address those constraints. Recognizing that formality is a process that actively disadvantages low-income groups enables us to acknowledge informality as a site where direct contestation against formality and other forms of resistance occur, as actors struggle to navigate and confront the failures of the formal.
2. See https://www.planetgold.org/ (accessed 15 June 2023). This project is funded by the Global Environment Facility (GEF) and operates under the 2013 Minamata Convention on Mercury, with the aim of ending the toxic trail of ASM through formalization and the elimination of mercury use. Its policy framework, which raises awareness of the harmful impacts of mercury use and provides alternative gold-processing technologies, could be enhanced by the strategic infusion of local knowledges so as to build trust and foster community engagement.

References

Abotchie, C., A. Awedoba, and I. K. Odotei. 2006. 'Perceptions on Chieftaincy', in Irene K. Odotei and Albert K. Awedoba (eds), *Chieftaincy in Ghana: Culture, Governance and Development*. Accra: Sub-Saharan Publishers, pp. 103–44.

Abraham, W. E. 1962. *The Mind of Africa*. Chicago: University of Chicago Press.

Abudulai, S. 2002. 'Land Rights, Land-Use Dynamics and Policy in Peri-urban Tamale, Ghana', in C. Toulmin, P. Lavigne-Delville and S. Traore (eds), *The Dynamics of Resource Tenure in West Africa*. London: IIED, pp. 72–85.

Acosta, Alberto. 2011. 'Extractivism and Neo-extractivism: Two Sides of the Same Curse', in M. Lang and D. Mokrani (eds), *Beyond Development: Alternative Visions from Latin America*. Amsterdam: TNI/Rosa Luxemburg Foundation, pp. 61–86.

Acquah, G. K. 2006. 'The Judicial Role of the Chief in Democratic Governance', in Irene K. Odotei and Albert K. Awedoba (eds), *Chieftaincy in Ghana: Culture, Governance and Development*. Accra: Sub-Saharan Publishers, pp. 65–80.

Adebisi, Foluke. 2016. 'Stop Researching Sub-Saharan Africa', *African Skies*, 29 July. Retrieved 22 November 2024 from https://folukeafrica.com/we-should-stop-researching-sub-saharan-africa/.

Ademolu, Edward. 2023. 'Birds of a Feather (Don't Always) Flock Together: Critical Reflexivity of "Outsiderness" as an "Insider" Doing Qualitative Research with One's "Own People"', *Qualitative Research* 24(2): 344–66.

Adogla-Bessa, Delali. 2017. 'Citi FM Launches #StopGalamseyNow Campaign', *Citinews*, 3 April. Retrieved 22 November 2024 from https://citifmonline.com/?p=307341.

Adom, Dickson, et al. 2018. 'The Conservation Ethos in the Asante Cultural and Artistic Elements for the Management of Ghana's Biodiversity', *International Journal of Humanities and Social Science Review* 4(3): 1–22.

Adotey, Edem. 2019. 'Parallel or Dependent? The State, Chieftaincy and Institutions of Governance in Ghana', *African Affairs* 184(473): 628–45.

Adu-Baffour, Ferdinand, Thomas Daum, and Regina Birner. 2021. 'Governance Challenges of Small-Scale Gold Mining in Ghana: Insights from a Process Net-Map Study', *Land Use Policy* 102: 1–16.

Adu-Baffour, Ferdinand, et al. 2025. 'Who Cleans Up the Mess? Exploring Community-Based Solutions for Rehabilitating Ghana's Artisanal and Small-Scale Mining Lands', *Environmental Development* 55: 1–15.

Adu-Gyamfi, Samuel, et al. 2020. 'British Land Policies in the Gold Coast and Her Relations with Asante', *Studia Historiae Oeconomicae* 38: 163–81.

Afeku, Charles, and Akua Asamoah Debrah. 2020. 'Policy Convergence on Development Minerals in Africa: A Study of Ghana's Regulatory Framework', *The Extractive Industries and Society* 7(2): 488–96.

Afriyie, Kwadwo, John K. Ganle, and Janet A. Adomako. 2016. 'The Good in Evil: A Discourse Analysis of the *Galamsey* Industry in Ghana', *Oxford Development Studies* 44(4): 493–508.

Ahwoi, Kwamena. 2010. *Local Government and Decentralisation in Ghana*. Accra: Unimax Macmillan.

Aidoo, Ama Ata. 2017. 'As the Dust Begins to Settle: An Afterword, Twenty Years On', in Helen Yitah (ed.), *After the Ceremonies: New and Selected Poems*. University of Nebraska Press, pp. 12–17.

Akabzaa, Thomas. 2009. 'Mining in Ghana: Implications for National Economic Development and Poverty Reduction', in Bonnie Campbell (ed.), *Mining in Africa: Regulation and Development*. London: Pluto Press, pp. 25–65.

Akabzaa, Thomas, and A. Darimani. 2001. 'Impact of Mining Sector Investment in Ghana: A Study of the Tarkwa Mining Region', SAPRI Draft Report.

Akafari, Albert Ayinpoya, et al. 2021. 'Land Appropriation, Customary Tenure and Rural Livelihoods: Gold Mining in Ghana', *Third World Quarterly* 42(11): 2572–92.

Ake, Claude. 1996. *Democracy and Development in Africa*. Washington, D.C.: Brookings Institution Press.

Akrong, Abraham. 2006. 'Religion and Traditional Leadership in Ghana', in Irene K. Odotei and Albert K. Awedoba (eds), *Chieftaincy in Ghana: Culture, Governance and Development*. Accra: Sub-Saharan Publishers, pp. 193–212.

Akurang-Parry, Kwabena O. 2006. '"Disrespect and Contempt for Our Natural Rulers": The African Intelligentsia and the Effects of British Indirect Rule on Indigenous Rulers in the Gold Coast c.1912–1920', *The International Journal of Regional and Local Studies* 2(1): 43–65.

Akyeampong, Emmanuel, and Pashington Obeng. 2005. 'Spirituality, Gender, and Power in Asante History', in Oyèrónkẹ́ Oyěwùmi (ed.), *African Gender Studies: A Reader.* New York: Palgrave Macmillan, pp. 23–48.

Alcoff, Linda. 1991–92. 'The Problem of Speaking for Others', *Cultural Critique* 20: 5–32.

Amanor, Kojo. 2004. 'Global and Local Land Markets: The Role of the Customary', in J. Quan, S. F. Tan and C. Toulmin (eds), *Land in Africa: Market Asset or Secure Livelihood? Proceedings and Summary of Conclusions from the Land in Africa Conference Held in London, November 8–9, 2004*. London: IIED, pp. 103–13.

———. 2008. 'The Changing Face of Customary Land Tenure', in Janine M. Ubink and Kojo S. Amanor (eds), *Contesting Land and Custom in Ghana: State, Chief and the Citizen*. Leiden: Leiden University Press, pp. 55–79.

———. 2009a. 'Securing Land Rights in Ghana', in Janine M. Ubink, André J. Hoekema and Willem J. Assies (eds), *Legalising Land Rights: Local Practices, State Responses and Tenure Security in Africa, Asia and Latin America*. Leiden: Leiden University Press, pp. 97–131.

———. 2009b. 'Tree Plantations, Agricultural Commodification, and Land Tenure Security in Ghana', in Janine M. Ubink, André J. Hoekema and Willem J. Assies (eds), *Legalising Land Rights: Local Practices, State Responses and Tenure Security in Africa, Asia and Latin America*. Leiden: Leiden University Press, pp. 133–61.

Amanor, Kojo, and Janine Ubink. 2008. 'Contesting Land and Custom in Ghana: Introduction', in Janine M. Ubink and Kojo S. Amanor (eds), *Contesting Land and Custom in Ghana: State, Chief and the Citizen*. Leiden: Leiden University Press, pp. 9–26.

Amin, Samir. 2009. *Eurocentrism*, 2nd edn. New York: Monthly Review Press.

Ampofo, Akosua Adomako. 2009. 'One Who Has Truth – She Has Strength: The Feminist Activist Inside and Outside the Academy in Ghana', in Akosua Adomako Ampofo and Signe Arnfred (eds), *African Feminist Politics of Knowledge: Tensions, Challenges, Possibilities*. Uppsala: Nordiska Afrikainstituet, pp. 28–51.

Andrew, Brook, and Jessica Neath. 2018. 'Encounters with Legacy Images: Decolonising and Re-imagining Photographic Evidence from the Colonial Archive', *History of Photography* 42(3): 217–38.

Andrews, Nathan. 2015. 'Digging for Survival and/or Justice? The Drivers of Illegal Mining Activities in Western Ghana', *Africa Today* 62(2): 3–24.

Anker, Kirsten. 2016. *Declarations of Interdependence: A Legal Pluralist Approach to Indigenous Rights*. London: Routledge.

Anofuechi, Benson O. 2022. 'A Critical Assessment of Ubuntu as a Source for Moral Formation in Contemporary Africa', Ph.D. dissertation. Cape Town: University of the Western Cape.

Antwi-Boateng, Osman, and Mamudu Abunga-Akudugu. 2020. 'Golden Migrants: The Rise and Impact of Illegal Chinese Small-Scale Mining in Ghana', *Politics & Policy* 48(1): 135–67.

Apoh, Wazi, et al. 2017. 'Law, Land and What Lies Beneath: Exploring Mining Impacts on Customary Law and Cultural Heritage Protection in Ghana and Western Australia', *African Identities* 15(4): 367–86.

Araújo, Sara. 2025. 'Legal Pluralism as Co-Presence: Disobeying the Hierarchies of the Western Canons', *Oñati Socio-Legal Series* 15(5): 1622–46.

Armah-Attoh, Daniel. 2017. 'Ghanaians Disapprove of Illegal Mining, Endorse Alternative Livelihood Support by Government', *Afrobarometer* Dispatch No. 175. Accra: CDD-Ghana.

Arnfred, Signe, and Akosua Adomako Ampofo. 2009. 'Introduction: Feminist Politics of Knowledge', in Akosua Adomako Ampofo and Signe Arnfred (eds), *African Feminist Politics of Knowledge: Tensions, Challenges, Possibilities*. Uppsala: Nordiska Afrikainstitutet, pp. 5–27.

Arthur-Holmes, Francis, et al. 2022. 'Graduate Unemployment, Artisanal and Small-Scale Mining, and Rural Transformation in Ghana: What Does the "Educated" Youth Involvement Offer?', *Journal of Rural Studies* 95: 125–39.

Arthur-Holmes, Francis, and Kwaku Abrefa Busia. 2022a. 'Safety Concerns and Occupational Health Hazards of Women in Artisanal and Small-Scale Mining in Ghana', *The Extractive Industries and Society* 10: 1–9.

———. 2022b. 'Women, North-South Migration and Artisanal and Small-Scale Mining in Ghana: Motivations, Drivers and Socio-economic Implications', *The Extractive Industries and Society* 10: 1–14.

Arthur-Holmes, Francis, and George Ofosu. 2024. 'Rethinking State-Led Formalisation of Artisanal and Small-Scale Mining (ASM): Towards Mining Licence Categorisation, Women Empowerment and Environmental Sustainability', *Resources Policy* 93: 1–15.

Aryee, Benjamin N. A., Bernard K. Ntibery, and Evans Atorkui. 2013. 'Trends in the Small-Scale Mining of Precious Minerals in Ghana: A Perspective on Its Environmental Impact', *Journal of Cleaner Production* 11: 131–40.

Aryee, R. J. 2007. 'Traditional Leadership and Local Governance in Africa: The Ghanaian Experience'. Presentation at the Fourth National Annual Local Government Conference, Southern Sun–Elangeni, Durban.

Asamoah, Kwame, and Alex Osei-Kojo. 2016. 'A Contextual Analysis of Implementation Challenges of Small-Scale Mining Laws in Ghana: A Case Study of Bekwai Municipality', *Sage Open* 6(3): 1–11.

'ASM Inventory: World Maps of Artisanal and Small-Scale Mining'. 2018. *The Artisanal and Small-scale Mining Knowledge Sharing Archive*. Retrieved October 2025 from http://artisanalmining.org.

Aubynn, Anthony. 2009. 'Sustainable Solution or a Marriage of Inconvenience? The Co-existence of Large-Scale Mining and Artisanal and Small-Scale Mining on the Abosso Goldfields Concession in Western Ghana', *Resources Policy* 34(1–2): 64–70.

Aubynn, T., et al. 2010. *Mainstreaming Artisanal and Small-Scale Mining: A Background to Policy Advocacy.* Draft Report. Accra: Ghana Chamber of Mines.

Awumbila, Mariama, and Dodzi Tsikata. 2010. 'Economic Liberalisation, Changing Resource Tenures and Gendered Livelihoods: A Study of Small-Scale Gold Mining and

Mangrove Exploitation in Rural Ghana', in Dodzi Tsikata and Pamela Golah (eds), *Land Tenure, Gender and Globalisation: Research Analysis from Africa, Asia and Latin America*. Ottawa: Zubaan, pp. 98–144.

Ayelazuno, Jasper Abembia, and Lord Mawuko-Yevugah. 2021. 'Between the Africa Mining Vision and the Neo-Patrimonial State: The Agency Gap in Ghana's Regulation of Artisanal and Small-Scale Mining', *South African Journal of International Affairs* 28(4): 555–82.

Baddianaah, Issah, Bernard Nuoleyeng Baatuuwie, and Raymond Adongo. 2022. 'Socio-demographic Factors Affecting Artisanal and Small-Scale Mining (Galamsey) Operations in Ghana', *Heliyon* 8: 1–12.

Banakar, Reza. 2011. 'Having One's Cake and Eating It: The Paradox of Contextualisation in Socio-legal Research', *International Journal of Law in Context* 7(4): 487–503.

———. 2015. *Normativity in Legal Sociology: Methodological Reflections on Law and Regulation in Late Modernity*. New York: Springer.

Banchirigah, Sadia Mohammed. 2006. 'How Have Reforms Fuelled the Expansion of Artisanal Mining? Evidence from Sub-Saharan Africa', *Resources Policy* 31(3): 165–71.

———. 2008. 'Challenges with Eradicating Illegal Mining in Ghana: A Perspective from the Grassroots', *Resources Policy* 33(1): 29–38.

Banchirigah, Sadia Mohammed, and Gavin Hilson. 2010. 'De-agrarianization, Re-agrarianization and Local Economic Development: Re-orienting Livelihoods in African Artisanal Mining Communities', *Policy Sciences* 43(2): 157–80.

Banks, Nicola, Melanie Lombard, and Diana Mitlin. 2020. 'Urban Informality as a Site of Critical Analysis', *The Journal of Development Studies* 56(2): 223–38.

Bansah, K. J. 2019. 'From Diurnal to Nocturnal: Surviving in a Chaotic Artisanal and Small-Scale Mining Sector', *Resources Policy* 64: 1–8.

Bansah, K. J., et al. 2018. 'Socioeconomic and Environmental Assessment of Informal Artisanal and Small-Scale Mining in Ghana', *Journal of Cleaner Production* 202: 465–75.

Bansah, K. J., Paul Junior Acquah, and Elsie Assan. 2022. 'Guns and Fires: The Use of Military Force to Eradicate Informal Mining', *The Extractive Industries and Society* 11: 1–12.

Bansah, K. J., A. B. Yalley, and N. Dumakor-Dupey. 2016. 'The Hazardous Nature of Small-Scale Underground Mining in Ghana', *Journal of Sustainable Mining* 15(1): 8–25.

Barbosa, Lia Pinheiro. 2022. 'Onto-Epistemic Paradigm of the Countryside and Social Theory: What Do Popular Movements of Latin American and the Caribbean Teach Us?', *Educational Studies* 58(5–6): 620–40.

Basu, Niladri, Elisha Renne, and Rachel N. Long. 2015. 'An Integrated Assessment Approach to Address Artisanal and Small-Scale Gold Mining in Ghana', *International Journal of Environmental Research and Public Health* 12(9): 11683–98.

Batterbury, Simon, and Frankline Ndi. 2018. 'Land-grabbing in Africa', in J. A. Binns, K. Lynch and E. Nel (eds), *The Routledge Handbook of African Development*. London: Routledge, pp. 573–82.

Benjamin, Charles E. 2008. 'Legal Pluralism and Decentralization: Natural Resource Management in Mali', *World Development* 36(11): 2255–76.

Benjamin, Nancy, and Ahmadou Aly Mbaye. 2014. 'Informality, Growth and Development in Africa', WIDER Working Paper No. 52.

Bennett, Jane. 2009. 'Connections to Research: The Southern African Network of Higher Education Institutions Challenging Sexual Harassment/Sexual Violence, 1996–2001', in Akosua Adomako Ampofo and Signe Arnfred (eds), *African Feminist Politics of Knowledge: Tensions, Challenges, Possibilities*. Uppsala: Nordiska Afrikainstitutet, pp. 52–82.

Bennet, T. W. 2009. 'Re-Introducing African Customary Law to the South African Legal System', *American Journal of Comparative Law* 57(1): 1–31.

Benton, Lauren. 1994. 'Beyond Legal Pluralism: Towards a New Approach to Law in the Informal Sector', *Social and Legal Studies* 3(2): 223–42.

———. 2009. *Law and Colonial Cultures: Legal Regimes in World History, 1400–1900*. Cambridge: Cambridge University Press.

Bentsi-Enchill, Kwamena. 1969. 'The Colonial Heritage of Legal Pluralism: The British Scheme', *Zambia Law Journal* 1(2): 1–30.

Benyera, Everisto. 2018. 'Colonialism, the Theft of History and the Quest for Justice for Africa', in Artwell Nhemachena, Tapiwa V. Warikandwa and Samuel K. Amoo (eds), *Social and Legal Theory in the Age of Decoloniality: (Re-)Envisioning Pan-African Jurisprudence in the 21st Century*. Bamenda: Langaa RPCIG, pp. 121–64.

Berman, Paul Schiff. 2007. 'Global Legal Pluralism', *Southern California Law Review* 80(6): 1155–238.

———. 2009. 'The New Legal Pluralism', *Annual Review of Law and Social Science* 5(1): 225–42.

Berry, Sara. 2000. *Chiefs Know Their Boundaries: Essays on Property, Power and the Past in Asante 1896–1996*. Oxford: James Currey.

Bhambra, Gurminder K. 2014. 'Postcolonial and Decolonial Dialogues', *Postcolonial Studies* 17(2): 115–21.

Biles, James J. 2009. 'Informal Work in Latin America: Competing Perspectives and Recent Debates', *Geography Compass* 3(1): 214–36.

Black, C. F. 2011. *The Land Is the Source of the Law: A Dialogic Encounter with Indigenous Jurisprudence*. London: Routledge.

Boafo, James, Sebastian Angzoorokuu Paalo, and Senyo Dotsey. 2019. 'Illicit Chinese Small-Scale Mining in Ghana: Beyond Institutional Weakness?', *Sustainability* 11(21): 1–18.

Boafo-Arthur, Kwame. 2003. 'Chieftaincy in Ghana: Challenges and Prospects in the 21st Century', *African and Asian Studies* 2(2): 125–53.

Boahen, Adu. 1975. *Ghana: Evolution and Change in the Nineteenth and Twentieth Centuries*. London: Longman.

Boamah, Festus. 2014. 'How and Why Chiefs Formalise Land Use in Recent Times: The Politics of Land Dispossession Through Biofuels Investment in Ghana', *Review of African Political Economy* 41(141): 406–23.

Boateng, Dennis Owusu, Francis Nana Yaw Codjoe, and Johnson Ofori. 2014. 'Impact of Illegal Small-Scale Mining (Galamsey) on Cocoa Production in Atiwa District of Ghana', *International Journal of Advanced Agricultural Research* 2: 89–99.

Boateng, Kwabena, and Stephen Afranie. 2020. 'Chieftaincy: An Anachronistic Institution Within a Democratic Dispensation? The Case of a Traditional Political System in Ghana', *Ghana Journal of Development Studies* 17(1): 25–47.

Boateng, Kwabena, Stephen Afranie, and Solomon Kofi Amoah. 2016. 'Social Mobilisation in the Midst of Social Change: The Case of Traditional Authorities in Ghana', *Journal of Educational and Social Research* 6(2): 103–12.

Boccheni, Amedeo Giusto, and Luisa Castaneda-Quintana. 2024. 'On the Ranchería with Keebet von Benda-Beckmann: Legal Pluralism, the Wiwa People, El Cercado, and Socio-spatial Relations in the Sierra Nevada de Santa Marta', *Legal Pluralism and Critical Social Analysis* 56(3): 370–95.

Boesten, Jelke, and Marsha Henry. 2018. 'Between Fatigue and Silence: The Challenges of Conducting Research on Sexual Violence in Conflict', *Social Politics: International Studies in Gender, State & Society* 25(4): 568–88.

Bourke, Lynsey, et al. 2009. 'Fieldwork Stories: Negotiating Positionality, Power and Purpose', *Feminist Africa* 13: 95–105.

Brempong, Arhin. 2001. *Transformations in Traditional Rule in Ghana (1951–1996)*. Accra: Sedco Publishing Limited.

Britwum, K. A. 1974. 'Kwadwo Adinkra of Gyaaman: A Study of the Relations between the Brong Kingdom of Gyaaman and Asante from c.1800–1818', *Transactions of the Historical Societies of Ghana* 15(2): 229–39.

Brobbey, S. A. 2008. *The Law of Chieftaincy in Ghana: Incorporating Customary Arbitration, Contempt of Court, Judicial Review*. Accra: Advanced Legal Publications.

Bromley, Daniel W. 2008. 'Formalising Property Relations in the Developing World: The Wrong Prescription for the Wrong Malady', *Land Use Policy* 26(1): 20–27.

Brooks, Jerome. 1994. 'Chinua Achebe: The Art of Fiction', *The Paris Review* 133(139). Retrieved 22 November 2024 from https://www.theparisreview.org/interviews/1720/the-art-of-fiction-no-139-chinua-achebe.

Bryceson, Deborah Fahy. 1996. 'Deagrarianization and Rural Employment in Sub-Saharan Africa: A Sectoral Perspective', *World Development* 24(1): 97–111.

———. 2018. 'Artisanal Gold-Rush Mining and Frontier Democracy: Juxtaposing Experiences in America, Australia, Africa and Asia', in Kuntala Lahiri-Dutt (ed.), *Between the Plough and the Pick: Informal, Artisanal and Small-Scale Mining in the Contemporary World*. Canberra: Australian National University Press, pp. 31–61.

Bryceson, Deborah Fahy, and Jesper Bosse Jønsson. 2010. 'Gold Digging Careers in Rural East Africa: Small-Scale Miners' Livelihood Choices', *World Development* 38(3): 379–92.

Buchanan, Rachel. 2007. 'Decolonizing the Archives: The Work of New Zealand's Waitangi Tribunal', *Public History Review* 14: 44–63.

Bush, R. 2009. '"Soon There Will Be No-One Left to Take the Corpses to the Morgue": Accumulation and Abjection in Ghana's Mining Communities', *Resources Policy* 34(1–2): 57–63.

Busia, Kofi Abrefa. 1951. *The Position of the Chief in the Modern Political System of Ashanti*. Oxford: Oxford University Press.

Buxton, Abbi. 2013. *Responding to the Challenge of Artisanal and Small-Scale Mining: How Can Knowledge Networks Help?* London: IIED.

Campbell, Bonnie. 2010. 'Revisiting the Reform Process of African Mining Law', *Canadian Journal of Development Studies* 30(1–2): 197–217.

Campbell, John. 2010. 'The "Problem" of Ethics in Contemporary Anthropological Research', *Anthropology Matters* 12(1): 1–17.

Carpi, Estella, and Portia Owusu. 2022. 'Slavery, Lived Realities, and the Decolonisation of Forced Migration Histories: An Interview with Dr Portia Owusu', *Migration Studies* 10(1): 87–93.

Centre for Development Studies. 2004. *Livelihoods and Policy in the Artisanal and Small-Scale Mining Sector – An Overview*. Swansea: University of Wales, Swansea.

Chanock, Martin. 1985. *Law, Custom, and Social Order: The Colonial Experience in Malawi and Zambia*. Cambridge: Cambridge University Press.

———. 1991. 'Paradigms, Policies and Property: A Review of the Customary Law of Land Tenure', in Kristin Mann and Richard Roberts (eds), *Law in Colonial Africa*. Portsmouth: Heinemann, pp. 61–84.

Chen, Martha (Marty) Alter. 2005. 'Rethinking the Informal Economy: From Enterprise Characteristics to Employment Relations', in Neema Kudva and Lourdes Beneria (eds), *Rethinking Informalization: Poverty, Precarious Jobs and Social Protection*. Ithaca: Cornell University Press, pp. 28–66.

———. 2007. 'Rethinking the Informal Economy: Linkages with the Formal Economy and the Formal Regulatory Environment', DESA Working Paper No. 46.

———. 2012. 'The Informal Economy: Definitions, Theories and Policies', WIEGO Working Paper No. 1.

———. 2020. 'COVID-19 Intensifies Global Need to Support Informal Workers in Their Struggle'. UNU-WIDER blog. Retrieved 3 November 2025 from https://www.wider.unu.edu/publication/covid-19-intensifies-global-need-support-informal-workers-their-struggle.

Chilisa, Bagele. 2005. 'Educational Research within Postcolonial Africa: A Critique of HIV/AIDS Research in Botswana', *International Journal of Qualitative Studies* 18(6): 659–84.

Chilisa, Bagele, Thenjiwe Emily Major, and Kelne Khudu-Petersen. 2017. 'Community Engagement with a Postcolonial, African-Based Relational Paradigm', *Qualitative Research* 17(3): 326–39.

Chilisa, Bagele, and Gabo Ntseane. 2010. 'Resisting Dominant Discourses: Implications of Indigenous, African Feminist Theory and Methods of Gender and Education Research', *Gender and Education* 22(6): 617–32.

Chimhowu, Admos. 2019. 'The "New" African Customary Land Tenure. Characteristic, Features and Policy Implications of a New Paradigm', *Land Use Policy* 81: 897–903.

Chinsinga, Blessings. 2006. 'The Interface Between Tradition and Modernity: The Struggle for Political Space at the Local Level in Malawi', *Civilisations* 54(1–2): 255–74.

Chirayath, Leila, Caroline Sage, and Michael Woolcock. 2005. 'Customary Law and Policy Reform: Engaging with the Plurality of Justice Systems', World Bank Development Report Background Paper. Washington, D.C.: World Bank.

Chiweshe, Malvern. 2018. 'African Men and Feminism: Reflections on Using African Feminism in Research', *Agenda* 32(2): 76–82.

Clapham, Christopher. 2020. 'Decolonising African Studies?', *Journal of Modern African Studies* 58(1): 137–53.

Clifford, Martin J. 2017. 'Assessing Releases of Mercury from Small-Scale Gold Mining Sites in Ghana', *The Extractive Industries and Society* 4(3): 497–505.

———. 2022. 'Artisanal and Small-Scale Mining and the Sustainable Development Goals: Why Nobody Cares', *Environmental Science and Policy* 137: 164–73.

Cotterell, Roger. 2006. *Law, Culture and Society: Legal Ideas in the Mirror of Social Theory*. Hampshire: Ashgate Publishing Ltd.

Cover, Robert M. 1983. 'Nomos and Narrative', *Harvard Law Review* 97(1): 4–68.

Crawford, Gordon, Coleman Agyeyomah, and Atinga Mba. 2017. 'Ghana – Big Man, Big Envelope, Finish: Chinese Corporate Exploitation in Small-Scale Mining', in Bettina Engels and Kristina Dietz (eds), *Contested Extractivism, Society and the State*. London: Palgrave Macmillan, pp. 69–99.

Crawford, Gordon, and Gabriel Botchwey. 2017. 'Conflict, Collusion and Corruption in Small-Scale Gold Mining: Chinese Miners and the State in Ghana', *Commonwealth and Comparative Politics* 55(4): 444–70.

Crook, Richard. 2005. 'The Role of Traditional Institutions in Political Change and Development', CDD/ODI Policy Brief No. 4.

———. 2008. 'Customary Justice Institutions and Local Alternative Dispute Resolution: What Kind of Protection Can They Offer to Customary Landholders?', in Janine M. Ubink and Kojo Sebastian Amanor (eds), *Contesting Land and Custom in Ghana: State, Chief and the Citizen*. Leiden: Leiden University Press, pp. 131–54.

Cunha, Teresa, and Isabel Casimiro. 2021. '"Cinderellas" of Our Mozambique Wish to Speak: A Feminist Perspective on Extractivism', *Feminist Africa* 2(1): 71–98.

Curtis, Mark. 2016. 'The New Colonialism: Britain's Scramble for Africa's Energy and Mineral Resources', *War on Want*. Retrieved 22 November 2024 from https://waronwant.org/sites/default/files/TheNewColonialism.pdf.

Dakubu, Mary Esther Kropp. 2012. 'The Portuguese Language on the Gold Coast, 1471–1807', *Ghana Journal of Linguistics* 1(1): 15–33.

Damonte, G. H. 2016. 'The "Blind" State: Government Quest for Formalization and Conflict with Small-Scale Miners in the Peruvian Amazon', *Antipode* 48(4): 956–76.

Damonte, Gerardo, et al. 2013. 'Small-Scale Gold Mining and Social and Environmental Conflict in the Peruvian Amazon', in L. Cremers, J. Kolen and M. E. M. de Theije (eds), *Small-Scale Mining in the Amazon: The Cases of Bolivia, Brazil, Colombia, Peru and Suriname*. Amsterdam: CEDLA, pp. 68–84.

Danquah, J. B. 1928. *Gold Coast: Akan Laws and Customs and the Akim Abuakwa Constitution*. London: George Routledge & Sons Ltd.

Davidson, Jeffrey. 1993. 'The Transformation and Successful Development of Small-Scale Mining Enterprises in Developing Countries', *Natural Resources Forum* 17(4): 315–26.

Davies, Gareth. 2020. 'The Relationship between Empirical Legal Studies and Doctrinal Legal Research', *Erasmus Law Review* 13(2): 3–12.

Davies, Margaret. 2005. 'The Ethos of Pluralism', *Sydney Law Review* 27(1): 87–112.

———. 2017a. *Asking the Law Question*, 4th edn. Adelaide: Thomson Reuters.

———. 2017b. *Law Unlimited: Materialism, Pluralism and Legal Theory*. New York: Routledge.

Davies, Oliver, and Donna J. Maier. 2024. 'Ghana', in *Encyclopaedia Britannica*. Retrieved 6 November 2025 from https://www.britannica.com/place/Ghana.

de Haan, Jorden, and Sara Geenen. 2016. 'Mining Cooperatives in Eastern DRC: The Interplay between Historical Power Relations and Formal Institutions', *The Extractive Industries and Society* 3(3): 823–31.

Dei, George J. Sefa. 2000a. 'African Development: The Relevance and Implications of Indigenousness', in George J. Sefa Dei, Budd L. Hall and Dorothy Goldin Rosenberg (eds), *Indigenous Knowledges in Global Contexts: Multiple Readings of Our World*. Toronto: University of Toronto Press, pp. 95–108.

———. 2000b. 'Rethinking the Role of Indigenous Knowledges in the Academy', *International Journal of Inclusive Education* 4(2): 111–32.

Dei, George Sefa, and Chizoba Imoka. 2018. 'Colonialism: Why Write Back?', *E-International Relations*, 3 January. Retrieved 22 November 2024 from https://www.e-ir.info/2018/01/03/colonialism-why-write-back/.

De Jong, Terah U., and Titus Sauerwein. 2021. 'State-Owned Minerals, Village-Owned Land: How a Shared Property Rights Framework Helped Formalize Artisanal Diamond Miners in Côte d'Ivoire Between 1986 and 2016', *Resources Policy* 70: 1–10.

Delmas-Marty, Mireille. 2009. *Ordering Pluralism: A Conceptual Framework for Understanding the Transnational Legal World*, trans. Naomi Norbeg. Oxford: Hart Publishing.

Dery, Isaac. 2020. 'Negotiating Positionality, Reflexivity and Power Relations in Research on Men and Masculinities in Ghana', *Gender, Place and Culture* 27(12): 1766–84.

de Soto, Hernando. 2000. *The Mystery of Capital: Why Capitalism Triumphs in the West and Fails Everywhere Else*. New York: Bantam Books.

Diala, Anthony C. 2017. 'The Concept of Living Customary Law: A Critique', *The Journal of Legal Pluralism and Unofficial Law* 49(2): 143–65.

Diala, Anthony C., and Christa Rautenbach. 2024. 'Introduction', in Anthony C. Diala and Christa Rautenbach (eds), *Reimagining Legal Pluralism in Africa: Balancing Indigenous, State, and Religious Laws*. Leiden: Brill, pp. 1–20.

Dillard, Cynthia B., and Amber Neal. 2020. 'I Am Because We Are: (Re)membering Ubuntu in the Pedagogy of Black Women Teachers from Africa to America and Back Again', *Theory Into Practice* 59(4): 370–78.

Dladla, Ndumiso. 2017. 'Towards an African Critical Philosophy of Race: Ubuntu as a Philo-praxis of Liberation', *Filosofia Theoretica: Journal of African Philosophy, Culture and Religions* 6(1): 39–68.

Donkor, Isaac. 2023. 'Missing Excavators: Attorney General Claiming No Evidence Despite Smoking Gun Evidence – NDC Suspects Cover-Up', *Modern Ghana*, 17 October. Retrieved 2 December 2024 from https://www.modernghana.com/news/1266459/missing-excavators-attorney-general-claiming-no.html.

Dreschler, Bernd. 2001. 'Small-Scale Mining and Sustainable Development within the SADC Region', IIED Working Paper No. 81.

Dube, Musa W. 1999. 'Searching for the Lost Needle: Double Colonization and Postcolonial African Feminisms', *Studies in World Christianity* 5(2): 213–28.

Dumett, Raymond E. 1998. *El Dorado in West Africa: The Gold Mining Frontier, African Labour and Colonial Capitalism in the Gold Coast 1875–1900*. Athens, Ohio: Ohio University Press.

Dupuis, Constance. 2022. 'Feminist Ethics Amid COVID-19: Unpacking Assumptions and Reflections on Risk in Research', in Wendy Harcourt, Karijn van den Berg, Constance Dupuis and Jacqueline Gaybor (eds), *Feminist Methodologies: Experiments, Collaborations and Reflections*. Cham: Palgrave Macmillan, pp. 47–61.
Dutta, Mohan Jyoti, and Mahuya Pal. 2020. 'Theorizing from the Global South: Dismantling, Resisting, and Transforming Communication Theory', *Communication Theory* 30(4): 349–69.
Echavarria, Cristina. 2014. *What is Legal? Formalising Artisanal and Small-Scale Mining in Colombia*. London: IIED.
Eduful, Michael, et al. 2020. 'The Illegal Artisanal and Small-Scale Mining (Galamsey) "Menace" in Ghana: Is Military-Style Approach the Answer?', *Resources Policy* 68: 1–14.
Ehrlich, Eugen. 1936. *Fundamental Principles of the Sociology of Law*. Cambridge, Massachusetts: Harvard University Press.
Elabor-Idemudia, P. 2000. 'The Retention of Knowledge of Folkways as a Basis for Resistance', in George J. Sefa Dei, Budd L. Hall and Dorothy Goldin Rosenberg (eds), *Indigenous Knowledges in Global Contexts: Multiple Readings of Our World*. Toronto: University of Toronto Press, pp. 102–19.
Elbra, Ainsley. 2017. *Governing African Gold Mining: Private Governance and the Resource Curse*. London: Palgrave Macmillan.
Ellimah, Richard. 2017. 'Stained Gold: A Story of Human Rights Violations in Ghana's Mining Industry', in C. Rodriguez-Garavito (ed.), *Fighting the Tide: Human Rights and Environmental Justice in the Global South*. Bogotá: Dejusticia, pp. 172–87.
Esdaile, Louisa, J., and Justin M. Chalker. 2017. 'The Mercury Problem in Artisanal and Small-Scale Gold Mining', *Chemistry: A European Journal* 24(27): 6905–16.
Eze, Chielozona. 2015. 'Feminist Empathy: Unsettling Cultural Norms in *The Secret Lives of Baba Segi's Wives*', *African Studies* 74(3): 310–26.
Fanon, Frantz. 1963. *The Wretched of the Earth*. New York: Grove Weidenfield.
———. 1986. *Black Skin, White Masks.* London: Pluto Press.
———. 1997. 'On National Culture', in Bart Moore-Gilbert, Gareth Stanton and Willy Maley (eds), *Postcolonial Criticism*. London: Routledge, pp. 91–111.
Feenan, Dermot. 2013. 'Exploring the "Socio" of Socio-legal Studies', in Dermot Feenan (ed.), *Exploring the 'Socio' of Socio-legal Studies*. London: Palgrave Macmillan, pp. 3–19.
Feintrenie, Laurène. 2013. 'Opportunities to Responsible Land-Based Investments in Central Africa', *Annual World Bank Conference on Land and Poverty, 8–11 April 2013*. Washington, D.C.: World Bank.
Ferring, David, Heidi Hausermann, and Emmanuel Effah. 2016. 'Site Specific: Heterogeneity of Small-Scale Gold Mining in Ghana', *The Extractive Industries and Society* 3(1): 171–84.
Few, April L. 2007. 'Integrating Black Consciousness and Critical Race Feminism into Family Studies Research', *Journal of Family Issues* 28(4): 452–73.
Few, April L., Dionne P. Stephens, and Marlo Rouse-Arnett. 2003. 'Sister-to-Sister Talk: Transcending Boundaries and Challenges in Qualitative Research with Black Women', *Family Relations* 52(3): 205–15.
Fisher, Eleanor. 2007. 'Occupying the Margins: Labour Integration and Social Exclusion in Artisanal Mining in Tanzania', *Development and Change* 8(4): 735–60.
———. 2008. 'Artisanal Gold Mining at the Margins of Mineral Resource Governance: A Case from Tanzania', *Development Southern Africa* 25(2): 199–213.
Flood, John. 2005. 'Socio-Legal Ethnography', in Reza Banakar and Max Travers (eds), *Theory and Method in Socio-Legal Research*. Oxford: Hart Publishing, pp. 33–48.
Fold, Neils, Jesper Bosse Jønsson, and Paul Yankson. 2014. 'Buying into Formalization? State Institutions and Interlocked Markets in African Small-Scale Gold Mining', *Futures* 62: 128–39.

Fosu, Richard. 2025. 'Towards a Critical Decolonial Turn/Theory: Beyond the Binary of the West Versus Africa', *Africa Spectrum* 60(1): 69–83.

Frempong, Alexander K. D. 2006. 'Chieftaincy, Democracy and Human Rights in Pre-Colonial Africa: The Case of the Akan System in Ghana', in Irene K. Odotei and Albert K. Awedoba (eds), *Chieftaincy in Ghana: Culture, Governance and Development*. Accra: Sub-Saharan Publishers, pp. 379–94.

French, Howard. 2021. *Born in Blackness: Africa, Africans, and the Making of the Modern World, 1471 to the Second World War*. New York: Liveright Publishing.

Frisso, Giovanna Maria. 2019. 'Third World Approaches to International Law: Feminists' Engagement with International Law and Decolonial Theory', in Susan Harris Rimmer and Kate Ogg (eds), *Research Handbook on Feminist Engagement with International Law*. Cheltenham: Edward Elgar Publishing, pp. 479–98.

Fuentes, Marisa J. 2016. *Dispossessed Lives: Enslaved Women, Violence and the Archive*. Philadelphia: University of Pennsylvania Press.

Fúnez-Flores, Jairo I. 2022. 'Decolonial and Ontological Challenges in Social and Anthropological Theory', *Theory Culture & Society* 39(6): 21–41.

Funoh, Kevin N. 2014. 'The Impacts of Artisanal Gold Mining on Local Livelihoods and the Environment in the Forested Areas of Cameroon', Centre for International Forestry Research Working Paper No. 150.

Geenen, Sara. 2012. 'A Dangerous Bet: The Challenges of Formalizing Artisanal Mining in the Democratic Republic of Congo', *Resources Policy* 37(3): 322–30.

Geoffrey, Samuel. 2009. 'Interdisciplinarity and the Authority Paradigm: Should Law Be Taken Seriously by Scientists and Social Scientists?', *Journal of Law and Society* 36(4): 431–59.

Ghana Statistical Service. 2024. 'Ghana 2021 Population and Housing Census: Population Projections 2021–2050'. Accra, Ghana.

Ghebru, Hosaena, and Isabel Lambrecht. 2017. 'Drivers of Perceived Land Tenure (In)security: Empirical Evidence from Ghana', *Land Use Policy* 66: 293–303.

Gocking, Roger S. 2005. *The History of Ghana*. London: Greenwood Press.

Griffiths, John. 1986. 'What Is Legal Pluralism?', *Journal of Legal Pluralism and Unofficial Law* 24: 1–55.

Grosfoguel, Ramón. 2007. 'The Epistemic Decolonial Turn: Beyond Political-Economy Paradigms', *Cultural Studies* 21(2–3): 211–33.

Guha-Khasnobis, Basudeb, Ravi Kanbur, and Elinor Ostrom. 2006. 'Beyond Formality and Informality', in Basudeb Guha-Khasnobis, Ravi Kanbur and Elinor Ostrom (eds), *Linking the Formal and Informal Economy: Concepts and Policies*. Oxford: Oxford University Press, pp. 1–18.

Guillemin, Marilys, and Lynn Gillam. 2004. 'Ethics, Reflexivity, and "Ethically Important Moments" in Research', *Qualitative Inquiry* 10(2): 261–80.

Gyekye, Kwame. 1997. *Tradition and Modernity: Philosophical Reflections on the African Experience.* Oxford: Oxford University Press.

Hamilton, Patricia. 2020. 'Now that I Know What You Are About: Black Feminist Reflections on Power in the Research Relationship', *Qualitative Research* 20(5): 519–33.

Hanisch, Carol. 1970. 'The Personal Is Political', in Shulamith Firestone and Anne Koedt (eds), *Notes from the Second Year: Women's Liberation: Major Writings of the Radical Feminists*. New York: Radical Feminism, pp. 76–78.

Haraway, Donna. 1988. 'Situated Knowledges: The Science Question in Feminism and the Privilege of Partial Perspective', *Feminist Studies* 14(3): 575–99.

Hardin, Garrett. 1968. 'The Tragedy of the Commons', *Science* 162(3859): 1243–248.

Harding, Sandra. (ed). 1987. *Feminism and Methodology*. Bloomington: Indiana University Press.

Harneit-Sievers, Axel. 1998. 'Igbo "Traditional Rulers": Chieftaincy and the State in Southeastern Nigeria', *Africa Spectrum* 33(1): 57–79.
Hart, Keith. 1973. 'Informal Income Opportunities and Urban Employment in Ghana', *Journal of Modern African Studies* 11(1): 61–89.
Hausermann, Heidi, Janet Adomako, and Maya Robles. 2020. 'Fried Eggs and All-Women's Gangs: The Geopolitics of Chinese Gold Mining in Ghana, Bodily Vulnerability, and Resistance', *Human Geography* 13(1): 60–73.
Hayford, J. E. Casely. 1903. *Gold Coast Native Institutions*. London: Sweet and Maxwell.
Hein, Kim A. A., and Todani A. Funyufunyu. 2014. 'Artisanal Mining in Burkina Faso: A Historical Overview of Iron Ore Extraction, Processing and Production in the Dem Region', *The Extractive Industries and Society* 1: 260–72.
Hentschel, Thomas, Felix Hruschka, and Michael Priester. 2002. *Global Report on Artisanal & Small-Scale Mining*. London: IIED.
———. 2003. *Artisanal and Small-Scale Mining: Challenges and Opportunities.* London: IIED.
Hilson, Gavin. 2002a. 'Land Use Competition Between Small- and Large-Scale Miners: A Case Study of Ghana', *Land Use Policy* 19(2): 149–56.
———. 2002b. 'Harvesting Mineral Riches: 1000 Years of Gold Mining in Ghana', *Resources Policy* 28(1–2): 13–26.
———. 2010. '"Once a Miner, Always a Miner": Poverty and Livelihood Diversification in Akwatia, Ghana', *Journal of Rural Studies* 26(3): 296–307.
———. 2011. 'Artisanal Mining, Smallholder Farming and Livelihood Diversification in Rural Sub-Saharan Africa: An Introduction', *Journal of International Development* 23(8): 1031–41.
———. 2013. 'Creating Rural Informality', *SAIS Review of International Affairs* 33(1): 51–64.
———. 2016. 'Farming, Small-Scale Mining and Rural Livelihoods in Sub-Saharan Africa: A Critical Overview', *The Extractive Industries and Society* 3(2): 547–63.
———. 2017. 'Shootings and Burning Excavators: Some Rapid Reflections on the Government of Ghana's Handling of the Informal Galamsey Mining "Menace"', *Resources Policy* 54: 109–16.
———. 2019. 'Why Is There a Large-Scale Mining "Bias" in Sub-Saharan Africa?', *Land Use Policy* 81: 852–61.
———. 2020. '"Formalization Bubbles": A Blueprint for Sustainable Artisanal and Small-Scale Mining (ASM) in Sub-Saharan Africa', *The Extractive Industries and Society* 7(4): 1624–38.
Hilson, Gavin, et al. 2017. 'Artisanal and Small-Scale Mining (ASM) in Sub-Saharan Africa: Re-conceptualizing Formalisation and "Illegal" Activity', *Geoforum* 83: 80–90.
Hilson, Gavin, et al. 2018. 'Formalizing Artisanal Gold Mining under the Minamata Convention: Previewing the Challenge in Sub-Saharan Africa', *Environmental Science and Policy* 85: 123–31.
Hilson, Gavin, et al. 2021a. 'Formalizing Artisanal and Small-Scale Mining in Mozambique: Concerns, Priorities and Challenges', *Resources Policy* 71: 1–15.
Hilson, Gavin, et al. 2021b. 'Artisanal and Small-Scale Mining, and COVID-19 in Sub-Saharan Africa: A Preliminary Analysis', *World Development* 139: 1–13.
Hilson, Gavin, Ekow Bartels, and Yanfei Hu. 2022. 'Brick by Brick, Block by Block: Building a Sustainable Formalization Strategy for Small-Scale Gold Mining in Ghana', *Environmental Science and Policy* 135: 207–25.
Hilson, Gavin, and Chris Garforth. 2013. '"Everyone Now Is Concentrating on the Mining": Drivers and Implications of Rural Economic Transition in the Eastern Region of Ghana', *The Journal of Development Studies* 49(3): 348–64.
Hilson, Gavin, and Angélique Gatsinzi. 2014. 'A Rocky Road Ahead? Critical Reflections on the Futures of Small-Scale Mining in sub-Saharan Africa', *Futures* 62(A): 1–9.

Hilson, Gavin, Halima Goumandakoye, and Penda Diallo. 2019. 'Formalizing Artisanal Mining "Spaces" in Rural Sub-Saharan Africa: The Case of Niger', *Land Use Policy* 80: 259–68.

Hilson, Gavin, and Abigail Hilson. 2017. 'Mining in Ghana: Critical Reflections on a Turbulent Past and Uncertain Future', in Ernest Aryeetey and Ravi Kunbar (eds), *The Economy of Ghana Sixty Years After Independence*. Oxford: Oxford University Press, pp. 260–76.

Hilson, Gavin, Abigail Hilson, and Eunice Adu-Darko. 2014. 'Chinese Participation in Ghana's Informal Gold Mining Economy: Drivers, Implications and Clarifications', *Journal of Rural Studies* 34: 292–303.

Hilson, Gavin, and Roy Maconachie. 2017. 'Formalising Artisanal and Small-Scale Mining: Insights, Contestations and Clarifications', *AREA* 49(4): 443–51.

———. 2020a. 'Artisanal and Small-Scale Mining and the Sustainable Development Goals: Opportunities and New Directions for Sub-Saharan Africa', *Geoforum* 111: 125–41.

———. 2020b. 'Entrepreneurship and Innovation in Africa's Artisanal and Small-Scale Mining Sector: Development and Trajectories', *Journal of Rural Studies* 78: 149–62.

———. 2020c. 'For the Environment: An Assessment of Recent Military Intervention in Informal Gold Mining Communities in Ghana', *Land Use Policy* 96: 1–12.

Hilson, Gavin, and James McQuilken. 2014. 'Four Decades of Support for Artisanal and Small-Scale Mining in Sub-Saharan African: A Critical Review', *The Extractive Industries and Society* 1(1): 104–18.

Hilson, Gavin, and Godfried Okoh. 2013. 'Artisanal Mining in Ghana: Institutional Arrangements, Resource Flows and Poverty Alleviation', in Bonnie K. Campbell (ed.), *Modes of Governance and Revenue Flows in African Mining*. London: Palgrave Macmillan, pp. 138–63.

Hilson, Gavin, and Clive Potter. 2005. 'Structural Adjustment and Subsistence Industry: Artisanal Gold Mining in Ghana', *Development and Change* 36(1): 103–31.

Hilson, Gavin, Titus Sauerwein, and John Owen. 2020. 'Large and Artisanal Scale Mine Development: The Case for Autonomous Co-existence', *World Development* 130: 1–19.

Hilson, Gavin, and Rickford Vieira. 2007. 'Challenges with Minimising Mercury Pollution in the Small-Scale Gold Mining Sector: Experiences from the Guianas', *International Journal of Environmental Health Research* 17(6): 429–41.

Hilson, Gavin, and Natalia Yakovleva. 2007. 'Strained Relations: A Critical Analysis of the Mining Conflict in Prestea, Ghana', *Political Geography* 26(1): 98–119.

Hinton, Jennifer J. 2005. *Communities and Small-Scale Mining: An Integrated Review for Development Planning*. Washington, D.C.: World Bank.

Hirons, Mark. 2014. 'Decentralising Natural Resource Governance in Ghana: Critical Reflections on the Artisanal and Small-Scale Mining Sector', *Futures* 62(A): 21–31.

———. 2020. 'How the Sustainable Development Goals Risk Undermining Efforts to Address Environmental and Social Issues in the Small-Scale Mining Sector', *Environmental Science and Policy* 114: 321–28.

Hoare, Quintin, and Geoffrey Nowell Smith (eds). 1971. *Selections from the Prison Notebooks* of *Antonio Gramsci*. New York: International Publishers.

Home, Robert, and Hilary Lim. 2004. 'Introduction: Demystifying the Mystery of Capital', in Robert Home and Hilary Lim (eds), *Demystifying the Mystery of Capital: Land Tenure and Poverty in Africa and the Caribbean*. London: Glasshouse Press, pp. 1–10.

hooks, bell. 1989. 'Choosing the Margin as a Space of Radical Openness', *Framework: The Journal of Cinema and Media* 36: 15–23.

———. 1994. *Teaching to Transgress: Education as the Practice of Freedom*. New York: Routledge.

Huggins, Chris, Doris Buss, and Blair Rutherford. 2017. 'A "Cartography of Concern": Place-Making Practices and Gender in the Artisanal Mining Sector in Africa', *Geoforum* 83: 142–52.
Hutchinson, Terry. 2013. 'Doctrinal Research: Researching the Jury', in Dawn Watkins and Mandy Burton (eds), *Research Methods in Law*. London: Routledge, pp. 8–39.
Igwe, Paul Agu, Nnamdi O. Madichie, and David Gamariel Rugara. 2022. 'Decolonising Research Approaches Towards Non-extractive Research', *Qualitative Market Research* 25(4): 453–68.
International Labour Organisation. 1999. 'Social and Labour Issues in Small-Scale Mines'. Geneva, Switzerland.
Israel, Mark. 2017. 'Research Ethics and Integrity in Socio-legal Studies and Legal Research', in Mike McConville and Wing Hong Chui (eds), *Research Methods for Law*. Edinburgh: Edinburgh University Press, pp. 180–204.
Jackson, Robert. 1992. 'New Mines for Old Gold: Ghana's Changing Mining Industry', *Geography* 77(2): 175–78.
Jenks, Angela C. 2022. 'Archives at the Margins: Toward a Liberatory Pedagogy in Anthropology', *Cultural Anthropology* 37(3): 387–94.
Johnson, Miranda. 2008. 'Making History Public: Indigenous Claims to Settler States', *Public Culture* 20(1): 97–117.
Jønsson, Jesper Bosse, and Neils Fold. 2011. 'Mining "From Below": Taking Africa's Artisanal Miners Seriously', *Geography Compass* 5(7): 479–93.
Kasanga, Kasim, and Nii A. Kotey. 2001. *Land Management in Ghana: Building on Tradition and Modernity*. London: IIED.
Kaufmann, Christoph, and Muriel Côte. 2021. 'Frames of Extractivism: Small-Scale Goldmining Formalization and State Violence in Colombia', *Political Geography* 91: 1–10.
Kelsen, Hans. 1967. *Pure Theory of Law*. Berkeley: University of California Press.
Kerner, Ina. 2013. 'Differences of Inequality: Tracing the Socioeconomic, the Cultural and the Political in Latin American Postcolonial Theory', International Research Network on Interdependent Inequalities in Latin America Working Paper Series 60.
Kimble, David. 1963. *A Political History of Ghana: The Rise of Gold Coast Nationalism 1850–1928*. Oxford: Clarendon Press.
Kinyondo, Abel, and Christopher Huggins. 2020. '"Centres of Excellence" for Artisanal and Small-Scale Gold Mining in Tanzania: Assumptions around Artisanal Entrepreneurship and Formalization', *The Extractive Industries and Society* 7(2): 758–66.
Ki-Zerbo, Joseph. 1981. 'General Introduction', in J. Ki-Zerbo (ed.), *General History of Africa: Methodology and African Prehistory*. Berkeley: University of California Press, pp. 1–23.
Kleinhans, Martha-Marie, and Roderick A. Macdonald. 1997. 'What is Critical Legal Pluralism?', *Canadian Journal of Law and Society* 12(2): 25–46.
Kludze, A. K. P. 1998. *The Modern Law of Succession in Ghana*. Dordrecht: Foris Publications.
Kotey, N. A. 1996. 'The 1992 Constitution and Compulsory Acquisition of Land in Ghana: Opening New Vistas', *Managing Land Tenure and Resource Access in West Africa: Proceedings of a Regional Workshop Held at Goree, Senegal, November 18–22 1996*. London: IIED.
Kpienbaareh, Daniel, et al. 2021. 'The Rise of the Fourth Estate: The Media, Environmental Policy, and the Fight Against Illegal Mining in Ghana', *Environmental Communication* 15(1): 69–84.
Kumah, Richard. 2022. 'Artisanal and Small-Scale Mining Formalization Challenges in Ghana: Explaining Grassroot Perspectives', *Resources Policy* 79: 1–10.
Kyeremanten, A. 1969. 'The Royal Stools of Ashanti', *Journal of the International African Institute* 39(1): 1–10.

Labonne, Beatrice. 2014. 'Who is Afraid of Artisanal and Small-Scale Mining (ASM)?', *The Extractive Industry and Society* 1: 121–23.

Lahiri-Dutt, Kuntala. 2008. 'Digging to Survive: Women's Livelihoods in South Asia's Small Mines and Quarries', *South Asian Survey* 15(2): 217–44.

———. 2014. 'Extracting Peasants from the Fields: Rushing for a Livelihood?', NUS Asia Research Institute Working Paper No. 216.

———. 2018. 'Reframing the Debate on Informal Mining', in Kuntala Lahiri-Dutt (ed.), *Between the Plough and the Pick: Informal, Artisanal and Small-Scale Mining in a Contemporary World*. Canberra: Australian National University Press, pp. 1–28.

Lartey, Nii Larte. 2022. 'We're Helping Farmers to Shun Exchanging Cocoa Farms for Galamsey-COCOBOD', *CitiNewsroom*, 6 October. Retrieved 22 November 2024 from https://citinewsroom.com/2022/10/were-helping-farmers-to-shun-exchanging-cocoa-farms-for-galamsey-cocobod-more-here-https-tinyurl-com-2punn3eo-citinewsroom/.

Lather, Patti. 2001. 'Postmodernism, Post-structuralism and Post(Critical) Ethnography: Of Ruins, Aporias and Angels', in Paul Atkinson, Amanda Coffey, Sara Delamont, John Lofland and Lyn Lofland (eds), *Handbook of Ethnography*. London: Sage Publications, pp. 477–92.

Liamputtong, Pranee. 2008. 'Doing Research in a Cross-Cultural Context: Methodological and Ethical Challenges', in Pranee Liamputtong (ed.), *Doing Cross-Cultural Research: Ethical and Methodological Perspectives*. Melbourne: Springer, pp. 1–20.

Liboiron, Max. 2021. *Pollution Is Colonialism*. Durham, North Carolina: Duke University Press.

Li, Tania Murray. 2014. 'What Is Land? Assembling a Resource for Global Development', *Transactions of the Institute of British Geographers* 39(4): 589–602.

Liu, Ruo-Fan. 2022. 'Hybrid Ethnography: Access, Positioning, and Data Assembly', *Ethnography* 0(0): 1–18.

Lochery, Emma. 2022. 'Situating Extraction in Capitalism: Blueprints, Frontier Projects, and Life-Making', *The Extractive Industries and Society* 11: 1–10.

Lodoh, C. H. K. 2002. 'A Case for the Formal Approach to Land Acquisition in Ghana', *Ghana School of Law Journal* 1: 56–75.

Logan, Carolyn. 2013. 'The Roots of Resilience: Exploring Popular Support for African Traditional Authorities', *African Affairs* 112(448): 353–76.

Lorde, Audre. 1984. *Sister Outsider: Essays and Speeches*. Berkeley: Crossing Press.

Lund, Christian. 2006. 'Twilight Institutions: Public Authorities and Local Politics in Africa', *Development and Change* 37(4): 685–705.

Mabe, Franklin N., Ebenezer Owusu-Sekyere, and Oluyemi Theophilus Adeosun. 2021. 'Livelihood Coping Strategies among Displaced Small-Scale Miners in Ghana', *Resources Policy* 74: 1–9.

Macarthy, Emmanuel Motese, and Ikpenmosa Uhumuavbi. 2025. 'Re-appraisal of Legal Systems in Sub-Saharan Africa: Questioning the Legal Pluralism Paradigm', *African Journal of Legal Studies* 17: 27–48.

Maconachie, Roy, and Tony Binns. 2007. '"Farming Miners" or "Mining Farmers"? Diamond Mining and Rural Development in Post-Conflict Sierra Leone', *Journal of Rural Studies* 23(3): 367–80.

Maconachie, Roy, and Gavin Hilson. 2011a. 'Artisanal Gold Mining: A New Frontier in Post-Conflict Sierra Leone?', *The Journal of Development Studies* 47(4): 595–616.

———. 2011b. 'Safeguarding Livelihoods or Exacerbating Poverty? Artisanal Mining and Formalisation in Africa', *Natural Resources Forum* 35(4): 293–303.

Mafundikwa, Saki. 2017. *Afrikan Alphabets: The Story of Writing in Africa*. Brussels: Mark Batty Publisher.

Maldonado-Torres, Nelson. 2007. 'On the Coloniality of Being: Contributions to the Development of a Concept', *Cultural Studies* 21(2–3): 240–70.

———. 2011. 'Thinking through the Decolonial Turn: Post-continental Interventions in Theory, Philosophy, and Critique – An Introduction', *Transmodernity* 1(2): 1–15.
Malinowski, Bronislaw. 1926. *Crime and Custom in Savage Society*. New York: Harcourt, Brace & Co.
Maloney, William F. 2004. 'Informality Revisited', *World Development* 32(7): 1159–78.
Mama, Amina. 2011. 'What Does It Mean to Do Feminist Research in African Contexts?', *Feminist Review* 98(1): 4–20.
Mamdani, Mahmood. 1996. *Citizen and Subject: Contemporary Africa and the Legacy of Late Colonialism*. New Jersey: Princeton University Press.
———. 1999. 'Historicising Power and Responses to Power: Indirect Rule and Its Reform', *Social Research* 66(3): 859–86.
———. 2012. *Define and Rule: Native as Political Identity*. Cambridge, Massachusetts: Harvard University Press.
Mantey, Jones, Kwabena Nyarko, and Frederick Owusu-Nimo. 2016. *Costed Reclamation and Decommissioning Strategy for Galamsey Operations in 11 Selected MDAs of the Western Region of Ghana*. London: International Growth Centre, LSE.
Mark-Thiesen, Cassandra. 2018. *Mediators, Contract Men, and Colonial Capital: Mechanized Gold Mining in the Gold Coast Colony, 1879–1909*. New York: Boydell and Brewer.
Marshall, Bruce, and Marcello M. Veiga. 2017. 'Formalization of Artisanal Miners: Stop the Train, We Need to Get Off!', *The Extractive Industries and Society* 4(2): 300–3.
Martin, Aryn, Natasha Myers, and Ana Viseu. 2015. 'The Politics of Care in Technoscience', *Social Studies of Science* 45(5): 625–41.
Martinez, Gerardo, Nicole M. Smith, and Aaron Malone. 2023. '"I Am Formal, What Comes Next?": A Proposed Framework for Achieving Sustainable Artisanal and Small-Scale Mining Formalization in Peru', *The Extractive Industries and Society* 13: 1–11.
Matemba, Yona Hisbon. 2014. 'Problems, Survival and Transformation: Religious Education in Scotland – A Historical Review, 1962–1992', *History of Education* 43(4): 542–60.
———. 2020. 'Gazing Back and Moving Forward', *British Journal of Religious Education* 42(2): 115–119.
Mawuko-Yevugah, Lord, and Harry Anthony Attipoe. 2021. 'Chieftaincy and Traditional Authority in Modern Democratic Ghana', *Southern African Journal of Philosophy* 40(3): 319–35.
Mbembe, Achille. 2002. 'On the Power of the False', *Public Culture* 14(3): 621–23.
McConville, Mike, and Wing Hong Chui. 2007. 'Introduction and Overview', in Mike McConville and Wing Hon Chui (eds), *Research Methods for Law*. Edinburgh: Edinburgh University Press, pp. 1–17.
McFadden, Patricia. 2007. 'African Feminist Perspectives on Post-Coloniality', *The Black Scholar: Journal of Black Studies and Research* 37(1): 36–42.
McFarlane, Colin, and Michael Waibel. 2012. 'Introduction: The Informal-formal Divide in Context', in Colin McFarlane and Michael Waibel (eds), *Urban Informalities: Reflections on the Formal and Informal*. London: Ashgate Publishing, pp. 1–12.
McQuilken, James, and Gavin Hilson. 2016. *Artisanal and Small-Scale Gold Mining in Ghana: Evidence to Inform an "Action Dialogue"*. London: IIED.
Meagher, Kate. 1995. 'Crisis, Informalization and the Urban Informal Sector in Sub-Saharan Africa', *Development and Change* 26(2): 259–84.
Medie, Peace A., and Alice J. Kang. 2018. 'Power, Knowledge and the Politics of Gender in the Global South', *European Journal of Politics and Gender* 1(1–2): 37–54.
Meinzen-Dick, Ruth S., and Rajendra Pradhan. 2001. 'Implications of Legal Pluralism for Natural Resource Management', *IDS Bulletin* 32(4): 10–17.
Menkel-Meadow, Carrie. 2020. 'Uses and Abuses of Socio-legal Studies', in Naomi Creutzfeldt, Marc Mason and Kirsten McConnachie (eds), *Routledge Handbook of Socio-Legal Theory and Methods*. London: Routledge, pp. 35–57.

Mensah, Albert K., et al. 2015. 'Environmental Impacts of Mining: A Study of Mining Communities in Ghana', *Applied Ecology and Environmental Sciences* 3(3): 81–94.
Mensah, Linda. 2021. 'Legal Pluralism in Practice: Critical Reflections on the Formalisation of Artisanal and Small-Scale Mining (ASM) and Customary Land Tenure in Ghana', *The Extractive Industries and Society* 8(4): 1–12.
Mensah-Bonsu, Henrietta Joy Abena Nyarko. 1993–1995. '*Avuugi v Abugri*: Some Customary Law Issues', *Review of Ghana Law* 19: 252–62.
Merry, Sally Engle. 1988. 'Legal Pluralism', *Law & Society Review* 22(5): 869–96.
———. 1991. 'Law and Colonialism', *Law & Society Review* 25(4): 889–922.
Mignolo, Walter. 2007. 'Introduction: Coloniality of Power and De-colonial Thinking', *Cultural Studies* 21(2–3): 155–67.
———. 2011a. *The Darker Side of Western Modernity: Global Futures, Decolonial Options*. Durham, North Carolina: Duke University Press.
———. 2011b. 'Geopolitics of Sensing and Knowing: On Decoloniality, Border Thinking and Epistemic Disobedience', *Postcolonial Studies* 14(3): 273–283.
Minerals Commission of Ghana. 2021. 'Small-Scale and Community Mining Operational Manual'. Accra, Ghana.
Ministry of Lands and Forestry, Ghana. 2003–2008. 'Implementation Manual for Land Administration Project (LAP-1)'. Accra, Ghana.
Mitchell, Clyde J. 1966. 'Theoretical Orientations in African Urban Studies', in Michael Banton (ed.), *The Social Anthropology of Complex Societies*. London: Routledge, pp. 37–68.
Mitchell, James. 2016. 'Pulling the Rug Out from Under: The Land Tenure Dynamics of Mining Concessions in Sub-Saharan Africa', *The Extractive Industries and Society* 3(4): 1117–29.
Mkabela, Queeneth. 2005. 'Using the Afrocentric Method in Researching the Indigenous African Culture', *The Qualitative Report* 10(1): 178–89.
Mkodzongi, Grasian, and Samuel Spiegel. 2019. 'Artisanal Gold Mining and Farming: Livelihood Linkages and Labour Dynamics after Land Reforms in Zimbabwe', *The Journal of Development Studies* 55(10): 2145–61.
Modiri, Joel. 2019. *Speech from Conference on Decolonisation and the Law School, University of Bristol, 13 September 2019*. Retrieved 22 November 2024 from Foluke Adebisi, 'Why I Say "Decolonisation Is Impossible"', *African Skies*, 17 December 2019. https://folukeafrica.com/why-i-say-decolonisation-is-impossible/.
Mohamed, Shakir, Marie-Therese Png, and William Isaac. 2020. 'Decolonial AI: Decolonial Theory as Sociotechnical Foresight in Artificial Intelligence', *Philosophy and Technology* 33(4): 659–84.
Mohammed, Wunpuni Fatimata. 2022. 'Bilchinsi Philosophy: Decolonizing Methodologies in Media Studies', *Review of Communication* 22(1): 7–24.
Moore, Niamh. 2012. 'The Politics and Ethics of Naming: Questioning Anonymisation in (Archival) Research', *International Journal of Social Research Methodology* 15(4): 331–40.
Moore, Sally Falk. 1978. *Law as Process: An Anthropological Approach*, 2nd edn. Münster–Hamburg: Lit with the IAI.
Morrison, Toni. 2007. *Beloved*. New York: Vintage Classics.
Mutemeri, Nellia, et al. 2016. 'Capacity Building for Self-Regulation of the Artisanal and Small-Scale Mining (ASM) Sector: A Policy Paradigm Shift Aligned with Development Outcomes and a Pro-Poor Approach', *The Extractive Industries and Society* 3(3): 653–58.
Nader, Laura. 1972. 'Up the Anthropologist: Perspectives Gained from Studying Up'. Retrieved 17 October 2025 from ERIC database, US Institute of Education Sciences.
Ndlovu-Gatsheni, Sabelo. 2013. 'Decolonising the University in Africa', *The Thinker* 51: 46–51.
———. 2017. 'The Emergence and Trajectories of Struggles for an "African University": The Case of Unfinished Business of African Epistemic Decolonisation', *Kronos* 43: 51–77.

Nekam, Alexander. 1967. 'Aspects of African Customary Law', *Northwestern University Law Review* 62(1): 45–56.
Nii-Aponsah, D. A. 1978. 'Law and Social Reality: The Effects of Marriage and Paternity on Membership of Family among Ga Mashi People', *Review of Ghana Law* 10(1): 32–46.
Nkrumah, Kwame. 1962. *Towards Colonial Freedom: Africa in the Struggle against World Imperialism*. London: Heinemann.
———. 1963. *Africa Must Unite*. New York: Frederick A. Praeger.
———. 1965. *Neocolonialism: The Last Stage of Imperialism*. London: Thomas Nelson & Sons Ltd.
Nnaemeka, Obioma. 1994. 'Bringing African Women into the Classroom: Rethinking Pedagogy and Epistemology', in Margaret R. Higgonet (ed.), *Borderwork: Feminist Engagements with Comparative Literature*. Ithaca, New York: Cornell University Press, pp. 301–18.
———. 2004. 'Nego-Feminism: Theorizing, Practicing, and Pruning Africa's Way', *Signs: Journal of Women in Culture and Society* 29(2): 357–85.
Norrie, Alan. 2005. *Law and the Beautiful Soul*. London: Glasshouse.
Nti, Kwaku. 2012. 'This Is Our Land: Land, Policy, Resistance, and Everyday Life in Colonial Southern Ghana, 1894–7', *Journal of Asian and African Studies* 48(1): 3–15.
Ntseane, Peggy Gabo. 2011. 'Culturally Sensitive Transformational Learning: Incorporating the Afrocentric Paradigm and African Feminism', *Adult Education Quarterly* 61(4): 307–23.
Nukunya, G. K. 2016. *Tradition and Change in Ghana: An Introduction to Sociology*. Accra: Woeli Publishing Services.
Nursoo, Ida. 2018. 'Indigenous Law, Colonial Injustice and the Jurisprudence of Hybridity', *The Journal of Legal Pluralism and Unofficial Law* 50(1): 56–70.
Nwokolo, Marie-Noelle. 2019. 'Ghana's Battle with Illegal Artisanal and Small-Scale Mining', LSE blog, 15 July. Retrieved 22 November 2024 from https://blogs.lse.ac.uk/africaatlse/2019/07/15/ghana-illegal-asm-artisanal-mining/.
Nyame, Frank K., and Joseph Blocher. 2010. 'Influence of Land Tenure Practices on Artisanal Mining Activity in Ghana', *Resources Policy* 35: 47–53.
Nyame, Frank K., and J. Andrew Grant. 2014. 'The Political Economy of Transitory Mining in Ghana: Understanding the Trajectories, Triumphs, and Tribulations of Artisanal and Small-Scale Operators', *The Extractive Industries and Society* 1(1): 75–85.
Obeng-Odoom, Franklin. 2016. 'Marketising the Commons in Africa: The Case of Ghana', *Review of Social Economy* 74(4): 390–419.
Odanga, René K. 2022. '(In)Validating Crises in African Studies: Certain Reflections on Disciplinary Stagnancy', *CODESRIA Bulletin* 12: 1–10.
O'Faircheallaigh, Ciaran, and Tony Corbett. 2016. 'Understanding and Improving Policy and Regulatory Responses to Artisanal and Small-Scale Mining', *The Extractive Industries and Society* 3(4): 961–71.
Ofori, Alesia D., Anna Mdee, and James Van Alstine. 2021. 'Politics on Display: The Realities of Artisanal Mining Formalisation in Ghana', *The Extractive Industries and Society* 8: 1–9.
Ofosu, George, et al. 2020. 'Socio-economic and Environmental Implications of Artisanal and Small-Scale Mining (ASM) on Agriculture and Livelihoods', *Environmental Science and Policy* 106: 210–20.
Ofosu, George, et al. 2024. 'Ban Mining, Ban Dining? Re(examining) the Policy and Practice of "Militarised Conservationism" on ASM Operations', *The Extractive Industries and Society* 17: 1–8.
Ofosu-Mensah, Emmanuel Ababio. 2010. 'Traditional Gold Mining in Adanse', *Nordic Journal of African Studies* 19(2): 124–47.
———. 2011. 'Gold Mining and the Socio-economic Development of Obuasi in Adanse', *African Journal of History and Culture* 3(4): 54–64.

Ogot, B. A. (ed.). 1992. *General History of Africa, Vol. V: Africa from the Sixteenth to Eighteenth Century*. London: Heinemann.

Okoh, Godfried Appiah. 2014. 'Grievance and Conflict in Ghana's Gold Mining Industry: The Case of Obuasi', *Futures* 62: 51–57.

Okoh, Godfried, and Gavin Hilson. 2011. 'Poverty and Livelihood Diversification: Exploring the Linkages between Smallholder Farming and Artisanal Mining in Rural Ghana', *Journal of International Development* 23(8): 1100–14.

Okrah, K. A. 2008. 'Sankofa: Cultural Heritage Conservation and Sustainable African Development', *The African Symposium* 8(2): 24–31.

Ollenu, N. A. 1962. *Principles of Customary Land Law in Ghana*. London: Sweet and Maxwell.

Omeje, Kenneth. 2008. 'Extractive Economies and Conflicts in the Global South: Re-Engaging Rentier Theory and Politics', in Kenneth Omeje (ed.), *Extractive Economies and Conflicts in the Global South: Multi-Regional Perspectives on Rentier Politics*. Hampshire: Ashgate, pp. 1–25.

Omosini, Olufemi. 1972. 'The Gold Coast Land Question, 1894–1900: Some Issues Raised on West Africa's Economic Development', *The International Journal of African Historical Studies* 5(3): 453–69.

Oomen, Barbara. 2000. '"We Must Now Go Back to Our History": Retraditionalisation in a Northern Province Chieftaincy', *African Studies* 59(1): 71–95.

Opoku-Agyemang, Kwabena. 2017. 'Looking Back while Moving Forward: The Case of Concrete Poetry and Sankofa', *Hyperrhiz New Media Studies* 16: 1–16.

Osei, Elisabeth Abena. 2020. 'Wakanda Africa Do You See? Reading *Black Panther* as a Decolonial Film Through the Lens of the Sankofa Theory', *Critical Studies in Media Communication* 37(4): 378–90.

Osei, Lydia, et al. 2021. 'Government's Ban on Artisanal and Small-Scale Mining, Youth Livelihoods and Imagined Futures in Ghana', *Resources Policy* 71: 1–10.

Osei, Lydia, Godwin Arku, and Isaac Luginaah. 2022. '"We Have Done Nothing Wrong": Youth Miners' Perceptions of the Environmental Consequences of Artisanal and Small-Scale Mining (ASM) in Ghana', *The Extractive Industries and Society* 12: 1–8.

Osei-Kojo, Alex, and Nathan Andrews. 2016. 'Questioning the Status Quo: Can Stakeholder Participation Improve Implementation of Small-Scale Mining Laws in Ghana?', *Resources* 5(33): 1–16.

Ostrom, Elinor. 1990. *Governing the Commons: The Evolution of Institutions for Collective Action*. Cambridge: Cambridge University Press.

Owusu, Obed, K. J. Bansah, and Albert Kobina Mensah. 2019. '"Small in Size, but Big in Impact": Socio-environmental Reforms for Sustainable Artisanal and Small-Scale Mining', *Journal of Sustainable Mining* 18(1): 38–44.

Owusu, Philip. 2019. 'Adinkra Symbols as "Multivocal" Pedagogical/Socialisation Tool', *Contemporary Journal of African Studies* 6(1): 46–58.

Owusu-Mensah, Isaac. 2014. 'Politics, Chieftaincy and Customary Law in Ghana's Fourth Republic', *Journal of Pan-African Studies* 6(7): 261–78.

Owusu-Sampah, Claudia. 2014. 'Adinkra', Ph.D. thesis. New York: Rochester Institute of Technology.

Oyěwùmi, Oyèrónké. 1997. *The Invention of Women: Making an African Sense of Western Gender Discourses*. Minneapolis: University of Minnesota Press.

———. 1998. 'De-Confounding Gender: Feminist Theorizing and Western Culture, a Comment on Hawkesworth's "Confounding Gender"', *Signs: Journal of Women in Culture and Society* 23(4): 1449–62.

Pala, Achola O. 1977. 'Definitions of Women and Development: An African Perspective', *Signs: Journal of Women in Culture and Society* 3(1): 9–13.

Parker, Charlie, Sam Scott, and Alistair Geddes. 2019. 'Snowball Sampling', in Paul Atkinson, Sara Delamont, Alexandru Cernat, Joseph W. Sakshaug and Richard A. Williams (eds), *Sage Research Methods Foundations*. London: Sage Publications, pp. 1–13.

Patel, K., et al. 2016. 'Evaluating Conflict Surrounding Mineral Extraction in Ghana: Assessing the Spatial Interactions of Large and Small-Scale Mining', *The Extractive Industries and Society* 3(2): 450–63.

Peltier, Cindy. 2018. 'An Application of Two-Eyed Seeing: Indigenous Research Methods with Participatory Action Research', *International Journal of Qualitative Research* 17: 1–12.

Pereira, Charmaine. 2002. 'Between Knowing and Imagining: What Space for Feminism in Scholarship on Africa?', *Feminist Africa* 1: 9–33.

Pereira, Charmaine, and Dodzi Tsikata. 2021. 'Extractivism, Resistance, Alternatives', *Feminist Africa* 21: 1–13.

Persaud, Anthony W., et al. 2017. 'Artisanal and Small-Scale Gold Mining in Senegal: Livelihoods, Customary Authority and Formalization', *Society & Natural Resources* 30(8): 980–93.

Pickering, Lucy, and Helen Kara. 2017. 'Presenting and Representing Others: Towards an Ethics of Engagement', *International Journal of Social Research Methodology* 20(3): 299–309.

Pijpers, Robert. 2014. 'Crops and Carats: Exploring the Interconnectedness of Mining and Agriculture in Sub-Saharan Africa', *Futures* 62(A): 32–39.

Pimentel, David. 2011. 'Legal Pluralism in Post-Colonial Africa: Linking Statutory and Customary Adjudication in Mozambique', *Yale Human Rights Development Journal* 14(1): 59–104.

Porter, Doug J. 2012. 'Some Implications of the Application of Legal Pluralism to Development Practice', in Brian Z. Tamanaha, Caroline Sage and Michael Woolcock (eds), *Legal Pluralism and Development: Scholars and Practitioners in Dialogue*. New York: Cambridge University Press, pp. 162–74.

Portes, Alejandro, Manuel Castells, and Lauren A. Benton (eds). 1989. *The Informal Economy: Studies in Advanced and Less Developed Countries*. Baltimore: Johns Hopkins University Press.

Portes, Alejandro, and Richard Schauffler. 1993. 'Competing Perspectives on the Latin American Informal Sector', *Population and Development Review* 19(1): 33–60.

Putzel, Louis, et al. 2015. 'Formalization as Development in Land and Natural Resource Policy', *Society and Natural Resources* 28(5): 453–72.

Quan, Julian, Janine Ubink, and A. Antwi. 2008. 'Risks and Opportunities of State Intervention in Customary Land Management: Emergent Findings from the Land Administration Project Ghana', in Janine M. Ubink and Kojo S. Amanor (eds), *Contesting Land and Custom in Ghana: State, Chief and Citizen*. Leiden: Leiden University Press, pp. 183–208.

Quan-Baffour, Poku Kofi. 2012. '*Sankofa*: "Gazing Back" to Indigenous Knowledge and Skills for Socio-economic Development of Ghana', *Studies of Tribes and Tribals* 10(1): 1–5.

Quijano, Aníbal. 2000. 'Coloniality of Power and Ethnocentrism in Latin America', *International Sociology* 15(2): 215–32.

Rajaee, Mozhgon, et al. 2015. 'Mercury Exposure Assessment and Spatial Distribution in a Ghanaian Small-Scale Gold Mining Community', *International Journal of Environmental Research and Public Health* 12(9): 10755–82.

Ranger, Terence. 1983. 'The Invention of Tradition in Colonial Africa', in Eric Hobsbawm and Terence Ranger (eds), *The Invention of Tradition*. Cambridge: Cambridge University Press, pp. 211–62.

Rathbone, Richard. 2000. 'Native Courts, Local Courts, Chieftaincy and the CPP in the 1950s', *Journal of African Cultural Studies* 13(1): 125–39.

Rattray, S. R. 1929. *Ashanti Law and Constitution*. Oxford: Clarendon Press.

Rose, Deborah Bird. 1996a. 'Land Rights and Deep Colonising: The Erasure of Women', *Aboriginal Law Bulletin* 3(85): 6–13.

———. 1996b. *Nourishing Terrains: Australian Aboriginal Views of Landscape and Wilderness*. Canberra: Australian Heritage Commission.

———. 2001. 'Settler Colonialism and the Transformation of Anthropology', *Postcolonial Studies: Culture, Politics, Economy* 4(2): 251–61.

Rosen, Lauren Coyle. 2020. *Fires of Gold: Law, Spirit and Sacrificial Labour in Ghana*. Oakland: University of California Press.

Roy, Ananya. 2009. 'The 21st-Century Metropolis: New Geographies of Theory', *Regional Studies* 43(6): 819–30.

Ruffin, Fayth. 2019. 'Land Governance in the Context of Legal Pluralism', in Adeoye O. Akinola and Henry Wissink (eds), *Trajectory of Land Reform in Post-Colonial African States: The Quest for Sustainable Development and Utilization*. Cham: Springer, pp. 91–108.

Rutazibwa, Olivia U. 2020. 'Hidden in Plain Sight: Coloniality, Capitalism and Race/ism as Far as the Eye Can See', *Millennium: Journal of International Studies* 48(2): 221–41.

Said, Edward W. 1978. *Orientalism*. New York: Vintage Books.

Salman, Ton, Felix Carrillo, and Carola Soruco. 2015. 'Small-Scale Mining Cooperatives and the State in Bolivia: Their Histories, Memories and Negotiation Strategies', *The Extractive Industries and Society* 2(2): 360–67.

Salo, Matti, et al. 2016. 'Local Perspectives on the Formalization of Artisanal and Small-Scale Mining in the Madre de Dios Gold Fields, Peru', *The Extractive Industries and Society* 3: 1058–66.

Santos, Boaventura de Sousa. 1977. 'The Law of the Oppressed: The Construction and Reproduction of Legality in Pasargada', *Law & Society Review* 12(1): 1–126.

———. 2014. *Epistemologies of the South: Justice Against Epistemicide*. New York: Routledge.

———. 2020. *Towards a New Legal Common Sense: Law, Globalisation and Emancipation*, 3rd edn. Cambridge: Cambridge University Press.

Sarat, Austin. 2004. 'Vitality Amidst Fragmentation: On the Emergence of Postrealist Law and Society Scholarship', in Austin Sarat (ed.), *The Blackwell Companion to Law and Society*. Oxford: Blackwell, pp. 1–11.

Sarat, Austin, and Susan Silbey. 1988. 'The Pull of the Policy Audience', *Law and Policy* 10(2–3): 97–166.

Sarpong, Sam. 2017. 'Sweat and Blood: Deific Interventions in Small-Scale Mining in Ghana', *Journal of Asian and African Studies* 52(3): 253–377.

Savornin, O., K. Niang, and A. Diouf. 2007. *Artisanal Gold Mining in the Tambacounda Region of Senegal: First Report on the Reduction of Mercury Emissions through Appropriate Technologies Training*. Kedougou, Senegal: Blacksmith Institute.

Schmidt, Peter R. 2014. 'Hardcore Ethnography: Interrogating the Intersection of Disease, Human Rights and Heritage', *Heritage and Society* 7(2): 170–88.

Schueler, Vivian, Tobias Kuemmerle, and Hilmar Shröder. 2011. 'Impacts of Surface Gold Mining on Land Use Systems in Western Ghana', *AMBIO: A Journal of the Human Environment* 40(5): 528–29.

Seccatore, Jacopo, et al. 2014. 'An Estimation of the Artisanal Small-Scale Production of Gold in the World', *Science of the Total Environment* 496: 662–67.

Seini, W. A. 2006. 'The Role of Traditional Authorities in Rural Development', in Irene K. Odotei and Albert K. Awedoba (eds), *Chieftaincy in Ghana: Culture, Governance and Development*. Accra: Sub-Saharan Publishers, pp. 547–64.

Sethuraman, S. V. 1976. 'The Urban Informal Sector: Concept, Measurement and Policy', *International Labour Review* 114(1): 69–81.

Shaban, Abdur Rahman Alfa. 2017. 'Ghana's Chief Justice Sets Up Specialized Courts to Deal with Illegal Mining', *Africanews*, 13 April. Retrieved 22 November 2024 from https://www.africanews.com/2017/04/13/ghana-s-chief-justice-sets-up-specialized-courts-to-deal-with-illegal-mining//.

Shivji, Issa. 2006. 'Lawyers in Neoliberalism: Authority's Professional Supplicants or Society's Amateurish Conscience?', *CODESRIA Bulletin* 3–4: 15–25.

Shumway, Rebecca. 2014. 'Palavers and Treaty Making in the British Acquisition of the Gold Coast Colony (West Africa)', in Saliha Belmessous (ed.), *Empire by Treaty: Negotiating European Expansion, 1600–1900*. New York: Oxford University Press, pp. 161–85.

Siegel, Shefa, and Marcello M. Veiga. 2009. 'Artisanal and Small-Scale Mining as an Extralegal Economy: De Soto and the Redefinition of "Formalization"', *Resources Policy* 34(1–2): 51–56.

Siwale, Agatha, and Twivwe Siwale. 2017. 'Has the Promise of Formalizing Artisanal and Small-Scale Mining (ASM) Failed? The Case of Zambia', *The Extractive Industries and Society* 4(1): 191–201.

Skeggs, Beverley. 2001. 'Feminist Ethnography', in Paul Atkinson, Amanda Coffey, Sarah Delamont, John Lofland and Lyn Lofland (eds), *Handbook of Ethnography*. London: Sage Publications, pp. 426–42.

Slater, Jennifer. 2019. 'Sankofa – The Need to Turn Back to Move Forward: Addressing Reconstruction Challenges that Face Africa and South Africa Today', *Studia Historae Ecclesiasticae* 45(1): 1–24.

Smith, Linda Tuhiwai. 1999. *Decolonising Methodologies: Research and Indigenous People*. London: Zed Books.

———. 2021. 'Decolonial Research Methods: Resisting Coloniality in Academic Knowledge Production'. Webinar delivered at the National Centre for Research Methods, University of Liverpool, 2 November.

Snyder, Francis G. 1981. 'Colonialism and Legal Form: The Creation of "Customary Law" in Senegal', *Journal of Legal Pluralism* 19: 49–90.

Sojková, Iva. 2022. 'Framing Illegal Artisanal and Small-Scale Gold Mining in the Ghanaian Media during the #StopGalamsey Campaign', *Journal of Modern African Studies* 60(3): 371–96.

Soko-de Jong, Thandi. 2022. 'Rememorying From the Academic Margins', *SocArXiv*. DOI: https://doi.org/10.31235/osf.io/wg5px.

Sonn, Christopher, Garth Stevens, and Norman Duncan. 2013. 'Decolonisation, Critical Methodologies and Why Stories Matter', in Gareth Stevens, Norman Duncan and Derek Hook (eds), *Race, Memory and the Apartheid Archive: Towards a Transformative Psychosocial Praxis*. Basingstoke: Palgrave Macmillan, pp. 295–314.

Spiegel, Samuel. 2015. 'Shifting Formalization Policies and Recentralizing Power: The Case of Zimbabwe's Artisanal Gold Mining Sector', *Society & Natural Resources* 28(5): 543–58.

Spiegel, Samuel, et al. 2014. 'Implications of the Minamata Convention on Mercury for Informal Gold Mining in Sub-Saharan Africa: From Global Policy Debates to Grassroots Implementation?', *Environment, Development and Sustainability* 14: 765–85.

Spivak, Gayatri C. 1985. 'The Rani of Sirmur: An Essay in Reading the Archives', *History and Theory* 24(3): 247–72.

Starr, June, and Jane F. Collier. 1989. 'Introduction: Dialogues in Legal Anthropology', in June Starr and Jane F. Collier (eds), *History and Power in the Study of Law: New Directions in Legal Anthropology*. Ithaca, New York: Cornell University Press, pp. 1–28.

Starr, June, and Mark Goodale (eds). 2002. *Practising Ethnography in Law: New Dialogues, Enduring Method*. London: Palgrave Macmillan.

Stoler, Ann Laura. 2002. 'Colonial Archives and the Arts of Governance', *Archival Science* 2: 87–109.

Tabak, Faruk, and Michaeline A. Crichlow. 2000. *Informalization: Process and Structure.* Baltimore: Johns Hopkins University Press.

Tamale, Sylvia. 2008. 'The Right to Culture and the Culture of Rights: A Critical Perspective on Women's Sexual Rights in Africa', *Feminist Legal Studies* 16(1): 47–69.

———. 2020. *Decolonization and Afro-Feminism*. Ottawa: Daraja Press.

Tamanaha, Brian Z. 1997. *Realistic Socio-Legal Theory: Pragmatism and a Social Theory of Law.* Oxford: Oxford University Press.

———. 2000. 'A Non-Essentialist Version of Legal Pluralism', *Journal of Law & Society* 27(2): 296–321.

———. 2001. *A General Jurisprudence of Law and Society*. Oxford: Oxford University Press.

———. 2021. 'Legal Pluralism across the Global South: Colonial Origins and Contemporary Consequences', *The Journal of Legal Pluralism and Unofficial Law* 53(2): 168–205.

Taylor, Ayowa Afrifa. 2006. 'An Economic History of the Ashanti Goldfields Corporation, 1895–2004: Land, Labour, Capital and Enterprise', Ph.D. dissertation. London: London School of Economics.

Taylor, D. B. 2020. 'A Timeline of the Coronavirus Pandemic', *New York Times*, 21 July. Retrieved 22 November 2024 from https://www.nytimes.com/article/coronavirus-timeline.html.

Telmer, Kevin H., and Marcello M. Veiga. 2008. 'World Emissions of Mercury from Artisanal and Small-Scale Mining', in Nicola Pirrone and Robert Mason (eds), *Mercury Fate and Transport in the Global Atmosphere: Emissions, Measurements and Models*. UNEP Global Mercury Partnership Interim Report, pp. 96–129.

Tetteh, Rebecca Addo. 2021. 'Galamsey: Real Perpetrators Are Not Those "Small Boys"; Arrest Barons – Ablakwa Says Burning Excavators Is a Futile Exercise', *Peace FM*, 24 May. Retrieved 22 November 2024 from https://radiooneghana.com/2021/05/galamsey-real-perpetrators-are-not-those-small-boys-arrest-barons-ablakwa-says-burning-excavators-is-a-futile-exercise/.

Teubner, Gunther. 1997. 'Global Bukowina: Legal Pluralism in the World Society', in Gunther Teubner (ed.), *Global Law without a State*. Brookfield: Dartmouth, pp. 1–22.

Thompson, Kwarkye Gyedu. 2016. 'Chieftaincy and Partisan Politics: The Case of Agona Ashanti Traditional Area', *Developing Country Studies* 6(11): 28–31.

Tlostanova, Madina. 2020. 'The Postcolonial Condition, the Decolonial Option, and the Post-Socialist Intervention', in Monika Albrecht (ed.), *Postcolonialism Cross-Examined: Multidirectional Perspectives on Imperial and Colonial Pasts and the Neocolonial Present*. London: Routledge, pp. 165–78.

Tokman, Victor E. 1978. 'An Exploration into the Nature of Informal–Formal Sector Relationships', *World Development* 6(9–10): 1065–75.

Torvikey, Gertrude Dzifa, Adwoa Yeboah Gyapong, and Faustina Obeng Adomaa. 2024. 'Wango! Women's Struggles Amidst Privatised and Extractivist Models of Salt Mining in Ghana', *Feminist Africa* 5(1): 50–73.

Tschakert, Petra. 2009. 'Recognizing and Nurturing Artisanal Mining as a Viable Livelihood', *Resources Policy* 34(1–2): 24–31.

Tschakert, Petra, and Kamini Singha. 2007. 'Contaminated Identities: Mercury and Marginalization in Ghana's Artisanal Mining Sector', *Geoforum* 38(6): 1304–21.

Tsing, Anna Lowenhaupt. 2005. *Friction: An Ethnography of Global Connections*. New Jersey: Princeton University Press.

Tsuma, William. 2010. *Gold Mining in Ghana: Actors, Alliances and Power*. Berlin: Lit Verlag.

Tuokuu, Francis Xavier Doku, et al. 2020. 'Criminalization of "Galamsey" and Livelihoods in Ghana: Limits and Consequences', *Natural Resources Forum* 44(1): 52–65.

Tweneboah, Seth. 2020. *Religion, Law, Politics and the State in Africa: Applying Legal Pluralism in Ghana*. New York: Routledge.

Twerefou, Daniel K. et al. 2015. 'Attitudes of Local People to Mining Policies and Interventions', LSE International Growth Centre Working Paper.
Twining, William. 2010. 'Normative and Legal Pluralism: A Global Perspective', *Duke Journal of Comparative & International Law* 20: 473–518.
Ubink, Janine M. 2008. *In the Land of the Chiefs: Customary Law, Land Conflicts, and the Role of the State in Peri-urban Ghana*. Leiden: Leiden University Press.
———. 2009. 'Legalising Customary Land Tenure in Ghana: The Case of Peri-urban Kumasi', in Janine Ubink, André Hoekema and William Assies (eds), *Legalising Land Rights: Local Practices, State Responses and Tenure Security in Africa, Asia and Latin America*. Leiden: Leiden University Press, pp. 163–91.
Ubink, Janine M., and Julian Quan. 2008. 'How to Combine Tradition with Modernity? Regulating Customary Land Management in Ghana', *Land Use Policy* 25: 198–213.
Ullo, Sixtus Dong. 2022. 'Afenyo Markin Challenges Politicians to Be Bold in Galamsey Fight', *CitiNewsroom*, September 22. Retrieved 22 November 2024 from https://citinewsroom.com/2022/09/afenyo-markin-challenges-politicians-to-be-bold-in-galamsey-fight/.
UAF-LAC (Urgent Action Fund for Latin America and the Spanish-Speaking Caribbean). 2021. 'Extractivism, the Pandemic and Other Possible Worlds: Economic Recovery and Alternatives from the Women Defenders of Territories in Latin America', UAF-LAC Women and Territories Program.
USAID. 2012. 'Country Profile: Property Rights and Resource Governance Ghana'. Washington, D.C.
Valsecchi, Pierluigi. 2007. '"He Who Sets the Boundary": Chieftaincy as a "Necessary" Institution in Modern Ghana', University of Teramo Department of Communication Working Paper No. 3.
Van Bockstael, Steven. 2014. 'The Persistence of Informality: Perspectives on the Future of Artisanal Mining in Liberia', *Futures* 62(A): 10–20.
———. 2019. 'Land Grabbing "From Below"? Illicit Artisanal Gold Mining and Access to Land in Post-Conflict Côte d' Ivoire', *Land Use Policy* 81: 904–14.
van Rouveroy van Nieuwaal, E. A. B., and R. A. van Dijk (eds). 1999. *African Chieftaincy in a New Socio-Political Landscape*. Hamburg: Lit Verlag.
Varley, Ann. 2013. 'Postcolonising Informality?', *Environment and Planning: Society and Space* 31(1): 4–22.
Vasquez-Brust, Diego Alfonso, Francis Arthur-Holmes, and Natalia Yakovleva. 2024. 'The Social and Environmental Responsibility of Informal Artisanal and Small-Scale Mining in Ghana: An Akan Philosophical Perspective', *Journal of Environmental Management* 360: 1–29.
Veiga, Marcello M., Gustavo Angeloci-Santos, and John A. Meech. 2014. 'Review of Barriers to Reduce Mercury Use in Artisanal Gold Mining', *The Extractive Industries and Society* 1(2): 351–61.
Verbrugge, Boris. 2015. 'The Economic Logic of Persistent Informality: Artisanal and Small-Scale Mining in the Southern Philippines', *Development and Change* 46(5): 1023–46.
Verbrugge, Boris, and Beverly Besmanos. 2016. 'Formalizing Artisanal and Small-Scale Mining: Whither the Workforce?', *Resources Policy* 47: 134–41.
Verbrugge, Boris, Jeroen Cuvelier, and Steven Van Bockstael. 2015. 'Min(d)ing the Land: The Relationship between Artisanal and Small-Scale Mining and Surface Land Arrangements in the Southern Philippines, Eastern DRC and Liberia', *Journal of Rural Studies* 37: 50–60.
Vergès, Françoise. 2021. *A Decolonial Feminism*, trans. Ashley J. Bohrer and Françoise Vergès. London: Pluto Press.
Vermette, D'Arcy. 2009. 'Colonialism and the Suppression of Aboriginal Voice', *Ottawa Law Review* 40(2): 225–65.

Vermeylen, Saskia. 2010. 'Law as a Narrative: Legal Pluralism and Resisting Euro-American (Intellectual) Property Law through Stories', *Journal of Legal Pluralism and Unofficial Law* 42(61): 53–78.

———. 2013. 'The Nagoya Protocol and Customary Law: The Paradox of Narratives in the Law', *Law, Environment and Development Journal* 9(2): 185–201.

Vermeylen, Saskia, and Gordon Clark. 2017. 'An Alternative Ethics for Research: Levinas and the Unheard Voices and Unseen Faces', *International Journal of Social Research Methodology* 20(5): 499–512.

von Benda-Beckmann, Franz. 2009. 'Riding or Killing the Centaur? Reflections on the Identity of Legal Anthropology', in Michael Freeman and David Napier (eds), *Law and Anthropology: Current Issues*. Oxford: Oxford University Press, pp. 13–46.

von Benda-Beckmann, Franz, K. von Benda-Beckmann, and H. L. J. Spiertz. 1997. 'Local Law and Customary Practices in the Study of Water Rights', International Water Management Institute Books Report H020134, pp. 221–42.

von Benda-Beckmann, Keebet. 2021. 'Relational Social Theories and Legal Pluralism', *The Indonesian Journal of Socio-Legal Studies* 1(1): 1–24.

von Benda-Beckmann, Keebet, and Bertram Turner. 2018. 'Legal Pluralism, Social Theory and the State', *Journal of Legal Pluralism and Unofficial Law* 50(3): 255–74.

Wakunuma, Kutoma, et al. 2025. 'Decoloniality as an Essential Trustworthy AI Requirement', in Damian Okaibedi Eke, Kutoma Wakunuma, Simisola Akintoye and George Okoh (eds), *Trustworthy AI: African Perspectives*. Basingstoke: Palgrave Macmillan, pp. 255–76.

Walker, Charles A. 2009. 'Lest We Forget: The Tuskegee Experiment', *Journal of Theory Construction & Testing* 13(1): 5–6.

Wane, Njoki. 2005. 'African Indigenous Knowledge: Claiming, Writing, Storing, and Sharing the Discourse', *Journal of Thought* 40(2): 27–46.

———. 2011. 'African Indigenous Feminist Thought: An Anticolonial Project', in Njoki Wane, Arlo Kempf and Marlon Simmons (eds), The *Politics of Cultural Knowledge*. Rotterdam: Sense Publishers, pp. 7–21.

Ward, W. E. F. 1991. *My Africa*. Accra: Ghana Universities Press.

Warikandwa, Tapiwa V., Artwell Nhemachena, and Nkosinothando Mpofu. 2017. 'Double Victimisation? Law, Decoloniality and Research Ethics in Post-Colonial Africa', *The Journal of Pan African Studies* 10(2): 64–81.

Watson, Irene. 2015. *Race Law: Aboriginal Peoples, Colonialism and International Law*. New York: Routledge.

Weng, Xiaoxue. 2015. 'The Rural Informal Economy: Understanding Drivers and Livelihood Impacts in Agriculture, Timber and Mining', IIED Working Paper.

White, Hylton. 2019. 'What is Anthropology that Decolonising Scholarship Should Be Mindful of It?', *Anthropology Southern Africa* 42(2): 149–60.

Whitehouse, David. 2019. 'Ghana Now Africa's Largest Gold Producer, but Reforms Await', *The Africa Report*, 8 October. Retrieved 22 November 2024 from https://www.theafricareport.com/18245/ghana-now-africas-largest-gold-producer-but-reforms-await/.

Wiredu, Kwasi. 1998. 'Towards Decolonizing African Philosophy and Religion', *African Studies Quarterly* 1(4): 17–46.

Woodman, Gordon R. 1987. 'How State Courts Create Customary Law in Ghana and Nigeria', in Bradford W. Morse and Gordon R. Woodman (eds), *Indigenous Law and the State*. Berlin: De Gruyter Mouton, pp. 181–220.

———. 1996. 'Legal Pluralism and the Search for the State', *Journal of African Law* 40(2): 152–67.

———. 2001. 'Customary Law in Common Law Systems', *IDS Bulletin* 32(1): 28–34.

———. 2011. 'A Survey of Customary Laws in Africa in Search of Lessons for the Future', in Jeanmarie Fenrich, Paolo Galizzi and Tracy Higgins (eds), *The Future of African Customary Law*. Cambridge: Cambridge University Press, pp. 9–30.

———. 2012a. 'Legal Pluralism in Africa: The Implications of State Recognition of Customary Laws Illustrated from the Field of Land Law', in H. Mostert and T. Bennet (eds), *Pluralism and Development: Studies in Access to Property in Africa*. Cape Town: JUTA, pp. 35–58.

———. 2012b. 'The Development "Problem" of Legal Pluralism: An Analysis and Steps Towards Solutions', in Brian Z. Tamanaha, Caroline Sage and Michael Woolcock (eds), *Legal Pluralism and Development: Scholars and Practitioners in Dialogue*. New York: Cambridge University Press, pp. 129–44.

World Bank. 1993. 'A Strategy for African Mining', Technical Paper No. WTP81. Washington D.C.

———. 2013. 'Understanding Poverty Extractive Industries: Artisanal and Small-Scale Mining'. Washington, D.C.

Wynn, L. L., and Mark Israel. 2018. 'The Fetishes of Consent: Signatures, Paper, and Writing in Research Ethics Review', *American Anthropologist* 120(4): 795–806.

Wynter, Sylvia. 2003. 'Unsettling the Coloniality of Being/Power/Truth/Freedom: Towards the Human, After Man, Its Overrepresentation – An Argument', *The New Centennial Review* 3(3): 257–337.

———. 2006. 'On How We Mistook the Map for the Territory, and Re-Imprisoned Ourselves in Our Unbearable Wrongness of Being, of *Désêtre*: Black Studies Toward the Human Project', in Lewis R. Gordon and Jane Anna Gordon (eds), *Not Only the Master's Tools: African-American Studies in Theory and Practice*. Boulder: Paradigm, pp. 107–69.

Yankson, Paul W. K., and Katherine V. Gough. 2019. 'Gold in Ghana: The Effect of Changes in Large-Scale Mining on Artisanal and Small-Scale Mining (ASM)', *The Extractive Industries and Society* 6: 120–28.

Ye, Jinzhong, et al. 2020. 'The Incursions of Extractivism: Moving from Dispersed Places to Global Capitalism', *Journal of Peasant Studies* 47(1): 155–83.

Yeboah, Charles Nixon. 2021. 'Review of Mining Act 703 in Offing, as 2021 West Africa Mining Conference Underway', *Joy Online,* 3 June. Retrieved 22 November 2024 from https://www.myjoyonline.com/review-of-mining-act-703-in-offing-as-2021-west-africa-mining-conference-underway/.

Yelpaala, Kaakpema, and Saleem H. Ali. 2005. 'Multiple Scales of Diamond Mining in Akwatia, Ghana: Addressing Environmental and Human Development Impact', *Resources Policy* 30(3): 145–55.

Youe, Chris. 2010. 'Mining Capital and Colonialism in Africa', *Canadian Journal of African Studies* 44(1): 179–87.

Zolnikov, Tara Rava. 2020. 'Effects of the Government Ban in Ghana on Women in Artisanal and Small-Scale Gold Mining', *Resources Policy* 65: 1–6.

Zvarivadza, T. 2018. 'Artisanal and Small-Scale Mining as a Challenge and Possible Contributor to Sustainable Development', *Resources Policy* 56: 49–58.

Zvarivadza, T., and A. S. Nhleko. 2018. 'Resolving Artisanal and Small-Scale Mining Challenges: Moving from Conflict to Cooperation for Sustainability in Mine Planning', *Resources Policy* 56: 78–86.

Index

www.ingramcontent.com/pod-product-compliance
Ingram Content Group UK Ltd.
Pitfield, Milton Keynes, MK11 3LW, UK
UKHW021837150926
8656IPUK00004B/29

9 781836 955122